PHILIP'S

50p

STREET ATLAS
S... [obscured] ...d
and ... [obscured] ...erham

www.philips-maps.co.uk

First published 2007 by

Philip's, a division of
Octopus Publishing Group Ltd
2-4 Heron Quays, London E14 4JP
www.octopusbooks.co.uk
An Hachette UK Company
www.hachettelivre.co.uk

First edition 2007
Second impression 2009

ISBN 978-0-540-09148-5
© Philip's 2007

Ordnance Survey®

This product includes mapping data licensed
from Ordnance Survey®, with the permission
of the Controller of Her Majesty's Stationery
Office.© Crown copyright 2007. All rights
reserved. Licence number 100011710

No part of this publication may be
reproduced, stored in a retrieval system or
transmitted in any form or by any means,
electronic, mechanical, photocopying,
recording or otherwise, without the
permission of the Publishers and the
copyright owner.

To the best of the Publishers' knowledge, the
information in this atlas was correct at the
time of going to press. No responsibility can
be accepted for any errors or their
consequences.

The representation in this atlas of a road,
track or path is no evidence of the existence
of a right of way.

Ordnance Survey and the OS symbol are
registered trademarks of Ordnance Survey,
the national mapping agency of Great Britain

Photographic acknowledgements:
VIII and IX Pete Hill / Alamy

Printed by Toppan, China

Contents

II **Key to map symbols**

III **Key to map pages**

IV **Route planning**

VIII **Illustrated guide to visitor attractions**

2 **Street maps** at 4½ inches to 1 mile

104 **Street maps of Sheffield city centre**
at 7 inches to 1 mile

108 **Index**

134 **List of numbered locations**

Key to map symbols

Roads

(12) **Motorway** with junction number

A34 **Primary route** – dual, single carriageway

A40 **A road** – dual, single carriageway

B1289 **B road** – dual, single carriageway

Through-route – dual, single carriageway

Minor road – dual, single carriageway

Rural track, private road or narrow road in urban area

Path, bridleway, byway open to all traffic, road used as a public path

Road under construction

Pedestrianised area

Gate or obstruction to traffic restrictions may not apply at all times or to all vehicles

P P&R **Parking, Park and Ride**

Railways

Railway

Miniature railway

Metro station, private railway station

Emergency services

Ambulance station, coastguard station

Fire station, police station

H ✚ **Hospital, Accident and Emergency entrance to hospital**

General features

✚ PO **Place of worship, Post Office**

i **Information centre** (open all year)

Bus or coach station, shopping centre

Important buildings, schools, colleges, universities and hospitals

Woods, built-up area

 Tumulus FORT **Non-Roman antiquity, Roman antiquity**

Leisure facilities

✗ ⊞ **Camping site, caravan site**

▶ ✗ **Golf course, picnic site**

Boundaries

• • • • • • **Postcode boundaries**

— • — **County and unitary authority boundaries**

Water features

 River Ouse **Tidal water, water name**

Non-tidal water – lake, river, canal or stream

< | **Lock, weir**

Enlarged mapping only

Railway or bus station building

Place of interest

Parkland

Scales

Blue pages: 4½ inches to 1 mile 1:14 080

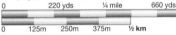

| 0 | 220 yds | ¼ mile | 660 yds | ½ r |

| 0 | 125m | 250m | 375m | ½ km |

Red pages: 7 inches to 1 mile 1:9 051

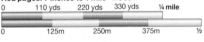

| 0 | 110 yds | 220 yds | 330 yds | ¼ mile |

| 0 | 125m | 250m | 375m | ½ k |

 62 **Adjoining page indicators** The colour of the arrow and the band indicates the scale of the adjoining page (see above)

Abbreviations

Acad	Academy	Mkt	Market
Allot Gdns	Allotments	Meml	Memorial
Cemy	Cemetery	Mon	Monument
C Ctr	Civic Centre	Mus	Museum
CH	Club House	Obsy	Observatory
Coll	College	Pal	Royal Palace
Crem	Crematorium	PH	Public House
Ent	Enterprise	Recn Gd	Recreation Ground
Ex H	Exhibition Hall	Resr	Reservoir
Ind Est	Industrial Estate	Ret Pk	Retail Park
IRB Sta	Inshore Rescue Boat Station	Sch	School
		Sh Ctr	Shopping Centre
Inst	Institute	TH	Town Hall/House
Ct	Law Court	Trad Est	Trading Estate
L Ctr	Leisure Centre	Univ	University
LC	Level Crossing	Wks	Works
Liby	Library	YH	Youth Hostel

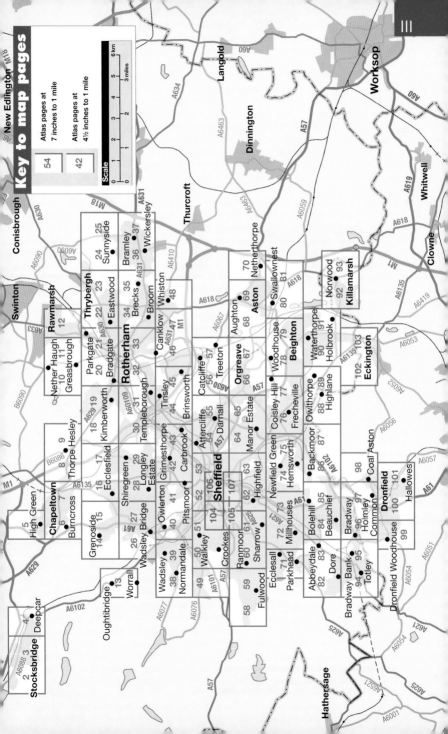

III

Scale

Atlas pages at
7 inches to 1 mile

54

Atlas pages at
4½ inches to 1 mile

42

0 1 2 3 4 5 6km
0 1 2 3miles

New Edlington

Worksop

Langold

Dinnington

Thurcroft

Whitwell

Clowne

Conisbrough

Swinton

Rawmarsh

Thrybergh

Sunnyside

Bramley

Wickersley

Netherthorpe

Norwood

Killamarsh

Nether Haugh

Greasbrough

Parkgate

Eastwood

Brecks

Whiston

Broom

Canklow

Aughton

Aston

Swallownest

Waterthorpe

Holbrook

Eckington

Rotherham

Bradgate

Kimberworth

Templeborough

Tinsley

Brinsworth

Catcliffe

Treeton

Orgreave

Woodhouse

Beighton

Owlthorpe

Highlane

Coal Aston

Chapeltown

Thorpe Hesley

Ecclesfield

Longley Estate

Grimesthorpe

Carbrook

Attercliffe

Darnall

Manor Estate

Coisley Hill

Frecheville

Backmoor

Dronfield

Hallowes

High Green

Burncross

Grenoside

Shiregreen

Owlerton

Pitsmoor

Sheffield

Highfield

Newfield Green

Hemsworth

Beauchief

Bradway

Holmley Common

Dronfield Woodhouse

Deepcar

Worrall

Wadsley Bridge

Wadsley

Normandale

Walkley

Crookes

Ranmoor

Sharrow

Ecclesall

Parkhead

Millhouses

Bolehill

Abbeydale

Dore

Totley

Bradway Bank

Stocksbridge

Oughtibridge

Fulwood

Hathersage

M18

M1

A60

A629

A6090

A6090

B6090

A633

B6086

M1

A6135

A629

A61

A6101

A57

A6102

A6077

A6076

A625

A6054

A6051

A625

A621

A6001

A57

A6025

A6625

A61

A6052

A6053

A6056

A6057

A6135

A618

A619

A60

A634

A6463

A6463

A6059

A631

A631

A631

A6410

A618

A6067

A57

A630

A618

A629

A6109

A6135

A630

A6088

5

6

7

8

9

10

11

12

13

14

15

16

17

18

19

20

21

22

23

24

25

26

27

28

29

30

31

32

33

34

35

36

37

38

39

40

41

42

43

44

45

46

47

48

49

50

51

52

53

54

55

56

57

58

59

60

61

62

63

64

65

66

67

68

69

70

71

72

73

74

75

76

77

78

79

80

81

82

83

84

85

86

87

88

89

90

91

92

93

94

95

96

97

98

99

100

101

102

103

104

105

106

107

2

3

4

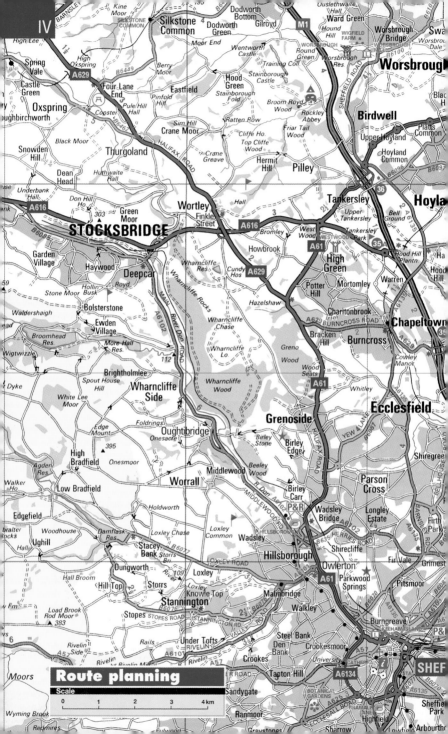

Route planning

Scale

0 1 2 3 4 km

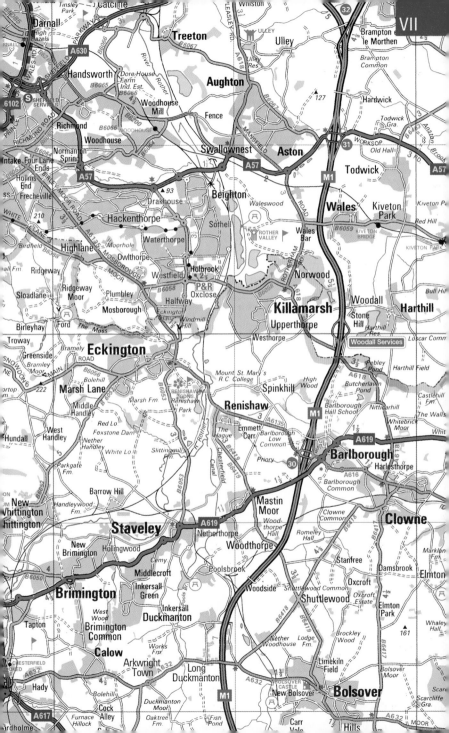

Visitor Attractions

Museums and Galleries

Bishops' House *Norton Lees Lane, Sheffield*
Bishops' House is the best preserved timber-framed house in Sheffield and was built around 1500. It is typical of the development of smaller English houses of the 16th and 17th centuries and looks much as it did in the 17th century. ☎0114 278 2600 🖥www.sheffieldgalleries.org.uk/coresite/html/bishops.asp 73 C3

Clifton Park Museum *Clifton Lane, Rotherham*
General museum housing such renowned exhibits as Nelson the Lion and the Rhinoceros Vase. Hands-on exhibits, high-tech displays and cookery lessons bring the history of Rotherham to life. ☎01709 336633 🖥www.rotherham.gov.uk 33 C4

Graves Art Gallery *Surrey Street, Sheffield* The Graves Art Gallery hold permanent displays from the city's collections of 19th- and 20th-century British and European Art, covering the development of modern art, as well as a programme of temporary exhibitions. 🖥www.sheffieldgalleries.org.uk/coresite/html/graves.asp ☎0114 278 2600 107 B3

Kelham Island Industrial Museum *Alma Street, Sheffield* Kelham Island Museum stands on a man-made island over 900 years old. Exhibitions, working machinery, activity areas and event days explore Sheffield's industrial heritage. ☎0114 2722106 🖥www.simt.co.uk 106 A5

Millennium Galleries *Arundel Gate, Sheffield*
An outstanding venue for the visual arts, craft and design, right in the heart of Sheffield with four galleries showing craft and designs, metalwork, temporary exhibitions and the collections of John Ruskin. 🖥www.sheffieldgalleries.org.uk/coresite/html/millennium.asp ☎0114 278 2600 106 B3

The Fire and Police Museum *Old Fire Station, West Bar, Sheffield* Houses memorabilia and old vehicles from fire brigades and police forces all over the country. ☎0114 2491 999 🖥www.firepolicemuseum.co.uk 106 A4

Weston Park Museum *Western Bank, Sheffield*
Very popular general museum, with interactive exhibits on subjects as wide-ranging as Egyptian mummies to a butcher's shop, as well as live ants and bees. 🖥www.sheffieldgalleries.org.uk/coresite/html/WPM.asp 104 A3

York and Lancaster Regimental Museum
Arts Centre, Walker Place, Drummond St, Rotherham Brings to life the history of the regiment from 1758–1968. ☎01709 336633 🖥www.rotherham.gov.uk 21 B1

Historic Sites

Abbeydale Industrial Hamlet *Abbeydale Road South, Sheffield* This unique 18th-century industrial works was one of the largest water-powered sites on the River Sheaf making agricultural tools. Its surviving features include waterwheels, tilt hammers, a grinding hull and the only intact crucible steel furnace in the world, as well as cottages, a counting house and a steam engine. ☎0114 2367731 🖥www.simt.co.uk 83 C2

Places of Worship

Cathedral Church of St Peter & St Paul *Church Street, Sheffield* A mainly Perpendicular, 15th-century cathedral with some 12th-century remnants. Highlights include the tomb of the sixth Earl of Shrewsbury and beautiful stained glass windows. ☎0114 275 3434 🖥www.sheffield-cathedral.co.uk 106 A4

Rotherham Minster *All Saints Square, Rotherham* A beautiful 14th–15th-century Perpendicular church with some Saxon and Norman parts, poppy-head chancel stalls, more than 30 Green Man carvings, beautiful tombs, a Jacobean pulpit, a Norman font of 1190 and several excellent stained-glass windows. 🖥www.rotherhamminster.org ☎01709 364737 33 A4

St John the Baptist *Church Street, Dronfield*
A fine 12th-century early Gothic church, with a beautiful Jacobean pulpit and lovely chancel. In the churchyard are the remains of an early preaching cross. ☎01246 412 328 🖥www.dwparish.org.uk 100 C3

St Peter and St Paul *Church Street, Eckington*
An exceptional church, dating back to 1100, with good examples from most architectural periods, an impressive tower and spire, beautiful Norman arcades and several important monuments to members of the Sitwell family. ☎01246 434 576 103 B2

Cathedral Church of St Marie *Norfolk Road, Sheffield* Sheffield's Roman Catholic cathedral since 1980, St Marie is a good example of a mid-19th-century church, when Catholic churches were allowed to be built for the first time since the Reformation. Although much of the Victorian woodwork has been removed, the majority of the stained-glass windows are original. 🖥www.stmariecathedral.org/joomla ☎0114 272 2522 107 C2

Other Sights

Magna Science Adventure Centre *Sheffield Road, Rotherham* The first science adventure centre in the UK, Magna is dedicated to making science fun, with attractions including rock moving races in JCBs, water cannons, a gyroscopic chair that spins you round, as well as multimedia displays ☎01709 720002 🖥www.visitmagna.co.uk 31 C2

Green Spaces

Cholera Monument Grounds & Clay Wood
Norfolk Road, Sheffield This small formal garden around the monument to the victims of the 1832 cholera outbreak offers fine views over the city, while the woodland is an SSSI. 🖥www.sheffield.gov.uk ☎0114 2860400 107 C2

Clifton Park *Clifton Lane, Rotherham* A highly popular urban park covering 56 acres around the Clifton Park Museum. Attractions include a fairground and children's play area and wide open spaces. The Rotherham Show is held here each September. ☎01709 382121 🖥www.rotherham.gov.uk 33 C4

Graves Park *Charles Ashmore Road, Sheffield*
The city's largest public park, Graves Park has ancient woodland, an animal farm, two playgrounds, sportsgrounds, formal gardens, lakes and a nature trail. 🖥www.sheffield.gov.uk 85 B3

Hillsborough Park *Penistone Road, Sheffield*
Park featuring a fishing lake, a bowling green with pavilion, a walled garden and a playground. 🖥www.sheffield.gov.uk 40 A3

Sheffield Botanical Gardens

Abbeydale Industrial Hamlet

other Valley Country Park and Nature eserve *Mansfield Road, Wales Bar, Sheffield* ff the A618 between Aston and Killamarsh, his country park and nature reserve offers wide range of watersports, cycle trails, children's play area, golf and quiet areas r birdwatching. ☎0114 2471452 www.rothervalley.f9.co.uk

heffield Botanical Gardens *Clarkehouse oad, Sheffield* A 19-acre garden first opened 1836. Originally designed by Robert arnock, the beautiful gardens contain a rge number of listed buildings, including he curvilinear Glass Pavilions and a number other interesting features. ☎0114 267 6496 www.sbg.org.uk 61 A3

ley Country Park *Pleasley Road, Rotherham* 47-acre park located on the A618 between ughton and Whiston, surrounding a former eservoir stocked for angling. There is a wide ariety of wildlife, especially wildfowl, and enty of space for rambling. ☎01709 365332 www.rotherham.gov.uk

ctivities

ramhall Lane Football Ground *Bramhall ane, Sheffield* Home of Sheffield United C. 🖳www.sufc.premiumtv.co.uk 0114-221-5757 62 B3

ineworld Sheffield *Valley Centretainment, roughton Lane, Sheffield* ☎0871 200 2000 www.cineworld.co.uk 44 A2

rystal Peaks Shopping Centre *off Eckington Vay, Sheffield* A large shopping centre which, fter major redevelopment, has more than 5 shops, a 100-stall market area and a ariety of restaurants. ☎0114 251 0457 www.crystalpeakscentre.com 90 C3

rucible Theatre *Norfolk Street, Sheffield* he largest Sheffield theatre, which stages l the major productions, as well as he annual snooker World Championships. www.sheffieldtheatres.co.uk 0114 249 5999 106 B3

on Valley Bowl *Worksop Road, Sheffield* pen-air venue for a variety of events. www.donvalleystadium.co.uk 0114 2233600 43 C1

on Valley Stadium *Worksop Road, Sheffield* ne of the UK's premier athletics grounds.

Also hosts other events and is home to Sheffield Eagles Rugby League Club. 🖳www.donvalleystadium.co.uk ☎0114 2233600 54 B4

English Institute of Sport *Coleridge Road, Sheffield* One of the country's most impressive indoor sports venues catering for both elite athletes and the general public and home to the Sheffield Sharks basketball team. 🖳www.eis2win.co.uk ☎0114 223 5600 43 B1

Goodwin Sports Centre *Northumberland Road, Sheffield* University sports and leisure centre, also open to the public. ☎0114 222 6958 🖳www.shef.ac.uk/usport 104 A3

Hallam FM Arena *Broughton Lane, Sheffield* Sheffield's premier venue for live music. 🖳www.hallamfmarena.co.uk ☎0114 256 56 56 43 C1

Heeley City Farm *Richards Road, Sheffield* Popular local attraction with unusual domestic animals, including large black pigs, Soay sheep, goats, an Exmoor pony and an Irish moiled cow. Also offers a play area for under-8s, garden centre, gardens and a renewable energy centre. 🖳www.heeleyfarm.org.uk ☎0114 258 0244 63 A1

Hillsborough Football Ground *Hillsborough, Sheffield* Home of Sheffield Wednesday FC 🖳www.swfc.premiumtv.co.uk ☎0870 999 1867 40 A4

Ice Sheffield *Coleridge Road, Sheffield* Ice-skating complex with 2 olympic-sized rinks, offering lessons and ice hockey. Home to the Sheffield Scimitars ice-hockey team. ☎0114 223 3900 🖳www.icesheffield.com 43 B1

Lyceum Theatre *Norfolk Street, Sheffield* The main venue for touring productions. 🖳www.sheffieldtheatres.co.uk ☎0114 249 5999 107 B3

Meadowhall Centre *Meadowhall Way, Sheffield* One of the largest shopping centres in Britain, with more than 270 shops, 30 restaurants and a Vue cinema. ☎0114 256 8800 🖳www.meadowhall.co.uk/website 44 A4

Millmoor Ground *Masbrough Street, Rotherham* Home of Rotherham United FC. 🖳www.themillers.premiumtv.co.uk/page/ Welcome ☎01709 512 434 32 B4

Octagon Centre *Western Bank, Sheffield* Multi-purpose conference venue which also hosts

art, fashion and motor shows, exhibitions, concerts and banquets. ☎0114 2228889 🖳www.shef.ac.uk/octagon 105 B3

Odeon Cinema *Sheffield Arundel Gate nr High Street, Sheffield* 🖳www.odeon.co.uk ☎0871 224 400 106 B3

Owlerton Stadium *Penistone Road, Sheffield* Greyhound racing stadium and home to the Sheffield Tigers speedway team. ☎0114 234 3074 🖳www.owlertonstadium.co.uk 40 B3

Ponds Forge International Sports Centre *Sheaf Street, Sheffield* Internationally-acclaimed sports centre, offering a variety of sports, including swimming, trampoline and diving. 🖳www.ponds-forge.co.uk ☎0114 223 3400 106 B3

Retail World Shopping Centre *Stadium Way, Parkgate, Rotherham* Thirty-plus big-name stores and restaurants 21 C3

Rotherham Civic Theatre *Catherine Street, Rotherham* Local theatre, staging a wide variety of events. ☎01709 823640 🖳www.rotherham.gov.uk 33 B4

Sheffield Ski Village *Vale Road, Sheffield* Dry ski slopes for skiing and snow boarding and Adventure Mountain adventure park for children. ☎0114 276 9459 🖳www.sheffieldskivillage.co.uk 41 A1

The Showroom Cinema *Paternoster Row, Sheffield* 🖳www.showroom.org.uk ☎0114 275 7727 107 B2

Studio Theatre *Norfolk Street, Sheffield* The smallest of the three Sheffield theatres, this venue hosts small-scale in-house and touring productions, as well as the Ensemble 360 annual music festival. ☎0114 249 5999 🖳www.sheffieldtheatres.co.uk 106 B3

Woodbourn Stadium *Stadium Way, Sheffield* Athletics and track facilities open to the public or for hire. Also stages major athletics events. 🖳www.donvalley-stadium.co.uk ☎0114 223637 54 A3

Information

Tourist Information
🛈 *Rotherham: Bridgegate* ☎01709 835904 🖳www.rotherham.gov.uk/graphics/ Visiting/Visitor+Centre 33 A1
🛈 *Sheffield: Norfolk Row* ☎(0)114 221 1900 🖳http://www.sheffield.gov.uk/out--about/tourist-information 106 A3

Rotherham Metropolitan Borough
Council Civic Building, Walker Place, Rotherham ☎01709 38212 www.rotherham.gov.uk 21 B1

Sheffield City Council Town Hall
Surrey Street, Sheffield ☎0114 272 6444 🖳www.sheffield.gov.uk 107 A3

Sheffield Supertram
☎0114 272 8282 🖳www.supertram.com

Travel South Yorkshire
☎01709 515151
🖳www.travelsouthyorkshire.com

National Rail Enquiries
☎0845 748 4950 🖳www.nationalrail.co.uk

NCP Car Parking
☎0870 606 7050 🖳www.ncp.co.uk

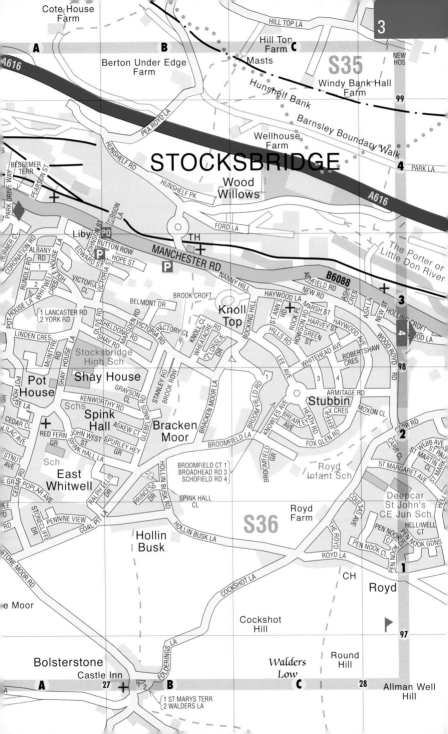

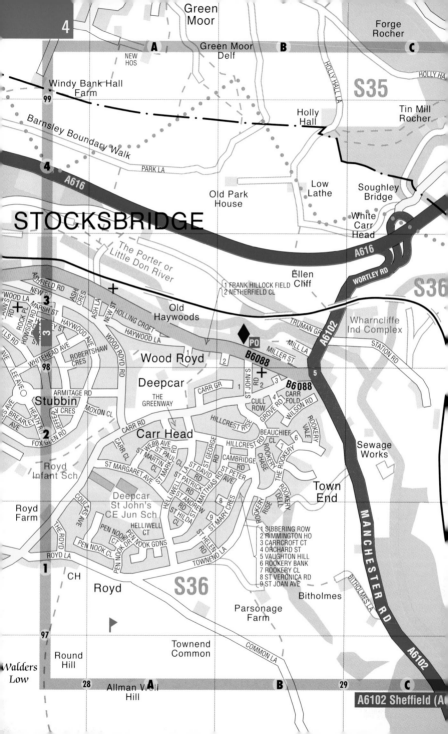

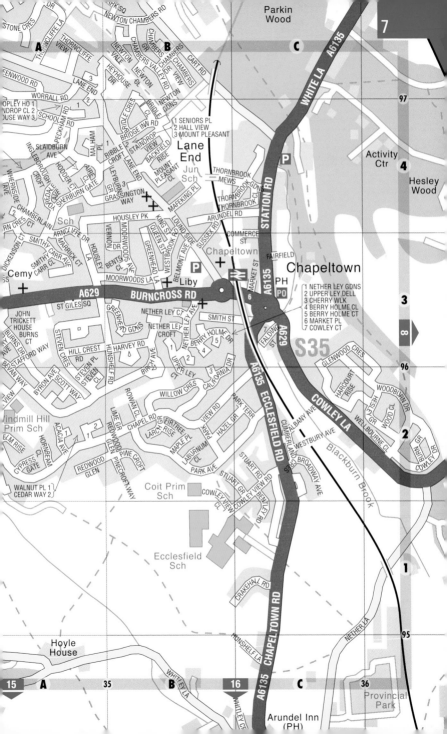

A   B   C

Hague
Wood

Shire Oaks
Wood

97

Trowles
Wood

4

rpe
ld
le

mwell
ouse

THORNWELL LA
THORNWELL WAY

2 KINGFISHER RISE

BITTERN
VIEW

AVOCET WAY

PEACOCK C
DUNLIN CL
SANDPIPER RD

RAVEN DR
PLOVER
RISE
CROFT

SWIFT WAY
MERLIN WAY

FULMAR
WAY

CURLEW
RISE

MARTIN
RISE
LAPWING

NIGHTINGALE
CROFT

VALE RISE

SHELDRAKE CL

CHAPELFIELD RD
CHAPELFIELD
CHAPELFIELD DR

KESTREL AVE

GOLDCREST
WLK

MALLARD CL

WENTWORTH RD

LINNET
MOUNT

Thorpe
Hesley

Sewage
Works

3

CHAPELFIELD RD
CHAPELFIELD
DR

CHAPELFIELD
MOUNT

WENTWORTH RD

KIRKCROFT
AVE

Upper Ox Close
Wood

S61

96

THORPE ST

THORPEFIELD
DR

THORPEFIELD
CL

OAKEN WOOD CL

Scholes
Paddock

2

SOUGH HALL AVE
SOUGH HALL

KIRKCROFT
CL

OAKEN WOOD RD

SCHOLES LA

THE PADDOCK

Scholes

SOUGH HALL RD

BROOK HILL

NEW ST
HILL SIDE

Thorpe
Hesley

SCHOLES GN

Bay Horse
(PH)

B6086

PIT LA

NEWTON PL

Nether Fold
Farm

1

Schole
Coppic

UPPER WORTLEY RD

SOR RD

TORNTREE RD
REE RD
BIRCHTREE
RD

LODGE LA

WINDMILL CT

PO

PH

95

Hesley Lodge
Farm

B6086

KIRKSTEAD ABBEY
MEWS

A629

LOUDEN CL

LOUDEN RD

UPPER WORTLEY RD

KEPPEL CL

KEPPEL RD

Grange
Lane
Farm

GRANGE LA

UPPER WORTLEY RD

Keppel's
Column

SCHOLES FIELD

KELVIN CT
MIDDLE
DR

KEPPEL
HTS

ADMIRALS CREST

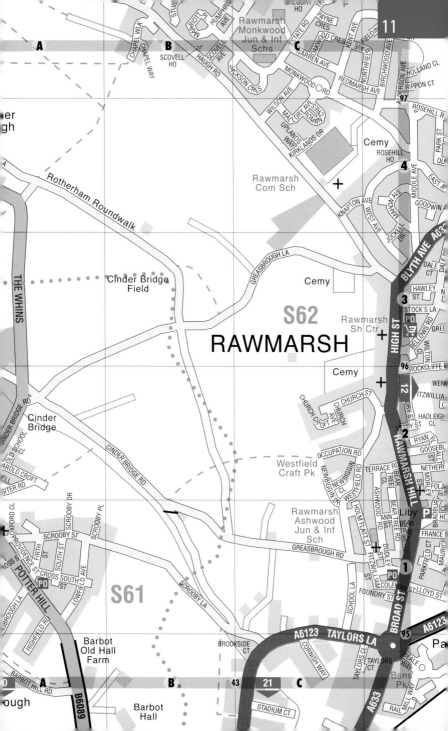

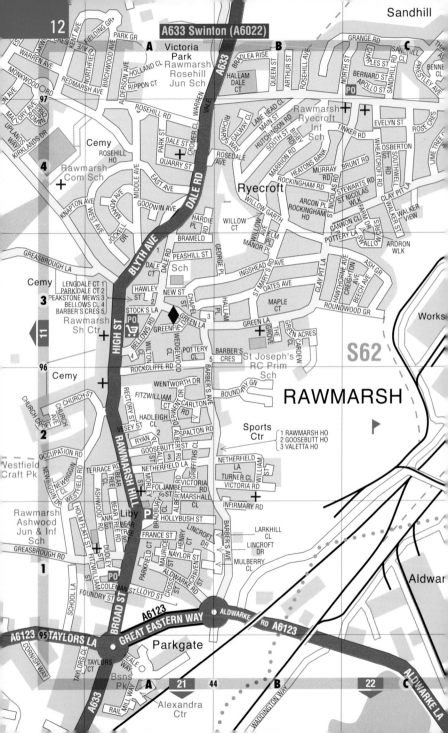

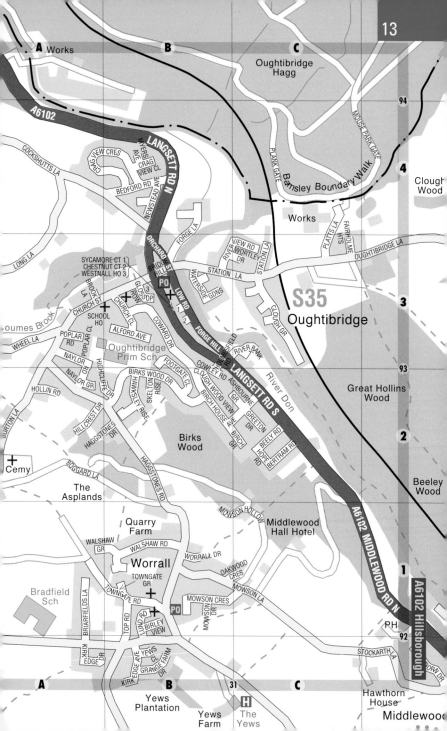

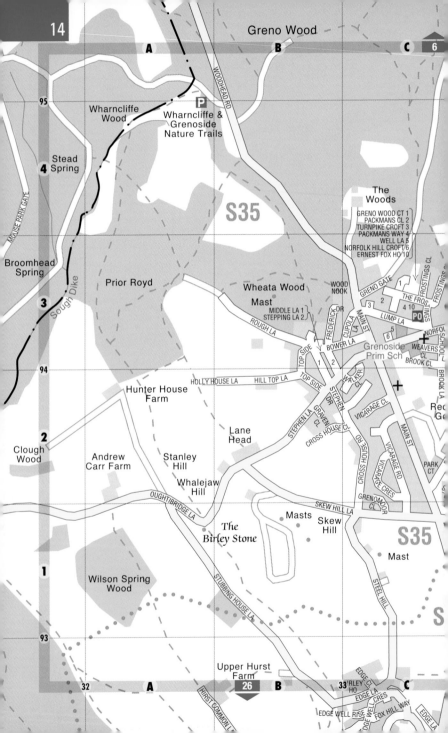

Greno Wood

A   **B**   **C**   **6**

95

WOODHEAD RD

Wharncliffe
Wood

P

Wharncliffe &
Grenoside
Nature Trails

4 Stead
Spring

MOUSE PARK GATE

The
Woods

GRENO WOOD CT 1
PACKMANS CL 2
TURNPIKE CROFT 3
PACKMANS WAY 4
WELL LA 5
NORFOLK HILL CROFT 6
ERNEST FOX HO 10

Broomhead
Spring

S35

3

Prior Royd

Sough Dike

Wheata Wood

Mast

MIDDLE LA 1
STEPPING LA 2

ROUGH LA

WOOD
NOOK

GRENO GATE

THE FROSTINGS

1

3   2   4 10

5 6

FRODERICK DR

CUPOLA LA

MAIN ST

LUMP LA

PO

FROSTINGS CL

FROSTINGS

SCHOOL

NORFOLK

TOP SIDE

BOWER LA

Grenoside
Prim Sch

WEAVERS
CL

BROOK CL

BROOK CL

94

HOLLY HOUSE LA

HILL TOP LA

TOP SIDE

1

2

+

Hunter House
Farm

STEPHEN LA

STEPHEN
DR

GRAVEN
CL

WALKER

WALKER

VICARAGE CL

Red
Go

2

Clough
Wood

Andrew
Carr Farm

Stanley
Hill

Lane
Head

CROSS HOUSE CL

CROSS HOUSE

VICARAGE RD

VICARAGE CRES

MAIN ST

PARK
CT

Whalejaw
Hill

OUGHTIBRIDGE LA

The
Birley Stone

Masts

SKEW HILL LA

Skew
Hill

GRENOMOOR
CL

S35

1

Wilson Spring
Wood

STUBBING HOUSE LA

Mast

STEEL HILL

93

32   **A**

HIRST COMMON L

Upper Hurst
Farm

26

B

33

RLEY
HO

EDGE CL

EDGE LA

EDGE WELL CRES

C

EDGE WELL RISE

EDGE WELL CRES

FOX HILL WAY

FOX HILL WAY

S

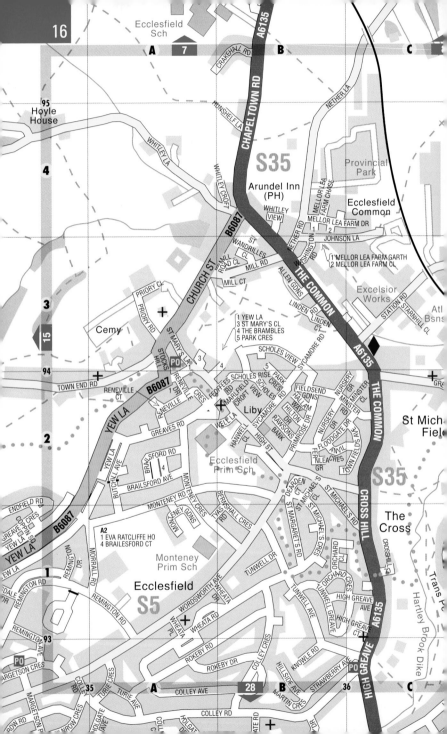

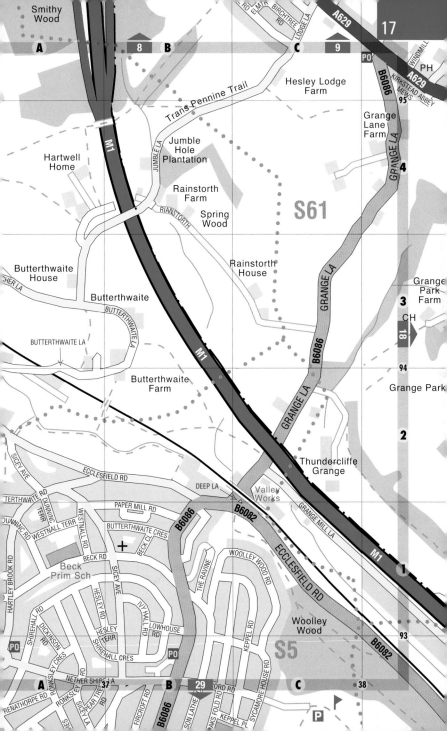

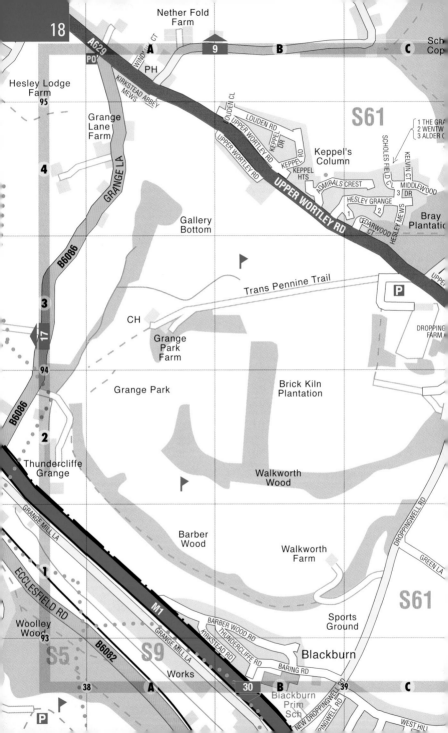

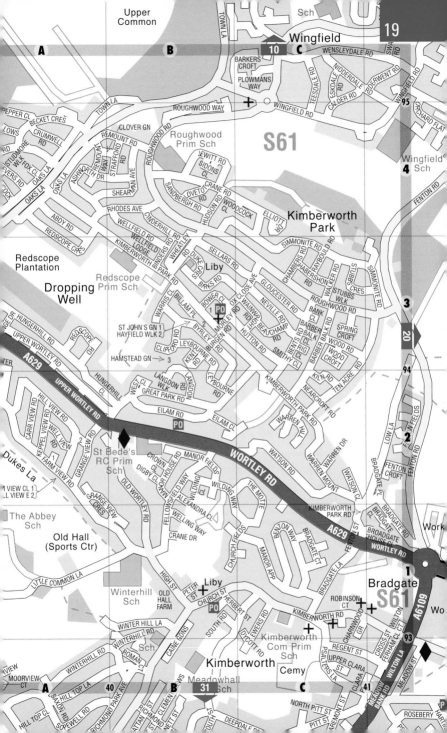

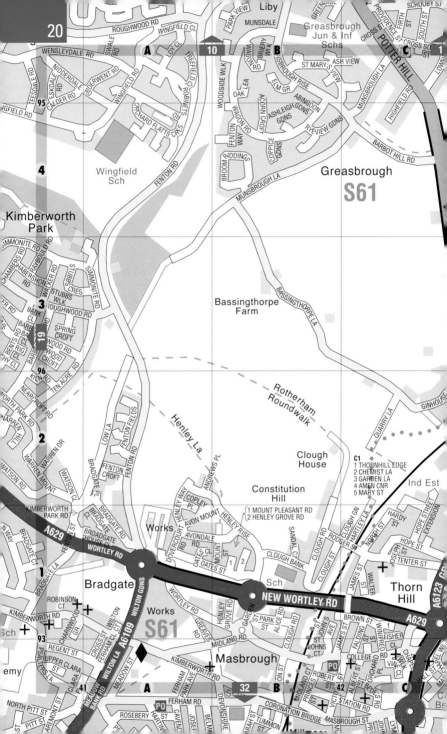

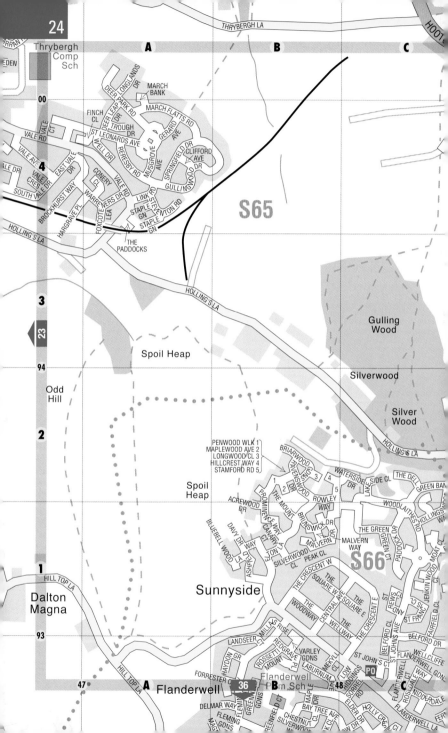

Ravenfield

A BOSVILE CL

B

C

25

Birk Lodge Farm

GARDEN LA

ARBOUR LA

B6093

95

4

Ravenfield Common

Braithwell Common

enfield m Sch

rside arm

Ravenfield Grange

3

MOOR LA N

FIELDSIDE CT

HOLLY'S HOUSE RD

COMMON LA

94

SANDRINGHAM PL

THE PADDOCKS

RADFORD CL

BELLWOOD CT

BRAITHWELL RD

MEADOW VIEW DR

CEDAR DR

Braithwell Common

ALLOTT CL

Ravenfield Common

MOOR LA N

POPLAR GR

HOWSON CL

OBORNE CL

WESTBY CL

Priests Bridge

PO

SMEATON CL

RANFIELD CT

Sewage Works

2

LONGFIELD DR

GRANSOV CL

HAZEL CT

BARBERRY WAY

FIRETHORN RISE

BLACKTHORN RISE

Hellaby Brook

LIDGET LA

REASBY AVE

COMMON FARM CL

SILVERMOOR DR

SPENCER DR

SANDERSON DR

S65

Hellaby Park Farm

STONE CL

HURLFIELD

GR SB CT

1

MOORFIELD MOORFIELD GR

MOOR LA S

MOORFIELD AVE

LIDGET LA

B6093

SCARBY RD

HAREWOOD GR

WAY

HELLABY VIEW

Spenwood Farm

93

Hella Ind E

M18

INDSOR RISE

NICHOLS

BROOK

MORAL WAY

COPPINS CL

AUNT DR

GALWIT CL

MILNER CL

ASKAM CT

Bramley Grange Farm

A 49

B 37

C 50

MGMORE

COPSE

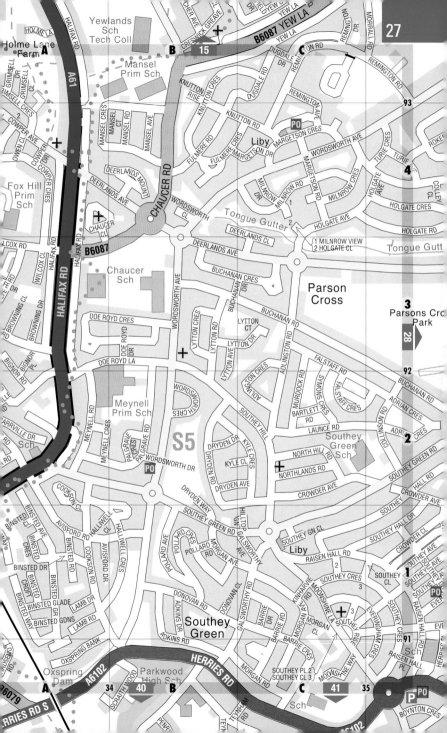

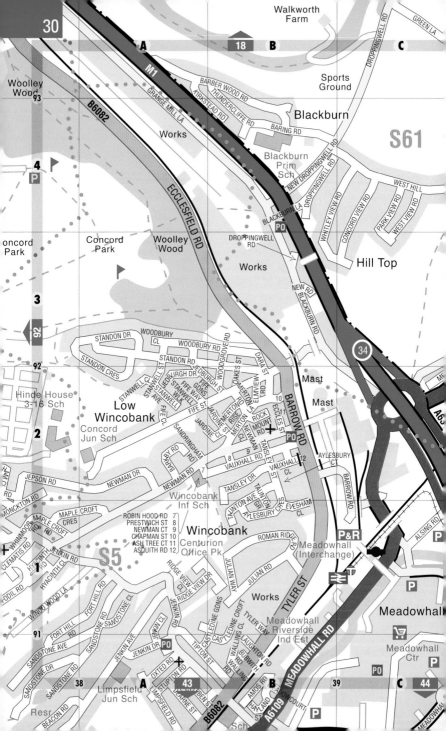

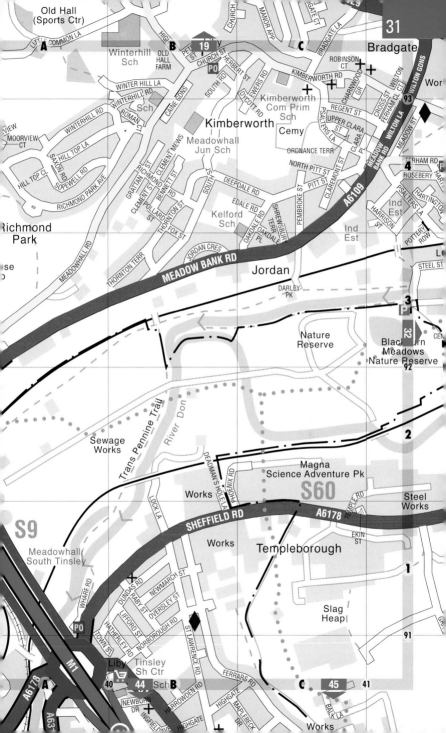

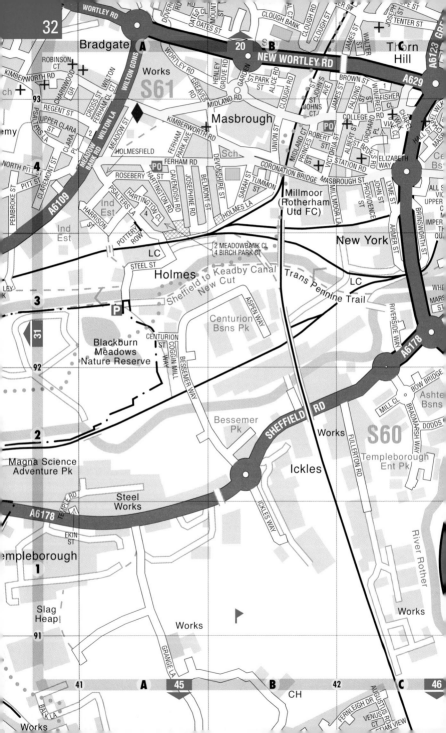

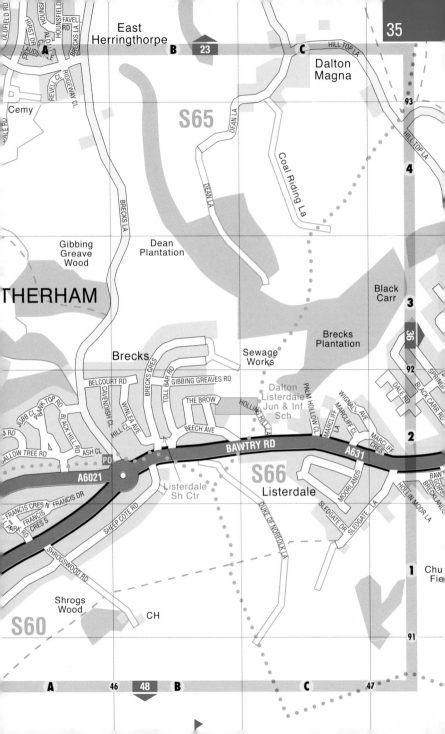

East
Herringthorpe

A **B** 23 **C** HILL TOP LA

Dalton
Magna

OLDFIELD RD
HIRST DR
HOUNDS
HOUNSFIELD
FAVELL
BRECKS LA

LAUDSDALE
CL
DALE RD

REVELL CL
RIDGEWAY CL

Cemy

S65

DEAN LA

93

DEAN LA

Coal Riding La

HILL TOP LA

4

BRECKS LA

Gibbing
Greave
Wood

Dean
Plantation

Black
Carr

3

THERHAM

Brecks
Plantation

36

Brecks

BRECKS CRES

Sewage
Works

92

SPRING

BELCOURT RD

TOLL BAR RD
GIBBING GREAVES RD

DALE RD

BLACK CARR RD

CAVENDISH CL

THE BROW

Dalton
Listerdale
Jun & Inf
Sch

PALM HOLLOW CL

WIGNALL AVE

MARCLIFF
LA

JUBB CL
BANK TOP RD

HILL LA
WINLEA AVE

BEECH AVE

HOLLING HILL LA

MARCLIFF
MARCLIFF CL

MARCLIFF
CRES

2

BLACK HILL RD
ASH CL

PO

BAWTRY RD

A631

BAW

GALLOW TREE RD

A6021

Listerdale
Sh Ctr

S66

Listerdale

MOORLANDS

GOTTS
BRECKLANDS

FRANCIS CRES N FRANCIS DR

FRANCIS
CRES S

SHEEP COTE RD

DUKE OF NORFOLK LA

SLEDGATE DR SLEDGATE LA

HOLLIN MOOR LA

1

Chu
Fie

PARK RD

SHROGSWOOD RD

Shrogs
Wood

CH

91

S60

A 46 48 **B** **C** 47

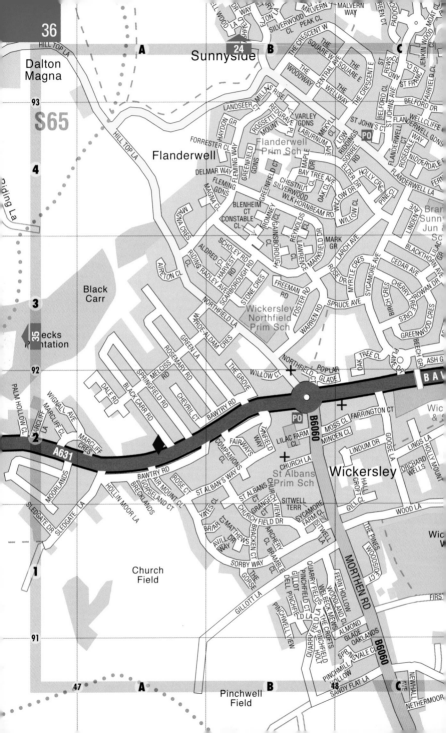

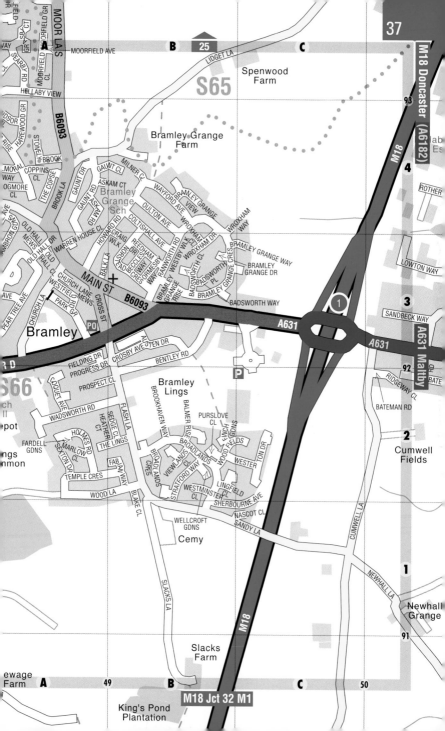

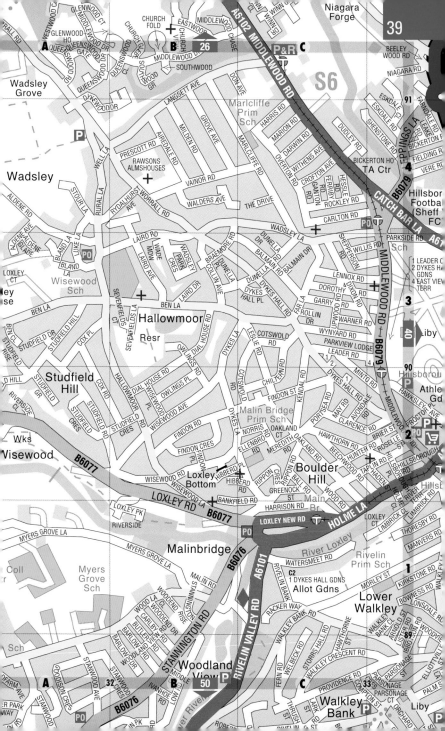

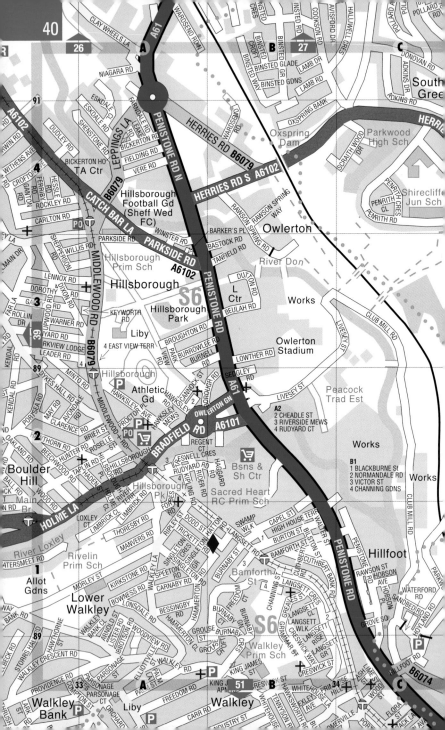

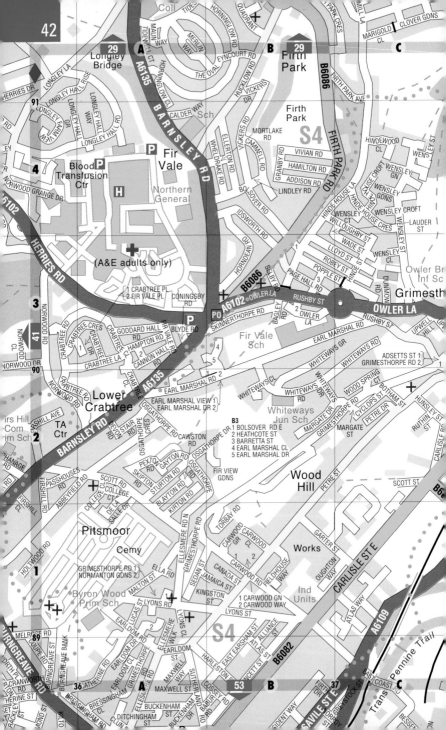

Coll
TIDE
HORNINGLOW RD
QUADRANT
PARK CRES
MILL
MARIGOLD CL CLOVER GDNS

MAIN
TIDEWAY
HORNINGLOW
MERLIN WAY
A6135
BARNSLEY RD
B6086
FIRTH PARK RD

29 Longley Bridge **A**
THE OVAL
EYNCOURT RD
HUCKLOW RD
VICKERS DR
Sch
FIRTH PARK AVE
B Firth Park **29** **C**

Longley La
LONGLEY HALL RISE
CALDER WAY
VICKERS RD
MORTLAKE RD
Firth Park
S4
HINDEWOOD CL
WENS
LEY ST

LONGLEY GR
LONGLEY HALL RD
LONGLEY HALL WAY
ELLERTON RD
WHELDRAKE RD
CAMMELL RD
GRANBY RD
VIVIAN RD
HINDE HOUSE LA
HINDE HOUSE CRES
WENSLEY GDNS
WENSLEY CROFT

91
LONGLEY FARM VIEW
BOLSOVER RD
HAMILTON RD
ADDISON RD
SE CROFT
WENSLEY GN
WENSLEY CT
LAUDER ST
WENSLEY CL

NORWOOD GRANGE DR
4
Blood Transfusion Ctr
P **P**
Fir Vale
Northern General
LINDLEY RD
WILLOUGHBY ST
WADE ST
LLOYD ST
ROBEY ST
POPPLE ST
WENSLEY CL

6102
H
IDSWORTH RD
HORNDEAN RD
PAGE HALL RD
Owler Br Inf Sc

HERRIES RD
(A&E adults only)
SELBY RD
B6086
Grimesth

3
1 Crabtree PL
2 Fir Vale PL
CONINGSBY RD
PO
A6102 OWLER LA
RUSHBY ST
OWLER LA
DUNMOW RD

NORWOOD RD
41
90
NORWOOD CL
NORWOOD DR
CRABTREE RD
CRABTREE CRES
GODDARD HALL RD
HAMPTON RD
CRABTREE LA
FIR VALE RD
BLYDE RD
SKINNERTHORPE RD
Fir Vale Sch
BAGLEY RD
2 OWLER LA
EARL MARSHAL RD
RUSHBY ST
UPWELL HILL

CANNON HALL RD
EARL MARSHAL RD
WHITEWAYS GR
WHITEWAYS RD
ADSETTS ST 1
GRIMESTHORPE RD 2

CRABTREE LA
Lower Crabtree
OSGATHORPE RD
CAWSTON RD
Whiteways Jun Sch
WHITEWAYS CL
WHITEWAYS DR
WHITEWAYS RD
MARGATE DR
GRIMESTHORPE RD
WOOD SPRING CT
BOTHAM ST
HUNSLEY ST

EARL MARSHAL VIEW 1
EARL MARSHAL DR 2
B3 1 BOLSOVER RD E
2 HEATHCOTE ST
3 BARRETTA ST
4 EARL MARSHAL CL
5 EARL MARSHAL DR
MARGATE ST
CYCLOPS ST
PETRE ST
RUTHIN ST
CARLISLE RD

2
BASHILL AVE
TA Ctr
BARNSLEY RD
DEVON STAIR
HIGHGROVE
OSGATHORPE RD
FIR VIEW GDNS
Wood Hill

PASSHOUSES RD
ABBEYFIELD RD
SCOTT RD
COLLEGE CT
PEXTON RD
GAYTON RD
STURTON RD
BLAYTON RD
KIRTON RD
OSGATHORPE RD
TORBAY RD
CARWOOD CL
CARWOOD GR
PETRE ST
SCOTT ST

FIRSHILL CL
FIRSHILL RD
College CT
DE LA SALLE DR
ELLESMERE RD N
GRIMESTHORPE RD
CARWOOD RD
FIELDHOUSE WAY
GARTER ST
Works
B6

Pitsmoor Cemy
ELLESMERE RD
ELLA RD
SEDAN ST
CANADA ST
JAMAICA ST
KINGSTON ST
OUGHTON WAY
CARLISLE ST E

HOLTWOOD RD
1
GRIMESTHORPE RD 1
NORMANTON GDNS 2
MALTON ST
LYONS RD
1 CARWOOD GN
2 CARWOOD WAY
Ind Units
ATLAS WAY
A6109

Byron Wood Prim Sch
EARL LUCAS ST
LYONS CL
LYONS ST
89
MELROSE RD
EARLDOM DR
EARLDOM ST
EAST EARSHAM ST
ALLIANCE ST
S4
B6082
Trans Pennine Trail

SPRINGREAVE RD
BURNGREAVE ST
LOUPE ST
BURNGREAVE BANK
EARLDOM RD
EARLDOM CL
GRIMESTHORPE RD
BRESSINGHAM RD
HARLESTON ST
EAST ST
COSSEY RD
FIRTH DR
COAST
BESSE

CRANWORTH RD
CATHERINE ST
36
A
MAXWELL ST
MAXWELL ST
SUTHERLAND RD
BABUR RD
53
B SAVILE ST E
37
BAGSTOCK ST
C

BUCKENHAM ST
DITCHINGHAM ST
BUCKINGHAM ST
CLUN

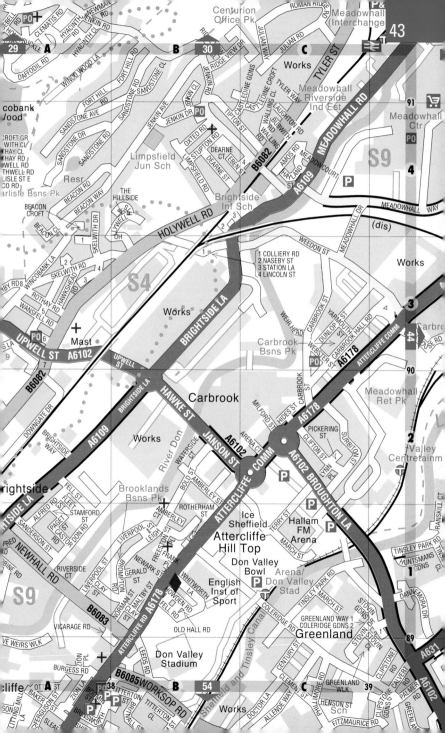

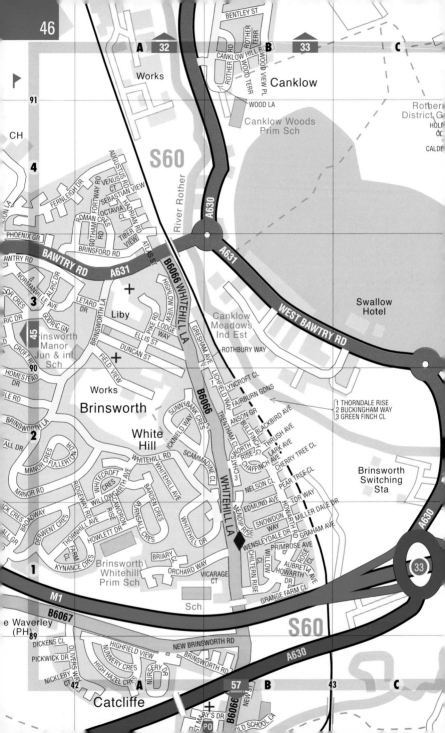

46

A 32
B 33
C

91

Works

CH

4

S60

BENTLEY ST
CANKLOW HILL RD
ROTHER TERR
WOOD VIEW PL
WOOD TERR
Canklow
WOOD LA
Canklow Woods
Prim Sch

River Rother

Rother
District G
HOL
OC
CALDE

AUGUSTUS RD
FERNLEIGH DR
VENUS CT
SEBASTIAN VIEW
FORTWAY RD
OCTAVIA CL
GOTHAM RD
ROMAN CRES
HADRIAN CL
TIBER VIEW
PHOENIX GR
BRINSFORD RD
ATLAS ST

AWTRY RD
BAWTRY RD A631

A630

A631

WEST BAWTRY RD

Swallow
Hotel

3

NORMANVILLE AVE
ALRIC DR
GODRIC GN
LETARD DR
B6066 WHITEHILL LA
HIGHLOW VIEW
PIKE RD
LODGE WAY
Liby
ELLIS ST
DUNCAN ST

RIC DR
45
insworth
Manor
Jun & inf
Sch

HOMESTEAD
DR
LE RD

90

FIELD VIEW
Works
Brinsworth

BRINSWORTH LA

Canklow
Meadows
Ind Est
ROTHBURY WAY

GRESHAM AVE

LICHFIELD WAY
LYNCROFT CL
FAIRBURN GDNS
ANSON GR

BRINSWORTH LA
2

White
Hill

SUNNY BANK CRES
ICKNIELD WAY
SCAMMADINE CL
B6066
TRENTHAM CL
ASHWORTH RISE
BULLFINCH CL
BLACKBIRD AVE
THRUSH AVE
LARK AVE
CHAFFINCH AVE
CHERRY TREE CL

1 THORNDALE RISE
2 BUCKINGHAM WAY
3 GREEN FINCH CL

Brinsworth
Switching
Sta

MANOR CRES
FULLERTON RD
MANOR RD
WHITECROFT CRES
WHITEHILL RD
RIDGEWAY RD
WILLOWGARTH AVE
CAWDRON RISE
BARDEN CRES
TYRNSALL CRES
WHITEHILL AVE
WHITEHILL DR
NELSON CL
PEAR TREE CL
TOR WAY
EDMUND AVE
SNOWDON WAY
HOWARTH RD
MILLER DALE DR
GRAHAM AVE
WENSLEYDALE DR
PRIMROSE AVE

DERWENT CRES
BROADWAY
THORNHILL AVE
HOWLETT DR
FARM CL
KYNANCE CRES
BRIARY
ORCHARD WAY
VICARAGE CT
Brinsworth
Whitehill
Prim Sch
MOTTIM
CHILTERN RISE
HOWARTH DR
AUBRETIA AVE
ROSE CL
GRANGE FARM CL

ICK CRES
ALL GR
ALL DR

1

M1

B6067

e Waverley
(PH)
89

DICKENS CL
PICKWICK DR
OLIVERS WAY
HIGHFIELD VIEW
NUNNERY CRES
HIGH HAZEL CRES
NICKLEBY
42
A
57
B
43
C

Catcliffe

NEW BRINSWORTH RD
BRINSWORTH RD
NURSERY DR

S60

A630

ST MARY'S DR
PO
OLD SCHOOL LA
B6066

WHITEHILL LA

NENDIP RISE

CHASWORTH RISE
3
LARL AVE

Sch

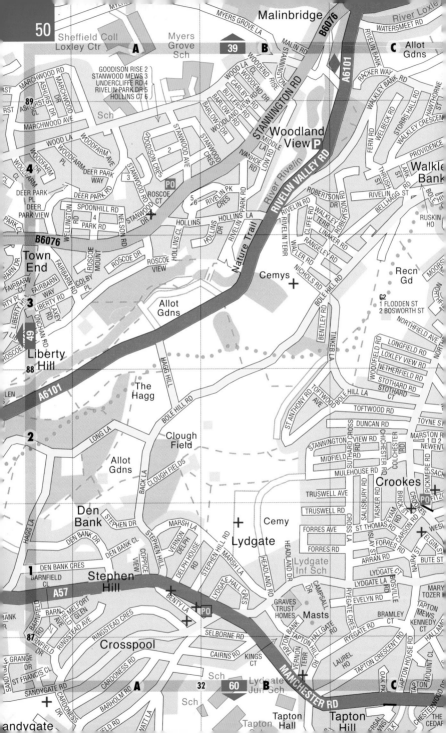

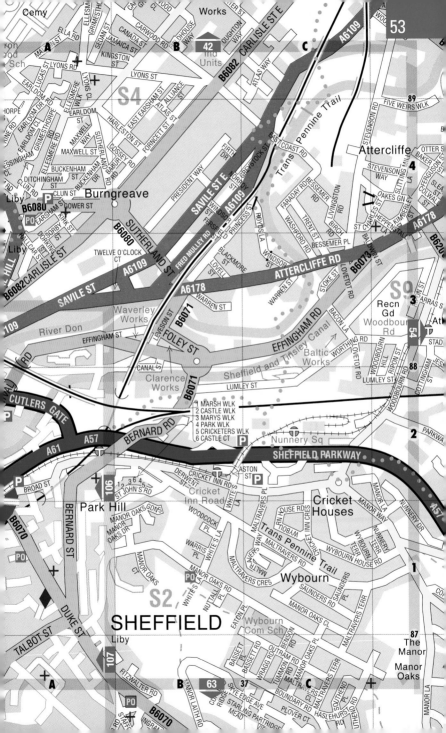

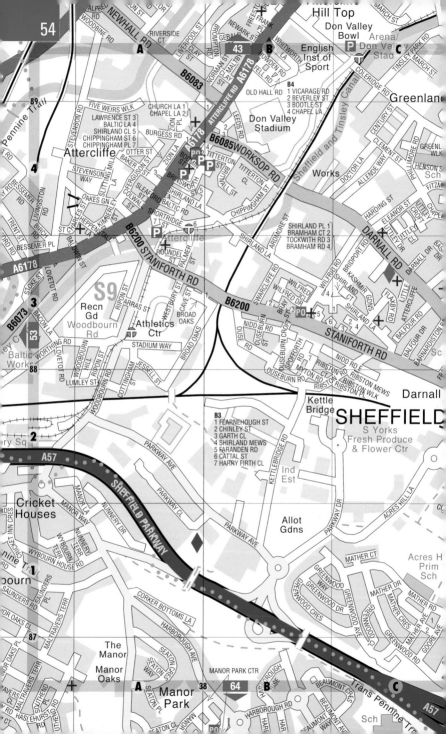

Tinsley
Marshalling Yd

A 45 **B** **C**

BRINSWORTH RD B6067

WOOD LA

GREEN LA

The Waverley
(PH)

89
EUROPA LINK

EUROPA CT

Sheffield
Airport
Bsns Pk

DICKENS C

PICKWICK

NICKLE

S9

EUROPA LINK

heffield Airport
Bsns Pk

4

Sheffield City
Airport

Sheffield City
Airport

SHEFFIELD PARKWAY

ans Pennine Trail

Superstore

3

B6533

POPLAR WA

55

B6066

88

Works

HIGH FIELD SPRING

SHEFFIELD PARKWAY

2

ls
k

LOW DR

E GR

TNUT AVE

DER LA

LARCH HILL

WAVERLEY
COTTS

A630

QUARRY RD

Sports
Gd

OAKLEY RD

HALESWORTH RD

87

B6066

FINCHWELL RD

S13

B6200

+

FINCHWELL RD

FINCHWELL CRES

A 41 66 **B** **C**

sworth

HALL

Orgreave

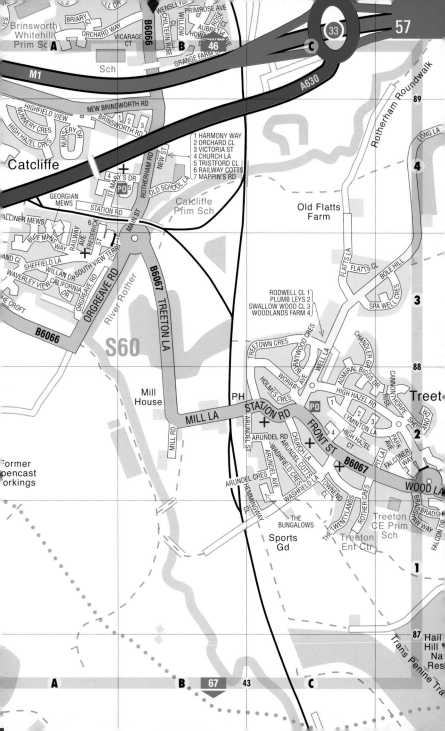

Brinsworth
Whitehill
Prim Sch **A**

BRIARY

WENSLEYD
WILLOW
CHILTERN RISE

PRIMROSE AVE
ROSE
AUBRETIA
HOW

ORCHARD WAY
VICARAGE
CT

B6066 **B** **46**

GRANGE FARM

33 **C**

M1

A630

Rotherham Roundwalk

89

HIGHFIELD VIEW
NUNNERY CRES
HIGH HAZEL CRES

NEW BRINSWORTH RD
BRINSWORTH RD

1 2 3

NURSERY DR

LONG LA

Catcliffe

ST MARY'S DR
PO

4 5

ROTHERHAM RD
NEW ST
OLD SCHOOL LA

1 HARMONY WAY
2 ORCHARD CL
3 VICTORIA ST
4 CHURCH LA
5 TRISTFORD CL
6 RAILWAY COTTS
7 MAPPIN'S RD

Catcliffe
Prim Sch

Old Flatts
Farm

4

GEORGIAN
MEWS

STATION RD

LLINER MEWS

BLUE MANS
WAY

RAILWAY
AVE

FREDERICK
ST

6

MAIN ST

SOUTH VIEW TERR

B6067

ORGREAVE RD

TREETON LA

FLATTS LA

FLATTS LA

BOLE HILL
CRES

SPA WELL

3

AND CL
SHEFFIELD LA
WILLAN DR
WAVERLEY VIEW
CALIFORNIA
DR
HE CROFT

River Rother

RODWELL CL 1
PLUMB LEYS 2
SWALLOW WOOD CL 3
WOODLANDS FARM 4

CHANDLER GR

B6066

S60

Mill
House

TREETOWN CRES

BANTWOOD CRES

WORRALL AVE

WELL LA

ADMIRAL BIGGS DR

CANNONTHORPE
RISE

88

Treet

PH

HOLMES CRES

STATION RD

PO

HIGH HAZEL RD

1

2 3

HIGH HAZEL
CT

LYMINTON LA

PARK
AVE

PIT LA

FALCONER
WAY

2

MILL LA

MILL RD

ARUNDEL ST

ARUNDEL RD

CHURCH LA

ARUNDEL COTTS

WASHFIELD CRES

ARUNDEL AVE

FRONT ST

4

B6067

TOWNEND
CL

ROTHER CRES

WOOD LA

BRADSH

BRADSHAW WAY

Former
pencast
orkings

ARUNDEL CRES

HEMMINGWAY
CL

WASHFIELD CL

THE
BUNGALOWS

THE TWENTYLANDS

Treeton
CE Prim
Sch

FALCON DR

Sports
Gd

Treeton
Ent Ctr

1

87 Hail
Hill
Na
Res

Trans Penine Tra

A **B** 67 **43** **C**

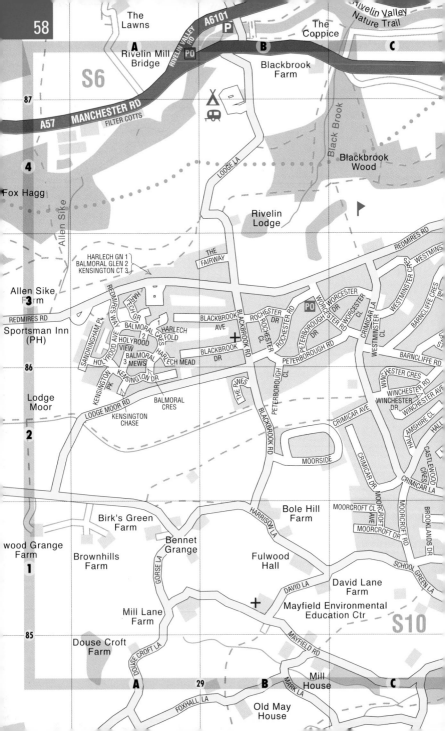

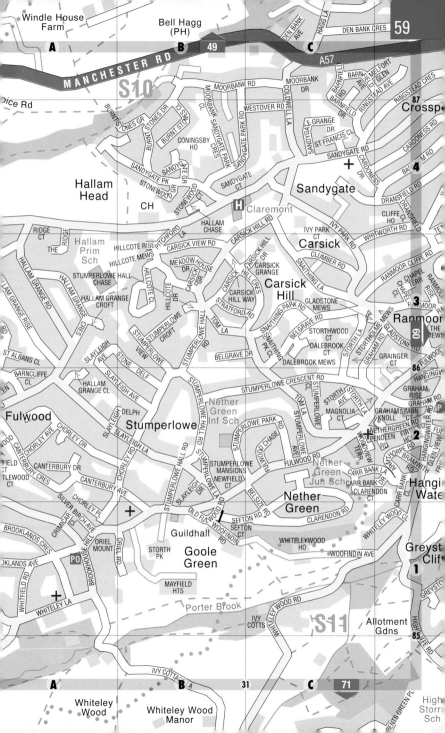

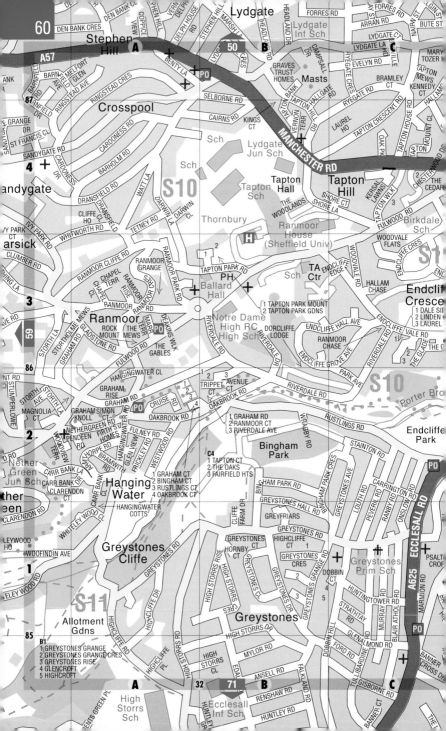

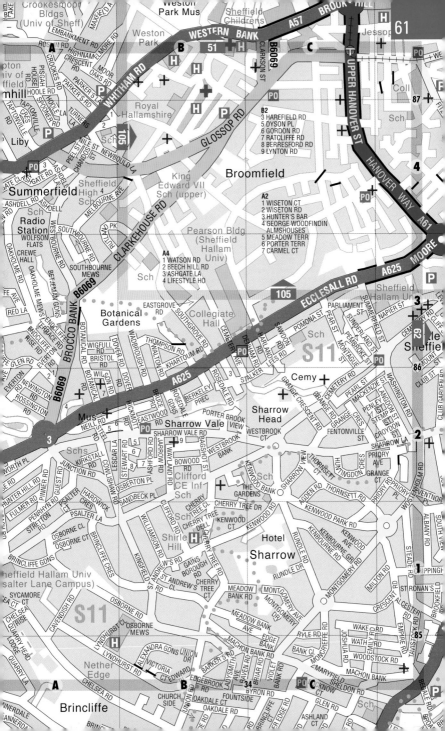

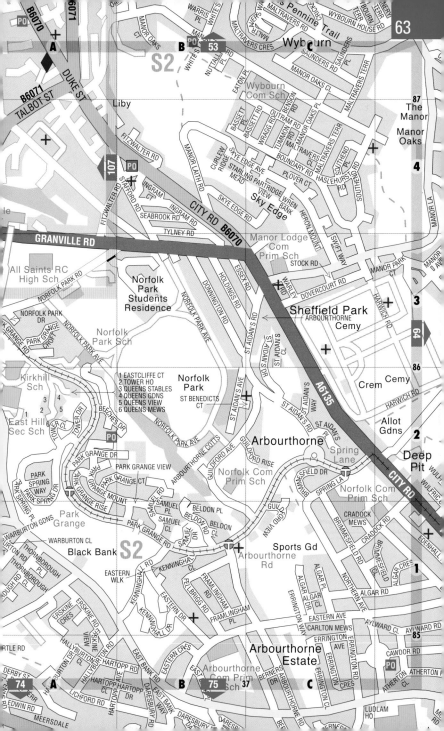

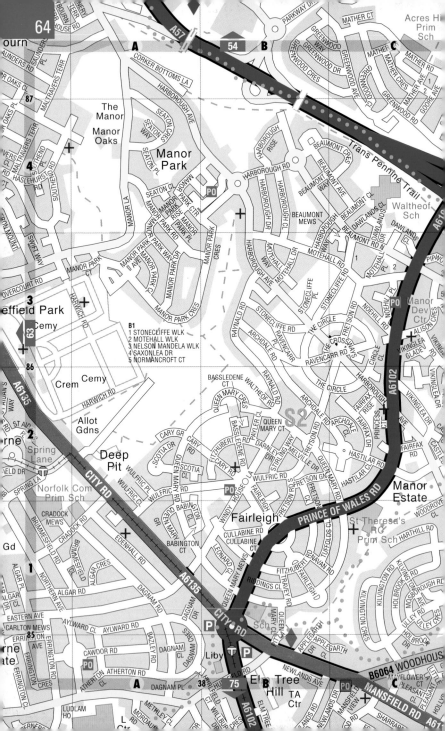

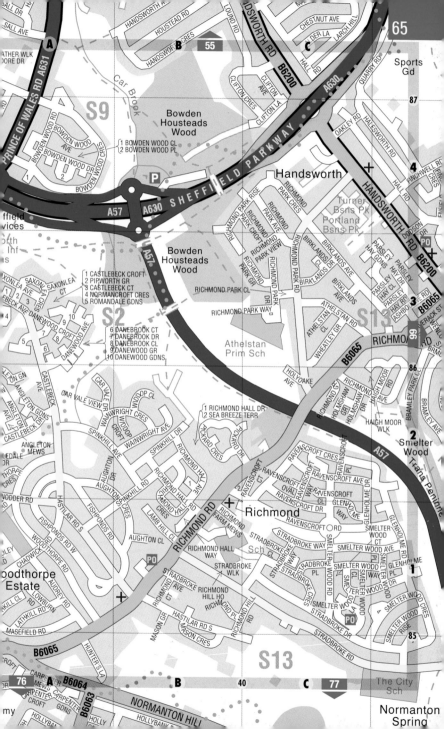

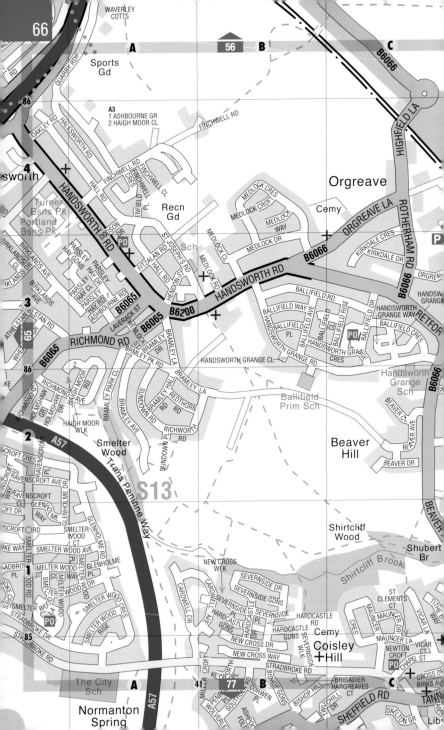

S60

A

B

B6067 WOOD LA

C

Treeton
Grange

87

Hail Mary
Hill Wood
Nature
Reserve

Trans Pennine Trail

Treeton Wood
Nature Reserve

4

Falconer
Wood

Mast

WES

Falconer
Farm

Falconer La

Smallage La

Smallage
Farm

Aston
Sc

3

67

86

Sewage
Works

Smallage
La

SHEFFIELD RD

FORD RD B6200

Works

2

Aston Fence
Jun & Inf
Sch

CHESTN

Liby

Works

S13

B6200

Fence
Farm

Sheffield Rd

Swallowne
Prim Sch

Trans Pennine Trail

River Rother

Timber
Yard

Park Hill
Farm

KINGFISHER
GR

KESTREL RISE

ROTHER VIEW
GDNS

ROTHER VIEW CL

PARK HILL
GDNS

N HIBBA
VE

BAXTER

HAIGH MOOR WAY

SOUTHWELL
GDNS

SJM

ST PARK DR

SORBY
RD

PARK
HILL GDNS

1

JOHN HIBBARD

CRES

RYAN DR

SWALLOW WOOD RD

PARK WISHING WELL

RUSSELL
CL

N RD

85

SOAP HOUSE LA

THORNCLIFFE
CL

LIDGET CL

A

44

79

B

C

B6200

aying
ield

Meadow Bank
Farm

A57

FIELD RD

CARR LA

A   B   C

S66

TURNSHAW RD

87

Turnshaw Plantation

4

Turnshaw Common

M1 Jct 32

Spring Wood

Mast

Brook

Burial Ground

ULLEY LA

3

69

86

S26

ULLEY LA

6067

New South Farm

2

AUGHTON LA

STANLEY GR

LARCH GR

MAPLE GR

WILLOW GR

ARLINGTON AVE

NORTH FARM CT

PIPER LA

OSBORNE AVE

CHRISTCHURCH

AVE

Cemy

SUDBURY DR

BELL ST

Conduit Moor or Common

Croft Farm

LEGION DR

COTSWOLD DR

HARDWICK

CHATSWORTH

THORESBY CL

Sch

MALTON DR

PO

B6067

WORKSOP RD

Yellow Lion (PH)

31

A57 / Worksop (A01)

PRIORY WAY

CHURCH VIEW

CL

CHURCH LA

GREEN LA

MELTON CT

1

LAYCOCK AVE

PORTLAND AVE

REGENTS WAY

CRADLEY DR

HADDON WAY

ALL SAINTS WAY

Netherthorpe

LAND VIEW

THE PADDOCKS

BURFORD CRES

WELBECK DR

WENTWORTH AVE

Aughton Court

Aston Park

M1

SOUTHLANDS

W 85

Aston

THE CHASE

WOODPECKER

FINCH RISE

CHURCH LA

Aston Park

R RISE

HERON

HILL

ROBIN

Aston Hall Jun & Inf Sch

A   47   81   B   C

BLUEBIRD

A57

Fiddle Neck Pond

M1 South

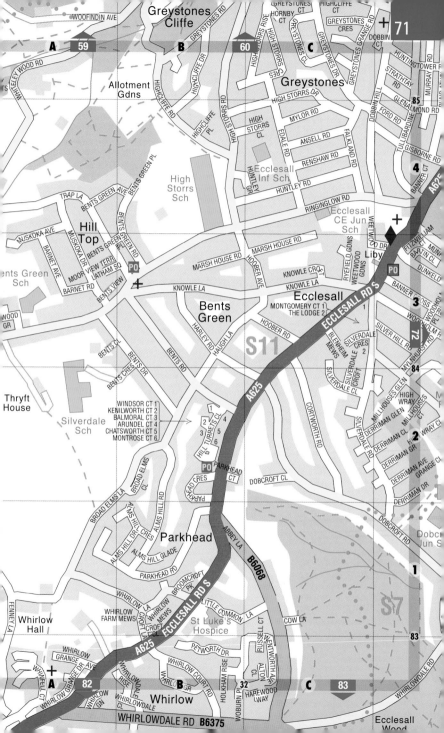

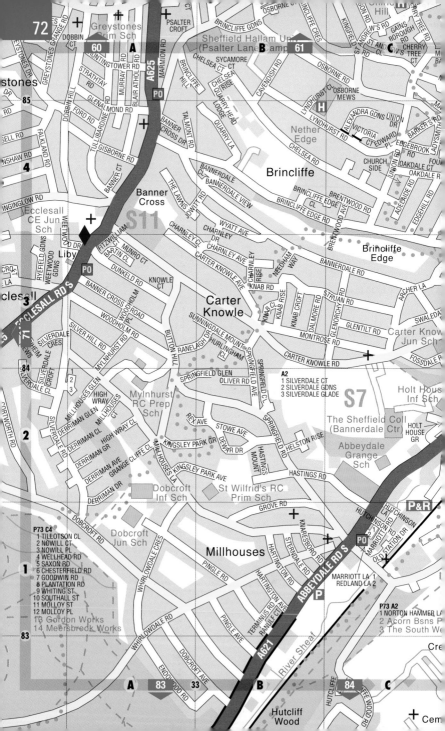

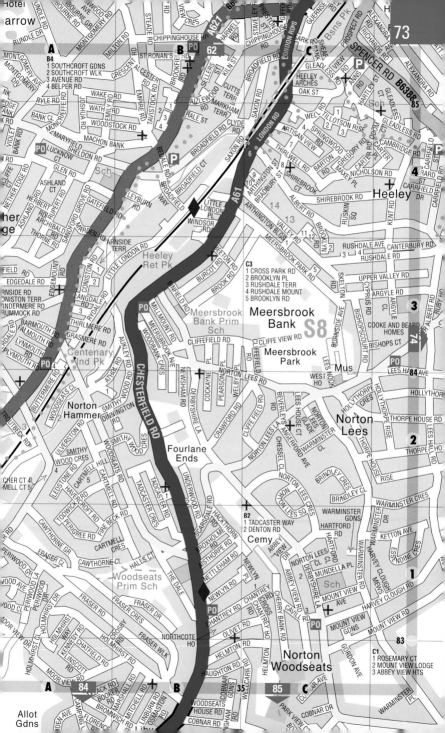

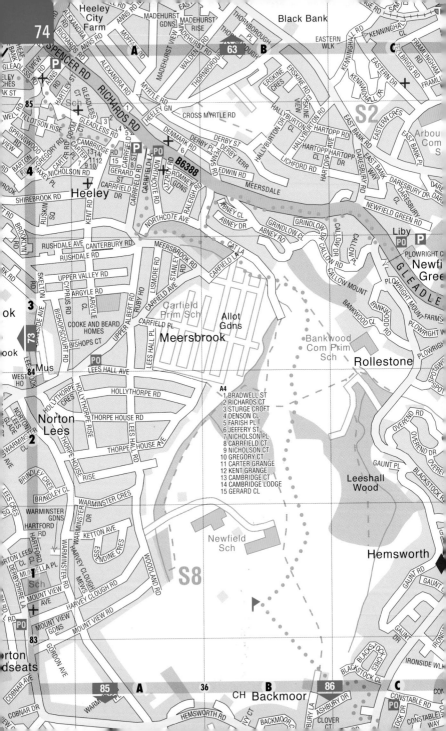

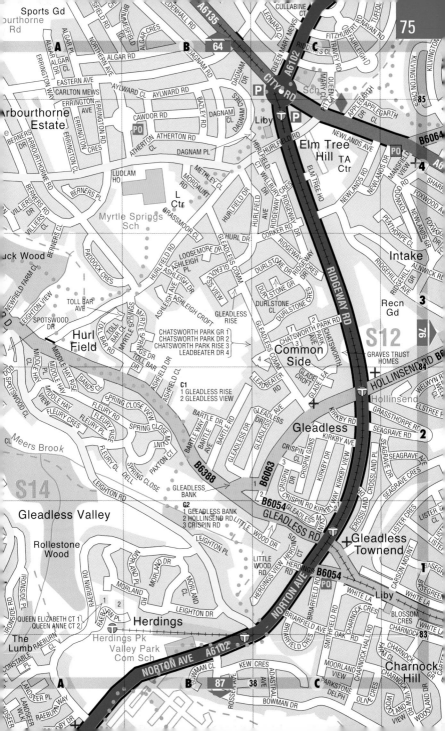

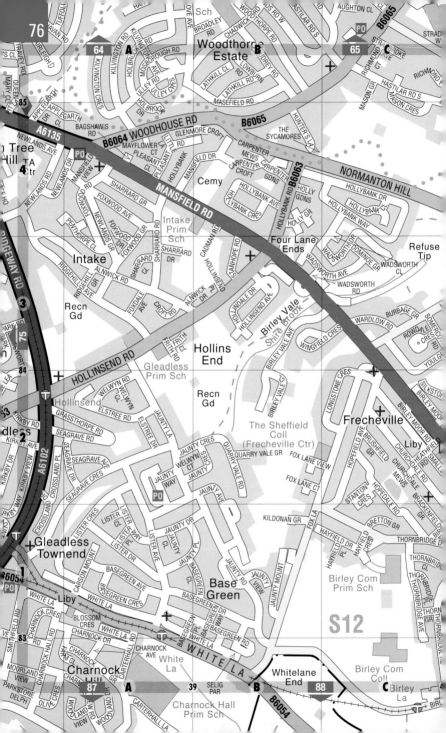

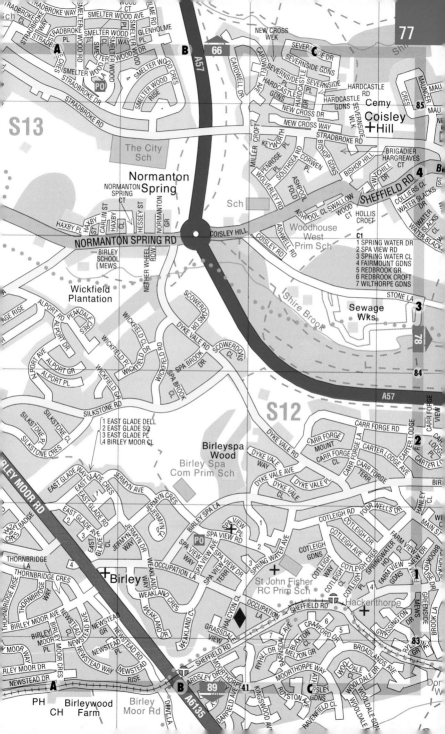

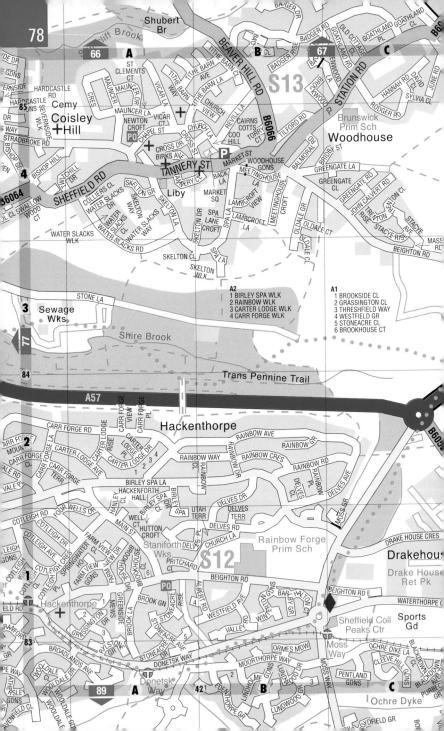

A B C

71

Limb Valley
Limb Brook

COIT LA

Rough
Standhills

Whirlow
Hall

83

WHIRLOW
GRANGE

Barberfields
Farm

Whirlow
Brook

P

WHIRLOW GRANGE DR

FENNEY LA

WHINFELL CT

S11

HOLLIS
HOSPL

Stand Hills

4

Whirlow
Bridge

LONG LINE

Moorview
Farm

Long Line
Farm

Sports
Gd

Moorside
Farm

HATHERSAGE RD

Sports
Gd

Sports
Gd

3

ASH HOUSE LA

LIMB LA

Dore Moor
Inn
(PH)

A625

CROSS LA

CROSS LA

Ash
House

82 HATHERSAGE RD

BRICKHOUSE LA

Brick Houses

Limb
Hill

KERWIN RD

PARKERS LA

LIMB LA

RYECROFT VIEW

Ry
F

RUSHLEY AVE

2

KERWIN CL

KERWIN DR

CAUSEWAY GLADE

CAUSEWAY
GDNS

CAUSEWAY
HEAD RD

RUSHLEY CL

RUSHLEY RD

RUSHLEY DR

S17

Causeway
Head

NEWFIELD CROFT

GREEN
PASTURES

DORE RD

MOORBANK

NEWFIELD LA

HEATHER LEA AVE

HEATHER LEA PL

THE
CAUSEWAY

RUSHLEIGH
CT

BURLINGTON GR

NEWFIELD CRES

MEADWAY DR

THE
MEADWAY

DORE HALL
CROFT

BURLINGTON
GLEN

SOUTH
CT

High
Greave

Recn
Gd

LEYFIELD RD

HIGH ST

BURLINGTON RD

BUR

1

NEWFIELD PL

DEVONSHIRE TERRACE
RD

VICARAGE LA

Dore

DEVONSHIRE
DR

Townhead

PO

HIGH TREES

SAVAGE LA

GILLEYFIELD AVE

V FERN GDNS

BUSHEY

KNOWLE GN

TOWNHEAD RD

MIDDLEFIELD
CROFT

DRURY LA

BUSHEY WOOD
GR

81

MIDDLEFIELD
CL

OVERDALE GDNS

CHURCH LA

Dore Prim
Sch

The Rowan
Sch

BLACKA MOOR VIEW

OVERDALE
RISE

SOUTHBOURNE
CT

Fairthorn

BLACKA MOOR RD

FURNISS AVE

FURNISS
MEWS

30

A

BLACKA MOOR CRES

94

B

31

C

Broadstorth

OLD HAY CL

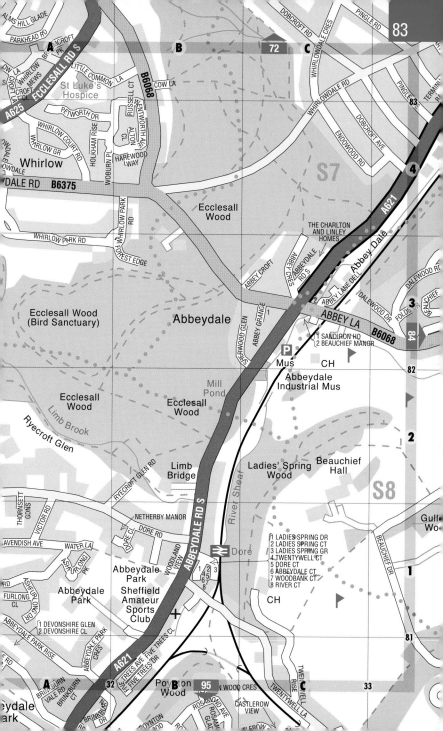

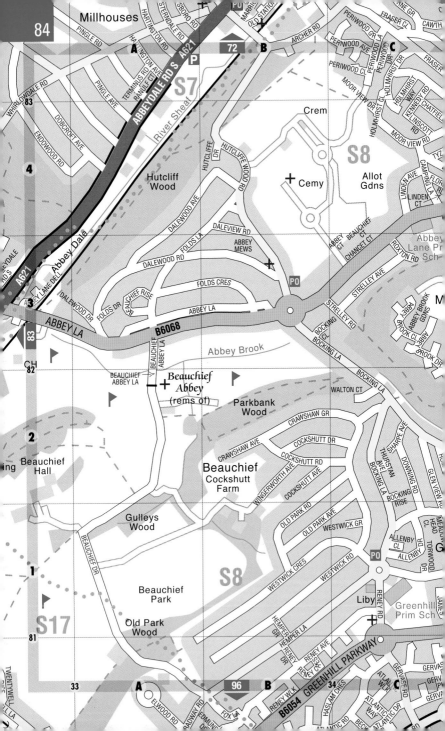

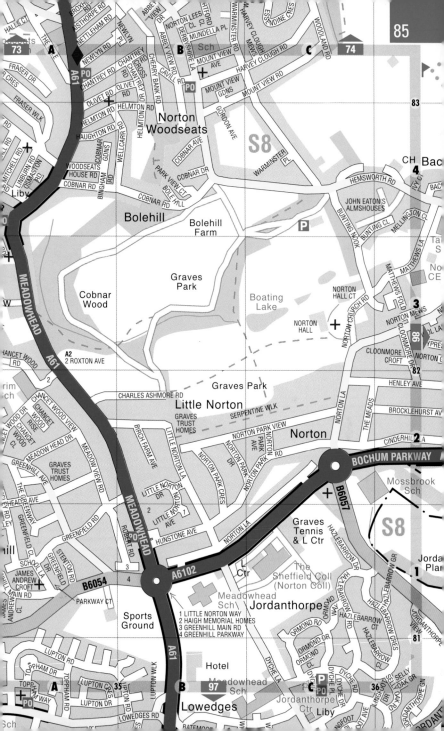

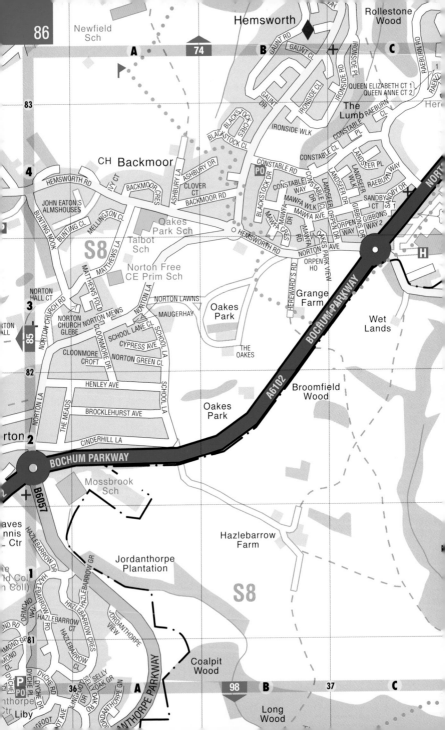

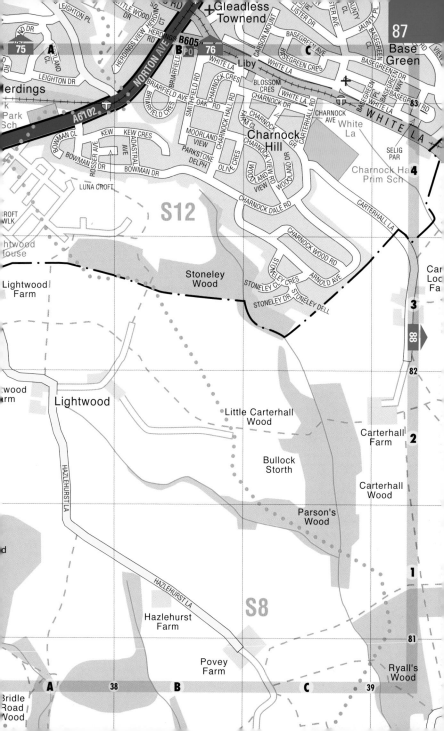

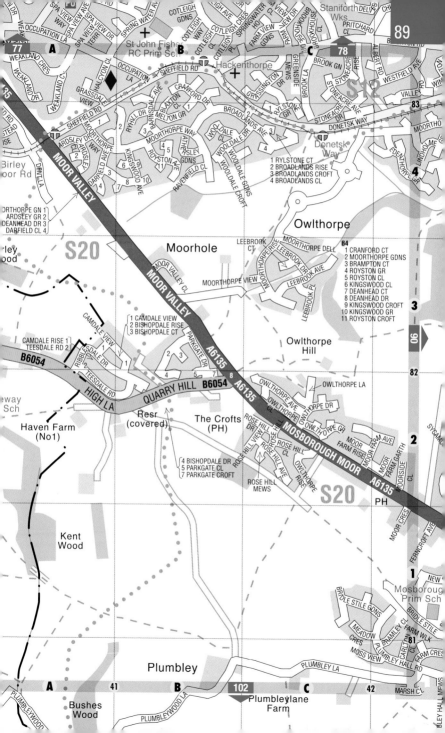

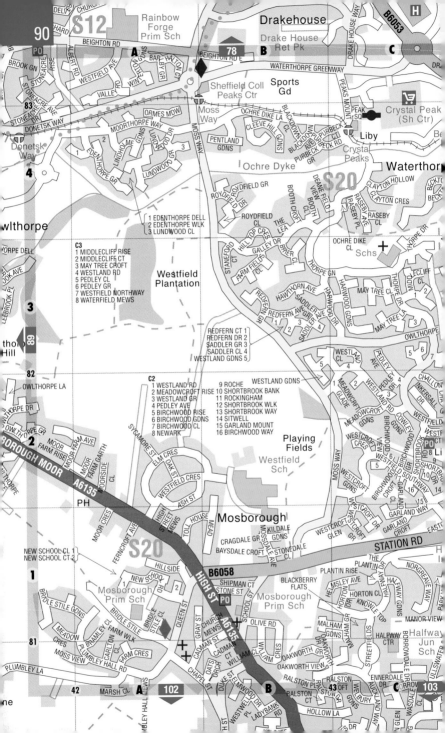

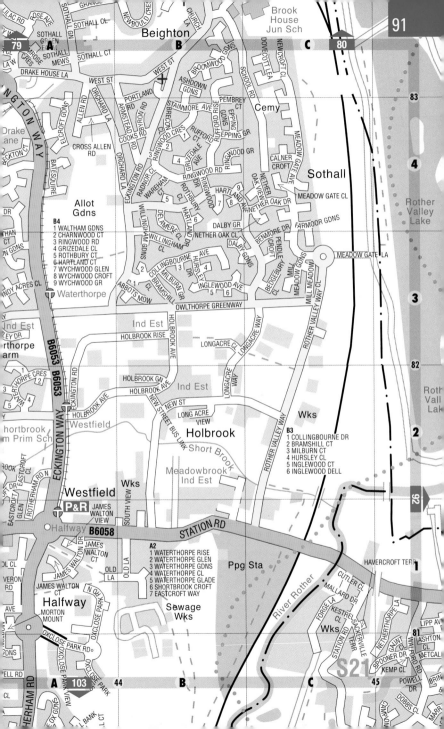

Brook House Jun Sch

Beighton

LILAC RD
ROSE AVE
SOTHALL GN
SOTHALL GRANGE
NEWBOULD CRES
CHURCH

SOTHALL GREEN
SOTHALL CL
SOTHALL MEWS
SOTHALL CT

MELROSE
CRES
DRAKE HOUSE LA

WEST ST
WEST ST

83

Drake Lane
Lane

ELCROFT GDNS
ALLEN RD
ORCHARD LA
BYRON RD
PORTLAND RD
ASHDOWN GDNS
STAINMORE AVE
BROOMWOOD GDNS
DOVECOTT LEA
NEWCROFT CL
SCHOOL RD

BRECON CT
PEMBREY CT
EPPING GDNS
EPPING GR

BECKTON CT
BATESQUIRE

CROSS ALLEN RD
COOKS RD
ARMSTEAD RD
RINGWOOD CRES
RUFFORD CT
RUFFORD RISE

Cemy

4

CROSS ALLEN RD
ECKINGTON LA
ORCHARD LA
RADNOR CL
RINGWOOD RD
GRIZEDALE AVE
RINGWOOD GR
CALNER CROFT

Sothall

MEADOW GATE AVE

83

DR
NATHAN CT
GDNS

Allot Gdns

WAREHAM CT
ROTHBURY CL
NETHER OAK VIEW
NETHER OAK DR
MEADOW GATE CL

Rother Valley Lake

B4
1 WALTHAM GDNS
2 CHARNWOOD CT
3 RINGWOOD RD
4 GRIZEDALE CL
5 ROTHBURY CT
6 HARTLAND CT
7 WYCHWOOD GLEN
8 WYCHWOOD CROFT
9 WYCHWOOD GR

WILLINGHAM GDNS
DELAMERE CL
HARTLAND DR
HARTLAND AVE
DALBY GR
NETHER OAK CL
FARMOOR GDNS

4

WINDY ACRES CL

WILLINGHAM CL
COLLINGBOURNE DR
MILBURN GR
HURSLEY AVE
INGLEWOOD AVE
DALBY GDNS
BENMORE DR
PENDLE CL
HEDGEBURY CL
MILL MEADOW GDNS

Waterthorpe

ABBOTS MDW
BRAMSHILL CT

5 6

OWLTHORPE GREENWAY

MILL MEADOW CL
ROTHER VALLEY WAY CL

MEADOW GATE LA

3

B6053
Ind Est
erthorpe Farm

HOLBROOK RISE
HOLBROOK AVE
LONGACRE CL
LONGACRE WAY
ROTHER VALLEY WAY

82

WATERTHORPE CRES
B6053

1 2
3
4 5

HOLBROOK GN
HOLBROOK AVE

Ind Est

Roth Vall Lak

HOLBROOK AVE
ECKINGTON RD
NEW STREET
NEW ST
LONG ACRE VIEW
BUS LINK

Ind Est

Wks

2

hortbrook m Prim Sch

Westfield

Short Brook

Holbrook

B3
1 COLLINGBOURNE DR
2 BRAMSHILL CT
3 MILBURN CT
4 HURSLEY CL
5 INGLEWOOD CT
6 INGLEWOOD DELL

92

ECKINGTON WAY

Meadowbrook Ind Est

Wks

ROTHERHAM CL
EASTCROFT CL
EASTCROFT GLEN

Westfield

SOUTH VIEW

P&R
JAMES WALTON DR

HAVERCROFT TERR

1

VERON RD
AVE

Halfway
B6058

STATION RD

River Rother

CUTLER CL
MALLARD DR

JAMES WALTON CT
JAMES WALTON VIEW
OLD LA

A2
1 WATERTHORPE RISE
2 WATERTHORPE GLEN
3 WATERTHORPE GDNS
4 WATERTHORPE CL
5 WATERTHORPE GLADE
6 SHORTBROOK CROFT
7 EASTCROFT WAY

Ppg Sta

FORGE LA
KESTREL CL
SPOONER DR
ACKERVILLE TERR
NETHERTHORPE LA
LIPP AVE

81

OL CL
JAMES WALTON CT
OLD LA

GAUNT CL
WALFORD RD
ASHTON CL
METCAL

Halfway
MORTON MOUNT

Sewage Wks

Wks
STATION RD

S21

ELL RD

OXCLOSE PARK DR
OXCLOSE PARK
OXCLOSE PARK RD
OXCLOSE PARK VIEW

KEMP CL
POWELL DR

DOBBS CL
CAMP
MARH
BRIN

A   Meadowgate Lake   **B**   **C**

PITHOUSE LA

County Dike

82

91

ROTHER VALLEY

Wks

Rother Valley Lake

Meadowgate Lake

4

S20

Killamarsh Meadows

Rother Valley Country Park

Nethermoor Lake

Killamarsh Jun Sch

Norwo Ind Es

ALDRED

NO CRE

SHERW

WOOD RD

SOUTH CRES

Nether Green

PRIMROSE LA

PRIMROSE CL

BARBER'S LA

NETHERGREEN CT 1
VALLEY DR 2
NETHERMOOR CL 3

58

Rother

3   CUTLER CL

HAVERCROFT TERR

NETHERTHORPE CL

MEADOWGATE PK

Parkside Sh Ctr

SHEFFIELD RD

NETHERGREEN AVE

NETHERGREEN GDNS

MURRAY RD

PINGLE RD

VALLEY RD

CHURCH VIEW

BELK LANE

B60

Killama Inf S

Chu Tow

MALLARD DR

FORGE LA

KESTREL CL

SACKERVILLE TERR

STATION RD

NETHERTHORPE LA

SPOONER DR

GAUNT

LIPP AVE

QUARRY RD

WALFORD RD

WAY

THE BUNGALOWS

BRIDGE ST

STANLEY ST

NETHERMOOR AVE

NETHERMOOR LA

L Ctr

Liby

KIRKCROFT DR

JUBILEE CRES

CHURCH MEWS

CHURCH LA

CHURCH LA

DALE RD

81

Wl

ASHTON CL

KEMP CL

METCALFE AVE

BRINDLEY CT

PEACOCK CL

WALKERS LA

THE MEADOWS

KIRKCROFT LA

KIRKCROFT AVE

NETHERMOOR LA

ROBINSON WAY 1
MUSARD WAY 2
MEYNELL WAY 3

POWELL DR

DOBBS CL

BAKER DR

CANAL BRIDGE

CANAL BRIDGE

CHANDOS CRES

ORCHARD PL

CURZON AVE

SHEEPCOTE HILL

MALINDER DR

IVY SIDE CL

IVY SIDE GDNS

BLINKERS HILL

ASHLEY LA

2

BRYONY CL

CAMPION DR

ASPEN CL

MARRISON DR

FOXCROFT CHASE 3

SHEEPCOTE RD

NETHER AVE

DELVES RD

ASHLEY CL

NORBURN DR

RECTORY GDNS

HIGH ST

Killamarsh

MULBERRY WAY

BETONY CL

ACACIA CRES

FIELD LA

CHESTNUT AVE

ELDER CL

ALMOND CRT

ACER CL

LABURNUM GR

ASH CL

FOXCROFT

FOXCROFT DR

Sch

SPRUCE RISE CL

FIR PL

JUNIPER

CYPRESS

CHERRY TREE DR

ROSE WAY

RECTORY RD

MANOR FARM CT

BIRCHLANDS DR

UPPERTHORPE VILLAS

S21

Upperthorpe

Cuckoo Way

Pennine Trail

1

HOLLY CL 1
WALNUT DR 2
YEW TREE DR 3

REDWOOD AVE

HAZEL AVE

POPLAR CL

MAPLE DR

LAUREL DR

BIRCH CL

CROFTERS CL

CEDAR CL

ELM CL

LIME TREE AVE

PINE CL

LARCH AVE

WILLOW RD

PEAR TREE CL

ROWAN TREE CL

OAK LA

BEECH CRES

WESTFIELD RD

HAWTHORNE CT

WESTHORPE RD

HEATH AVE

SIMCREST AVE

GORSE DR

MOSS RD

BRIARS CL

MANOR RD

DUMBLETON RD

FANNY AVE

UPPERTHORPE RD

80

PH

BOILEY LA

Westthorpe

ROWAN TREE RD

SPINKHILL RD

45   **A**   **B**   46   **C**

A   **B**   **C**

CH

M1 to Jct 31

M1

NSFIELD RD

82

NS RD

BEDGRAVE CL

Angel Inn
(PH)

Nor
Wood

4

ROTHERHAM RD

Norwood

PEATFIELD RD

WOODSIDE AVE

Baugy
Hill

NORWOOD CRES

CROSS ST

NORWOOD PL

Highmoor
Farm

3

WALSEKER LA

Top
Farm

CINDER LA

DAWBER LA

Gannow
Hill

Pop
Far

81

Killamarsh
Pond

Woodall
Pond

2

MANSFIELD RD

Woodall

KILLAMARSH LA

Low
Plantation

Sewage
Wks

High Moor

S26

Traveller's
Rest
(PH)

WOODALL RD

Woodall
Bottoms

DOWCAR LA

1

A618

Woodall
Service Area

80

Woodall
Common

HUT LA

M1

A   **B**   **C**

Comberwood
Farm

MANSFIELD
RD

47

A618 Clowne

M1 Nottingham (A610)

48

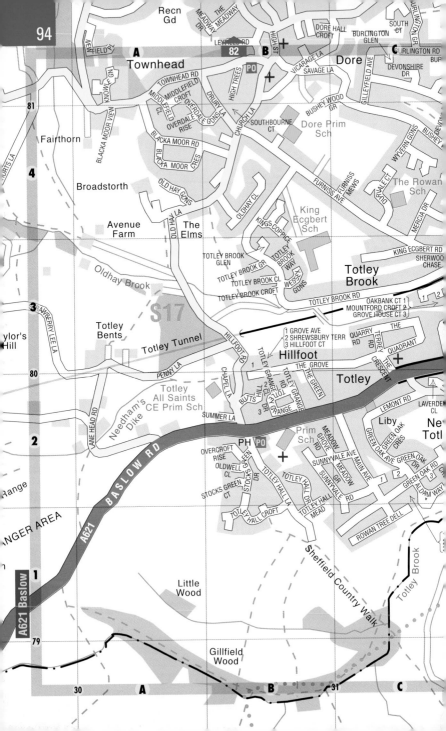

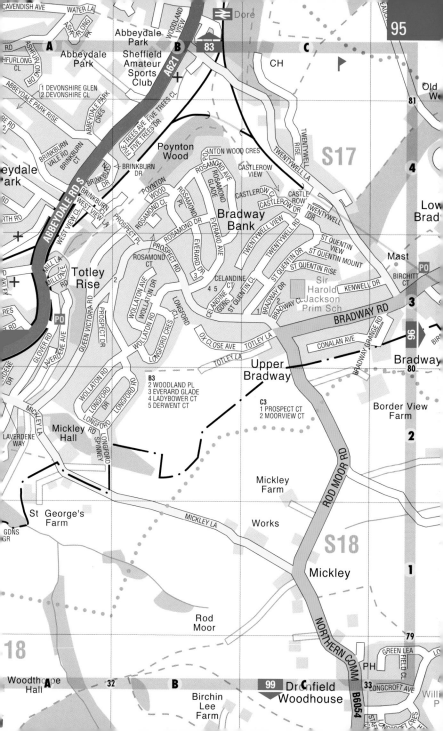

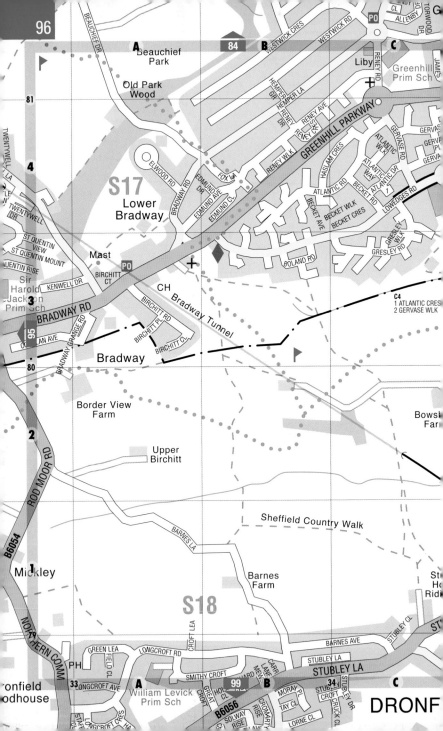

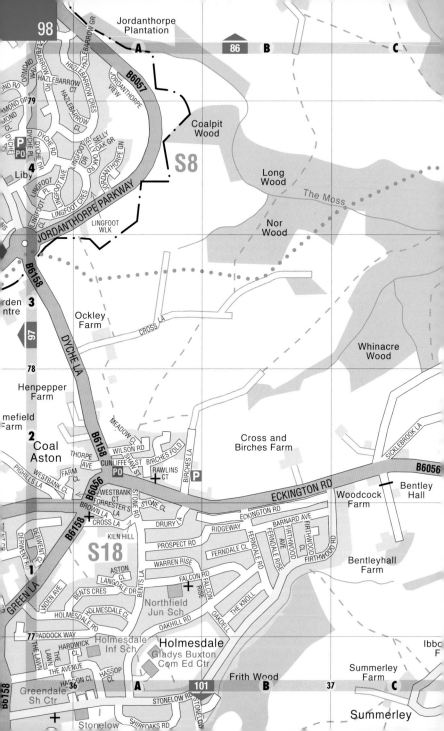

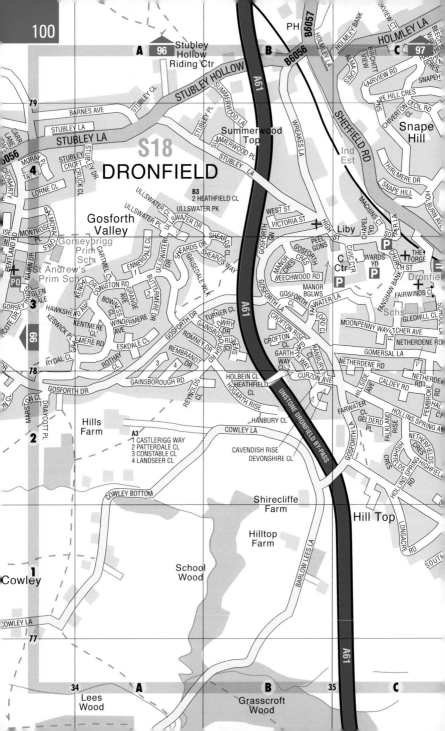

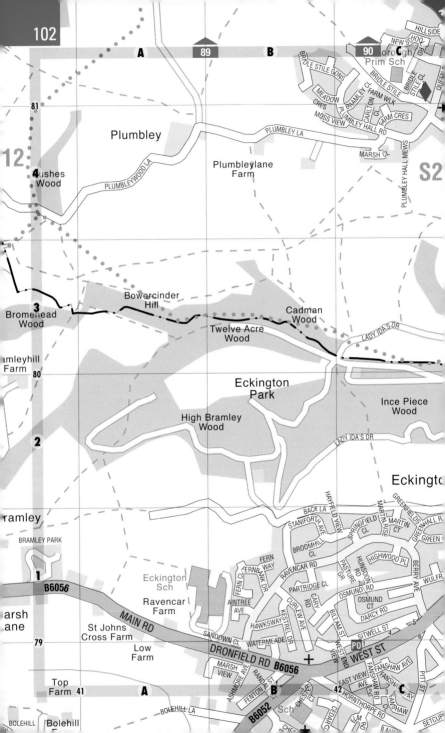

HILLSIDE
NEW SCHOOL
NEW SCHOOL RD
oroGgh
90
Prim Sch

BRIDLE STILE GDNS

MEADOW CRES

BRAMLEY CL

CARLTON CL

FARM CL

BRIDLE STILE

BRIDLE STILE CL

QUEEN

BRAMLEY WLK

PLUMBLEY HALL RD

FARM CRES

MOSS VIEW

MARSH CL

PLUMBLEY HALL MEWS

S2

81

Plumbley

PLUMBLEY LA

12

4ushes Wood

PLUMBLEYWOOD LA

Plumbleylane Farm

Bowercinder Hill

3

Bromehead Wood

Cadman Wood

Twelve Acre Wood

LADY IDA'S DR

amleyhill Farm

80

Eckington Park

Ince Piece Wood

2

High Bramley Wood

LADY IDA'S DR

Eckingto

Eckington

ramley

BACK LA

HAYFIELD VIEW

GREENFIELDS

BRAMLEY PARK

STANIFORTH AVE

SPRINGFIELD CL

MARTIN RISE

MARTIN CT

GREENHALL R

GREEN

BROOMHILL CL

HIGHWOOD PL

BERRY AVE

FERN WAY

RAVENCAR RD

HUNSDON RD

PASTURE GR

WULFR

FERNBANK DR

PARTRIDGE CL

OSMUND RD

1

Eckington Sch

FERN CL

AINTREE AVE

CURLEW AVE

CARY RD

OSMUND CT

DARCY RD

BILLAM ST

SITWELL ST

B6056

Ravencar Farm

HAWKSWAY

KESTREL DR

WEST END

WEST ST

MAIN RD

SANDOWN CL

WATERMEADE

PO

arsh ane

St Johns Cross Farm

Low Farm

79

DRONFIELD RD B6056

FANSHAW AVE

MARSH VIEW

ASHMORE AVE

RANDA

FENTON CL

EAST VIEW

FANSH

HORNTHORPE RD

FANSHAW RD

FANSHI

PITT ST

Top Farm 41

A

42

C

BOLEHILL LA

B6052

CEDAR C

ELM R

Sch

BOLEHILL Bolehill

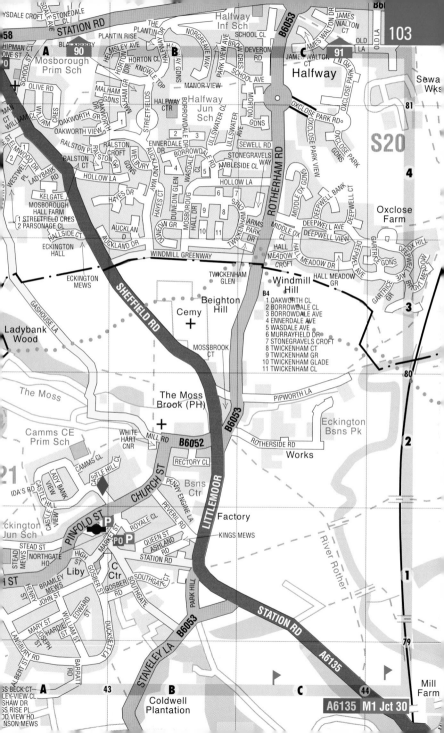

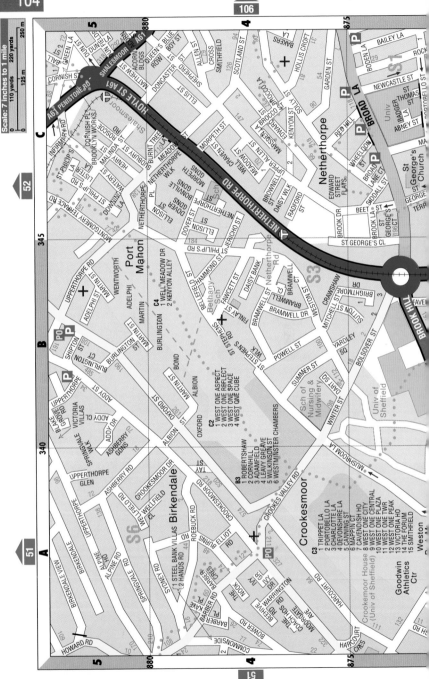

One-way streets

62

HIGH ST

House numbers 59

WHITHAM RD
SEVERN RD
BEAUFORT RD
TREE ROOT WLK
SEVERN CT
WELLESLEY RD
Sheffield Children's
Dental
DURHAM LA
CLARKSON ST
DURHAM RD
B6069
GLOSSOP RD
EMMET HO
PEEL TERR
WILKINSON ST
Royal Hallamshire
PALMERSTON RD
SHEARWOOD RD
CLAREMONT PL
CLAREMONT CRES
PAXTON COLLEGE
King Edward VII Sch
BEECH HILL RD
ST MARK'S CRES
BROOMFIELD RD
RUTLAND CT
WATSON RD
NEWBOULD LA
MELBOURNE AVE
CLARKEHOUSE RD
BROOMGROVE CRES
ANTRIM AVE
PARK CRES
PARK LA
COLLEGIATE CRES
BROOMGROVE RD
BROOMGROVE LA
CLARKEGROVE RD
SOUTHGROVE RD
EASTGROVE RD
ASH GR
EDEN
THE CHASE
CLARKE DELL
HALLAM CT
CLARKE DR
Sheffield High School
Birkdale Prep Sch
Botanical Gardens
Pearson Bldg (Sheffield Hallam Univ)
OAKBURN CT
BROOMHALL RD
VICTORIA RD
Broomfield
GLOUCESTER ST
GLOUCESTER CRES
DORSET ST
RUTH SQ
HOLBERRY GDNS
HAVELOCK ST
BROOMSPRING LA
BRUNSWICK ST
WILKINSON ST
FILEY ST
FILEY LA
MONMOUTH ST
HOLBERRY CL
WHARNCLIFFE RD
TRAVIS PL
CLARKE ST
HANOVER ST
BROOMHALL ST
CLINTON PL
CLINTON WLK
BROOM ST
WILLIAM ST
EXETER PL
EXETER DR
SUMMERFIELD ST
POMONA ST
ECCLESALL RD
SUNNY BANK
Univ
NAPIER ST
HARROW ST
MOORE ST
HANOVER WAY
UPPER HANOVER ST
HANOVER SQ
HEADFORD GDNS
HEADFORD ST
BROOMHALL PL
BROOMHALL RD
BATH
MEWS
BROOM WLK
BROOM GN
BOLTON ST
CAVENDISH ST
CAVENDISH CT
CONWAY ST
CONWAY PL
VICTORIA ST
WILKINSON LA
GELL ST
BROOMSPRING LA
BROOMSPRING CL
Springfield Prim Sch
CONVENT
BROOMHALL RD
EGERTON ST
EGERTON WLK
EGERTON LA
EGERTON CT
FITZWILLIAM ST
BROOMHALL ST
EVANS ST
HEDFORD ST
WELLINGTON ST
BOWDON ST
THOMAS ST
MILTON ST
MILTON LA
HODGSON ST
FITZWILLIAM GATE
FITZWILLIAM ST
YOUNG ST
BISHOP ST
SOUTH LA
HERMITAGE ST
ST MARY'S GATE
ST MARY'S RD
LONDON RD
B6388
BEELEY RD
CEMETERY RD
HANOVER WAY
ELDON ST
DEVONSHIRE ST
DEVONSHIRE CTYD
TRAFALGAR ST
DIVISION ST
FLOCKTON HO
WEST ST
WESTFIELD TERR
WESTHILL LA
PORTLAND LA
GLOSSOP RD
VICTORIA
BROOMSPRING LA
THE GRANARY
BARLEY HO
DRAYMANS CT
THE MALTINGS
THE BREW HO
COOPERS HO
MACKENZIE CRES
WILTON PL
SANDON VIEW
FAIRFIELD LO

61
870
865
2
1
A61
A57
B6069

Scale: 7 inches to 1 mile
0 110 yards 220 yards
0 125 m 25

C

A6178 ATTERCLIFFE RD 29

B5
1 JOHNSON LA
2 SCHOLEY ST
3 ANDREW LA
4 PINSENT

5 REDGRAVE
6 CRACKNELL
7 FOSTER

B6073

SUSSEX RD

SUSSEX ST

CADMAN ST

EFFINGHAM ST

EFFINGHAM LA

SAVILE ST

River Don

B6092

SPITAL HILL A6135

A6109

BRUNSWICK RD

360

A6135

A6109

WALKER ST

72

105

A57

A61

BLAST LA

C4
1 LINK ROW
2 RUBENS ROW
3 BERNARD GDNS
4 HIGH PAVEMENT ROW

A61 SHEFFIELD PARKWAY

CRICKET INN RD

B6071

Hyde

Park Hill

HYDE PARK WLK

ST JOHN'S RD

BERNARD ST

BLACKWELL PL

OLD ST

STEPNEY ST

BROAD ST

NEW STREET LA

BARD ST

HIGH STREET LA

CROWN CT

BLACKWELL CT

B6070

NORWICH ST

ANSON ST

Pennine Trail

Victoria Quays

WHARF ST

EXCHANGE PL

B6073

UPPER CASTLE FOLDS

Ponds Forge

Fitzalan Sq

COMMERCIAL ST

PARK SQ

POND ST

Ponds Forge Int Sports Ctr

B

CUTLERS GATE

FURNIVAL RD

VICTORIA STATION RD

SHELDON ROW

WILLEY ST

WICKER LA

BLONK ST

CASTLEGATE

Castle Mkt

The Gallery

DIXON LA

EXCHANGE ST

BROAD ST

SHUDE HILL

JEW LA

BAKERS HILL

FLAT ST

ESPERANTO PL

S4

Bsn Ctr

126

12

STANLEY LA

STANLEY ST

JOHNSON ST

GUN LA

JONES ST

NURSERY LA

NURSERY ST

SPITALFIELDS

108

S3

MILLSANDS

A3
1 CITY WHARF
2 ROYAL VICTORIA BLDGS
3 ROYAL EXCHANGE
4 CORPORATION BLDGS
5 CORPORATION MEWS
6 HARTSHEAD SQ

BRIDGE ST

LADY'S BRIDGE

WAINGATE

CASTLE GN

CASTLE ST

KING ST

HAYMARKET

MARKET PL

ANGEL ST

SNIG HILL

BANK ST

S Yorks Pol HQ

Cts

FITZALAN SQ

HIGH ST

CASTLE SQ

MULBERRY ST

GEORGE ST

HIGH CT

WATSONS WLK

ALDINE CT

NEW ST

PETER'S CLO

YORK ST

BLACK SWAN WLK

CHAPEL WLK

S1

Studio

A

355

CHATHAM ST

SWINTON ST

BRIDGEHOUSES

B6074

CORPORATION ST

Kelham Island

Kelham Island Ind Mus

COTTON ST

KELHAM ISLAND

COTTON MILL WLK

ALMA ST

RUSSELL ST

MOORFIELDS FLATS

A4
1 WHEATS LA
2 FIG TREE LA

GIBRALTAR BLDGS

STEELHOUSE LA

BOWER SPRING

SPRING ST

WATER ST

LOVE ST

PLUM ST

PLUM LA

BRIDGE ST

WORKHOUSE LA

Law Cts

WEST BAR

SCARGILL CROFT

MEETING HOUSE LA

HARTSHEAD

NEW ST

NORTH CHURCH ST

QUEEN ST

PARADISE ST

SILVER ST

PARADISE SQ

CAMPO LA

ST JAMES ROW

CHURCH ST

Cath Cathedral

EAST PAR

CHURCH ST

ORCHARD ST

ORCHARD

LEOPOLD ST

EXCHANGE GATEWAY

City Hall

A61

MOORFIELDS

A4

GREEN LA

DUN ST

ACORN ST

SPENCER BDY

BOWLING GREEN ST

EBENEZER PL

JOINER LA

COPPER ST

TRINITY ST

SNOW LA

SMITHFIELD

ALLEN ST

SCOTLAND ST

Fire & Police Mus

FURNACE HILL

CUPOLA

LAMBERT ST

WESTBAR

TENTER ST

SILVER ST HEAD

LEE CROFT

VICAR LA

HOLLY ST

PINFOLD ST

BELL'S SQ

HAWLEY ST

The SIMS

Pennine Croft Ctr

CROFT BLDGS

TOWNHEAD ST

City Plaza

TRIPPET LA

Hall

TRINITY La City

BAILEY ST

HOLLIS CROFT

WHITE CROFT

BAKERS HILL

875

5 880 **4**

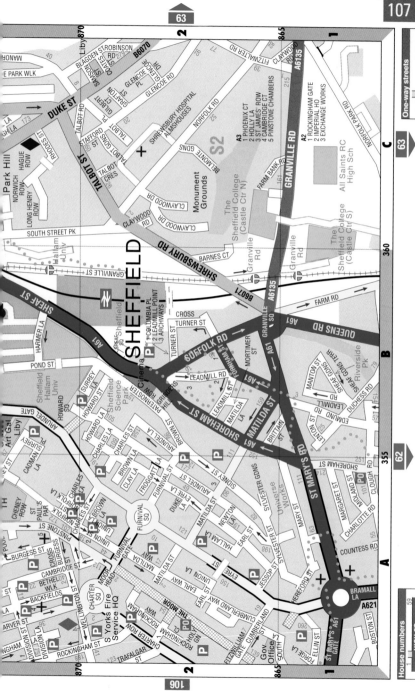

One-way streets

House numbers
1 — 59
HIGH ST

SHEFFIELD

S2

Sheffield

A3
1 PHOENIX CT
2 LILLA
3 ST JAMES' ROW
4 CAMBRIDGE CT
5 PINSTONE CHAMBERS

A2
1 ROCKINGHAM GATE
2 IMPERIAL HO
3 EXCHANGE WORKS

P 1 COLUMBIA PL
2 LEADMILL POINT
3 ARCHWAYS

Index

Street names are listed alphabetically and show the locality, the Postcode district, the page number and a reference to the square in which the name falls on the map page

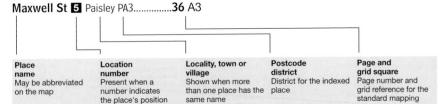

Maxwell St 5 Paisley PA3..............36 A3

Place name	Location number	Locality, town or village	Postcode district	Page and grid square
May be abbreviated on the map	Present when a number indicates the place's position in a crowded area of mapping	Shown when more than one place has the same name	District for the indexed place	Page number and grid reference for the standard mapping

Towns and villages are listed in CAPITAL LETTERS
Public and commercial buildings are highlighted in magenta. **Places of interest** are highlighted in blue with a star ★

Abbreviations used in the index

Acad	**Academy**	Ct	**Court**	Hts	**Heights**
App	**Approach**	Ctr	**Centre**	Ind	**Industrial**
Arc	**Arcade**	Ctry	**Country**	Inst	**Institute**
Ave	**Avenue**	Cty	**County**	Int	**International**
Bglw	**Bungalow**	Dr	**Drive**	Intc	**Interchange**
Bldg	**Building**	Dro	**Drove**	Junc	**Junction**
Bsns, Bus	**Business**	Ed	**Education**	L	**Leisure**
Bvd	**Boulevard**	Emb	**Embankment**	La	**Lane**
Cath	**Cathedral**	Est	**Estate**	Liby	**Library**
Cir	**Circus**	Ex	**Exhibition**	Mdw	**Meadow**
Cl	**Close**	Gd	**Ground**	Meml	**Memorial**
Cnr	**Corner**	Gdn	**Garden**	Mkt	**Market**
Coll	**College**	Gn	**Green**	Mus	**Museum**
Com	**Community**	Gr	**Grove**	Orch	**Orchard**
Comm	**Common**	H	**Hall**	Pal	**Palace**
Cott	**Cottage**	Ho	**House**	Par	**Parade**
Cres	**Crescent**	Hospl	**Hospital**	Pas	**Passage**
Cswy	**Causeway**	HQ	**Headquarters**	Pk	**Park**

Pl	**Place**
Prec	**Precinct**
Prom	**Promenade**
Rd	**Road**
Recn	**Recreation**
Ret	**Retail**
Sh	**Shopping**
Sq	**Square**
St	**Street**
Sta	**Station**
Terr	**Terrace**
TH	**Town Hall**
Univ	**University**
Wk, Wlk	**Walk**
Wr	**Water**
Yd	**Yard**

Index of towns, villages, streets, hospitals, industrial estates, railway stations, schools, shopping centres, universities and places of interest

108 Abb–Ald

A

Abbey Brook Cl S8....84 C3
Abbey Brook Ct S8......84 C3
Abbey Brook Dr S8 ....84 C2
Abbey Brook Gdns S8...84 C3
Abbey Cres S7..........83 C3
Abbey Croft S7 ....83 C3
Abbey Ct S8.............84 C3
ABBEYDALE 83 B3
Abbeydale Grange Sch
S7.....................72 C2
Abbeydale Industrial
Mus ★ S7................83 C2
ABBEYDALE PARK 95 A4
Abbeydale Park Cres
S17....................95 A4
Abbeydale Park Rise
S17....................95 A4
Abbeydale Prim Sch
S7.....................73 A4
Abbeydale Rd S7 ....73 A3
Abbeydale Rd S S7 .....83 C3

Abbeyfield Rd S4........41 C2
Abbey Grange S7........83 C3
Abbey La S7, S8, S11.....83 C3
Abbey Lane Dell S8......83 C3
Abbey Lane Prim Sch
S8.....................84 C4
Abbey Mews S8 ....84 B3
Abbey Sch The S61......19 A1
Abbey View Dr S8.......73 C1
Abbey View Hts 3 S8 ...73 C1
Abbey View Rd S8 ......73 C1
Abbots Mdw S20 ....91 B3
Abdy Rd S61.............19 A4
Abingdon Gdns S61.....20 B4
Abney Cl S14 ....74 B4
Abney Dr S14...........74 B4
Abney Rd S14 ....74 B4
Abney St S1 ....104 C3

Acacia Ave
Chapeltown S35 ....7 A2
Rotherham S66..........36 C3
Acer Cl S21 ....92 A1
Ackworth Dr S9 ....45 A3
Acorn Bldgs S3........104 C5
Acorn Bsns Pk 2 S3 ....73 A2
Acorn Croft S61 ....20 B4

Acorn Dr S6.............38 A1
Acorn Hill S6............38 B1
Acorn St S3 ....106 A5
Acorn Way S6 ....49 A4
Acre Gate S35 ....6 B4
Acres Hill La S9 ....54 C2
Acres Hill Prim Sch
S9.....................54 C1
Acres Hill Rd S9 ....55 A2
Acres View S65 ....34 B1
Acrewood Dr S66........24 B1
Acton Cl S26 ....69 B3
Adamfield 3 S3........104 B3
Adastral Ave S12 ....87 B4
Addison Rd S5 ....42 B4
Addy Cl S6 ....104 B5
Addy Dr S6 ....104 B5
Addy St S6 ....104 B5
Adkins Dr S5 ....27 B1
Adkins Rd S5 ....27 B1
Adlington Cres S5.......27 C2
Adlington Rd S5.........27 C3
Admiral Biggs Dr S60...57 C2
Admirals Crest S61 .....18 B4

Adrian Cres S5 ....28 A2
Adsetts St S4............42 C3
Agden Rd S7 ....61 C2
Ainsley Rd S10 ....51 A2
Ainsty Rd 3 S7..........62 A1
Aintree Ave S21 ....102 B1
Aire Cl S35 ....7 A4
Airedale Rd S6 ....39 B4
Aireton Cl S66..........36 A3
Air Mount Cl S66 ....36 A2
Aisthorpe Rd S8........73 B1
Aizlewood Rd S8 ....62 A1
Akley Bank Cl S17 ......95 A3
Albanus Croft 1 S6 ....49 A4
Albanus Ridge S6 ......49 A4
Albany Ave S35 ....7 C2
Albany Rd
Sheffield S7 ....62 A1
Stocksbridge S36........3 A3
Albany St S65 ....33 B4
Albert Rd
Rawmarsh S62..........12 A2
Sheffield, Hackenthorpe
S12....................78 B1
Sheffield, Heeley S8....73 C4
Albert St S60 ....32 C4
Albert Terrace Rd S6....51 C3
Albion S6 ....104 B4

Albion Rd S60 ....33 B4
Albion Row S6 ....49 B2
Albion St S6...........104 B4
Alcester Rd S7 ....62 A1
Aldam Cl
Rotherham S65..........23 A1
Sheffield S17 ....94 C2
Aldam Croft S17........94 C2
Aldam Rd S17 ....95 A2
Aldam Way S17.........94 C2
Aldene Ave S6..........39 A3
Aldene Glade S6 ....39 A3
Aldene Rd S6...........39 A4
Alder Chase S61........18 C4
Alder La S9 ....55 C1
Alderney Rd 3 S8 ......62 B1
Alders Gn S6 ....38 B3
Alderson Pl S2 ....62 B2
Alderson Rd S2.........62 B2
Alderson Rd N S2.......62 B2
Aldfield Way S5 ....41 C4
Aldine Ct S1...........106 B4
Aldred Cl
Killamarsh S21 ....92 C4
Rotherham S66..........36 B3
Aldred Ct S60 ....33 B3
Aldred Rd S10..........51 A3
Aldred St S60...........33 B3

ALDWARKE 12 C1
Aldwarke La S62, S65 . . . . .22 B4
Aldwarke Rd S62 . . . . .12 A1
Alexandra Cl S61 . . . . .19 B2
Alexandra Ctr S62 . . . . . . .21 C4
Alexandra Gdns S11 . . . .72 C4
Alexandra Rd
  Aston S26 . . . . .69 A2
  Dronfield S18 . . . . .101 A4
  Sheffield S2 . . . . .62 C1
Alford Ave S35 . . . . .13 B3
Alfred Rd S9 . . . . .43 A1
Algar Cl S2 . . . . .63 C1
Algar Dr S2 . . . . .63 C1
Algar Pl S2 . . . . .63 C1
Algar Rd S2 . . . . .63 C1
Alice Rd S61 . . . . .20 B1
Alison Cl S26 . . . . .69 B1
Alison Cres S2 . . . . .64 C3
Alison Dr S26 . . . . .69 B1
Allan St S65 . . . . .33 B4
Allenby Cl S8 . . . . .84 C1
Allenby Dr S8 . . . . .84 C1
Allendale Rd S65 . . . . .34 C2
Allende Way S9 . . . . .54 C4
Allen Gdns S35 . . . . .16 B3
Allen Rd S20 . . . . .91 A4
Allen St S3 . . . . .104 C4
Allestree Dr S18 . . . . .99 B3
Alliance St S4 . . . . .42 B1
Allott Cl S65 . . . . .25 A2
All Saints RC High Sch
  S2 . . . . .107 C1
All Saints' Sq S60 . . . . .33 A4
All Saints Way S26 . . . . . . .70 A1
Allt St S62 . . . . .12 A2
Alma Cres S18 . . . . .97 B1
Alma Rd
  Chapeltown S35 . . . . .5 B1
  Rotherham S60 . . . . .33 A3
Alma Row S60 . . . . .48 A3
Alma St S3 . . . . .106 A5
Almond Dr S21 . . . . .92 A1
Almond Glade S66 . . . . . . .36 C1
Alms Hill Cres S11 . . . . . . .71 B1
Alms Hill Dr S11 . . . . .71 B1
Alms Hill Glade S11 . . . . . .71 B1
Alms Hill Rd S11 . . . . .71 B1
Alney Pl S6 . . . . .27 A2
Alnwick Dr S12 . . . . .76 B3
Alnwick Rd S12 . . . . .76 A3
Alpha Rd S65 . . . . .22 B1
Alpine Cl S36 . . . . .2 C3
Alpine Croft S36 . . . . .2 C3
Alpine Ho S6 . . . . .104 A5
Alpine Rd
  Sheffield S6 . . . . .104 A5
  Stocksbridge S36 . . . . .3 A3
Alport Ave S12 . . . . .77 A3
Alport Dr S12 . . . . .77 A3
Alport Gr S12 . . . . .77 A3
Alport Pl S12 . . . . .77 A2
Alport Rd S12 . . . . .77 A3
Alport Rise S18 . . . . .99 C4
Alric Dr S60 . . . . .45 C3
Alrich Mews S36 . . . . .2 B4
Alsing Rd S9 . . . . .30 C1
Alton Cl
  Dronfield S18 . . . . .99 C2
  Sheffield S11 . . . . .83 B4
Amberley Cl S9 . . . . .43 B1
Amberley St S9 . . . . .43 B2
Ambler Rise S26 . . . . .69 A3
Ambleside Cl
  Brinsworth S60 . . . . .45 B2
  Sheffield S20 . . . . .103 B4
Amen Cnr
  ■ Rotherham S60 . . . . .21 A1
  ◆ Rotherham, Thorn Hill
  S60 . . . . .20 C1
Amos Rd S9 . . . . .43 C4
Andover Dr S3 . . . . .52 B4
Andover St
  Sheffield S3 . . . . .52 C4
  Sheffield, Woodside S3 . . . .52 B4
Andrew La S3 . . . . .106 B5
Andrews Pl S61 . . . . .20 A2
Angel St S3 . . . . .106 B4
Angerford Ave S8 . . . . .73 C2
Anglesey Rd S18 . . . . .100 C2
Angleton Ave S2 . . . . .65 A2
Angleton Cl S2 . . . . .65 A2

Angleton Gdns S2 . . . . . .65 A2
Angleton Gn S2 . . . . .65 A2
Angleton Mews S2 . . . . . .65 A2
Angram Bank Prim Sch
  S35 . . . . .5 A1
Angram Rd S35 . . . . .5 B2
Annat Pl S35 . . . . .5 A1
Annesley Cl S8 . . . . .85 A1
Annesley Rd S8 . . . . .85 A1
Anns Grove Prim Sch
  S2 . . . . .62 B1
Anns Rd S2 . . . . .62 B1
Anns Rd N S2 . . . . .62 C1
Ann St S62 . . . . .12 A1
Ansell Rd S11 . . . . .71 C4
Anson Gr S60 . . . . .46 B2
Anson St S2 . . . . .106 C3
Antrim Ave S10 . . . . .105 A2
Anvil Cl S6 . . . . .49 C4
Anvil Cres S35 . . . . .16 B2
Applegarth Cl S12 . . . . . . .75 C4
Applegarth Dr S12 . . . . . . .75 C4
Appleton Cl S65 . . . . .23 A3
Appletree Dr S18 . . . . . . .100 C3
ARBOURTHORNE 63 C2
Arbourthorne S2 . . . . .63 C3
Arbourthorne Com Prim
  Sch S2 . . . . .74 C4
Arbourthorne Cotts
  S2 . . . . .63 B2
ARBOURTHORNE
  ESTATE 75 A4
Arbourthorne Rd S2 . . . . .75 A4
Archdale Cl S2 . . . . .64 C2
Archdale Rd S2 . . . . .64 B2
Archer Ct S8 . . . . .73 A2
Archer Gate S6 . . . . .38 B3
Archer Ho ■ S65 . . . . .21 B1
Archer La S2 . . . . .72 C3
Archer Rd S8 . . . . .73 A1
Archery Cl S66 . . . . .36 B1
Archibald Rd S7 . . . . .73 A4
Archway Ctr S1 . . . . .107 B3
Archways S2 . . . . .107 B2
Arcon Pl S62 . . . . .12 B4
Arcubus Ave S26 . . . . .69 B2
Ardmore St S9 . . . . .54 B3
Ardron Wlk S62 . . . . .12 C4
Ardsley Ave S26 . . . . .69 C1
Ardsley Cl S20 . . . . .89 A4
Ardsley Dr S20 . . . . .89 A4
Ardsley Gr S20 . . . . .89 A4
Arena Ct S9 . . . . .43 C2
Argyle Cl S8 . . . . .74 A3
Argyle Rd S8 . . . . .74 A3
Arley St S2 . . . . .62 B3
Arlington Ave S26 . . . . . . .70 A2
Armer St S60 . . . . .32 C3
Armitage Rd S26 . . . . .3 C2
Arms Park Dr S20 . . . . . . .103 C4
Armstead Rd S20 . . . . .91 B4
Armthorpe Rd S11 . . . . . . .60 A2
Arncliffe Dr S35 . . . . .7 A4
Arnold Ave S12 . . . . .87 C3
Arnold Rd S65 . . . . .34 B4
Arnold St S6 . . . . .51 A4
Arnside Rd ■ S8 . . . . .73 A3
Arnside Terr S8 . . . . .73 A3
Arran Rd S10 . . . . .50 C1
Arras St S9 . . . . .54 A3
Arrowsmith Ho ■
  S65 . . . . .21 B1
Arthington Blgs S2 . . . . . .73 C4
Arthington St S8 . . . . .73 C4
Arthur Rd S36 . . . . .2 C3
Arthur St S26 . . . . .69 B1
Artisan View S8 . . . . .73 C4
Arundel Ave
  Rotherham S65 . . . . .23 A3
  Treeton S60 . . . . .57 C2
Arundel Cl S18 . . . . .99 C3
Arundel Cres S60 . . . . .57 C2
Arundel Ct S11 . . . . .71 B2
Arundel Gate S1 . . . . .107 B3
Arundel La S1 . . . . .107 B2
Arundel Rd
  Chapeltown S35 . . . . .7 B4
  Rotherham S60, S65 . . . . . .33 C3
  Treeton S60 . . . . .57 C2
Arundel St
  Sheffield S1 . . . . .107 A2

Arundel St continued
  Treeton S60 . . . . .57 C2
Ascot St S1 . . . . .62 B3
Ashberry Gdns S6 . . . . . . .104 A5
Ashberry Rd S6 . . . . .104 A5
Ashbourne Gr
  Oughtibridge S35 . . . . .13 C2
  ■ Sheffield S13 . . . . .66 A3
Ashbourne Rd S13 . . . . . . .66 A3
Ashbury Dr S8 . . . . .86 A4
Ashbury La S8 . . . . .86 A4
Ash Cl
  Killamarsh S21 . . . . .92 A1
  Rotherham S65 . . . . .35 A2
Ash Cres S36 . . . . .3 C3
Ashdell S10 . . . . .61 A4
Ashdell La S10 . . . . .61 A4
Ashdell Prep School
  S10 . . . . .60 C4
Ashdell Rd S10 . . . . .61 A4
Ashdown Gdns S20 . . . . . .79 C1
Asher Rd S4 ■ 62 A2
Ashfield Cl S12 . . . . .75 B2
Ashfield Dr S12 . . . . .75 B2
Ashfield Rd S36 . . . . .3 C3
Ashfield Way S66 . . . . .24 B1
Ashford Cl S18 . . . . .99 C2
Ashford Rd
  Dronfield S18 . . . . .99 C2
  Dronfield S18 . . . . .99 C3
  Sheffield S11 . . . . .61 B2
Ashfurlong Cl S17 . . . . . . .83 A1
Ashfurlong Dr S17 . . . . . . .83 A1
Ashfurlong Pk S17 . . . . . . .83 A1
Ashfurlong Rd S17 . . . . . . .83 A1
Ashgate Cl S10 . . . . .61 A4
Ashgate La ■ S10 . . . . .61 A4
Ashgate Rd S10 . . . . .61 A4
Ash Gr
  Rawmarsh S62 . . . . .12 C3
  Rotherham S66 . . . . .36 C3
  Sheffield S10 . . . . .105 A2
Ash House La S17 . . . . .82 B3
Ash La S36 . . . . .4 A3
Ashland Ct S7 . . . . .73 A4
Ashland Rd
  Eckington S21 . . . . .103 B1
  Sheffield S7 . . . . .73 A4
Ashleigh Ave S12 . . . . .75 B3
Ashleigh Croft S12 . . . . . . .75 B3
Ashleigh Dr S12 . . . . .75 B3
Ashleigh Gdns S61 . . . . . . .20 B4
Ashleigh Pl S12 . . . . .75 B3
Ashley Cl S21 . . . . .92 B2
Ashley Gr S26 . . . . .69 B1
Ashley Ind Est S60 . . . . . . .21 A1
Ashley La S21 . . . . .92 B2
Ashmount S6 . . . . .26 C2
Ashpool Cl S13 . . . . .77 C4
Ashpool Fold S13 . . . . .77 C4
Ash St
  Sheffield, Mosborough
  S20 . . . . .90 A2
  Sheffield S6 . . . . .51 C4
Ashtenne Bsns Ctr
  S60 . . . . .32 C2
Ashton Cl S21 . . . . .92 A2
Ash Tree Cl S9 . . . . .30 B2
Ashurst Cl S6 . . . . .49 C4
Ashurst Dr S6 . . . . .38 C1
Ashurst Pl S6 . . . . .49 C4
Ashurst Rd S6 . . . . .38 C1
Ash View
  Chapeltown S35 . . . . .7 A2
  Rotherham S61 . . . . .10 C1
Ashwell Gr S65 . . . . .22 B2
Ashwell Rd S13 . . . . .77 C4
Ashwood Cl S35 . . . . .5 A2
Ashwood Rd
  Chapeltown S35 . . . . .5 A2
  Rawmarsh S62 . . . . .12 A1
Ashworth Dr S61 . . . . .19 A4
Askam Gr S66 . . . . .37 A4
Askam Rd S66 . . . . .37 A4
Askew Ct S66 . . . . .3 B2
Asline Rd S2 . . . . .62 B2
Aspen Cl S21 . . . . .92 A2
Aspen Way S60 . . . . .32 B3
Asquith Rd S9 . . . . .30 B2
Aster Cl S20 . . . . .79 B1
ASTON 81 A4

Aston CE Jun & Inf Sch
  S26 . . . . .69 C1
Aston Cl S18 . . . . .98 A1
ASTON COMMON 80 C4
Aston Comp Sch S26 . . . .69 A2
Aston Fence Jun & Inf
  Sch S13 . . . . .68 B2
Aston Hall Junior &
  Infant Sch S26 . . . . .81 B4
Aston La S26 . . . . .69 B3
Aston Lodge Prim Sch
  S26 . . . . .80 C4
Aston Springwood Prim
  Sch S26 . . . . .69 C2
Aston St S2 . . . . .53 B2
Astwell Gdns S35 . . . . .6 C4
Athelstan Cl S13 . . . . .65 C3
Athelstan Prim Sch
  S13 . . . . .65 C3
Athelstan Rd S13 . . . . .65 C3
Athersley Gdns S20 . . . . . .89 B4
Atherton Cl S2 . . . . .75 B4
Atherton Rd S2 . . . . .75 B4
Athol Rd S8 . . . . .73 A2
Athron Dr S65 . . . . .34 C2
Atkin Pl S2 . . . . .62 B2
Atkinson Mews S21 . . . . .102 C3
Atlantic Cres ■ S8 . . . . . . .96 C4
Atlantic Dr S8 . . . . .96 C4
Atlantic Way S8 . . . . .96 C4
Atlantic Wlk S8 . . . . .96 C4
Atlas Bsns Pk S35 . . . . . . .16 C3
Atlas St
  Brinsworth S60 . . . . .46 A3
  Sheffield S4 . . . . .53 B4
Atlas Way S4 . . . . .42 C1
ATTERCLIFFE 54 A4
Attercliffe Comm S9 . . . . .43 B2
ATTERCLIFFE HILL
  TOP .43 C1
Attercliffe Rd S4, S9 . . . . .53 C3
Aubretia Ave S60 . . . . .46 B1
Auckland Ave S6 . . . . .38 C2
Auckland Dr S20 . . . . .103 B3
Auckland Rise S20 . . . . . .103 B3
Auckland Way S20 . . . . . .103 B4
Audrey Rd S13 . . . . .65 A1
AUGHTON 69 B3
Aughton Ave S26 . . . . .69 A3
Aughton Cl S13 . . . . .65 B1
Aughton Cres S13 . . . . .65 B1
Aughton Dr S13 . . . . .65 B2
Aughton La S26 . . . . .69 C2
Aughton Prim Sch
  S26 . . . . .69 A3
Aughton Rd S26 . . . . .69 A3
Augustus Rd S60 . . . . .46 A4
Aukley Rd S8 . . . . .73 B3
Aunby Dr S25 . . . . .84 C4
Austen Dr S66 . . . . .37 B3
Austin Cl S6 . . . . .38 C2
Austin Ct S6 . . . . .38 C2
Avenue Cl S11 . . . . .60 B2
Avenue Rd ■ S7 . . . . .73 B4
Avenue The
  Dronfield S18 . . . . .101 A4
  Sheffield S10 . . . . .58 A3
  Sheffield, Beighton S20 . . . .79 B2
  Sheffield, Darnall S9 . . . . . .55 A2
Avill Way S66 . . . . .36 B1
Avisford Dr S5 . . . . .27 A1
Avisford Rd S5 . . . . .27 A1
Avocet Way S61 . . . . .9 A4
Avon Cl S18 . . . . .97 C1
Avondale Rd
  Rotherham S61 . . . . .20 A1
  Sheffield S6 . . . . .39 C2
Avon Gr S5 . . . . .6 C4
Avon Mount S61 . . . . .20 A1
Aylesbury Cres S9 . . . . .30 B1
Aylesbury Ct S9 . . . . .30 B2
Aylsham Dr S26 . . . . .69 C1
Aysgarth Rd S6 . . . . .26 C3
Aysgarth Rise S26 . . . . . . .69 A2

B

Babur Rd S4 . . . . .53 B4
Backfield Rise S35 . . . . .7 B4
Backfields S1 . . . . .107 A3
Back La
  Eckington S21 . . . . .102 B1
  Rawmarsh S62 . . . . .11 A4

Back La continued
  Sheffield, Den Bank
  S10 . . . . .50 A2
  Sheffield S13 . . . . .78 B4
BACKMOOR 86 A4
Backmoor Cres S8 . . . . . . .86 A4
Backmoor Rd S8 . . . . .86 B4
Bacon La S9 . . . . .53 C3
Baden St S60 . . . . .20 C1
Badger Cl S13 . . . . .67 A1
Badger Dr S13 . . . . .67 A1
Badger La S1 . . . . .104 C3
Badger Pl S13 . . . . .67 B1
Badger Rd S13 . . . . .67 A1
Badger Rise S13 . . . . .67 A1
Badsley Ct ■ S65 . . . . .33 C4
Badsley Moor Jun & Inf
  Schs S65 . . . . .34 B4
Badsley Moor La S65 . . . . .34 A4
Badsley St S S65 . . . . .33 C3
Badsley St S65 . . . . .33 C4
Badsworth Cl S66 . . . . .37 B3
Badsworth Pl S66 . . . . .37 B3
Badsworth Way S66 . . . . . .37 B3
Bagley Rd S4 . . . . .42 B3
Bagshaw's Rd S12 . . . . . . .76 A4
Bagshot St S11 . . . . .61 B2
Bailey Dr S21 . . . . .92 C4
Bailey La S1 . . . . .104 C3
Bailey St S1 . . . . .106 A3
Baker Dr S21 . . . . .92 A2
Bakers Hill S1 . . . . .106 B3
Bakers La S1 . . . . .104 C4
Baker St S9 . . . . .54 A4
Balaclava La ■ S6 . . . . .51 C4
Balaclava Rd S6 . . . . .51 C4
Baldwin St S9 . . . . .53 C3
Balfour Dr S9 . . . . .54 C3
Balfour Ho S36 . . . . .3 A3
Balfour Rd S9 . . . . .54 C3
Balk La
  Brinsworth S60 . . . . .45 B4
  Rotherham S66 . . . . .37 B4
Ballard Hall (Sheffield
  Hallam Univ) S10 . . . . . . .60 B3
Ballifield Ave S13 . . . . .66 B3
Ballifield Cl S13 . . . . .66 C3
Ballifield Cres S13 . . . . . . .66 C3
Ballifield Dr S13 . . . . .66 C3
Ballifield Pl S13 . . . . .66 B3
Ballifield Prim Sch
  S13 . . . . .66 B2
Ballifield Rd S13 . . . . .66 B3
Ballifield Rise S13 . . . . . . .66 C3
Ballifield Way S13 . . . . .66 B3
Ball Rd S6 . . . . .39 C2
Ball St S3 . . . . .52 A3
Balmain Dr S6 . . . . .39 C3
Balmain Rd S6 . . . . .39 C3
Balmer Rise S66 . . . . .37 B2
Balm Gn S1 . . . . .106 A3
Balmoral Cres
  Dronfield S18 . . . . .99 C4
  Sheffield S10 . . . . .58 A3
Balmoral Ct S11 . . . . .71 B2
Balmoral Glen S10 . . . . . . .58 A3
Balmoral Mews S10 . . . . . .58 A3
Balmoral Rd S13 . . . . .78 B4
Balmoral Way S66 . . . . . . .37 A4
Baltic La S9 . . . . .54 A4
Baltic Rd S9 . . . . .54 A4
Baltic Works S9 . . . . .53 C3
Bamforth St S6 . . . . .40 B1
Bank Cl
  Rotherham S61 . . . . .10 A1
  Sheffield S7 . . . . .73 A4
Bankfield La S6 . . . . .49 A4
Bankfield Rd S6 . . . . .39 C2
Bank House Rd S6 . . . . . . .51 A3
Bank St S1 . . . . .106 B4
Bank Terr ■ S10 . . . . .51 A1
Bank Top Rd S65 . . . . .35 A2
Bank View S60 . . . . .47 C3
Bankwood Cl S14 . . . . .74 C3
Bankwood Com Prim Sch
  S14 . . . . .74 C3
Bankwood Rd S14 . . . . .74 C3
Banner Cross Dr S11 . . . . .72 A2

Banner Cross Road
S11 . . . . 72 A3
Banner Ct S11 . . . . 72 A4
Bannerdale Cl S11 . . . . 72 B4
Bannerdale Rd S7, S11 . . . 72 C3
Bannerdale View S11 . . . . 72 B4
Bannham Rd S9 . . . . 55 B2
Barber Balk Cl S61 . . . . 10 A1
Barber Balk Rd S61 . . . . 10 A1
Barber Cres S10 . . . . 104 A4
Barber Pl S10 . . . . 104 A4
Barber Rd S10 . . . . 104 A4
Barberry Way S65 . . . . 25 B2
Barber's Ave S62 . . . . 12 B1
Barber's Cres S62 . . . . 12 B3
Barber's La S21 . . . . 92 B3
Barber Wood Rd S61 . . . . . 18 B1
Barbot Hall Ind Est
S61 . . . . 21 A3
Barbot Hill Rd S61 . . . . 20 C4
Barden Cres S60 . . . . 46 A1
Bard St S2 . . . . 106 C3
Bardwell Rd S3 . . . . 52 A4
Barfield Ave S60 . . . . 47 B3
Barholm Rd S10 . . . . 60 A4
Baring Rd S61 . . . . 30 B4
Barkby Rd S9 . . . . 30 A2
Barkers Croft S61 . . . . 10 A3
Barker's Pl S6 . . . . 40 A3
Barker's Pool S1 . . . . 107 A3
Barker's Rd S7 . . . . 72 C4
Barlby Gr S12 . . . . 78 B1
Barley Ho 2 S11 . . . . 105 C1
Barley Mews S19 . . . . 44 A4
Barleywood Rd S9 . . . . 55 A4
Barlow Dr S6 . . . . 50 B4
Barlow Lees La S18 . . . . . . 100 B1
Barlow Rd S6 . . . . 50 B4
Barlow View S18 . . . . 101 A1
Barmouth Rd S7 . . . . 73 A3
Barnard Ave S18 . . . . 98 B1
Barnardiston Rd S9 . . . . . . 54 C3
Barncliffe Cl S10 . . . . 59 A2
Barncliffe Cres S10 . . . . . . 58 C3
Barncliffe Dr S10 . . . . 58 C3
Barncliffe Glen S10 . . . . . . 59 A2
Barncliffe Rd S10 . . . . 58 C3
Barnes Ave S18 . . . . 100 A4
Barnes Ct S2 . . . . 107 B2
Barnes Green S35 . . . . 6 B1
Barnes Hall Rd S35 . . . . 6 A4
Barnes La S18 . . . . 96 A1
Barnet Ave S11 . . . . 71 A3
Barnet Rd S11 . . . . 71 A3
Barnfield Ave S10 . . . . 49 C1
Barnfield Cl S10 . . . . 49 C1
Barnfield Dr S10 . . . . 59 C4
Barnfield Rd S10 . . . . 49 C1
Barnsdale Ave S20 . . . . 89 B4
Barnsley Rd
Sheffield S5 . . . . 28 C2
Wentworth S61 . . . . 8 C4
Baron St S1 . . . . 62 B3
Barrack La S6 . . . . 51 C4
Barrat Cnr 3 S65 . . . . 34 B3
Barretta St 3 S4 . . . . 42 B3
Barrie Cres S5 . . . . 41 A4
Barrie Dr S5 . . . . 27 C1
Barrie Rd S5 . . . . 27 C1
Barrowby Rd S60 . . . . 34 B1
Barrow Rd
Sheffield S9 . . . . 30 B2
Sheffield S9 . . . . 30 C2
Bartholomew Cl S60 . . . . . . 48 B4
Bartin Cl S11 . . . . 72 A3
Bartle Ave S12 . . . . 75 B2
Bartle Dr S12 . . . . 75 B2
Bartle Rd S12 . . . . 75 B2
Bartlett Cl S6 . . . . 49 A3
Bartlett Rd S5 . . . . 27 C2
Bartle Way S12 . . . . 75 B2
Barton Rd S8 . . . . 73 C4
BASE GREEN 76 B1
Basegreen Ave S12 . . . . 76 A1
Basegreen Cl S12 . . . . 76 B1
Basegreen Cres S12 . . . . . . 76 A1
Basegreen Dr S12 . . . . 76 B1
Basegreen Pl S12 . . . . 76 A1
Basegreen Rd S12 . . . . 76 B1

Basegreen Way S12 . . . . . . 76 B1
Basford Cl S9 . . . . 55 A4
Basford Dr S9 . . . . 54 C3
Basford Mews S9 . . . . 55 A3
Basford Pl S9 . . . . 54 C3
Basford St S9 . . . . 54 C3
Basil Griffith Ct S4 . . . . 41 C2
Baslow Rd S17 . . . . 94 A2
Bassett Pl S2 . . . . 63 B4
Bassett Rd S2 . . . . 63 C4
Bassingthorpe La S61 . . . . . 20 B3
Bassledene Ct S2 . . . . 64 B2
Bassledene Rd S2 . . . . 64 B2
Bastock Rd S6 . . . . 40 B3
BATEMOOR 97 B3
Batemoor Cl S8 . . . . 97 B4
Batemoor Dr S8 . . . . 97 B4
Batemoor Pl S8 . . . . 97 B4
Batemoor Rd S8 . . . . 97 B3
Batemoor Wlk S8 . . . . 97 B4
Batesquire S20 . . . . 91 A4
Bates St S10 . . . . 51 A3
Bath St S3 . . . . 105 C2
Batt St 3 S8 . . . . 62 B2
Batworth Dr S5 . . . . 41 B2
Batworth Rd S5 . . . . 41 B2
Baulk Farm Cl S61 . . . . 10 C2
Bawtry Gate S9 . . . . 44 C4
Bawtry Rd
Brinsworth S60 . . . . 45 C3
Rotherham S66 . . . . 36 C2
Baxter Cl
Sheffield, Birley Carr
S6 . . . . 26 C2
Sheffield S26 . . . . 68 B1
Baxter Dr S6 . . . . 26 C2
Baxter Mews S6 . . . . 26 C2
Baxter Rd S6 . . . . 26 C2
Bay Ct S21 . . . . 92 A1
Baysdale Croft S20 . . . . 90 B1
Bay Tree Ave S66 . . . . 36 B4
Bazley Rd S2 . . . . 75 B4
Beacon Cl S9 . . . . 43 A3
Beacon Croft S9 . . . . 43 A3
Beacon Dr S9 . . . . 43 A4
Beaconsfield Rd S60 . . . . . . 34 A1
Beacon Way S9 . . . . 43 A4
Beale Way S62 . . . . 21 C4
Bear Tree Cl S62 . . . . 12 A2
Bear Tree Rd S62 . . . . 12 A1
Bear Tree St S62 . . . . 12 A1
Beauchamp Rd S61 . . . . 10 A1
BEAUCHIEF 84 B2
Beauchief Abbey La
S8 . . . . 84 A3
Beauchief Abbey (rems
of) ✱ S8 . . . . 84 A2
Beauchief Cl S8 . . . . 4 B2
Beauchief Ct S8 . . . . 84 C3
Beauchief Dr S17 . . . . 84 A1
Beauchief Manor S7 . . . . . . 83 C3
Beauchief Rise S8 . . . . 84 A3
Beaufort Rd S10 . . . . 105 A3
Beaumont Ave S2 . . . . 64 C4
Beaumont Cl S2 . . . . 64 C4
Beaumont Cres S2 . . . . 64 C4
Beaumont Dr S65 . . . . 34 B3
Beaumont Mews S2 . . . . . . 64 C3
Beaumont Rd N S2 . . . . 64 C3
Beaumont Way S2 . . . . 64 B4
Beaver Ave S13 . . . . 66 C2
Beaver Cl S13 . . . . 66 C2
Beaver Dr S13 . . . . 66 C2
BEAVER HILL 66 C2
Beaver Hill Rd S13 . . . . 66 C1
Beccles Way S66 . . . . 37 B3
Beck Cl S5 . . . . 17 B1
Becket Ave S8 . . . . 96 B4
Becket Cres
Rotherham S61 . . . . 19 A4
Sheffield S8 . . . . 96 C4
Becket Rd S8 . . . . 96 C4
Becket Wlk S8 . . . . 96 C4
Beck Prim Sch S5 . . . . 17 A1
Beck Rd S5 . . . . 17 A1
Beckton Ave S20 . . . . 90 C4
Beckton Ct S20 . . . . 91 A4
Beckton Gr S20 . . . . 90 C4
Beckwith Rd S65 . . . . 23 A1
Bedale Ct S60 . . . . 33 C2
Bedale Rd S8 . . . . 73 B4
Bedford Rd S35 . . . . 13 B4

Bedford St S6 . . . . 52 A3
Bedgebury Cl S20 . . . . 91 C3
Bedgrave Cl S21 . . . . 93 A4
Beech Ave
Rawmarsh S62 . . . . 12 C3
Rotherham S65 . . . . 35 B2
Beech Cres S21 . . . . 92 B1
Beech Ct S10 . . . . 105 A2
Beeches Dr S2 . . . . 63 A2
Beeches Gr S20 . . . . 79 C1
Beeches The S26 . . . . 69 B1
Beechfern Cl S35 . . . . 5 B2
Beech Gr S66 . . . . 36 C3
Beech Hill Rd
2 Sheffield S10 . . . . 61 A4
Sheffield S10 . . . . 105 A2
Beech Way
Aston S26 . . . . 69 A2
Dronfield S18 . . . . 97 B1
Beechwood Cl S5 . . . . 21 C1
Beechwood Rd
Chapeltown S35 . . . . 6 C4
Dronfield S18 . . . . 100 B3
Rotherham S60 . . . . 34 A2
Sheffield S6 . . . . 39 C2
Stocksbridge S36 . . . . 3 A2
Beehive Rd S10 . . . . 104 A4
Beeley St S11 . . . . 105 C1
Beeley Wood La S35,
S6 . . . . 26 A2
Beeley Wood Rd S6 . . . . 26 C1
Beely Rd S35 . . . . 13 C2
Beeston Cl S18 . . . . 99 B4
Beeton Rd S8 . . . . 73 B3
Beet St S3 . . . . 104 C3
Beeversleigh 3 S65 . . . . . . 33 B4
Beevers Rd S61 . . . . 19 A4
BEIGHTON 79 C1
Beighton Com Hospl
S20 . . . . 79 A1
Beighton Inf Sch S20 . . . . . 79 C3
Beighton Rd
Sheffield, Hackenthorpe
S12 . . . . 78 B1
Sheffield, Woodhouse
S13 . . . . 78 C3
Beighton Rd E S20 . . . . 78 C1
Belcourt Rd S65 . . . . 35 A2
Beldon Cl S2 . . . . 63 B1
Beldon Pl S2 . . . . 63 B1
Beldon Rd S2 . . . . 63 B1
Belford Cl S66 . . . . 36 C4
Belford Dr S66 . . . . 36 C4
Belgrave Dr S10 . . . . 59 B3
Belgrave Pl S2 . . . . 69 B1
Belgrave Rd S10 . . . . 59 C3
Belgrave Sq 6 S2 . . . . 62 B2
Belklane St S21 . . . . 92 C3
Bellamy Cl S65 . . . . 34 B3
Bellefield St S3 . . . . 104 B4
Bellfields The S61 . . . . 8 C3
Bellhagg Rd S6 . . . . 50 C4
Bellhouse Rd S5 . . . . 29 B3
Bellows Cl S62 . . . . 12 A3
Bellows Rd S62 . . . . 12 A3
Bellscroft Ave S65 . . . . 23 B4
Bells Sq S1 . . . . 106 A3
Bell St S26 . . . . 70 A1
Bellwood Ct S65 . . . . 25 B2
Belmont Ave S35 . . . . 7 B3
Belmont Dr S36 . . . . 3 B3
Belmonte Gdns S2 . . . . 107 C2
Belmont St S61 . . . . 32 A4
Belper Rd 4 S7 . . . . 73 B4
Belsize Rd S10 . . . . 59 C1
Belton Cl S18 . . . . 99 B3
Belvedere Par S66 . . . . 36 C4
Ben Cl S6 . . . . 39 A3
Ben La S6 . . . . 39 B3
Benmore Dr S20 . . . . 91 C3
Bennett St
Rotherham S61 . . . . 31 B4
3 Sheffield S10 . . . . 62 A2
Benson Rd S2 . . . . 63 C4
Bentfield Ave S60 . . . . 34 C1
Bent Lathes Ave S60 . . . . . . 34 C1
Bentley Rd
Chapeltown S35 . . . . 7 C1
Rotherham S66 . . . . 37 B3
Sheffield S6 . . . . 50 B3
Bentley St S60 . . . . 33 A1
Benton Way S61 . . . . 19 C1

Bents Cl
Chapeltown S35 . . . . 7 B3
Sheffield S11 . . . . 71 A3
Bents Cres
Dronfield S18 . . . . 98 A1
Sheffield S11 . . . . 71 B3
Bents Dr S11 . . . . 71 B3
BENTS GREEN 71 B3
Bents Green Ave S11 . . . . . 71 A4
Bents Green Pl S11 . . . . 71 A3
Bents Green Rd S11 . . . . . . 71 B3
Bents Green Sch S11 . . . . . 71 A3
Bents La S18 . . . . 98 A1
Bents Rd
Rotherham S61 . . . . 10 A1
Sheffield S11 . . . . 71 B3
Bents View S11 . . . . 71 A3
Benty La S10 . . . . 50 A1
Berkeley Prec S11 . . . . 61 B2
Bernard Gdns 3 S2 . . . . . 106 C4
Bernard Rd S2, S4 . . . . 53 B2
Bernard St
Rotherham S60 . . . . 33 B3
Sheffield S2 . . . . 106 C3
Berners Cl S2 . . . . 75 A4
Berners Dr S2 . . . . 75 A4
Berners Pl S2 . . . . 75 A4
Berners Rd S2 . . . . 75 A4
Bernshall Cres S5 . . . . 16 B1
Berresford Rd 8 S11 . . . . . 61 B2
Berry Ave S21 . . . . 102 C1
Berry Holme Cl S35 . . . . 7 B3
Berry Holme Ct S35 . . . . 7 B3
Berry Holme Dr S35 . . . . 7 B3
Bertram Rd S35 . . . . 13 C2
Bessemer Pk S60 . . . . 32 B2
Bessemer Pl S9 . . . . 53 C3
Bessemer Rd S9 . . . . 53 C4
Bessemer Terr S36 . . . . 3 A4
Bessemer Way S60 . . . . 32 A2
Bessingby Rd S6 . . . . 40 A1
Bethany Sch S3 . . . . 104 B4
Bethel Rd S65 . . . . 21 C2
Bethel Wlk S1 . . . . 107 A3
Betjeman Gdns S10 . . . . . . 61 A3
Beulah Rd S6 . . . . 40 B3
Bevan Ho S60 . . . . 47 A4
Bevan Way S35 . . . . 7 A2
Bevercotes Rd S5 . . . . 29 B1
Beverley Cl S26 . . . . 69 B1
Beverley Rd S8 . . . . 73 C2
Beverley St 2 S9 . . . . 54 B4
Bevin Pl S62 . . . . 12 C4
Bickerton Ho S6 . . . . 40 A4
Bickerton Rd S6 . . . . 40 A4
Bigby Way S66 . . . . 25 A1
Bignor Pl S6 . . . . 27 A3
Bignor Rd S6 . . . . 27 A2
Billam Pl S61 . . . . 19 B3
Billam St S21 . . . . 102 B1
Bilston St S6 . . . . 40 B1
Binders Rd S61 . . . . 19 B3
Binfield Rd S8 . . . . 73 B3
Bingham Ct S11 . . . . 60 A2
Bingham Park Cres
S11 . . . . 60 B2
Bingham Park Rd S11 . . . . . 60 B2
Bingham Rd S8 . . . . 85 A4
Binsted Ave S5 . . . . 27 A1
Binsted Cl S5 . . . . 27 A1
Binsted Cres S5 . . . . 27 A1
Binsted Croft S5 . . . . 27 A1
Binsted Dr S5 . . . . 27 A1
Binsted Gdns S5 . . . . 27 A1
Binsted Glade S5 . . . . 27 A1
Binsted Gr S5 . . . . 27 A1
Binsted Rd S5 . . . . 27 A1
Binsted Way S5 . . . . 27 A1
Birchall Ave S60 . . . . 47 C3
Birch Ave S35 . . . . 7 B3
Birch Cl S21 . . . . 92 A1
Birch Cres S66 . . . . 36 C3
Birchen Cl S18 . . . . 99 C3
Birches Fold S18 . . . . 98 A2
Birches La S18 . . . . 98 A2
Birch Farm Ave S8 . . . . 85 B2
Birch Gr S35 . . . . 13 C2
Birch House Ave S35 . . . . . 13 B2
Birchitt Cl S17 . . . . 96 A3
Birchitt Ct S17 . . . . 96 A3
Birchitt Pl S17 . . . . 96 A3
Birchitt Rd S17 . . . . 96 A3

Birchitt View S18 . . . . 97 B1
Birchlands Dr S21 . . . . 92 B1
Birch Park Ct S61 . . . . 32 A4
Birch Rd S9 . . . . 53 C4
Birchtree Rd S61 . . . . 9 A1
Birch Tree Rd S36 . . . . 3 A1
Birchvale Rd S12 . . . . 76 C1
Birchwood Cl 7 S20 . . . . . 90 C2
Birchwood Croft S20 . . . . . 90 C2
Birchwood Dr S65 . . . . 25 C2
Birchwood Gdns 6
S20 . . . . 90 C2
Birchwood Gr S20 . . . . 90 C2
Birchwood Rise 5
S20 . . . . 90 C2
Birchwood View S20 . . . . . . 90 C2
Birchwood Way 18
S20 . . . . 90 C2
Birdwell Rd 5 S4 . . . . 43 A3
Birkbeck Ct S13 . . . . 5 B2
Birkdale Prep Sch
S10 . . . . 105 A1
Birkdale Sch S10 . . . . 61 A4
BIRKENDALE 104 A4
Birkendale S6 . . . . 104 A5
Birkendale Rd S6 . . . . 51 B3
Birkendale View S6 . . . . . . 104 A5
Birklands Ave S13 . . . . 65 C3
Birklands Cl S13 . . . . 65 C3
Birklands Dr S13 . . . . 65 C3
Birks Ave S13 . . . . 78 A4
Birks Rd S61 . . . . 19 B3
Birks Wood Dr S35 . . . . 13 B2
BIRLEY 77 B1
BIRLEY CARR 26 C2
Birley Com Coll S12 . . . . . . 88 B4
Birley Com Prim Sch
S12 . . . . 76 C1
BIRLEY EDGE 26 C4
Birley Ho S6 . . . . 26 C4
Birley La S12 . . . . 88 B4
Birley Moor Ave S12 . . . . . . 77 A1
Birley Moor Cl S12 . . . . 88 C4
Birley Moor Cres S12 . . . . . 88 C4
Birley Moor Dr S12 . . . . 88 C4
Birley Moor Pl S12 . . . . 88 C4
Birley Moor Rd S12 . . . . 88 C4
Birley Moor Way S12 . . . . . . 88 C4
Birley Rise Cres S6 . . . . 26 C2
Birley Rise Rd S6 . . . . 26 C2
Birley School Mews
S13 . . . . 77 A3
Birley Spa Cl S12 . . . . 78 A2
Birley Spa Com Prim Sch
S12 . . . . 77 B2
Birley Spa Dr S12 . . . . 78 A2
Birley Spa La S12 . . . . 78 A2
Birley Spa Wlk 1 S12 . . . . 78 A2
Birley Vale Ave S12 . . . . 76 B3
Birley Vale Cl S12 . . . . 76 B2
Birley View S35 . . . . 13 B1
Bisby Rd S62 . . . . 12 B4
Bishopdale Ct S20 . . . . 89 B3
Bishopdale Dr S20 . . . . 89 B2
Bishopdale Rise S20 . . . . . . 89 B3
Bishop Gdns S13 . . . . 77 C4
Bishop Hill S13 . . . . 77 C4
Bishopscourt Rd S8 . . . . 73 C3
Bishops Ct S8 . . . . 74 A3
Bishopsholme Cl S5 . . . . . . 41 B4
Bishopsholme Rd S5 . . . . . . 41 C4
Bishops House Mus ✱
S8 . . . . 73 C2
Bishop St S3 . . . . 105 C2
Bishopstoke Ct 1
S65 . . . . 22 A1
Bitholmes La S36 . . . . 4 C1
Bittern View S61 . . . . 9 B4
Blacka Moor Cres S17 . . . . 94 A4
Blacka Moor Rd S17 . . . . . . 94 A4
Blacka Moor View
S17 . . . . 94 A4
Blackberry Flats S20 . . . . . . 90 C1
Blackbird Ave S60 . . . . 46 B2
Blackbrook Ave S10 . . . . . . 58 B3
Blackbrook Dr S10 . . . . 58 B3
Blackbrook Rd S10 . . . . 58 B2
BLACKBURN 30 B4
Blackburn Cres S35 . . . . 7 A4
Blackburn Croft S35 . . . . 7 A4
Blackburn Dr S35 . . . . 6 C4
Blackburne St 1 S6 . . . . . . 40 B1

Blackburn La S61 . . . . 30 B4
Blackburn Prim Sch
 S61 . . . . 30 B4
Blackburn Rd S61 . . . . 30 B3
Black Carr Rd S66 . . . . 36 A2
Blackdown Ave S20 . . . . . . 90 B4
Blackdown Cl S20 . . . . 90 B4
Black Hill Rd S65 . . . . 35 A2
Black La S6 . . . . 38 B1
Blackmoor Cres S60 . . . . . 45 C3
Blackmore St S4 . . . . 53 B3
Blacksmith La S35 . . . . . . 14 C2
Blackstock Cl S14 . . . . 86 B4
Blackstock Cres S14 . . . . . 86 B4
Blackstock Dr S14 . . . . 86 B4
Blackstock Rd S14 . . . . . . 74 C2
Black Swan Wlk S1 . . . . 106 A3
Blackthorn Ave S66 . . . . . 36 C3
Blackthorn Cl S35 . . . . . . 5 B2
Blackthorn Rise S25 . . . . . 82 B2
Blackwell Cl S2 . . . . 106 C3
Blackwell Ct S2 . . . . 106 C3
Blackwell Pl S2 . . . . 106 C3
Blagden St S2 . . . . 107 C2
Blair Athol Rd S11 . . . . . . 60 C1
Blake Cl S66 . . . . 37 B2
Blake Grove Rd S6 . . . . . 104 B5
Blakeney Rd S10 . . . . 51 A1
Blake St S6 . . . . 51 B3
Bland La S6 . . . . 39 A3
Bland St S4 . . . . 42 C2
Blaxton Cl S20 . . . . 89 B4
Blayton Rd S4 . . . . 42 A2
Blenheim Cl S66 . . . . 24 C1
Blenheim Ct S66 . . . . 36 B4
Blenheim Mews S11 . . . . 71 C3
Blonk St S1 . . . . 106 B4
Blossom Cres S12 . . . . 76 A1
Bluebell Cl S5 . . . . 29 C1
Bluebell Rd S5 . . . . 29 C1
Bluebell Wood La S66 . . 24 B1
Bluebird Hill S26 . . . . 81 A4
Blue Boy St S3 . . . . 104 C4
Blue Mans Way S60 . . . . . 57 A3
Blyde Rd S5 . . . . 42 A3
Blyth Ave S62 . . . . 12 A3
Blyth Cl S60 . . . . 48 B3
Bochum Parkway S8 . . . . 86 A2
Bocking Cl S8 . . . . 84 B3
Bocking Hill S36 . . . . 3 C3
Bocking La
 Sheffield, Greenhill
 S8 . . . . 84 C2
 Sheffield S8 . . . . 84 B3
Bocking Rise S8 . . . . 84 C2
Boden La S1 . . . . 104 C3
Boden Pl S9 . . . . 55 A3
Boggard La S35 . . . . 13 A2
Boland Rd S8 . . . . 96 B3
Bold St S9 . . . . 43 B2
BOLEHILL 85 B4
Bole Hill S6 . . . . 85 B4
Bole Hill Cl S6 . . . . 50 C4
Bolehill La S10 . . . . 50 C2
Bole Hill Rd S6 . . . . 50 B3
Bolsover Rd S5 . . . . 42 B4
Bolsover Rd E 1 S5 . . . . . 42 B3
Bolsover St S3 . . . . 104 B3
Bolton St S3 . . . . 105 C2
Bond S6 . . . . 104 B4
Bonet La S60 . . . . 45 B3
Bonville Gdns S3 . . . . . . 104 C4
Booker Rd S8 . . . . 84 C4
Booth Cl S20 . . . . 90 B4
Booth Croft S20 . . . . 90 B4
Booth Rd S35 . . . . 5 A1
Booth St S61 . . . . 10 C2
Bootle St 3 S9 . . . . 54 B4
Borough Mews S6 . . . . . . 52 A3
Borough Rd S6 . . . . 40 B2
Borrowdale Ave 3
 S20 . . . . 103 B4
Borrowdale Cl 2
 S20 . . . . 103 B4
Borrowdale Dr S20 . . . . 103 B4
Borrowdale Rd S20 . . . . 103 B4
Boston Castle Gr S60 . . 33 B2
Boston Castle Terr
 S60 . . . . 33 B2
Boston St S2 . . . . 62 B3
Bosville Rd S10 . . . . 50 C1

Bosville St S65 . . . . 23 A2
Boswell Cl S35 . . . . 5 A2
Boswell St S65 . . . . 33 C3
Bosworth St 2 S10 . . . . . 50 C2
Botanical Gardens
 (Sheffield) * S11 . . . . 61 B3
Botanical Rd S11 . . . . 61 A3
Botham St S4 . . . . 42 C2
Botsford St S3 . . . . 52 B4
Boulder Gn S62 . . . . 12 B2
Boundary Dr S62 . . . . 12 B2
Boundary Rd S2 . . . . 63 C4
Boundary Wlk S60 . . . . . 45 B2
Bourne Rd S5 . . . . 28 C2
Bow Bridge Cl S60 . . . . . 32 C2
Bowden Wood Ave S9 . . 65 A4
Bowden Wood Cl S9 . . . . 65 A4
Bowden Wood Cres
 S9 . . . . 65 A4
Bowden Wood Dr S9 . . . 65 A4
Bowden Wood Pl S9 . . . . 65 A4
Bowden Wood Rd S9 . . . 65 A4
Bowdon St S1 . . . . 105 C2
Bowen Dr S65 . . . . 23 C4
Bowen Rd S65 . . . . 21 C2
Bower Cl S61 . . . . 19 B3
Bower La S35 . . . . 14 B3
Bower Rd S10 . . . . 104 A4
Bower Spring S3 . . . . . . 106 A4
Bower St S3 . . . . 106 A4
Bowfield Ct S5 . . . . 28 C2
Bowfield Rd S5 . . . . 29 A2
Bowland Dr S35 . . . . 6 C3
Bowling Green St S3 . . 106 A5
Bowman Cl S12 . . . . 87 A4
Bowness Cl S18 . . . . 100 A3
Bowness Rd S6 . . . . 40 A1
Bowood Rd S11 . . . . 61 B2
BOWSHAW 97 A2
Bowshaw S18 . . . . 97 A2
Bowshaw Ave S8 . . . . 97 B3
Bowshaw Cl S8 . . . . 97 B3
Bowshaw View S8 . . . . . . 97 B3
Boyce St S6 . . . . 51 B3
Boyland St S3 . . . . 52 A4
Boynton Cres S5 . . . . 41 B4
Boynton Rd S5 . . . . 41 B4
Bracken Ct S66 . . . . 36 B1
Brackenfield Gr S12 . . . . 76 C1
Bracken Hill S35 . . . . 6 B2
Bracken Moor La S36 . . . 3 B2
Bracken Rd S20 . . . . 29 B1
Brackley St S3 . . . . 52 C4
Bradbury's Cl S62 . . . . . . 12 A1
Bradbury St S8 . . . . 73 C4
Bradfield Rd S6 . . . . 40 A2
Bradfield Sch S35 . . . . . . 13 A1
BRADGATE 20 A1
Bradgate Cl S61 . . . . 20 A1
Bradgate Ct S61 . . . . 19 C1
Bradgate La S61 . . . . 19 C1
Bradgate Pl S61 . . . . 20 A2
Bradgate Rd S61 . . . . 20 A1
Bradley St S10 . . . . 51 A3
Bradmarsh Way S60 . . . 32 C2
Bradshaw Ave S60 . . . . . 57 D1
Bradshaw Way S60 . . . . . 57 D1
Bradstone Rd S65 . . . . . . 22 C2
BRADWAY 96 A3
BRADWAY BANK 95 B4
Bradway Cl S17 . . . . 95 C3
Bradway Dr S17 . . . . 95 C3
Bradway Grange Rd
 S17 . . . . 96 A3
Bradway Rd
 Sheffield, Bradway
 S17 . . . . 95 C3
 Sheffield, Lower Bradway
 S17 . . . . 96 A4
Bradwell Cl S18 . . . . 99 B3
Bradwell St 1 S2 . . . . 74 A4
Braemore Rd S6 . . . . 39 B3
Brailesford Ct 4 S5 . . . . 16 A2
Brailsford Ave S5 . . . . 16 A2
Brailsford Rd S5 . . . . 16 A2
Braithwell Rd S65 . . . . . . 25 B2
Bramall Ct S2 . . . . 62 B2
Bramall La
 Sheffield S2 . . . . 62 B2
 Stocksbridge S36 . . . . . . 2 B5

Bramall Lane Football Gd
 S2 . . . . 62 B3
Bramble Cl S66 . . . . 36 B1
Brambles The S35 . . . . . . 16 B3
Brameld Rd S62 . . . . 12 A3
Bramham Ct S9 . . . . 54 C3
Bramham Rd S9 . . . . 54 C3
BRAMLEY 37 A3
Bramley Ave
 Aston S26 . . . . 69 C2
 Sheffield S13 . . . . 64 A2
Bramley Cl S20 . . . . 90 A1
Bramley Ct S10 . . . . 50 C1
Bramley Dr S13 . . . . 66 A3
Bramley Grange Cres
 S66 . . . . 37 B3
Bramley Grange Dr
 S66 . . . . 37 B3
Bramley Grange Prim
 Sch S66 . . . . 37 B3
Bramley Grange Rise
 S66 . . . . 37 B3
Bramley Grange View
 S66 . . . . 37 B3
Bramley Grange Way
 S66 . . . . 37 B3
Bramley Hall Rd S13 . . . 64 A2
Bramley La S13 . . . . 66 A2
Bramley Mews S21 . . . . 103 A1
Bramley Park Cl S13 . . . 66 A3
Bramley Park Rd S13 . . 66 A3
Bramley Sunnyside Jun
 & Inf Schs S66 . . . . 36 C4
Brampton Ct 3 S20 . . . . 89 B4
Bramshill Cl S20 . . . . 91 B3
Bramshill Ct 2 S20 . . . . 91 B3
Bramwell Cl S3 . . . . 104 B4
Bramwell Dr S3 . . . . 104 B4
Bramwell St
 Rotherham S65 . . . . 21 B1
 Sheffield S3 . . . . 104 B4
Bramwith Rd S11 . . . . . . 60 A2
Brandeth Rd S6 . . . . 51 C3
Brandon St S3 . . . . 41 C1
Brandreth Cl S6 . . . . 51 C3
Bransby St S6 . . . . 51 B3
Brantwood Sch S7 . . . . . 61 C2
Brathay Cl 3 S4 . . . . 43 A3
Brathay Rd 4 S4 . . . . 43 A3
Bray St S9 . . . . 54 B3
Bray Wlk S61 . . . . 18 C4
Brearley Ave S36 . . . . 3 C2
Brecklands
 Rotherham S65 . . . . 34 C2
 Rotherham, Wickersley
 S66 . . . . 36 A2
BRECKS 35 B3
Brecks Cres S65 . . . . 35 B2
Brecks La S65 . . . . 35 B4
Brecon Cl S20 . . . . 91 B4
Brentwood Ave S11 . . . . 72 C4
Brentwood Rd S11 . . . . . 72 C4
Bressingham Cl S4 . . . . . 53 A4
Bressingham Rd S4 . . . . 53 A4
Bretton Gr S12 . . . . 76 C1
Brew Ho The S11 . . . . . . 105 B1
Briar Ct S66 . . . . 36 B1
Briarfield Ave S12 . . . . . . 75 C1
Briarfield Cres S12 . . . . . 87 B4
Briarfield Rd S12 . . . . 75 C1
Briarfields La S35 . . . . . . 13 A1
Briar Rd S7 . . . . 73 A4
Briars Cl S21 . . . . 92 B1
Briarwood Gdns S66 . . . 24 B2
Briary Ave S35 . . . . 5 B1
Briary Cl S60 . . . . 46 A1
Brickhouse La S17 . . . . . . 82 A2
BRICK HOUSES 82 B2
Brick St S10 . . . . 50 C1
Bridby St S13 . . . . 78 B4
Bridgegate S60 . . . . 21 A1
Bridge Hill S35 . . . . 13 B3
Bridgehouses S3 . . . . . . 106 A5
Bridge Inn Rd S35 . . . . . . 4 C2
Bridge St
 Killamarsh S21 . . . . 92 B2
 Rotherham S60 . . . . 21 A1
 Sheffield S3 . . . . 106 B4
Bridle Cl S35 . . . . 7 B4
Bridle Cres S35 . . . . 7 B4
Bridle Stile S20 . . . . 90 A1

Bridle Stile Cl S20 . . . . . . 90 A1
Bridle Stile Gdns S20 . . 89 C1
Bridport Rd S9 . . . . 54 C3
Brier Cl S20 . . . . 90 B3
Brierly Rd S65 . . . . 23 B3
Brier St S6 . . . . 40 A2
Briery Wlk S61 . . . . 10 C1
Brigadier Hargreaves Ct
 S13 . . . . 77 C4
Brightmore Dr S3 . . . . . 104 B3
Brighton Terrace Rd
 S10 . . . . 51 A2
BRIGHTSIDE 43 A2
Brightside Inf Sch S9 . . . 43 C4
Brightside La S9 . . . . 43 A1
Brightside Way S9 . . . . . . 43 A2
Brimmesfield Dr S2 . . . . 63 C2
Brimmesfield Rd S2 . . . . 63 C1
BRINCLIFFE 72 B4
Brincliffe Cres S11 . . . . . 61 A1
Brincliffe Ct S7 . . . . 73 A4
Brincliffe Edge Cl S11 . . 72 B4
Brincliffe Edge Rd S7,
 S11 . . . . 72 B4
Brincliffe Gdns S11 . . . . 61 A1
Brincliffe Hill S11 . . . . . . 60 C1
Brindley Cl S8 . . . . 73 C2
Brindley Cres S8 . . . . 73 C2
Brindley Ct S21 . . . . 92 A2
Brinkburn Cl S17 . . . . 95 A4
Brinkburn Ct S17 . . . . . . 95 A4
Brinkburn Dr S17 . . . . . . 95 A4
Brinkburn Vale Rd
 S17 . . . . 95 A4
Brinsford Rd S60 . . . . 46 A3
BRINSWORTH 45 A2
Brinsworth Comp Sch
 S60 . . . . 45 B2
Brinsworth Grange
 S60 . . . . 45 B3
Brinsworth Hall Ave
 S60 . . . . 45 C2
Brinsworth Hall Cres
 S60 . . . . 45 C2
Brinsworth Hall Dr
 S60 . . . . 45 C2
Brinsworth Hall Gr
 S60 . . . . 45 C1
Brinsworth Howarth
 Prim Sch S60 . . . . 46 A1
Brinsworth La S60 . . . . . . 45 C2
Brinsworth Manor Jun &
 Inf Sch S60 . . . . 46 A3
Brinsworth Rd
 Catliffe S60 . . . . 45 C1
 Catliffe S60 . . . . 57 A4
Brinsworth St
 Rotherham S60 . . . . 32 C4
 Sheffield S9 . . . . 54 A4
Brinsworth Whitehill
 Prim Sch S60 . . . . 46 A1
Bristol Rd S11 . . . . 61 A3
Britannia Rd S9 . . . . 55 A2
Britnall St S9 . . . . 54 B4
Brittain St S2 . . . . 107 B2
Broadcroft Cl S20 . . . . . . 80 A1
Broad Elms Cl S11 . . . . . 71 B2
Broad Elms La S11 . . . . . 71 A1
Broadfield Ct S8 . . . . 73 B4
Broadfield Rd S8 . . . . 73 B4
Broadfield Way S8 . . . . . 73 B4
Broadgate House Cl
 S61 . . . . 20 A1
Broadhead Rd S36 . . . . . . 3 C2
Broad Inge Cres S35 . . . . 6 C3
Broad La S1 . . . . 106 A4
Broadlands S66 . . . . 37 B2
Broadlands Ave S20 . . . . 89 C4
Broadlands Cl S20 . . . . . . 89 C4
Broadlands Cres S66 . . . 37 B2
Broadlands Croft S20 . . 89 C4
Broadlands Rise S20 . . . 89 C4
Broad Lane Ct S11 . . . . 104 C3
Broadley Rd S13 . . . . 65 A1
Broad Oaks S9 . . . . 54 A3
Broad St
 Rawmarsh S62 . . . . 12 A1
 Sheffield, Park Hill S2 . 106 C4
 Sheffield S2 . . . . 106 B4
Broadway
 Brinsworth S60 . . . . 45 C1
 Rotherham S65 . . . . 22 B1

Broadway Ave S35 . . . . . . 7 C2
Broadway E S65 . . . . 22 B1
Brocco Bank S11 . . . . 61 A3
Brocco La S11, S3 . . . . . 104 C4
Brocco St S1, S3 . . . . . . 104 C4
Brockhurst Way S65 . . . 23 C4
Brocklehurst Ave S8 . . . 86 A2
Brockwood Cl S13 . . . . . . 67 A1
Brompton Rd S9 . . . . 43 B1
Bromwich Rd S8 . . . . 85 A4
Brook Cl
 Aston S26 . . . . 69 C1
 Sheffield S35 . . . . 14 C3
Brook Croft S36 . . . . 3 B3
Brook Ct S61 . . . . 9 A2
Brook Dr S3 . . . . 104 C4
Brookfield Cl S65 . . . . . . 23 A3
Brookfield Rd S7 . . . . 62 A1
Brook Gn S12 . . . . 78 A1
Brookhaven Way S66 . . 37 B2
Brook Hill
 Rotherham S61 . . . . 9 A2
 Sheffield S3 . . . . 104 B3
Brookhouse Cl S12 . . . . . 78 A1
Brookhouse Ct 6 S12 . . 78 A1
Brookhouse Dr S12 . . . . 78 A1
Brookhouse Hill S10 . . . 59 A1
Brook House Jun Sch
 S20 . . . . 80 A1
Brookhouse Rd S26 . . . . 80 C4
Brook La
 Oughtibridge S35 . . . . . 13 A3
 Rotherham S66 . . . . 37 A4
 Sheffield, Grenoside
 S35 . . . . 14 C3
 Sheffield, Hackenthorpe
 S12 . . . . 78 A1
 Sheffield S3 . . . . 104 C3
Brooklands Ave S10 . . . 59 A1
Brooklands Bsns Pk
 S9 . . . . 43 B1
Brooklands Cres S10 . . . 59 A1
Brooklands Dr S10 . . . . . 58 C1
Brooklyn Pl 2 S8 . . . . . . 73 C3
Brooklyn Rd 5 S8 . . . . . 73 C3
Brooklyn Works S3 . . . 104 C5
Brook Rd
 Chapeltown S35 . . . . 6 C4
 Rotherham S65 . . . . 22 B2
 Sheffield S8 . . . . 73 B3
Brook Row S36 . . . . 3 B3
Brookside S65 . . . . 34 C3
Brookside Cl 1 S12 . . . . 78 A1
Brookside Ct S61 . . . . 21 B4
Brook St S60 . . . . 47 C3
Brookview Ct S18 . . . . . . 97 B1
BROOM 34 A2
Broom Ave S60 . . . . 34 B1
Broom Chase S60 . . . . . . 33 C2
Broom Cl
 Rotherham S60 . . . . 24 C1
 Sheffield S11 . . . . 62 A3
Broom Cres S60 . . . . 33 C2
Broomcroft Pk S11 . . . . . 71 B1
Broom Ct S60 . . . . 34 A2
Broom Dr S60 . . . . 34 B1
BROOMFIELD 105 B2
Broomfield Ct S36 . . . . . . 3 C2
Broomfield Gr
 Rotherham S60 . . . . 33 C3
 Stocksbridge S36 . . . . . . 3 C2
Broomfield La S36 . . . . . . 3 B2
Broomfield Rd
 Sheffield S10 . . . . 105 A2
 Stocksbridge S36 . . . . . . 3 C2
Broom Gn S3 . . . . 105 C2
Broom Gr S60 . . . . 33 C3
Broom Grange S60 . . . . . 34 A2
Broomgrove Cres
 S10 . . . . 105 A2
Broomgrove La S10 . . . 105 A1
Broomgrove Rd S10 . . . 105 A1
Broomhall Pl S10 . . . . . 105 B1
Broomhall Rd S10 . . . . . 105 B1
Broomhall St
 Sheffield, Broomhill
 S3 . . . . 105 B2
 Sheffield S10 . . . . 105 C2
BROOMHILL 51 A1

Broomhill Cl S21 . . . . .102 B1
Broomhill Inf Sch S10 . . . .61 A4
Broom La S60 . . . . 34 B1
Broom Rd S60 . . . . 33 C3
Broom Riddings S61 . . . . . 20 B4
Broomspring Cl S3 . . . . .105 B2
Broomspring La S10 . . . .105 C2
Broom St S10 . . . . .105 B2
Broom Terr S60 . . . . 33 C3
Broom Valley Jun & Inf
  Schs 33 C2
Broom Valley Rd S60 . . . . 34 A1
Broom Wlk S3 . . . . .105 C2
Broomwood Cl **3** S20 . . 79 C1
Broomwood Gdns S20 . . . 79 C1
Brotherton St S3 . . . . 52 C4
Broughton La S9 . . . . 43 C2
Broughton Rd S6 . . . . 40 A3
Brow Cres S20 . . . . 91 A1
Brownell St S3 . . . . .104 C4
Browning Cl S3 . . . . 27 A3
Browning Ct **2** S65 . . . . 34 B3
Browning Dr
  Rotherham S65 . . . . 34 B4
  Sheffield S6 . . . . 27 A3
Browning Rd
  Rotherham S65 . . . . 34 B3
  Sheffield S6 . . . . 27 A3
Brown La
  Dronfield S18 . . . . 98 A1
  Sheffield S1 . . . . .107 A2
Brown St
  Rotherham S60 . . . . 20 C1
  Sheffield S1 . . . . .107 B2
Brow The S65 . . . . 35 A2
Broxholme Rd S8 . . . . 73 B1
Bruce Rd S11 . . . . 61 B2
Brunswick Dr S66 . . . . 24 B1
Brunswick Prim Sch
  S13 . . . . .78 C4
Brunswick Rd
  Rotherham S60 . . . . 33 C2
  Sheffield S3 . . . . 52 C3
Brunswick St S10 . . . . . .105 B2
Brunt Rd S62 . . . . 12 C4
Brushfield Gr S12 . . . . 76 C2
Bubwith Rd S9 . . . . 43 C4
Buchanan Cres S5 . . . . 27 B3
Buchanan Dr S5 . . . . 27 B3
Buchanan Rd S5 . . . . 27 B3
Buckenham Dr S4 . . . . 53 A4
Buckenham St S4 . . . . 53 A4
Buckingham Cl **2**
  S18 . . . . 99 C4
Buckingham Way S60 . . . . 46 B2
Buck Wood View S14 . . . . 74 C3
Bullen Rd S6 . . . . 26 C3
Bullfinch Cl S60 . . . . 46 B2
Bungalows The
  Killamarsh S21 . . . . 92 A2
  Treeton S60 . . . . 57 C2
Bunkers Hill S21 . . . . 92 C2
Bunting Cl S8 . . . . 85 C4
Bunting Nook S8 . . . . 85 C3
Burbage Cl S18 . . . . 99 C4
Burbage Gr S12 . . . . 76 C3
Burcot Rd S8 . . . . 73 B3
Burford Cres S26 . . . . 69 C1
Burgen Rd S61 . . . . 19 B3
Burgess Rd S9 . . . . 54 A4
Burgess St S1 . . . . .107 A3
Burgoyne Cl S6 . . . . 51 B4
Burgoyne Rd S6 . . . . 51 B4
Burlington S6 . . . . .104 B4
Burlington Cl S17 . . . . 82 C1
Burlington Gr S17 . . . . 82 C1
Burlington Glen S17 . . . . . 82 C1
Burlington Gr S17 . . . . 82 C1
Burlington Rd S17 . . . . 82 C1
Burlington St S6 . . . . .104 B3
Burnaby Cres S6 . . . . 40 B1
Burnaby Ct S6 . . . . 40 B1
Burnaby Gn S6 . . . . 40 B1
Burnaby St S6 . . . . 40 B1
Burnaston Ct S18 . . . . 99 B3
BURNCROSS 6 C2
Burncross Dr S35 . . . . 7 A3
Burncross Gr S35 . . . . 6 C3
Burncross Rd S35 . . . . 6 C3

Burnell Rd S6 . . . . 40 A3
Burn Gr S35 . . . . 8 A2
BURNGREAVE 53 A4
Burngreave Bank S4 . . . . . 52 C4
Burngreave Rd S3 . . . . 52 C4
Burngreave St S3 . . . . 52 C4
Burngrove Pl S3 . . . . 41 C1
Burnsall Cres S60 . . . . 46 A1
Burns Ct S35 . . . . 7 A3
Burns Dr
  Chapeltown S35 . . . . 7 A3
  Dronfield S18 . . . . .101 B2
  Rotherham S65 . . . . 34 B4
Burnside Ave S8 . . . . 73 C3
Burns Rd
  Rotherham S65 . . . . 34 B4
  Sheffield S6 . . . . 51 B4
Burnt Stones Cl S10 . . . . . 59 B4
Burnt Stones Dr S10 . . . . . 59 B4
Burnt Stones Gr S10 . . . . . 59 B4
Burnt Tree La S3 . . . . . . .104 C5
Burntwood Cres S60 . . . . . 57 C3
Burrell St S60 . . . . 33 A4
Burrowlee Rd S6 . . . . 40 A3
Burrows Dr S5 . . . . 41 B4
Burton La S35 . . . . 13 A2
Burton Rd S3 . . . . 52 A4
Burton St S6 . . . . 40 B1
Bushey Wood Gr S17 . . . . 82 B1
Bushey Wood Rd S17 . . . . 94 C4
Busk Knoll S5 . . . . 41 B4
Busk Mdw S5 . . . . 41 B4
Busk Meadow Inf Sch
  S5 . . . . 41 B3
Busk Pk S5 . . . . 41 B4
Butchill Ave S5 . . . . 16 A2
Bute St S10 . . . . 50 C1
Butler Rd S6 . . . . 50 B4
Butler Way S21 . . . . 92 A2
Buttermere Dr S18 . . . . .100 A3
Buttermere Rd S7 . . . . 73 A2
Butterthwaite Cres S5 . . . 17 B1
Butterthwaite La S35 . . . . 17 A3
Butterthwaite Rd S5 . . . . . 17 A2
Button Hill S11 . . . . 72 A3
Button Row S36 . . . . 3 B3
Butts Hill S17 . . . . 94 B2
Byrley Rd S61 . . . . 19 B3
Byron Ave S35 . . . . 7 A2
Byron Cl S18 . . . . .101 B1
Byron Dr S65 . . . . 34 A4
Byron Rd
  Sheffield, Beighton
  S20 . . . . 91 B4
  Sheffield, Nether Edge
  S7 . . . . .73 A4
Byron Wood Prim Sch
  S4 . . . . 42 A1

C

Cadman Ct S20 . . . . .103 A4
Cadman La S1 . . . . .107 B3
Cadman Rd S12 . . . . 76 B4
Cadman St
  Sheffield, Park Hill
  S4 . . . . .106 C4
  Sheffield S20 . . . . .103 A4
Caernarvon Rd S18 . . . . .101 A2
Caine Gdns S61 . . . . 31 B4
Cairns Cotts S13 . . . . 78 B4
Cairns Rd
  Sheffield, Beighton
  S20 . . . . .79 B2
  Sheffield S10 . . . . 60 B4
Calcot Gr S35 . . . . 7 A3
Caldbeck Gr S35 . . . . 5 B2
Calder Ct S60 . . . . 46 C4
Calder Rd S61 . . . . 10 A3
Calder Way S5 . . . . 41 A4
Caldey Rd S18 . . . . .100 C2
California Dr
  Catliffe S60 . . . . .57 A3
  Chapeltown S35 . . . . 7 B2
Callow Dr S14 . . . . 74 C3
Callow Mount S14 . . . . 74 C3
Callow Pl S14 . . . . 74 C3
Callow Rd S14 . . . . 74 B3
Callum Ct S62 . . . . 21 B4
Callywhite La S18 . . . . . .101 B3
Calner Croft S20 . . . . 91 C4
Calvert Rd S9 . . . . 55 A4

Camborne Cl S6 . . . . 26 C3
Camborne Rd S6 . . . . 26 C3
Cambridge Cres S65 . . . . . 22 A1
Cambridge Ct
  13 Sheffield, Heeley
  S8 . . . . .74 A4
  4 Sheffield S1 . . . . . . .107 A3
Cambridge Lodge **14**
  S8 . . . . .74 A4
Cambridge Pl S65 . . . . 22 A1
Cambridge Rd
  Sheffield S8 . . . . 74 A4
  Stocksbridge S36 . . . . 4 B2
Cambridge St
  Rotherham S65 . . . . 22 A1
  Sheffield S1 . . . . .107 A3
Cambron Gdns S66 . . . . . . 37 A4
Camdale Rise S12 . . . . 89 A3
Camdale View S12 . . . . . . 89 B3
Cammell Rd S5 . . . . 42 B4
Camms CE Prim Sch
  S21 . . . . .103 A2
Camms Cl S21 . . . . .103 A2
Camm St S6 . . . . 51 A4
Campbell Dr S65 . . . . 34 B4
Campbell St S61 . . . . 11 A2
Camping La S8 . . . . 84 C4
Campion Dr S21 . . . . 92 A2
Campo La S1 . . . . .106 A4
Campsall Dr S10 . . . . 50 B1
Canada St S4 . . . . 42 B1
Canal Bridge S21 . . . . 92 B2
Canal St S4 . . . . 53 B2
Canary Ct S66 . . . . 24 B1
CANKLOW 33 A1
Canklow Hill Rd S60 . . . . . 33 A1
Canklow Meadows Ind
  Est S60 . . . . 46 B3
Canklow Rd S60 . . . . 33 A2
Canklow Woods Prim
  Sch S60 . . . . 46 B4
Canning St **5** S1 . . . . . .105 C3
Cannock St S6 . . . . 40 A2
Cannon Cl S62 . . . . 12 C4
Cannon Hall Rd S5 . . . . . . 42 A3
Cannonthorpe Rise
  S60 . . . . .57 D2
Canterbury Ave S10 . . . . . 59 A2
Canterbury Cl **1** S65 . . 34 B3
Canterbury Cres S10 . . . . . 59 A2
Canterbury Dr S10 . . . . . . 59 A2
Canterbury Rd S8 . . . . 74 A3
Cantilupe Cres S26 . . . . . . 69 B2
Capel St S6 . . . . 40 B1
CARBROOK 43 B2
Carbrook Bsns Pk S9 . . . . 43 C3
Carbrook Hall Rd S9 . . . . . 43 C3
Carbrook St S9 . . . . 43 C3
Cardew Cl S62 . . . . 12 B3
Cardoness Dr S10 . . . . 59 C4
Cardoness Rd S10 . . . . 60 A4
Cardwell Ave S13 . . . . 66 B1
Cardwell Dr S13 . . . . 64 A1
Carfield Ave S8 . . . . 74 A3
Carfield La S8 . . . . 74 B3
Carfield Pl S8 . . . . 74 A3
Carfield Prim Sch S8 . . . . . 74 A3
Car Hill S61 . . . . 20 C4
Carlby Rd S6 . . . . 39 B1
Carley Dr S20 . . . . 91 A3
Carlingford Rd S60 . . . . . . 34 A1
Carlin St S13 . . . . 77 A4
Carlisle Bsns Pk **9**
  S9 . . . . 43 A3
Carlisle Pl **5** S65 . . . . . . 21 B1
Carlisle Rd S4 . . . . 42 C2
Carlisle St E S4 . . . . 42 C1
Carlisle St
  Rotherham S65 . . . . 21 B1
  Sheffield S4 . . . . 53 A3
Carlthorpe Gr S35 . . . . 5 A1
Carlton Ave S65 . . . . 33 C3
Carlton Cl S20 . . . . .102 C4
Carlton Mews S2 . . . . 63 C1
Carlton Rd
  Rawmarsh S62 . . . . 12 A2
  Sheffield S6 . . . . 39 C4
Carmel Ct **7** S11 . . . . . . 61 A2
Carnaby Rd S6 . . . . 40 A1
Carnarvon St S6 . . . . 51 C3
Carpenter Croft S12 . . . . . 76 B4
Carpenter Gdns S12 . . . . . 76 B4

Carpenter Mews S12 . . . .76 B4
Carr Bank Cl S11 . . . . 60 A2
Carr Bank Dr S11 . . . . 60 A2
Carr Bank La S11 . . . . 59 C2
Carr Cl
  Brinsworth S60 . . . . 45 B2
  Stocksbridge S36 . . . . 4 A2
Carrcroft Ct S36 . . . . 4 B2
Carrfield Ct **8** S8 . . . . . 74 A4
Carrfield Dr S8 . . . . 74 A4
Carrfield La S8 . . . . 74 A4
Carrfield Rd S8 . . . . 74 A4
Carrfield St S8 . . . . 74 A4
Carr Fold S36 . . . . 4 B2
Carr Forge Cl S12 . . . . 77 C2
Carr Forge La S12 . . . . 77 C2
Carr Forge Mount
  S12 . . . . 77 C2
Carr Forge Pl S12 . . . . 78 A2
Carr Forge Rd S12 . . . . 78 A2
Carr Forge Terr S12 . . . . . 77 C2
Carr Forge View S12 . . . . . 78 A2
Carr Forge Wlk **4**
  S12 . . . . 78 A2
Carr Gr S36 . . . . 4 A2
CARR HEAD 4 A2
Carrill Dr S6 . . . . 26 C4
Carrill Rd S6 . . . . 26 C4
Carrington Rd S11 . . . . 60 C2
Carrington St S65 . . . . 33 C3
Carr La S18 . . . . 99 B4
Carr Lane Mews S18 . . . . . 99 C4
Carr Rd
  Sheffield S6 . . . . 51 A4
  Stocksbridge S36 . . . . 4 A2
Carr View Rd S61 . . . . 19 A2
Carrville Dr S6 . . . . 27 A2
Carrville Rd S6 . . . . 27 A2
Carrville Rd W S6 . . . . 26 C2
Carrwell La S6 . . . . 26 C1
CARSICK 59 C3
Carsick Gr S10 . . . . 59 B3
Carsick Grange S10 . . . . . . 59 C3
CARSICK HILL 59 C2
Carsick Hill Cres S10 . . . . . 59 C3
Carsick Hill Dr S10 . . . . . . 59 C3
Carsick Hill Rd S10 . . . . . . 59 C4
Carsick Hill Way S10 . . . . . 59 B3
Carsick View Rd S10 . . . . . 59 B3
Carson Mount S12 . . . . . . 76 A1
Carson Rd S10 . . . . 50 C1
Carter Grange **11** S8 . . 74 A4
Carterhall La S12 . . . . 88 A4
Carterhall Rd S12 . . . . 87 C4
CARTER KNOWLE 72 B3
Carter Knowle Ave
  S11 . . . . 72 B3
Carter Knowle Jun Sch
  S7 . . . . 72 C3
Carter Knowle Rd S7,
  S11 . . . . 72 B3
Carter Lodge Ave S12 . . . 78 A2
Carter Lodge Dr S12 . . . . . 78 A2
Carter Lodge Pl S12 . . . . . 78 A2
Carter Lodge Rise
  S12 . . . . 78 A2
Carter Lodge Wlk **3**
  S12 . . . . 78 A2
Carter Pl S8 . . . . 74 A4
Carter Rd S8 . . . . 73 C4
CARTLEDGE 99 A1
Cartmel Cl S18 . . . . .100 A3
Cartmel Cres S8 . . . . 73 B1
Cartmel Ct S8 . . . . 73 A2
Cartmel Hill S8 . . . . 73 A2
Cartmell Rd S8 . . . . 73 A2
Car Vale Dr S13 . . . . 65 A2
Car Vale View S13 . . . . 65 A2
Carver La S1 . . . . .107 A3
Carver St S1 . . . . .107 A3
Carwood Cl S4 . . . . 42 B1
Carwood Gn S4 . . . . 42 B1
Carwood Gr S4 . . . . 42 B1
Carwood Park Ind Units
  S4 . . . . 42 B1
Carwood Rd S4 . . . . 42 B1
Carwood Way S4 . . . . 42 B1
Cary Rd
  Eckington S21 . . . . .102 B1
  Sheffield S2 . . . . 64 B2
Castle Ave S60 . . . . 33 A1
Castlebeck Ave S2 . . . . . . 65 A3

Castlebeck Croft S2 . . . . . 65 A3
Castlebeck Ct S2 . . . . 65 A3
Castlebeck Dr S2 . . . . 65 A2
Castle Ct S2 . . . . 53 B2
Castledale Croft S2 . . . . . 64 C2
Castledale Gr S2 . . . . 65 A2
Castledale Pl S2 . . . . 64 C2
Castledine Croft S9 . . . . . 43 C4
Castledine Gdns S9 . . . . . 43 C4
Castlegate S3 . . . . .106 B4
Castle Gn S3 . . . . .106 B4
Castle Hill S21 . . . . .103 A2
Castle Hill Cl S21 . . . . . . .103 A2
Castle Mkt S3 . . . . .106 B4
Castlerigg Way **1**
  S18 . . . . .100 A3
Castle Row S17 . . . . 95 C4
Castlerow Cl S17 . . . . 95 C4
Castlerow Dr S17 . . . . 95 C4
Castlerow View S17 . . . . . 95 C4
Castle Sq S1 . . . . .106 B3
Castle St S3 . . . . .106 B4
Castle View S11 . . . . .103 A1
Castle Wlk S2 . . . . 53 B2
Castlewood Cres S10 . . . . 58 C2
Castlewood Ct S10 . . . . . . 59 A2
Castlewood Dr S10 . . . . . . 58 C2
Castlewood Rd S10 . . . . . . 58 C2
Castor Rd S9 . . . . 43 A1
Catch Bar La S6 . . . . 40 A4
Catcliffe Prim Sch
  S60 . . . . .57 B4
Catcliffe Rd S9 . . . . 55 A2
Catherine Ave S26 . . . . . . 69 B1
Catherine Rd S4 . . . . 53 A4
Catherine St
  2 Rotherham S65 . . . . . 33 B4
  Sheffield S3 . . . . 52 C4
Cat La S2, S8 . . . . 74 B3
Catley Rd
  Sheffield, Darnall S9 . . . . 55 A3
  Sheffield S9 . . . . 55 B3
CATLIFFE 57 A4
Cattal St **8** S9 . . . . 54 B3
Catterick Ho S65 . . . . 21 C1
Causeway Gdns S17 . . . . . 82 B2
Causeway Glade S17 . . . . 82 A2
CAUSEWAY HEAD 82 A2
Causeway Head Rd
  S17 . . . . 82 B2
Causeway The S17 . . . . . . 82 B1
Cavendish Ave
  Sheffield, Abbeydale Park
  S17 . . . . .83 A1
  Sheffield, Loxley S6 . . . . 38 C3
Cavendish Cl S65 . . . . 35 A2
Cavendish Ct S3 . . . . . . .105 C2
Cavendish Ho **7** S1 . . .105 C3
Cavendish Rd
  Rotherham S61 . . . . 32 A4
  Sheffield S11 . . . . 61 A1
Cavendish Rise S18 . . . . .100 B3
Cavendish St S3 . . . . . . .105 C3
Cave St S9 . . . . 54 A3
Cavill Rd S8 . . . . 73 C1
Cawdor Rd S2 . . . . 75 B4
Cawdron Cl S65 . . . . 23 A3
Cawdron Rise S60 . . . . 46 A1
Cawston Rd S4 . . . . 42 A2
Cawthorne Cl
  Rotherham S65 . . . . 22 C1
  Sheffield S8 . . . . 73 A1
Cawthorne Gr S8 . . . . 73 A1
Cawthorne Rd S65 . . . . . . 22 C1
Caxton La S10 . . . . 61 A4
Caxton Rd S10 . . . . 61 A4
Cecil Ave S18 . . . . .100 C4
Cecil Rd S18 . . . . .100 C4
Cecil Sq S2 . . . . 62 A2
Cedar Ave S66 . . . . 36 C3
Cedar Cl
  Killamarsh S21 . . . . 92 A1
  Stocksbridge S36 . . . . 3 A2
Cedar Dr S65 . . . . 25 C2
Cedar Rd S36 . . . . 3 A2
Cedars The S10 . . . . 60 C4
Cedar Way S35 . . . . 7 A2
Cedarwood Cl S18 . . . . . .100 C4
Celandine Ct S17 . . . . 95 B3
Celandine Gdns S17 . . . . . 95 B3
Cemetery Ave S11 . . . . . . 61 B3

Cemetery Rd
Dronfield S18 . . . . **101** A2
Sheffield S11 . . . . **62** A3
Sheffield S11 . . . . **105** C1
Centenary Ind Pk S8 . . . . **73** A3
Centenary Market Hall
S65 . . . . **21** B1
Centenary Way S60 . . . . . **33** A2
Central Ave
Rotherham, East Dene
S65 . . . . **34** B4
Rotherham, Sunnyside
S66 . . . . **24** B1
Central Bsns Pk S60 . . . **32** C4
Central Par S65 . . . . **34** B4
Central Rd S60 . . . . **21** A1
Centre The S66 . . . . **37** A3
Centurion Bsns Pk
S60 . . . . **32** B3
Centurion Office Pk
S9 . . . . **30** B1
Centurion St S60 . . . . **32** A3
Century St S9 . . . . **54** C4
Century View S60 . . . . . . **45** B2
Chaddesden Cl S18 . . . . . **99** B3
Chadwick Rd S13 . . . . **65** A1
Chaff Cl S60 . . . . **47** C3
Chaffinch Ave S60 . . . . . . **46** B2
Chaff La S60 . . . . **47** C3
Challiner Mews S60 . . . . . **57** A4
Challoner Gn S20 . . . . **90** C2
Challoner Way S20 . . . . . **90** C2
Chamberlain Ct S35 . . . . . **7** A4
Chambers La S4 . . . . **43** A3
Chambers Rd S61 . . . . **10** A1
Champion Cl S5 . . . . **29** A4
Champion Rd S5 . . . . **29** A4
Chancet Ct S8 . . . . **84** C3
Chancet Wood Cl S8 . . . **85** A2
Chancet Wood Dr S8 . . . **85** A2
Chancet Wood Rd S8 . . . **85** A3
Chancet Wood Rise
S8 . . . . **85** A2
Chancet Wood View
S8 . . . . **85** A2
Chandler Gr S60 . . . . **57** C3
Chandos Cres S21 . . . . . . **92** B2
Chandos St S10 . . . . **61** A4
Channing Gdns ❹ S6 . . . **40** B1
Channing St S6 . . . . **40** B1
Chantrey Rd S8 . . . . **73** B1
Chapel Bank Apartments
❸ S6 . . . . **51** A4
Chapel Cl
Chapeltown S35 . . . . **6** C3
Rotherham S61 . . . . **10** B2
Sheffield S10 . . . . **60** A3
Chapelfield Cres S61 . . . . **9** A3
Chapelfield Dr S61 . . . . . . **9** A3
Chapelfield La S61 . . . . . . **9** A3
Chapelfield Mount S61 . . **9** A3
Chapelfield Pl S61 . . . . . . **9** A3
Chapelfield Rd S61 . . . . . . **9** A4
Chapelfield Way S61 . . . . . **9** A3
Chapel Hill S60 . . . . **47** C3
Chapel La
Rotherham S60 . . . . **32** C4
Sheffield, Hillfoot S17 . . . **94** B2
❹ Sheffield S9 . . . . **54** B4
Chapel Rd
Chapeltown, Mortomley
S35 . . . . **5** C2
Chapeltown S35 . . . . **7** A2
Chapel St
Rawmarsh S62 . . . . **12** A3
Rotherham S60 . . . . **10** C2
Sheffield, Coisley Hill
S13 . . . . **78** A4
Sheffield S20 . . . . **102** C4
Chapel Terr S10 . . . . **60** A3
CHAPELTOWN **7** C3
Chapeltown Rd S35 . . . . **16** B4
Chapeltown Sta S35 . . . . . **7** C3
Chapel Wlk
Rotherham S60 . . . . **32** C4
Sheffield S1 . . . . **107** B3
Chapelwood Rd S9 . . . . . **54** C4
Chapel Yd S18 . . . . **100** C4
Chapman St S9 . . . . **30** B2
Charles Ashmore Rd
S8 . . . . **85** B2

Charles Clifford Dental
Hospl The S10 . . . . **105** A3
Charles La S1 . . . . **107** B2
Charles Sq S35 . . . . **5** B1
Charles St
Dronfield S1 . . . . **107** A3
Sheffield S1 . . . . **107** B2
Charlotte Ct S2 . . . . **62** C2
Charlotte La ❸ S1 . . . . . **105** C3
Charlotte Rd S1, S2 . . . . . **62** C3
CHARLTONBROOK **6** C4
Charlton Brook Cres
S35 . . . . **6** C3
Charlton Clough S35 . . . . . **6** B3
Charlton Dr S35 . . . . **6** C4
Charlton Hill Rise S35 . . . **6** B3
Charlton & Linley Homes
The S7 . . . . **83** C2
Charnley Ave S11 . . . . **72** B3
Charnley Cl S11 . . . . **72** A3
Charnley Dr S11 . . . . **72** B3
Charnley Rise S11 . . . . **72** B3
Charnock Ave S12 . . . . **87** A4
Charnock Cres S12 . . . . . . **75** C1
Charnock Dale Rd
S12 . . . . **87** C4
Charnock Dr S12 . . . . **76** A1
Charnock Gr S12 . . . . **87** C4
Charnock Hall Prim Sch
S12 . . . . **87** C4
Charnock Hall Rd S12 . . . **87** B4
CHARNOCK HILL **87** A4
Charnock View Rd
S12 . . . . **87** C4
Charnock Wood Rd
S12 . . . . **87** C3
Charnwood Ct ❷ S20 . . **91** B4
Charnwood Gr S61 . . . . . . **19** C1
Charter Row S1 . . . . **107** A2
Charter Sq S1 . . . . **107** A2
Chase Ct S6 . . . . **38** B2
Chase Rd S6 . . . . **38** B3
Chase The
Aston S26 . . . . **81** A4
Sheffield, Loxley S6 . . . . . **38** B2
Sheffield S10 . . . . **105** A1
Chatfield Rd S8 . . . . **84** C4
Chatham St
Rotherham S35 . . . . **33** B4
Sheffield S3 . . . . **106** A5
Chatsworth Cl S26 . . . . . . **70** A1
Chatsworth Ct S11 . . . . . . **71** B2
Chatsworth Park Ave
S12 . . . . **75** C3
Chatsworth Park Dr
S12 . . . . **75** C3
Chatsworth Park Gr
S12 . . . . **75** C3
Chatsworth Park Rd
S12 . . . . **75** C3
Chatsworth Park Rise
S12 . . . . **75** C3
Chatsworth Pl S18 . . . . . . **99** C4
Chatsworth Rd S17 . . . . . . **95** A4
Chatsworth Rise S60 . . . . **46** B2
Chatterton Dr S65 . . . . . . **34** B2
Chaucer Cl S5 . . . . **27** A4
Chaucer Dr S18 . . . . **101** B3
Chaucer Rd
Rotherham S65 . . . . **34** B3
Sheffield S5 . . . . **27** B4
Chaucer Sch S5 . . . . **27** B3
Cheadle St ❷ S6 . . . . . . **40** A2
Chelmsford Ave S26 . . . . **69** C2
Chelsea Ct S11 . . . . **61** A1
Chelsea Rd S11 . . . . **72** B4
Chelsea Rise S11 . . . . **61** A1
Chemist La ❷ S60 . . . . . . **20** C1
Cheney Row S1 . . . . **107** A3
Cherry Bank Rd S8 . . . . . . **73** C1
Cherry Brook S65 . . . . **22** B2
Cherry St S S2 . . . . **62** B2
Cherry St S2 . . . . **62** B2
Cherry Tree Cl
Brinsworth S60 . . . . **46** B2
Sheffield S11 . . . . **61** B1
Cherry Tree Cres S66 . . . **36** C3
Cherry Tree Ct S11 . . . . . . **61** B1
Cherry Tree Dell S11 . . . . **61** B1
Cherry Tree Dr
Killamarsh S21 . . . . **92** B1
Sheffield S11 . . . . **61** B1

Cherry Tree Rd S11 . . . . . **61** B1
Cherry Wlk S35 . . . . **7** B2
Chessel Cl S8 . . . . **73** C2
Chesterfield Rd
Aston S26 . . . . **80** A4
Dronfield S18 . . . . **101** A3
Sheffield S8 . . . . **73** B2
Chesterfield Rd S S8 . . . **97** B4
Chesterhill Ave S65 . . . . . **23** B3
Chesterton Rd S65 . . . . . . **22** A3
Chesterton Way S65 . . . . **22** B3
Chesterwood Dr S10 . . . . **60** C4
Chestnut Ave
Killamarsh S21 . . . . **92** A1
Rotherham S65 . . . . **22** B1
Sheffield, Beighton S20 . . **79** B3
Sheffield, Handsworth Hill
S9 . . . . **55** C1
Stocksbridge S36 . . . . **3** A2
Chestnut Cl
Dronfield S18 . . . . **101** B2
Rotherham S66 . . . . **36** B4
Chestnut Ct S35 . . . . **13** B3
Chestnut Dr S35 . . . . **7** A2
Chestnut Rd S26 . . . . **68** C2
Chevril Ct S66 . . . . **36** A2
Chichester Rd S10 . . . . . . **50** C2
Chiltern Ho S10 . . . . **33** A4
Chiltern Rd S6 . . . . **39** C2
Chiltern Rise S60 . . . . **46** B1
Chinley St ❷ S9 . . . . **54** B3
Chippingham Pl S9 . . . . . . **54** A4
Chippingham St S9 . . . . . . **54** B4
Chippinghouse Rd S7,
S8 . . . . **62** A1
Chiverton Cl S18 . . . . **100** C4
Chorley Ave S10 . . . . **59** A2
Chorley Dr S10 . . . . **59** A2
Chorley Pl S10 . . . . **59** A1
Chorley Rd S10 . . . . **59** B2
Christchurch Ave S26 . . . **69** C2
Christ Church Rd S3 . . . . **41** C1
Church Ave S62 . . . . **11** C2
Church Cl
Oughtibridge S35 . . . . . . **13** B3
Ravenfield S65 . . . . **24** C5
Church Croft S62 . . . . **11** C2
Churchdale Mews
S12 . . . . **76** C2
Churchdale Rd S12 . . . . . . **76** C2
Church Field Dr S66 . . . . . **36** B1
Church Fold S6 . . . . **19** B1
Church Glebe S6 . . . . **26** A1
Church Hill S60 . . . . **48** A3
Churchill Rd
Sheffield S10 . . . . **51** A1
Stocksbridge S36 . . . . **2** B4
Church La
Aston S26 . . . . **81** B4
Catliffe S60 . . . . **57** A4
Eckington S21 . . . . **88** C1
Killamarsh S21 . . . . **92** C2
Rotherham, Bramley
S66 . . . . **37** A3
Rotherham, Wickersley
S66 . . . . **36** B2
Sheffield, Beighton S20 . . **79** C1
Sheffield S9 . . . . **54** A4
Sheffield, Townhead
S17 . . . . **94** B4
Sheffield, Woodhouse
S13 . . . . **78** B4
Treeton S60 . . . . **57** C2
Church Lane Mews
S66 . . . . **37** A3
Church Mews
Killamarsh S21 . . . . **92** C3
Sheffield S20 . . . . **90** B1
Church Side S7 . . . . **72** C4
Church St
Dronfield S18 . . . . **100** C4
Eckington S21 . . . . **103** B2
Oughtibridge S35 . . . . . . **13** A3
Rawmarsh S62 . . . . **11** C2
Rotherham, Kimberworth
S61 . . . . **19** B1
Rotherham S60 . . . . **33** A4
Rotherham, Wingfield
S61 . . . . **10** C2
Sheffield, Ecclesfield
S35 . . . . **16** A3

Church St continued
Sheffield S1 . . . . **106** A3
Sheffield, Stannington
S6 . . . . **49** A3
CHURCH TOWN **92** C3
Church View
Aston S26 . . . . **70** A1
Killamarsh S21 . . . . **92** C3
Rotherham, Wickersley
S66 . . . . **36** B1
Sheffield S6 . . . . **26** A1
Sheffield, Woodhouse
S13 . . . . **78** B4
Cinder Bridge Rd S62 . . . **11** B2
Cinderhill La S8 . . . . **86** A2
Cinder Hill La S35 . . . . **15** B3
Cinderhill Rd S61 . . . . **19** B4
Cinder La S21 . . . . **93** A3
Circle Cl S2 . . . . **64** C3
Circle The
Chapeltown S35 . . . . **5** C1
Sheffield S2 . . . . **64** B3
City Plaza S1 . . . . **106** A3
City Sch The S13 . . . . **77** B4
City Wharf S3 . . . . **106** B4
City View S18 . . . . **100** C3
Claire Ct S60 . . . . **21** A1
Clara Pl S61 . . . . **31** C4
Claremont Cres S10 . . . . **105** A3
Claremont Hospl S10 . . . **59** B4
Claremont Pl S10 . . . . . . **105** A3
Claremont St S61 . . . . **31** C4
Clarence Rd S6 . . . . **39** C2
Clarence Works S4 . . . . . . **53** B3
Clarendon Ct S10 . . . . **59** C2
Clarendon Rd
Rotherham S65 . . . . **21** C1
Sheffield S10 . . . . **59** C1
Clarke Dell S10 . . . . **105** A1
Clarke Dr S10 . . . . **105** A1
Clarkegrove Rd S10 . . . . **105** A1
Clarkehouse Rd S10 . . . **105** A2
Clarke Sq ❻ S11 . . . . **62** A2
Clarke St S10 . . . . **105** B2
Clark Gr S6 . . . . **49** B4
Clarkson St S10 . . . . **105** B3
Clay La S1 . . . . **107** A2
Clay Pit La S62 . . . . **12** C4
Clay St S9 . . . . **43** B1
Clayton Cres S20 . . . . **90** C4
Clayton Hollow S20 . . . . . **90** C4
Clay Wheels La S6 . . . . . . **26** B1
Claywood Dr S2 . . . . **107** C2
Claywood Rd
Sheffield S2 . . . . **107** C1
Sheffield S2 . . . . **107** C2
Cleeve Hill Gdns S20 . . . **90** B4
Clematis Rd S5 . . . . **29** C1
Clement Mews S61 . . . . . . **31** B4
Clementson Rd S10 . . . . . **51** A2
Clement St
Rotherham S61 . . . . **31** B4
Sheffield S9 . . . . **54** C4
Cleveland St S6 . . . . **51** C3
Cliffe Farm Dr S11 . . . . . . **60** B1
Cliffefield Rd S8 . . . . **73** C3
Cliffe Field Rd S8 . . . . **73** C2
Cliffe Ho S10 . . . . **60** A4
Cliffe House Rd S5 . . . . . . **28** B2
Cliffe Rd S6 . . . . **50** B4
Cliffe View Rd S8 . . . . **73** C3
Clifford Ave S65 . . . . **24** A4
Clifford CE Inf Sch
S11 . . . . **61** B2
Clifford Rd
Rotherham S61 . . . . **19** B3
Sheffield S11 . . . . **61** B1
Cliff Rd S6 . . . . **49** B4
Cliff St S11 . . . . **62** A3
CLIFTON **21** C1
Clifton Ave
Rotherham S65 . . . . **34** A4
Sheffield S9 . . . . **55** C1
Clifton Bank S60 . . . . **33** B4
Clifton Com Arts Sch
S65 . . . . **22** A1
Clifton Comp Upper Sch
S65 . . . . **22** A2
Clifton Cres S9 . . . . **55** B1
Clifton Cres N S65 . . . . . . **33** C4
Clifton Cres S S65 . . . . . . **33** C4
Clifton Gr S65 . . . . **33** C4

Clifton La
Rotherham S65 . . . . **33** B4
Sheffield S9 . . . . **65** C4
Clifton Mount S65 . . . . . . **33** B4
Clifton Park Mus ★
S65 . . . . **33** C4
Clifton St S9 . . . . **43** C2
Clifton Terr S65 . . . . **33** B4
Clinton Pl S10 . . . . **105** B2
Clinton Wlk S10 . . . . **105** B2
Clipstone Gdns S9 . . . . . . **55** A4
Clipstone Rd S9 . . . . **55** A4
Cloonmore Croft S8 . . . . . **86** A3
Cloonmore Dr S8 . . . . **86** A3
Clough Bank
Rotherham S61 . . . . **20** B1
Sheffield S2 . . . . **62** C2
Clough Fields S10 . . . . **50** A2
Clough Gn S61 . . . . **20** C1
Clough Gr S35 . . . . **13** C3
Clough Rd
Rotherham S61 . . . . **20** B1
Sheffield S1, S2 . . . . **62** B3
Clough St S61 . . . . **20** B1
Clough Wood View
S35 . . . . **13** B2
Clover Ct S8 . . . . **86** A4
Clover Gdns S5 . . . . **29** B1
Clover Gn S61 . . . . **19** B4
Club Garden Rd S11 . . . . . **62** A2
Club Garden Wlk ❷
S11 . . . . **62** A3
Club Mill Rd S6 . . . . **40** C1
Club St S11 . . . . **62** A2
Clumber Rd S10 . . . . **59** C3
Clumber Rise S26 . . . . **81** A4
Clun Rd S4 . . . . **53** A4
Clun St S4 . . . . **53** A4
Clyde Rd S8 . . . . **73** B4
Coach Houses The
S10 . . . . **104** A4
Coach Rd S61 . . . . **10** C1
COAL ASTON **97** C2
Coalbrook Ave S13 . . . . . . **67** B2
Coalbrook Gr S13 . . . . **67** B2
Coalbrook Rd S13 . . . . **67** B2
Coal Pit La S36 . . . . **3** A1
Coates St S2 . . . . **107** C2
Cobden Pl S10 . . . . **51** A2
Cobden Terr S10 . . . . **51** A2
Cobden View Rd S10 . . . . **51** A2
Cobnar Ave S8 . . . . **85** B4
Cobnar Dr S8 . . . . **85** B4
Cobnar Gdns S8 . . . . **85** A4
Cobnar Rd S8 . . . . **85** A4
Cockayne Pl S8 . . . . **73** B2
Cockshot La S36 . . . . **3** C1
Cockshutt Ave S8 . . . . **84** B2
Cockshutt Dr S8 . . . . **84** B2
Cockshutt Rd S8 . . . . **84** B2
Cockshutts La
Oughtibridge S35 . . . . . . **13** A4
Wharncliffe Side S35 . . . . **13** A4
Coggin Mill Way S60 . . . . **32** A3
COISLEY HILL **78** A4
Coisley Hill S13 . . . . **77** B4
Coisley Rd S13 . . . . **77** C3
Coit Prim Sch S35 . . . . **7** B2
Coke Hill S60 . . . . **33** A3
Coke La S60 . . . . **33** A3
Colby Pl S6 . . . . **50** A3
Colchester Rd S10 . . . . . . **50** C2
Coldwell La S10 . . . . **59** C4
Coleford Rd S9 . . . . **55** B3
Coleman St S62 . . . . **12** A1
Coleridge Gdns S9 . . . . . . **44** A1
Coleridge Prim Sch
S65 . . . . **22** A2
Coleridge Rd
Rotherham S65 . . . . **21** C1
Sheffield S9 . . . . **43** C1
Colister Dr S9 . . . . **55** A2
Colister Gdns S9 . . . . **55** A1
College Cl S4 . . . . **42** A2
College Ct S4 . . . . **42** A2
College Park Cl S60 . . . . . **33** B2
College Rd
Rotherham, Masbrough
S60 . . . . **32** C4

College Rd continued
Rotherham S60. . . . . .20 C1
College St
Rotherham S60. . . . . .33 A4
Sheffield S10 . . . . .105 A2
College Wlk 7 S60 . . . . . . .21 A1
Collegiate Cres S10. . . . . .105 A2
Collegiate Hall (Sheffield
Hallam Univ) S10. . . . . . . .61 B3
Colley Ave S5. . . . . .28 A4
Colley Cl S5 . . . . .28 A4
Colley Cres S5. . . . . .28 B4
Colley Dr S5. . . . . .28 B4
Colley Rd S5 . . . . .28 A4
Colliers Cl S13 . . . . .78 A4
Colliery Rd S9. . . . . .43 B3
Collin Ave S6. . . . . .39 B3
Collingbourne Ave
S20. . . . . .91 B3
Collingbourne Dr 1
S20. . . . . .91 B3
Collingham Rd S26 . . . . . . .80 B4
Collinson Rd S5 . . . . .28 A2
Collins Yd S18. . . . . .101 A3
Colne Ct S60 . . . . .46 C4
Coltishall Ave S66 . . . . . . .37 B4
Columbia Pl S11. . . . . .107 B2
Colver Rd S2 . . . . .62 B2
Colwall St S9. . . . . .54 A4
Commerce St S35 . . . . .7 C3
Commercial St S1. . . . . . . .104 A3
Common Farm Cl S65. . . . .25 A2
Commonside S10. . . . . . . .104 A4
COMMON SIDE 75 C3
Common The S35. . . . . .16 B3
Companions Cl S66. . . . . . .36 B2
Compton St S6 . . . . .51 A4
Conalan Ave S17 . . . . .95 C3
Concord Jun Sch S9. . . . . .30 A2
Concord Rd S5 . . . . .29 B4
Concord Sports Ctr
S5 .29 B2
Concord View Rd S61 . . . . .30 C4
Conduit La S10 . . . . .51 A2
Conduit Rd S10. . . . . .51 A2
Conery Cl S65 . . . . .24 A4
Congress St S1 . . . . .104 C3
Coningsby Ho S10 . . . . .59 B4
Coningsby Rd S5 . . . . .42 A3
Coniston Rd
Dronfield S18. . . . . .100 A3
Sheffield S8 . . . . .73 A3
Coniston Terr 2 S8. . . . . . .73 A3
Constable Cl
3 Dronfield S18. . . . . . . .100 A3
Rotherham S66. . . . . .36 B3
Sheffield S14 . . . . .86 C4
Constable Dr S14. . . . . . . .86 B4
Constable Pl S14 . . . . .86 C4
Constable Rd S14. . . . . . . .86 B4
Constable Way
Rotherham S65. . . . . .22 C3
Sheffield S14 . . . . .86 B4
Convent Pl S3 . . . . .105 C3
Convent Wlk S3 . . . . .105 C3
Conway Cres S65 . . . . .22 C2
Conway St S3 . . . . .105 B3
Conyers Dr S26. . . . . .69 B2
Coo Hill S13. . . . . .78 B4
Cooke & Beard Homes
S8. .74 A3
Cookson Cl S5. . . . . .27 A2
Cookson Rd S5 . . . . .27 A1
Cooks Rd S20 . . . . .91 B4
Cooks Wood Rd S3 . . . . . . .41 B1
Coombe Pl S10 . . . . .51 A1
Coombe Rd S10 . . . . .51 A1
Coopers Ho S11 . . . . .105 B1
Copley Pl S6 . . . . .20 A1
Copper Beech Cl 1
S20 . . . . .79 C1
Copper St S3. . . . . .106 A4
Coppice Cl S36 . . . . .9 D4
Coppice Gdns S61 . . . . .20 B4
Coppice The S61. . . . . .19 A4
Coppice View S10. . . . . . . .50 A1
Coppins Cl S66 . . . . .37 A4
Coppin Sq S5. . . . . .15 C1
Copse The S66. . . . . .37 A4

Coquet Ave S66 . . . . .37 A2
Coral Cl S26. . . . . .69 A4
Coral Dr S26 . . . . .69 A4
Coral Pl S26. . . . . .69 A4
Coral Way S26 . . . . .69 A4
Corby Rd S4. . . . . .43 A3
Corker Bottoms La S2 . . . .54 A1
Corker Rd S12. . . . . .75 C4
Cornhill 2 S3 . . . . .104 B3
Cornish Pl S3 . . . . .104 C5
Cornish St S3 . . . . .52 A3
Cornish Way S62 . . . . .21 B4
Coronation Bridge S60,
S61. . . . . .32 B4
Coronation Rd S36 . . . . .3 A3
Corporation Bldgs
S3 .106 B4
Corporation St
Rotherham S60. . . . . .33 A4
Sheffield S3 . . . . .106 A4
Cortworth Rd S11 . . . . .71 C2
Corwen Pl S13 . . . . .77 C4
Cossey Rd S4. . . . . .53 B4
Cotleigh Ave S12 . . . . .77 C1
Cotleigh Cl S12 . . . . .77 C1
Cotleigh Cres S12 . . . . .77 C1
Cotleigh Dr S12 . . . . .77 C1
Cotleigh Gdns S12. . . . . . . .77 C1
Cotleigh Pl S12. . . . . .77 C1
Cotleigh Rd S12 . . . . .77 C1
Cotleigh Way S12. . . . . . . .77 C1
Cotswold Ave S35. . . . . .6 C3
Cotswold Cres S60. . . . . . .48 A4
Cotswold Dr S26. . . . . .69 C1
Cotswold Rd S6 . . . . .39 C2
Cottam Cl S60. . . . . .48 A3
Cottam Rd S35 . . . . .5 B1
Cottenham Rd S65. . . . . . . .21 C1
Cottingham St S9 . . . . .54 A2
Cotton Mill Row S3 . . . . . .106 A5
Cotton Mill Wlk S3 . . . . . .106 A5
Cotton St S3 . . . . .106 A5
Coultas Ave S36 . . . . .3 C1
Countess Rd S1 . . . . .62 B3
Coupe Rd S3 . . . . .52 C4
Coupland Rd S65 . . . . .22 C2
Coventry Rd S9. . . . . .55 A3
Coverdale Rd S7. . . . . .73 A3
Coward Dr S35 . . . . .13 B3
Cow La S11. . . . . .71 C1
COWLEY 99 C1
COWLEY BAR. 99 A2
Cowley Bottom S18. . . . . .100 A2
Cowley Cl S35. . . . . .7 C3
Cowley Dr S35. . . . . .8 A2
Cowley Gdns S20 . . . . .90 C2
Cowley Hill S35, S61. . . . . . .8 B2
Cowley La
Chapeltown S35 . . . . .7 C2
Holmesfield S18. . . . . .99 C1
Cowley Rd S35 . . . . .13 B2
Cowley View Cl S35 . . . . . . .7 B2
Cowley View Rd S35 . . . . . .7 C2
Cowlishaw Rd S11. . . . . . . .61 A2
Cowper Ave S6 . . . . .27 A4
Cowper Cres S6 . . . . .27 A4
Cowper Dr
Rotherham S65. . . . . .34 B2
Sheffield S6 . . . . .27 A4
Cowrakes Cl S60. . . . . .48 A3
Cow Rakes La S60 . . . . . . .48 A3
Cox Pl S6 . . . . .39 A3
Cox Rd S6 . . . . .39 A2
Crabtree Ave S5 . . . . .42 A3
Crabtree Cl S5 . . . . .42 A3
Crabtree Cres S5 . . . . .41 C3
Crabtree Dr S5 . . . . .42 A3
Crabtree La S5 . . . . .42 A3
Crabtree Pl S5 . . . . .42 A3
Crabtree Rd S5. . . . . .42 A3
Cracknell 6 S3 . . . . .106 B5
Cradley Dr S35 . . . . .69 C1
Cradock Mews S2 . . . . .63 C1
Cragdale Gr S20 . . . . .90 B1
Crag View Cl S35 . . . . .13 B4
Crag View Cres S35 . . . . . .13 A4
Craig Wlk S66 . . . . .37 B3
Crakehall Rd S35 . . . . .7 C1
Crane Dr S61. . . . . .19 B1
Crane Rd S61. . . . . .19 B4
Cranford Ct 1 S20 . . . . . . .89 B4
Cranford Dr S20 . . . . .77 C1

Cranworth Cl S65. . . . . . . .22 A1
Cranworth Pl S3. . . . . .52 C4
Cranworth Rd
Rotherham S65. . . . . .21 C2
Sheffield S3 . . . . .52 C4
Craven Cl S9 . . . . .55 A3
Craven St
Rawmarsh S62. . . . . .12 A1
Sheffield S3 . . . . .104 C4
Crawford Rd S8 . . . . .73 B2
Crawshaw S3. . . . . .104 C4
Crawshaw Ave S8 . . . . . . .84 B2
Crawshaw Gr S8. . . . . .84 B2
Cream St S2. . . . . .62 C3
Creighton Ave S2 . . . . .12 C3
Crescent E The S66 . . . . . .24 C1
Crescent Rd S7. . . . . .62 A1
Crescent The S17. . . . . . . .94 C3
Crescent W The S66 . . . . . .24 B1
Cresswell Rd S9 . . . . .55 A2
Crest Rd S5 . . . . .28 C2
Crestwood Ct S5 . . . . .28 C2
Crestwood Gdns S5. . . . . . .28 C2
Creswick Ave S5. . . . . .15 C1
Creswick Cl S65 . . . . .23 A2
Creswick Greave S35 . . . . .15 B1
Creswick Greave Cl
S35. . . . . .15 B1
Creswick La S35. . . . . .15 B1
Creswick Rd S65 . . . . .23 A2
Creswick St S6 . . . . .51 B4
Creswick Way S6 . . . . .51 B4
Crewe Hall S10 . . . . .61 A3
Cricketers Wlk S2 . . . . .53 B2
CRICKET HOUSES. 53 C1
Cricket Inn Cres S2 . . . . . . .53 C1
Cricket Inn Rd S2 . . . . .53 B2
Crimicar Ave S10 . . . . .58 C2
Crimicar Cl S10. . . . . .59 A1
Crimicar Dr S10 . . . . .58 C2
Crimicar La S10 . . . . .58 C2
Crispin Cl S12 . . . . .75 C2
Crispin Dr S12. . . . . .75 C2
Crispin Gdns S12 . . . . .75 C2
Crispin Rd 3 S12. . . . . . . .75 C2
Croft Cl S11 . . . . .71 B1
Croft La S11. . . . . .71 B1
Croft Lea S18. . . . . .99 A2
Crofton Ave S6 . . . . .39 C4
Crofton Cl S18. . . . . .100 B3
Crofton Rise
Chapeltown S35 . . . . .6 B4
Dronfield S18. . . . . .100 B3
Croft Rd
Brinsworth S60 . . . . .45 C3
Sheffield, Intake S12 . . . . . .76 A3
Sheffield S6 . . . . .49 B4
Crofts Bldgs S3. . . . . .106 A4
Crofts Dr S65. . . . . .23 B4
Croft St S61 . . . . .10 C2
Crofts The
Rotherham S60. . . . . .33 A4
Rotherham, Wickersley
S66. . . . . .36 B1
Croft The S60. . . . . .57 A3
Cromarty Rise S18. . . . . . . .99 C4
Cromer Cl S62. . . . . .12 A4
Cromford St S2. . . . . .62 C3
Cromwell St S6. . . . . .51 A3
CROOKES 50 C2
Crookes S10. . . . . .50 C1
CROOKESMOOR. 104 A4
Crookesmoorbldgs (Univ
of Sheff) S10. . . . . .51 A1
Crookesmoor Bldgs
(Univ of Sheffield)
S10. . . . . .51 A1
Crookesmoor Dr S6 . . . . . .104 A4
Crookesmoor House
(Univ of Sheffield)
S10. . . . . .105 A3
Crookesmoor Rd S10,
S6. . . . . .104 A4
Crookes Rd S10 . . . . .51 A1
Crookes Valley Rd S3,
S10. . . . . .104 A4
Crosby Ave S66 . . . . .37 B3
Crosby Rd S8 . . . . .73 B1
Cross Allen Rd S20 . . . . . . .91 A4
Cross Bedford St S6 . . . . . .52 A3
Cross Burgess St S1. . . . .107 A3
Cross Chantrey Rd S8 . . . .73 C1

Cross Dr S13 . . . . .78 A4
Crossfield Gdns S35 . . . . . . .5 B4
Cross Gilpin St 2 S6 . . . . .51 C4
Cross Hill S35 . . . . .16 C1
Crosshill Cl S35 . . . . .16 C1
Cross House Cl S35 . . . . . .14 B2
Cross House Rd S35 . . . . . .14 C2
Cross La
Dronfield, Coal Aston
S18. . . . . .98 A1
Dronfield, Quoit Green
S18. . . . . .101 A3
Dronfield S18 . . . . .98 A3
Sheffield, Brick Houses
S17. . . . . .82 A3
Sheffield S10 . . . . .50 C1
Stocksbridge S36 . . . . .2 A4
Crossland Dr S12. . . . . .75 C1
Crossland Pl S12 . . . . .75 C2
Cross Myrtle Rd S2 . . . . . . .62 C1
Cross Park Rd 1 S8 . . . . . .73 C3
CROSSPOOL. 60 A4
Cross Smithfield S3. . . . . .104 C4
Cross South St S61 . . . . . . .11 A1
Cross St
Killamarsh S21 . . . . .93 A3
Rawmarsh S62. . . . . .12 A1
Rotherham, Bradgate
S61 .32 A4
Rotherham, Bramley
S66. . . . . .37 A3
Rotherham, Greasbrough
S61 .11 A1
Rotherham, Whinney Hill
S65. . . . . .23 B4
Sheffield S3 . . . . .78 A4
Cross Turner St S2 . . . . . . .107 B2
Crossways S2 . . . . .64 C3
Crowder Ave S5 . . . . .28 A2
Crowder Cl S5. . . . . .28 A1
Crowder Cres S5. . . . . .28 A1
Crowder Rd S5 . . . . .28 B1
Crowland Rd S5. . . . . .28 B2
Crown Cl S61. . . . . .19 B2
Crownhill Rd S60 . . . . .45 C3
Crown Pl S2. . . . . .106 C3
Crown Works S20 . . . . .79 C3
Crowther Pl 7 S7 . . . . .62 B2
Croydon St S11. . . . . .62 A2
Crucible Theatre ★
S1. . . . . .106 B3
Cruck Cl S18 . . . . .100 A4
Cruise Rd S11 . . . . .60 A2
Crummock Rd 4 S7. . . . . . .73 A3
Crumpsall Dr S5. . . . . .41 A3
Crumpsall Rd S5 . . . . .41 A3
Crumwell Rd S61 . . . . .19 A4
Crystal Peaks (Sh Ctr)
S20. . . . . .90 C4
Cullabine Ct S2. . . . . .64 B1
Cullabine Rd S2 . . . . .64 B1
Cull Row S36 . . . . .4 B2
Cumberland Cres S35. . . . . .7 C2
Cumberland St S1 . . . . . . .107 A2
Cumberland Way S1. . . . . .107 A2
Cundy St S6. . . . . .51 B4
Cunliffe St S18 . . . . .98 A2
Cupola S3. . . . . .106 A4
Cupola La S35. . . . . .14 C3
Cupola Yd S60. . . . . .32 C4
Curlew Ave S21. . . . . .102 B1
Curlew Ridge S2 . . . . .63 B4
Curlew Rise S61. . . . . .9 B4
Curzon Ave S18. . . . . .100 B2
Curzon Cl S21 . . . . .92 B2
Cuthbert Bank Rd S6 . . . . .40 B1
Cuthbert Rd S6. . . . . .40 B1
Cutler Cl S21 . . . . .91 C1
Cutlers Gate S3, S4 . . . . . .106 C4
Cutts Terr S8 . . . . .62 A1
Cyclops St S4 . . . . .42 C2
Cypress Ave S8. . . . . .86 A3
Cypress Cl S21 . . . . .92 A1
Cypress Gate S35. . . . . .7 A2
Cyprus Rd S8. . . . . .73 C3
Cyprus Terr S6. . . . . .51 B4

D

Daffodil Rd S5. . . . . .29 C1
Dagnam Cl S2. . . . . .75 B4
Dagnam Cres S2 . . . . .75 B4

Dagnam Pl S2. . . . . .75 B4
Daisy Bank S3. . . . . .104 B4
Daisy Wlk
Sheffield, Beighton
S20. . . . . .79 B1
Sheffield, Netherthorpe
S3. . . . . .104 C4
Dalbury Rd S18. . . . . .99 B3
Dalby Gdns S20. . . . . .91 B3
Dalby Gr S20 . . . . .91 B4
Dale Ave S65 . . . . .34 C3
Dalebrook Ct S10. . . . . .59 C3
Dalebrook Mews S10 . . . . .59 C3
Dale Ct S62 . . . . .12 A3
Dale Rd
Dronfield S18 . . . . .101 A2
Killamarsh S21 . . . . .92 C2
Rawmarsh S62. . . . . .12 A4
Rotherham, Brecks S65 . . . .34 C2
Rotherham, Wickersley
S66. . . . . .36 A2
Dale Side S10 . . . . .60 C3
Dale St S62. . . . . .12 A4
Dale The S8 . . . . .73 B1
Daleview Rd S8 . . . . .84 B4
Dalewood Ave S8. . . . . .84 A4
Dalewood Dr S8 . . . . .84 A3
Dalewood Rd S8. . . . . .84 A3
Dalmore Rd S7 . . . . .72 B3
DALTON 23 A3
Dalton Ct 9 S8 . . . . .62 A1
Dalton Foljambe Prim
Sch S65. . . . . .23 B3
Dalton La S65 . . . . .23 A2
Dalton Listerdale Jun &
Inf Sch S65. . . . . .35 C2
DALTON MAGNA 23 C1
DALTON PARVA 23 A2
Damer St S10 . . . . .104 A3
Danebrook Cl S2 . . . . .65 A3
Danebrook Ct S2. . . . . .65 A3
Danebrook Dr S2 . . . . .65 A3
Danewood Ave S2 . . . . .65 A3
Danewood Croft S2. . . . . . .65 A3
Danewood Gdns S2. . . . . . .65 A3
Danewood Gr S2 . . . . .65 A3
Daniel Hill S6 . . . . .51 C3
Daniel Hill St S6. . . . . .51 B3
Daniel Hill St S6 . . . . .51 B3
Daniel Hill Terr S6 . . . . .51 C3
Daniel La S61 . . . . .10 C4
Daniels Dr S26 . . . . .69 A3
Dannemora Dr S9 . . . . .44 A1
Danum Dr S65. . . . . .21 C1
Dara St S61 . . . . .30 B3
Darcy Cl S25 . . . . .69 B2
Darcy Rd S21 . . . . .102 C1
Daresbury Cl S2. . . . . .74 C4
Daresbury Dr S2. . . . . .74 C4
Daresbury Pl S2 . . . . .74 C4
Daresbury Rd S2 . . . . .74 C4
Daresbury View S2. . . . . . . .74 C4
Darfield Ave S20 . . . . .89 A4
Darfield Cl S20 . . . . .89 A4
Darley Gr S6 . . . . .49 B4
Darley Pk S61 . . . . .31 C3
DARNALL. 54 C2
Darnall Dr S9 . . . . .54 C3
Darnall Rd S9 . . . . .54 C3
Darnall Sta S9 . . . . .55 A2
Darnley Dr S2 . . . . .64 B2
Dart Sq S3 . . . . .104 B2
Darwall Cl S35 . . . . .5 B2
Darwin Cl S10 . . . . .60 A4
Darwin La S10 . . . . .60 A4
Darwin Rd S6 . . . . .39 C4
David Cl S13 . . . . .67 B1
David La S10 . . . . .58 B1
Davis Cl S65. . . . . .23 A3
Davis St S65. . . . . .22 A1
Davy Dr S66. . . . . .24 B1
Dawber La S21 . . . . .93 A3
Dawlands Cl S2 . . . . .64 C3
Dawlands Dr S2 . . . . .64 C3
Deadman's Hole La
S9. .31 B1
Deakins Wlk S10 . . . . .60 A3
Deane Field View S20 . . . . .90 B4
Deanhead Ct 7 S20. . . . . . .89 B4
Deanhead Dr 8 S20 . . . . . .89 B4
Dean La S65. . . . . .35 B4
Dearden Ct S35. . . . . .16 B2

Dearne Ct S9 . . . . 43 B4
Dearne St S9 . . . . 43 B4
DEEPCAR 4 A2
Deepcar St John's CE
  Jun Sch S36. . . . . 4 A2
Deepdale Rd S61 . . . . 31 C4
Deep La S5. . . . . 17 C2
Deepwell Ave S20 . . . . . 103 C4
Deepwell Bank S20 . . . . . 103 C4
Deepwell Ct S20 . . . . 103 C4
Deepwell View S20 . . . . . 103 C4
Deerlands Ave
  Sheffield S5 . . . . 27 B4
  Sheffield S5 . . . . 28 B4
Deerlands Cl S5 . . . . 27 C4
Deerlands Mount S5. . . . . . 27 B4
Deer Park View S6. . . . . . . 49 C4
Deer Park Cl S6 . . . . 49 C4
Deer Park Pl S6 . . . . 49 C4
Deer Park Rd
  Rotherham S65. . . . . 24 A4
  Sheffield S6 . . . . 50 A4
Deer Park Way S6 . . . . 50 A4
Delamere Cl S20. . . . . 91 B4
De La Salle Dr S4 . . . . 42 A1
Delf St S2 . . . . 62 C1
Dell The S66. . . . . 24 C2
Delmar Way S66 . . . . 36 B4
Delph House Rd S10 . . . . . . 50 A1
Delta Pl S65. . . . . 22 B1
Delves Ave S12 . . . . 78 C2
Delves Cl S12. . . . . 78 B2
Delves Dr S12 . . . . 78 B2
Delves Pl S12. . . . . 78 A1
Delves Rd
  Killamarsh S21. . . . . 92 A2
  Sheffield S12 . . . . 78 B1
Delves Terr S12. . . . . 78 B1
DEN BANK. 50 A1
Den Bank Ave S10 . . . . 49 C1
Den Bank Cl S10. . . . . 50 A1
Den Bank Cres S10 . . . . 49 C1
Den Bank Dr S10 . . . . 50 A1
Denby St S2. . . . . 62 B3
Dene Cres S65 . . . . 22 B2
Dene La S3. . . . . 105 C2
Dene Rd S65 . . . . 22 B2
Denham Rd S11 . . . . 61 C3
Denholme Cl S3 . . . . 52 C3
Denman St S65. . . . . 21 B2
Denman Rd S4 . . . . 74 A4
Denson Cl S2 . . . . 74 A4
Dent La S12 . . . . 89 A4
Denton Rd S8 . . . . 73 B2
Derby Pl S2 . . . . 74 B4
Derbyshire La S8 . . . . 73 C1
Derby St S2 . . . . 74 B4
Derby Terr S2 . . . . 74 B4
Derriman Ave S11 . . . . 72 A2
Derriman Cl S11. . . . . 72 A2
Derriman Dr S11 . . . . 72 A2
Derriman Glen S11 . . . . 71 C2
Derriman Gr S11 . . . . 72 A2
Derwent Cl S18. . . . . 97 C1
Derwent Cres S60 . . . . 45 C1
Derwent Ct
  Rotherham S60. . . . . 47 A4
  Sheffield S17. . . . . 95 B3
Derwent Dr
  Chapeltown S35 . . . . 6 C3
  Rawmarsh S62 . . . . 12 A2
Derwent Rd
  Dronfield S18 . . . . 97 C1
  Rotherham S61. . . . . 10 B1
Derwent St S2. . . . . 53 B2
Deveron Rd S20 . . . . 91 A1
Devon Rd S4 . . . . 42 A2
Devonshire Cl
  Dronfield S18 . . . . 100 B2
  Sheffield S17. . . . . 95 A4
Devonshire Ctyd S1. . . . . 105 C2
Devonshire Dr S17. . . . . . . 82 C1
Devonshire Glen S17 . . . . . 95 A4
Devonshire Gr S17. . . . . . . 94 C4
Devonshire La S1 . . . . . 105 C3
Devonshire Rd S17 . . . . . . 95 A4
Devonshire St
  Rotherham S61. . . . . 32 B4
  Sheffield S3. . . . . 105 C3

Devonshire Terrace Rd
  S17. . . . . 82 B1
Dewar Dr S7 . . . . 72 B2
Dewhill Ave S60 . . . . 47 C3
Dial Cl S5 . . . . 28 C2
Dial House Rd S6 . . . . 39 B3
Dial The S5. . . . . 29 A3
Dial Way S5 . . . . 28 C2
Dickens Cl S60 . . . . 56 C4
Dickenson Ct S35. . . . . 7 A3
Dickinson Rd S5. . . . . 17 A1
Digby Cl S61 . . . . 19 B2
Dikelands Mount S35 . . . . . 6 B4
Dinnington Rd S8 . . . . 73 B2
Ditchingham St S4 . . . . 53 A4
Division La S1 . . . . 107 A3
Division St S1 . . . . 107 A3
Dixon La S1 . . . . 106 B4
Dixon Rd S6. . . . . 39 C3
Dixon St
  Rotherham S65. . . . . 21 B1
  Sheffield S3. . . . . 52 A3
Dobbin Cl S11. . . . . 60 C1
Dobbin Hill S11. . . . . 72 A4
Dobbs Cl S21. . . . . 92 A2
Dobcroft Ave S7 . . . . 83 C4
Dobcroft Cl S11 . . . . 71 C2
Dobcroft Inf Sch S7 . . . . . . 72 A2
Dobcroft Jun Sch S7 . . . . . 72 A1
Dobcroft Rd S7,S11,. 72 A1
Doctor La S9 . . . . 54 C4
Dodds Cl S60 . . . . 32 C2
Dodd St S6 . . . . 40 A1
Dodson Dr S13 . . . . 66 A4
Doe Royd Cres S5 . . . . 27 A3
Doe Royd Dr S5 . . . . 27 B3
Doe Royd La S5 . . . . 27 B3
Doles La S60 . . . . 48 C1
Domine La S60 . . . . 33 A4
Dominoe Gr S12. . . . . 76 C3
Don Ave S6. . . . . 26 A1
Doncaster Gate S61. . . . . . 33 B4
Doncaster Gate Hospl
  S65 . . . . 33 B4
Doncaster Pl S65 . . . . 22 A1
Doncaster Rd
  Rotherham, Eastwood
    S65. . . . . 22 A2
  Rotherham S65. . . . . 22 C3
Doncaster St S3 . . . . 104 C4
Donetsk Way S12,S20 . . . . 89 C4
Donnington Rd S2 . . . . 63 B3
Donovan Cl S5 . . . . 27 B1
Donovan Rd S5. . . . . 27 B1
Don Rd S9 . . . . 43 A1
Don St S60 . . . . 33 A4
Don Valley Bowl S9. . . . . . 43 C1
Don Valley Stadium
  S1. . . . . 54 B4
Don View Ho S65 . . . . 22 A2
Dorcliffe Lodge S10 . . . . . . 60 B3
DORE 82 C1
Dore Cl S17 . . . . 83 B1
Dore Ct S17 . . . . 83 B1
Dore Hall Croft S17 . . . . . . 82 B1
Dore House Ind Est
  S3 . . . . 67 A3
Dore Prim Sch S17 . . . . . . 94 B4
Dore Rd S17. . . . . 82 C2
Dore Sta S17. . . . . 83 B1
Dorking St S4 . . . . 53 A3
Dorothy Rd S6. . . . . 39 C3
Dorset St S10 . . . . 105 B2
Douglas Rd S3 . . . . 41 A1
Douglas St S60 . . . . 33 B4
Dovecote La S65. . . . . 24 C5
Dovecott Lea S20. . . . . . . 80 A1
Dovedale Rd
  Rotherham S65. . . . . 34 C3
  Sheffield S7. . . . . 72 C3
Dove La S26. . . . . 81 A4
Dovercourt Rd
  Rotherham S65. . . . . 20 A1
  Sheffield S2. . . . . 63 C3
Dover Gdns S3 . . . . 104 C4
Dover Rd S11. . . . . 61 B3
Dover St S3 . . . . 104 C4
Dowland Ave S35 . . . . 5 C2
Dowland Cl S35 . . . . 5 C2
Dowland Ct S35 . . . . 5 B2
Dowland Gdns S35 . . . . . . 5 C2
Downgate Dr S4. . . . . 43 A2

Downham Rd S5. . . . . 29 A1
Downing La S3 . . . . 104 C5
Downing Rd S8. . . . . 84 C2
Down's Row S60. . . . . 33 A4
Drake Cl S35 . . . . 6 C3
DRAKEHOUSE 78 C1
Drake House Cres
  S20 . . . . 78 C1
Drake House La S20 . . . . . . 79 B1
Drake House La W
  S20. . . . . 79 B1
Drake House Ret Pk
  S20. . . . . 78 C1
Drake House Way S20 . . . . 79 A1
Dransfield Cl S10. . . . . 60 A4
Dransfield Rd S10 . . . . 60 A4
Draycott Pl S18. . . . . 99 C2
Draymans Ct S11. . . . . . . 105 C1
Drive Colley S5. . . . . 28 B4
Driver St S13 . . . . 67 B1
Drive The S6 . . . . 39 C4
DRONFIELD 100 A4
Dronfield Inf Sch
  S18 . . . . 100 C3
Dronfield Jun Sch
  S18 . . . . 100 C3
Dronfield Sta S18 . . . . . . 100 C3
DRONFIELD
  WOODHOUSE 99 A4
DROPPING WELL 19 A3
Droppingwell Farm Cl
  S61 . . . . 19 A3
Droppingwell Rd
  Rotherham S61. . . . . 18 C1
  Sheffield S61. . . . . 30 B3
Drover Cl S35 . . . . 6 C4
Drummond Cres S5 . . . . . . 28 B3
Drummond Rd S5 . . . . 28 B3
Drummond St
  Rotherham S65. . . . . 21 B1
  Rotherham, St Ann's
    S60 . . . . 21 A1
Drury La
  Dronfield S18 . . . . 98 A1
  Sheffield S17. . . . . 82 B1
Dryden Ave S5 . . . . 27 B2
Dryden Dr S5 . . . . 27 B2
Dryden Rd
  Rotherham S65. . . . . 34 B2
  Sheffield S5. . . . . 27 B2
Dryden Way S5 . . . . 27 B1
Duchess Rd S2 . . . . 107 B1
Duckham St S2 . . . . 81 A4
Dudley Rd S62 . . . . 12 A1
Dudley St S62 . . . . 12 A1
Duke Cres S61. . . . . 19 B3
Duke La S1. . . . . 107 A2
Duke Of Norfolk La
  S60. . . . . 35 C1
Dukes Pl S65 . . . . 34 B3
Duke St
  Sheffield, Park Hill
    S2. . . . . 107 C3
  Sheffield S20 . . . . 103 A4
Dumbleton Rd S21 . . . . . . 92 C1
Duncan Rd S10. . . . . 50 C2
Duncan St S60 . . . . 46 A3
Duncombe St S6 . . . . 51 B3
Dundas Rd S9 . . . . 31 B1
Dunedin Glen S20 . . . . . . 103 B4
Dunedin Gr S20 . . . . 103 B4
Dunella Dr S6 . . . . 39 C3
Dunella Pl S6 . . . . 39 B3
Dunella Rd S6 . . . . 39 C3
Dun Fields S3 . . . . 104 C5
Dunkeld Rd S11 . . . . 72 A3
Dunkerley Rd S6 . . . . 38 B3
Dun La S3. . . . . 104 C5
Dunlin Cl S61. . . . . 9 A4
Dunlop St S9 . . . . 43 C3
Dunmow Rd S4. . . . . 42 C3
Dunninc Rd S5 . . . . 17 A1
Dunninc Terr S5 . . . . 17 A1
Dun St S3. . . . . 104 C5
Durham La S10. . . . . 105 B3
Durham Pl S65 . . . . 34 B2
Durham Rd S10. . . . . 105 B3
Durlstone Cl S12 . . . . 75 C3
Durlstone Cres S12 . . . . . . 75 C3
Durlstone Dr S12 . . . . 75 C3

Durlstone Gr S12 . . . . 75 C3
Durmast Gr 6 S6. . . . . 49 A4
Durvale Ct S17 . . . . 94 C4
Dutton Rd S6. . . . . 40 B3
Dyche Cl S8 . . . . 97 C4
Dyche Dr S8. . . . . 97 C4
Dyche La S8, S18. . . . . 97 C3
Dyche Pl S8 . . . . 97 C4
Dyche Rd S8 . . . . 97 C4
Dycott Rd S61 . . . . 19 C1
Dykes Hall Gdns 1
  S6. . . . . 39 C2
Dykes Hall Pl S6 . . . . 39 C2
Dykes Hall Rd S6 . . . . 39 C2
Dykes La S6. . . . . 39 C2
Dyke Vale Ave S12 . . . . . . 77 C2
Dyke Vale Cl S12 . . . . 77 C2
Dyke Vale Pl S12 . . . . 77 C2
Dyke Vale Rd S12 . . . . 77 B3
Dyke Vale Way S12 . . . . . . 77 C2
Dykewood Dr S6. . . . . 39 A4
Dyson Pl 5 S11 . . . . 61 B2

E

Eagleton Dr S35. . . . . 5 C2
Eagleton Rise S35 . . . . 5 C2
Eagle View S26 . . . . 81 A4
Earldom Cl S4. . . . . 53 A4
Earldom Dr S4 . . . . 53 A4
Earldom Rd S4 . . . . 42 A1
Earldom St S4. . . . . 53 A4
Earl Marshal Cl 4 S4. . . . . 42 B3
Earl Marshal St 5 S4. . . . . 42 B3
Earl Marshal Rd S4 . . . . . . 42 B3
Earl Marshal View S4 . . . . . 42 B3
Earl St S1 . . . . 107 A2
Earl Way S1 . . . . 107 A2
Earsham St S4 . . . . 53 B4
East Ave S62 . . . . 12 A4
East Bank Pl S2 . . . . 74 C4
East Bank Rd S2 . . . . 74 C4
East Bank Way S2 . . . . 74 C4
East Bawtry Rd S60 . . . . . . 48 A4
Eastcliffe Ct S2. . . . . 63 A2
East Coast Rd S9 . . . . 53 C4
East Cres
  Rotherham S65. . . . . 22 B1
  Stocksbridge S36. . . . . . . 2 C3
Eastcroft Cl S20 . . . . 91 A2
Eastcroft Dr S20 . . . . 91 A2
Eastcroft Glen S20. . . . . . . 91 A2
Eastcroft View S20. . . . . . . 91 A2
Eastcroft Way 7 S20 . . . . . 91 A2
EAST DENE 22 B1
East Dene JMI Sch
  S65 . . . . 22 A1
Eastern Ave S2 . . . . 63 C1
Eastern Cres S2 . . . . 74 C4
Eastern Dr S2 . . . . 63 B1
Eastern Wlk S2 . . . . 63 B1
Eastfield Rd
  Dronfield S18 . . . . 101 B2
  Sheffield S10 . . . . 51 A3
Eastgate Ct S65 . . . . 34 B4
East Glade Ave S12 . . . . . . 77 A1
East Glade Cl S12. . . . . 77 A1
East Glade Cres S12 . . . . . . 77 A1
East Glade Dell S12. . . . . . . 77 A1
East Glade Pl S12 . . . . 77 A1
East Glade Rd S12 . . . . 77 A1
East Glade Sq S12 . . . . 77 A1
East Glade Way S10. . . . . . 77 A1
Eastgrove Rd S10. . . . . . . 105 A1
EAST
  HERRINGTHORPE. 23 B1
East Hill Sec Sch S2. . . . . . 63 A2
Eastleigh 3 S65. . . . . 22 A1
East Par S1 . . . . 106 A3
East Rd
  Rotherham S65. . . . . 22 B2
  Sheffield S2. . . . . 62 C1
East Terr S26 . . . . 81 B1
East Vale Dr S65 . . . . 23 C4
East View Terr S6 . . . . 40 A3
EAST WHITWELL 3 A2
EASTWOOD 21 C2
Eastwood Dr S6 . . . . 26 A1
Eastwood Ct S65 . . . . 22 A2
Eastwood La S65 . . . . 21 C2
Eastwood Mount S65 . . . . . 34 A4
Eastwood Rd S11. . . . . 61 B2

Eastwood Trad Est
  S65. . . . . 22 A3
Eastwood Vale S65. . . . . . . 22 A2
Eastwood View 2
  S65. . . . . 22 B2
Eaton Pl S2 . . . . 53 B1
Ebenezer Pl S3 . . . . 106 A5
Ebenezer St S3 . . . . 106 A5
Eben St S9 . . . . 43 B4
ECCLESALL 71 C3
Ecclesall CE Jun Sch
  S11 . . . . 71 C4
Ecclesall Inf Sch S11 . . . . . 71 C4
Ecclesall Rd S11 . . . . 60 C1
Ecclesall Rd S S11 . . . . 71 B1
ECCLESFIELD. 16 A1
Ecclesfield Prim Sch
  S5. . . . . 16 A2
Ecclesfield Rd
  Chapeltown S35 . . . . 7 C2
  Sheffield S5. . . . . 17 B2
Ecclesfield Sch S35 . . . . . . 7 B1
Eccles St S9 . . . . 30 B2
ECKINGTON 102 C2
Eckington Bsns Pk
  S21. . . . . 103 C2
Eckington Hall S20 . . . . . 103 A3
Eckington Jun Sch
  S21. . . . . 103 A3
Eckington Mews S20 . . . . 103 A3
Eckington Rd
  Dronfield S18 . . . . 98 B2
  Sheffield S20 . . . . 91 B4
Eckington Sch S21. . . . . . 102 A1
Eckington Way S20 . . . . . . 79 B1
Edale Rd
  Rotherham S11 . . . . 31 C4
  Sheffield S11 . . . . 71 C4
Eden Ct S10. . . . . 105 A2
Eden Dr S6 . . . . 38 C2
Eden Glade S26 . . . . 69 B2
Eden Gr S26. . . . . 69 B2
Edensor Rd S5. . . . . 41 C4
Edenthorpe Dell S20. . . . . . 90 A4
Edenthorpe Gr S20 . . . . . . 90 A4
Edenthorpe Wlk S20. . . . . . 90 A4
Edge Bank S7 . . . . 73 A4
Edgebrook Rd S7. . . . . 72 C4
Edge Cl S6 . . . . 26 C4
Edgedale Rd S7 . . . . 73 A3
Edgefield Rd S7 . . . . 73 A3
Edgehill Rd S7 . . . . 72 C4
Edge La S6 . . . . 26 C4
Edgemount Rd S7 . . . . 73 A3
Edge Well Cl S6 . . . . 26 C4
Edge Well Cres S6 . . . . 26 C4
Edge Well Dr S6 . . . . 26 C4
Edge Well Pl S6 . . . . 26 C4
Edge Well Rise S6 . . . . 26 C4
Edge Well Way S6 . . . . 26 C4
Edmund Ave
  Brinsworth S60 . . . . 46 B1
  Sheffield S17. . . . . 96 B4
Edmund Cl S17 . . . . 96 B4
Edmund Dr S17. . . . . 96 B4
Edmund Rd S2 . . . . 107 B1
Edward Pl S17 . . . . 72 C4
Edward St
  Eckington S21. . . . . 103 A1
  Sheffield S3. . . . . 104 C4
  Stocksbridge S36. . . . . . . 3 A3
Edward Street Flats
  S3 . . . . 104 C4
Edwin Rd S2 . . . . 74 B4
Effingham La S4. . . . . 106 C4
Effingham Rd S4, S9 . . . . . . 53 B3
Effingham Sq 8 S65. . . . . . 21 A1
Effingham St
  Rotherham S65. . . . . 21 A1
  Rotherham, St Ann's
    S65 . . . . 21 B2
  Sheffield S4. . . . . 106 C5
Egerton Cl S3 . . . . 105 C2
Egerton La S3 . . . . 105 C2
Egerton Rd
  Aston S26. . . . . 69 B1
  Dronfield S18 . . . . 101 A4
Egerton St S3 . . . . 105 C2
Egerton Wlk S3 . . . . 105 C2

Eilam Cl S61. . . . . 19 B2
Eilam Rd S61 . . . . 19 B2
Ekin St S9 . . . . 31 C1
Elcroft Gdns S20. . . . . 91 A4
Elder Ct S21. . . . . 92 A1
Elder Dr S66 . . . . 36 C4
Eldertree Rd S61 . . . . 9 A1
Eldon Cl S1 . . . . 105 C3
Eldon Rd S65 . . . . 21 C2
Eldon St S1 . . . . 105 C3
Eleanor St S9 . . . . 54 C4
Elgin St S10 . . . . 50 C1
Elizabeth Rd S26 . . . . 80 C4
Elizabeth Way S60 . . . . . . 32 C4
Ella Rd S4 . . . . 42 A1
Ellenbro Rd S6 . . . . 39 C2
Ellerton Rd S5. . . . . 42 B4
Ellesmere Rd S4. . . . . 53 A4
Ellesmere Rd N S4. . . . . . 42 A1
Ellesmere Terr 4 S65. . . 33 C4
Ellesmere Wlk S4. . . . . . . 53 A4
Ellin St S1 . . . . 107 A1
Elliot La S35. . . . . 6 C1
Elliot Rd S6 . . . . 104 A4
Elliott Ct 10 S65 . . . . 21 B1
Elliott Dr S61 . . . . 10 A2
Elliott La S35 . . . . 6 B2
Elliottville St S6 . . . . 51 A4
Ellisons Rd S21. . . . . 93 A4
Ellison St S3 . . . . 104 C4
Ellis St
  Brinsworth S60 . . . . 46 A3
  Sheffield S3 . . . . 104 C4
Ellorslie Dr S36. . . . . 3 B3
Elm Cl S21 . . . . 92 A1
Elm Cres S20 . . . . 90 A2
Elm Dr S21 . . . . 92 A1
Elmfield Ave S5 . . . . 28 B2
Elm Gr S61. . . . . 10 C1
Elmham Rd S9 . . . . 55 B2
Elmhirst Dr S65 . . . . 34 C2
Elm La S5 . . . . 28 B2
Elmore Rd S10 . . . . 51 A1
Elm Pl S62 . . . . 12 B3
Elm Rd S20. . . . . 79 C2
Elm Rise S35 . . . . 7 A2
Elm Tree Cres S18 . . . . . . 97 B1
ELMTREE HILL 75 C4
Elm Tree Ho S12 . . . . 75 C4
Elmtree Rd S61. . . . . 9 A1
Elmview Rd S19 . . . . 30 B2
Elmwood Dr S20. . . . . . . 103 A4
Elsham Cl S66 . . . . 25 A1
Elstree Dr S12 . . . . 76 A2
Elstree Rd S12. . . . . 76 A2
Elton La S66. . . . . 24 B1
Elvaston Cl S18. . . . . 99 A3
Elwood Rd S17 . . . . 96 A4
Embankment Rd S10 . . . . 51 A1
Emerson Cl S5 . . . . 28 B3
Emerson Cres S5 . . . . 28 B2
Emerson Dr S5 . . . . 28 B2
Emily Rd S7 . . . . 73 A4
Emmanuel Jun Sch
  S20. . . . . 90 C3
Emmet Ho S10 . . . . 105 B3
Empire Rd S7 . . . . 73 B4
Endcliffe Ave S10. . . . . . . 61 A3
Endcliffe Cres S10 . . . . . . 60 C3
ENDCLIFFE
  CRESCENT 60 C3
Endcliffe Edge S10 . . . . . 60 C3
Endcliffe Glen Rd S11. . . 61 A3
Endcliffe Grove Ave
  S10. . . . . 60 C3
Endcliffe Hall Ave S10 . . 60 C3
Endcliffe Rise Rd S11. . . 61 A3
Endcliffe Terrace Rd
  S11. . . . . 61 A3
Endcliffe Vale Ave
  S11. . . . . 61 A2
Endcliffe Vale Rd S10 . . . 60 C3
Endfield Rd S5 . . . . 15 C1
Endowood Rd S7 . . . . 83 C4
Enfield Pl S13 . . . . 66 A4
English Institute of Sport
  S9 . . . . 43 B2

Ennerdale Ave 4
  S20. . . . . 103 B4
Ennerdale Cl S18 . . . . . . 100 A3
Ennerdale Dr S20. . . . . . 103 B4
Entwhistle Rd S35 . . . . . . 5 C1
Epping Gdns S20 . . . . 91 B4
Epping Gr S20. . . . . 91 B4
Ernest Copley Ho S35. . . . 7 A4
Ernest Fox Ho S35 . . . . . 14 C3
Errington Ave S2 . . . . 75 A4
Errington Cl S2. . . . . 75 A4
Errington Cres S2 . . . . . . 75 A4
Errington Rd S2 . . . . 75 A4
Errington Way S2. . . . . . . 63 C1
Erskine Cres S2 . . . . 63 A1
Erskine Rd
  Rotherham S65. . . . . 21 B2
  Sheffield S2 . . . . 63 A1
Erskine View S2 . . . . 63 A1
Eskdale Cl
  Dronfield S18 . . . . 100 A3
  Sheffield S6 . . . . 40 A4
Eskdale Rd
  Rotherham S65. . . . . 10 A3
  Sheffield S6 . . . . 40 A4
Eslaforde Terr S65 . . . . . . 22 A2
Esperanto Pl S1 . . . . 106 B3
Essendine Cres S8. . . . . . 74 A1
Essex Rd S2 . . . . 63 B3
Estone Dr S26 . . . . 69 B2
Etwall Way S5. . . . . 28 C2
Europa Cl S9 . . . . 56 B4
Europa Dr S9 . . . . 44 B1
Europa Link S9 . . . . 55 C4
Evans St S3 . . . . 105 C2
Eva Ratcliffe Ho 1
  S5. . . . . 16 A2
Evelyn Rd S10 . . . . 50 C1
Evelyn St S62. . . . . 12 C4
Everard Ave S17 . . . . 95 B3
Everard Dr S17 . . . . 95 B3
Everard Glade 3 S17. . . 95 B3
Everingham St S28. . . . . . 28 A1
Everingham Cres S28. . . . 28 A1
Everingham Pl S5 . . . . . . 28 A1
Everingham Rd S5. . . . . . 28 A1
Everton Rd S11. . . . . 61 A2
Evesham Cl S9 . . . . 30 B1
Ewers Rd S61 . . . . 19 C1
Excelsior Works S35. . . . . 16 C3
Exchange Gateway
  S1. . . . . 106 A3
Exchange Pl S2. . . . . 106 B4
Exchange St S2. . . . . 106 B4
Exchange Works 3
  S1. . . . . 107 A2
Exeter Dr S3 . . . . 105 C1
Exeter Pl S3. . . . . 105 B2
Exeter Way S3. . . . . 105 B2
Exley Ave S6 . . . . 51 B4
Eyam Rd S10 . . . . 50 C1
Eyncourt Rd S5. . . . . 29 A1
Eyre Gdns S35. . . . . 6 B4
Eyre La S1 . . . . 107 A2
Eyre St S1. . . . . 107 A2

Fabian Way S66 . . . . 37 B2
Fairbank Rd S5. . . . . 41 C3
Fairbank View S60 . . . . . . 48 A3
Fairbarn Cl S6. . . . . 49 C3
Fairbarn Dr S6 . . . . 49 C3
Fairbarn Pl S6. . . . . 49 C3
Fairbarn Rd S6 . . . . 49 C3
Fairbarn Way S6. . . . . 49 C3
Fairburn Gdns S60. . . . . . 46 B2
Fairfax Dr S2 . . . . 64 C2
Fairfax Rd S2 . . . . 64 C2
Fairfax Rise S2 . . . . 64 C2
Fairfield S35 . . . . 7 C3
Fairfield Cl S66. . . . . 24 C1
Fairfield Hts 3 S10 . . . . . 60 C4
Fairfield Lo S10 . . . . 105 B2
Fairfield Rd S6 . . . . 51 C4
Fairholme Hts S35. . . . . . 13 C3
FAIRLEIGH. 64 B1
Fairleigh S2. . . . . 64 B2
Fairleigh Dr S60. . . . . 33 B2
Fairmount Gdns 4
  S12. . . . . 77 C1
Fairthorn Rd S5 . . . . 29 A2

Fair View Dr S26. . . . . 69 C1
Fairview Rd S18 . . . . 97 B1
Fairways S66. . . . . 36 B2
Fairways The S10. . . . . . . 58 B3
Fairwinds Cl S18 . . . . . . 100 C3
Falcon Dr S60 . . . . 57 D1
Falconer La S13 . . . . 68 A3
Falconer Way S60 . . . . . . 57 D2
Falcon Rd S18 . . . . 98 A1
Falcon Rise S18 . . . . 98 B1
Falding St
  Chapeltown S35. . . . . 7 C3
  Rotherham S60. . . . . 32 C4
Falkland Rd S11 . . . . 71 C4
Falkland Rise S18 . . . . . 100 C2
Fallon Rd S6 . . . . 49 B4
Falmouth Rd S7 . . . . 73 A3
Falstaff Cres S5 . . . . 27 C2
Falstaff Rd S5 . . . . 27 C3
Fane Cres S26 . . . . 69 B2
Fanny Ave S21. . . . . 92 C1
Fanshaw Bank S18 . . . . . 100 C3
Fanshaw Rd S18 . . . . . . 101 A4
Faraday Rd S9. . . . . 53 C4
Faranden Rd 5 S9 . . . . . 54 B3
Far Cres S65 . . . . 22 B1
Farcroft Gr 1 S4 . . . . . . 43 A3
Far Dalton La S65 . . . . . . 23 C2
Fardell Gdns S66 . . . . 37 A2
Far Field Rd S65. . . . . 34 C3
Fargate S1 . . . . 106 A3
Farish Pl 5 S2 . . . . 74 A4
Far La
  Rotherham S65. . . . . 22 B1
  Sheffield S6 . . . . 39 C3
Farlow Croft S35 . . . . 5 A2
Farm Bank Rd S2 . . . . . . 107 C2
Farm Cl
  Brinsworth S60 . . . . 45 C1
  Dronfield S18 . . . . 97 C2
  Sheffield S12 . . . . 87 B4
Farm Cres S20. . . . . 102 C4
Farm Dr S62. . . . . 12 C4
Farm Fields Cl S20. . . . . . 90 B3
Farmoor Gdns S20. . . . . . 91 C4
Farm Rd S2 . . . . 107 B1
Farmstead Cl S14. . . . . . . 74 C3
Farm View Cl
  Rotherham S61. . . . . 19 A2
  Sheffield S12 . . . . 78 A1
Farm View Dr S12. . . . . . . 78 A1
Farm View Gdns S12. . . . 78 A1
Farm View Rd S61 . . . . . . 19 A2
Farm Wlk S20 . . . . 90 A1
Farnaby Dr S35. . . . . 5 B2
Farnaby Gdns S35. . . . . . . 5 B2
Farndale Rd S6 . . . . 40 A4
Farnley Ave S5 . . . . 27 A2
Farnsworth Rd S65 . . . . . 22 C1
Far Pl S65. . . . . 22 B1
Farrar Rd 2 S7 . . . . 62 A1
Farrier Gate S6 . . . . 6 C4
Farrington Ct S66 . . . . . . 36 C2
Far View Rd S5 . . . . 28 B2
Farwater Cl S18 . . . . 100 C2
Farwater La S18. . . . . . . 100 B3
Favell Rd
  Rotherham S65. . . . . 23 A1
  Sheffield S3 . . . . 104 B3
Fawcett St S3 . . . . 104 B4
Fearnehough St 1 S9 . . 54 B3
Fellbrigg Rd S2. . . . . 63 B1
Fellowsfield Way S61 . . . 19 B2
Fell Rd S9 . . . . 43 B1
Fell St S9 . . . . 43 A2
Fenney La S11. . . . . 82 C4
Fenton Croft S61 . . . . 20 A2
Fenton Fields S61 . . . . . . 20 A2
Fenton Rd S61. . . . . 20 A4
Fenton St S61 . . . . 19 C1
Fentonville St S11 . . . . . . 61 C2
Fenton Way S61 . . . . 20 B4
Feoffees Rd S35 . . . . 16 B2
Ferguson St S9 . . . . 54 A4
Ferham Cl S61 . . . . 32 A4
Ferham Park Ave S61 . . . 32 A4
Ferham Prim Sch S61 . . 32 B4
Ferham Rd S61. . . . . 32 A4
Fern Ave S20 . . . . 79 B2
Fernbank Dr S21 . . . . . . 102 B1
Fern Cl S21. . . . . 102 B1
Ferncroft Ave S20 . . . . . . 90 A1

Ferndale Cl S18 . . . . 98 B1
Ferndale Dr S66. . . . . 36 C4
Ferndale Rd S18 . . . . 98 B1
Ferndale Rise S18 . . . . . . 98 B1
Fern Hollow S66. . . . . 36 C1
Fernlea Gr S35 . . . . 16 B2
Fernleigh Dr S60 . . . . 45 C4
Fern Rd S6 . . . . 50 C4
Fern Way S21 . . . . 102 B1
Ferrars Cl S9 . . . . 45 A4
Ferrars Dr S9 . . . . 45 A3
Ferrars Rd S9 . . . . 45 A4
Ferrars Way S9 . . . . 45 A3
Ferriby Rd S6 . . . . 39 C4
Fersfield St S4 . . . . 53 B3
Field Cl S18 . . . . 99 B4
Fielder News S 29 B2
Fieldhead Rd S8. . . . . 62 B1
Fieldhouse Way S4 . . . . . 42 B1
Fielding St S66. . . . . 37 A3
Fielding Rd S6 . . . . 40 A4
Fieldsend Gdns S35. . . . . 16 B2
Fieldside Ct S65 . . . . 25 A3
Field View S60. . . . . 46 A2
Field Way S60 . . . . 21 A2
Fife Cl S9 . . . . 30 A2
Fife Gdns S9 . . . . 30 A2
Fife St S9 . . . . 30 A2
Fife Way S9 . . . . 30 A2
Fig Tree La 2 S1 . . . . . 106 A4
Filey La S33 . . . . 105 B2
Filey St S10 . . . . 105 B2
Filter Cotts S6. . . . . 58 A4
Finch Cl S65. . . . . 24 A4
Finch Gdns S66. . . . . 37 B2
Finch Rise S26 . . . . 81 A4
Finchwell Cl S13 . . . . 66 A4
Finchwell Cres S13 . . . . . 66 A4
Finchwell Rd S13. . . . . . . 66 A4
Findon Cres S6 . . . . 39 B2
Findon Pl S6 . . . . 39 B2
Findon Rd S6. . . . . 39 B2
Findon St S6. . . . . 39 C2
Finlay Rd S65. . . . . 22 A2
Finlay St S3 . . . . 104 B4
Fircroft Ave S5 . . . . 29 A3
Fircroft Rd S5 . . . . 29 B4
Firebeck Rd S8 . . . . 73 A1
Firethorn Rise S65 . . . . . . 25 B2
Fir Pl S21 . . . . 92 A1
Firshill Ave S4 . . . . 41 C2
Firshill Cl S4 . . . . 41 C2
Firs Hill Com Prim Sch
  S3 . . . . 41 C2
Firshill Cres S4 . . . . 41 B2
Firshill Croft S4 . . . . 41 B2
Firshill Gdns S4 . . . . 41 B2
Firshill Glade S4. . . . . 41 B2
Firshill Mews S4 . . . . 41 C2
Firshill Rd S4. . . . . 41 C2
Firshill Rise S4 . . . . 41 C2
Firshill Way S4 . . . . 41 B2
Firshill Wlk S4 . . . . 41 C2
Fir St S6 . . . . 51 A3
First Ave S65 . . . . 22 A1
First La S66 . . . . 36 C1
Firth Dr S4 . . . . 53 B4
FIRTH PARK 29 A1
Firth Park Ave S5 . . . . . . 29 A1
Firth Park Com Arts Coll
  S5 . . . . 29 A1
Firth Park Cres S5 . . . . . . 29 A1
Firth Park Rd S5. . . . . 42 C4
Firth's Homes S11. . . . . . 60 A2
Firth St S61 . . . . 11 A1
Firthwood Ave S18 . . . . . 98 B1
Firthwood Cl S18 . . . . 98 B1
Firthwood Rd S18 . . . . . . 98 B1
Firtree Rise S35 . . . . 7 B2
FIR VALE. 42 A4
Fir Vale Pl S5 . . . . 42 A3
Fir Vale Rd S5 . . . . 42 A3
Fir Vale Sch S4 . . . . 42 B3
Fir View Gdns S4 . . . . . . 42 B2
Fisher Cl S60 . . . . 20 C1
Fisher La S9 . . . . 55 A3
Fishponds Rd S13 . . . . . . 65 A1
Fishponds Rd W S13. . . . 65 A1
Fitzalan Rd S13. . . . . 66 A3
Fitzalan Sq S1 . . . . 106 B3
Fitzgerald Rd S10 . . . . . . 50 C2

Fitzhubert Rd
  Sheffield S2 . . . . 64 B1
  Sheffield S2 . . . . 64 B2
Fitzmaurice Rd S9 . . . . . . 54 C4
Fitzroy Rd S2. . . . . 74 A4
Fitzwalter Rd S2. . . . . 63 B4
Fitzwilliam Ct
  Rawmarsh S62. . . . . 12 A2
  Sheffield S11 . . . . 72 A3
Fitzwilliam Gate S1. . . . 107 A2
Fitzwilliam Rd S65. . . . . . 22 A2
Fitzwilliam Sq S61. . . . . . 10 C2
Fitzwilliam St
  Rawmarsh S62. . . . . 12 A1
  Sheffield S1 . . . . 105 C2
Five Trees Ave S17 . . . . . 95 B4
Five Trees Cl S17. . . . . . . 95 B4
Five Trees Dr S17 . . . . . . 95 B4
Five Weirs Wlk S9 . . . . . . 54 A4
Flanders Ct S61 . . . . 9 A3
FLANDERWELL 36 A4
Flanderwell Ave S66 . . . . 37 A3
Flanderwell Ct S66 . . . . . 36 C4
Flanderwell Gdns S66 . . 36 C4
Flanderwell La S66. . . . . . 36 C4
Flanderwell Prim Sch
  S66 . . . . 36 B4
Flash La S66. . . . . 37 B2
Flask View S6 . . . . 38 A1
Flat La S60 . . . . 47 C3
Flat St S1 . . . . 106 B3
Flatts Cl S60 . . . . 57 C3
Flatts La S60 . . . . 57 C3
Flaxby Rd S9 . . . . 54 C3
Fleet St S9 . . . . 43 A1
Fleming Gdns S66 . . . . . . 36 B4
Fleming Way S66 . . . . . . 36 B4
Fletcher Ave S18 . . . . . . 100 C3
Fletcher Ho 2 S65 . . . . . 21 B1
Fleury Cl S14 . . . . 75 A2
Fleury Cres S14 . . . . 75 A2
Fleury Pl S14 . . . . 75 A2
Fleury Rd S14 . . . . 75 A2
Fleury Rise S14. . . . . 75 A2
Flockton Ave S14 . . . . . . 67 A2
Flockton Cres S13 . . . . . . 67 A2
Flockton Ct S1 . . . . 105 C3
Flockton Dr S13 . . . . 67 A2
Flockton Ho S1. . . . . 105 C3
Flockton Rd S13. . . . . 67 A2
Flodden St 1 S10 . . . . . . 50 C2
Floodgate Dr S35. . . . . . . 16 B2
Flora St S1 . . . . 51 C4
Florence Ave S26 . . . . . . 69 B1
Florence Rd S8. . . . . 74 A4
Folds Cres S8 . . . . 84 B3
Folds Dr S8 . . . . 84 A3
Folds La S8 . . . . 84 A3
Fold The S65 . . . . 23 A2
Foley St S4 . . . . 53 B3
Foljambe Dr S65 . . . . 23 B3
Foljambe Rd S65. . . . . . . 22 B2
Foljambe St S62. . . . . 12 A2
Folkwood Gr S11 . . . . 71 A3
Follett Rd S5 . . . . 28 C3
Footgate Cl S35 . . . . 13 B2
Forbes Rd S6. . . . . 40 A2
Ford Cl S18. . . . . 100 B3
Ford La S36 . . . . 3 B4
Ford Rd S11. . . . . 72 A4
Foremark Rd S5 . . . . 29 A2
Forest Edge S7 . . . . 83 B3
Forge Hill S35 . . . . 13 B3
Forge La
  Killamarsh S21. . . . . 91 C1
  Oughtibridge S35. . . . . . 13 B4
  Rotherham S60. . . . . 33 A4
  Sheffield S1 . . . . 107 A3
Forge Student Village 7
  S2. . . . . 62 A3
Forge The S18. . . . . 100 C3
Forncett St S4. . . . . 53 B4
Fornham St S2. . . . . 107 B2
Forres Ave S10 . . . . 50 C1
Forres Rd S10 . . . . 50 C1
Forrester Cl S66 . . . . 36 A3
Forrester's La S18. . . . . . . 98 A2
Forth Ave S18 . . . . 22 A2
Fort Hill Rd S9 . . . . 30 A1
Fortway Rd S60 . . . . 46 A4
Forum The 14 S1. . . . . . 105 C3
Fossdale Rd S7. . . . . 72 C3

Foster [7] S3 . . . . 106 B5
Foster Rd S66 . . . . . . 36 B3
Fosters The S35 . . . . . 5 B1
Foster Way S35 . . . . . 5 B1
Foundry Ct S3 . . . . . . 41 C1
Foundry St S2 . . . . . . 12 A1
Fountain Prec S1 . . . . . 106 A3
Fountside S7 . . . . 72 C4
Four Wells Dr S12 . . . . 78 A2
Fox Cl S61 . . . . 19 A4
Foxcote Lea S65 . . . . . 24 A4
Foxcroft Chase S21 . . . 92 A2
Foxcroft Dr S21 . . . . . 92 A1
Foxcroft Gr S21 . . . . . 92 A2
Foxdale Ave S12 . . . . . 76 A3
Fox Glen Rd S36 . . . . . 3 C2
Foxglove Rd S5 . . . . . 29 B2
Fox Hill S3 . . . . 52 B4
Fox Hill Ave S6 . . . . . . 26 C3
Fox Hill Cl S6 . . . . . . 26 C3
Fox Hill Cres S6 . . . . . 26 C3
Fox Hill Dr S6 . . . . . . 26 C3
Fox Hill La S6 . . . . . . 26 C4
Fox Hill Prim Sch S6 . . . 27 A4
Fox Hill Rd S6 . . . . . . 26 C3
Fox Hill Way S6 . . . . . 26 C4
Fox La
  Sheffield, Base Green
  S12 . . . . 76 B1
  Sheffield, Lower Bradway
  S17 . . . . 96 B4
Fox Lane Ct S12 . . . . . 76 B2
Fox Lane View S12 . . . . 76 B2
Fox Rd S6 . . . . 51 C4
Fox St
  Rotherham S61 . . . . . 31 B4
  Sheffield S3 . . . . . . 52 C4
Fox Wlk S6 . . . . 51 B4
Foxwood Ave S12 . . . . 76 A4
Foxwood Dr S12 . . . . . 76 A4
Foxwood Gr S12 . . . . . 76 A3
Foxwood Rd S12 . . . . . 76 A4
Framlingham Pl S2 . . . . 63 B1
Framlingham Rd S2 . . . . 63 B1
France Rd S6 . . . . 38 B3
Frances St S60 . . . . . . 33 B3
Francis St S62 . . . . . . 12 A1
Francis Cres N S60 . . . . 35 A1
Francis Cres S S60 . . . . 35 A1
Francis Dr S60 . . . . . . 35 A2
Francis Gr S35 . . . . . . 5 B1
Frank Hillock Field S36 . . 4 A3
Frank Pl S9 . . . . 43 B1
Fraser Cl S8 . . . . 73 A1
Fraser Cres S8 . . . . . . 73 B1
Fraser Dr S8 . . . . 73 B1
Fraser Rd
  Rotherham S60 . . . . . 33 C3
  Sheffield S8 . . . . . . 73 A1
Fraser Wlk S8 . . . . . . 85 A4
FRECHEVILLE 76 C2
Frederick Dr S35 . . . . . 14 B3
Frederick Rd [10] S7 . . . 62 A1
Frederick St
  Catliffe S60 . . . . 57 A3
  Rotherham S60 . . . . . 21 A1
  Sheffield S9 . . . . . . 54 C2
Fred Mulley Rd S4 . . . . 53 B4
Freedom Ct S6 . . . . . . 40 B1
Freedom Rd S6 . . . . . . 51 A4
Freeman Gdns S35 . . . . 6 B4
Freeman Rd S66 . . . . . 36 B3
Freeston Pl S9 . . . . . . 43 B1
Fretson Cl S2 . . . . 64 B2
Fretson Gn S2 . . . . . . 64 B2
Fretson Rd S2 . . . . . . 64 B2
Fretson Rd S S2 . . . . . 64 B2
Fretwell Rd S65 . . . . . . 22 C2
Friar Cl S6 . . . . 49 B4
Frickley Rd S11 . . . . . . 60 A2
Frith Cl S12 . . . . 76 A3
Frith Rd S12 . . . . 76 A3
Frithwood Dr S18 . . . . . 101 B4
Froggatt La S1 . . . . . . 107 A2
Frogmore Cl S66 . . . . . 37 A4
Front St S60 . . . . 57 C2
Frostings Cl S35 . . . . . 14 C3
Frostings The S35 . . . . 14 C3
Fulford Cl S9 . . . . 55 A3
Fulford Pl S9 . . . . 55 A3
Fullerton Dr S60 . . . . . . 45 C2
Fullerton Rd S60 . . . . . 32 C2

Fulmer Way S61 . . . . . 9 B4
Fulmere Cres S5 . . . . . 27 B4
Fulmere Rd S5 . . . . . . 27 B4
Fulmer Rd S11 . . . . . . 61 A1
Fulney Rd S11 . . . . 60 A2
Fulton Rd S6 . . . . 51 B3
FULWOOD 59 A2
Fulwood Chase S10 . . . . 59 C2
Fulwood Rd S10 . . . . . 60 C4
Furnace Hill S3 . . . . . . 106 A4
Furnace La S13 . . . . . . 67 C1
Furness Cl S6 . . . . . . 38 B1
Furness Rd S35 . . . . . . 5 A1
Furniss Ave S17 . . . . . 94 B4
Furniss Mews S17 . . . . 94 C4
Furnival Gate S1 . . . . . 107 A2
Furnival Rd S4 . . . . . . 106 C4
Furnival Sq S1 . . . . . . 107 A2
Furnival St S1 . . . . . . 107 A2
Furnival Way S60 . . . . . 48 B3

G

Gables The S10 . . . . . . 60 A3
Gainsborough Cl S66 . . . 36 B3
Gainsborough Rd
  Dronfield S18 . . . . . 100 A2
  Dronfield S18 . . . . . 100 A3
  Sheffield S11 . . . . . 61 B1
Gainsford Rd S9 . . . . . 55 A2
Gallery The S3 . . . . . . 106 B4
Galley Dr S20 . . . . 90 B3
Gallow Tree Rd S65 . . . 35 A2
Galsworthy Ave S5 . . . . 27 C1
Galsworthy Rd S5 . . . . 27 C1
Galway Cl S62 . . . . . . 12 B4
Gamston Rd S [8] S8 . . . 62 A1
Gannow Cl S21 . . . . . . 93 A3
Ganton Rd S6 . . . . . . 39 C4
Garbroads Cres S65 . . . 23 B4
Garden Cl S60 . . . . . . 47 B4
Garden Cres S60 . . . . . 47 B4
Garden La [3] S60 . . . . 20 C1
Garden St
  Rotherham S61 . . . . . 20 B1
  Sheffield S1 . . . . . . 104 C4
Gardens The S11 . . . . . 61 C2
GARDEN VILLAGES 2 C3
Garden Wlk
  Rotherham S60 . . . . . 47 B4
  Sheffield S20 . . . . . 79 C1
Gardom Cl S18 . . . . . . 99 C3
Garfield Mount S65 . . . . 33 C3
Garland Cl S20 . . . . . . 90 C1
Garland Croft S20 . . . . 90 C1
Garland Dr S6 . . . . . . 38 C3
Garland Mount [13]
  S20 . . . . 90 C2
Garland Way S20 . . . . . 90 C1
Garry Rd S6 . . . . 39 C3
Garter St S4 . . . . 42 B1
Garth Cl [3] S9 . . . . . . 54 B3
Garth Way S18 . . . . . . 100 B3
Garth Way Cl S18 . . . . . 100 B3
Gashouse La
  Eckington S20, S21 . . . 103 A3
  Sheffield S20, S21 . . . 103 A3
Gatefield Rd S7 . . . . . . 73 A4
Gateway Cl S62 . . . . . . 21 B4
Gateway Ct S62 . . . . . . 21 B4
Gateway The S62 . . . . . 21 B4
Gatty Rd S5 . . . . 17 A1
Gaunt Cl
  Killamarsh S21 . . . . . 92 A2
  Rotherham S66 . . . . . 37 B4
  Sheffield S14 . . . . . 74 C1
Gaunt Dr
  Rotherham S66 . . . . . 37 A4
  Sheffield S14 . . . . . 74 C1
Gaunt Pl S14 . . . . 74 C2
Gaunt Rd
  Rotherham S66 . . . . . 37 A4
  Sheffield S14 . . . . . 74 C1
Gaunt Way S14 . . . . . . 74 C1
Gayton Rd S4 . . . . 42 A2
Gelderd Pl S18 . . . . . . 100 C2
Gell St S3 . . . . 105 B3
George Pl S62 . . . . . . 12 B3
George St
  [2] Rotherham S60 . . . 21 A1
  Sheffield S1 . . . . . . 106 B3

George Woodfindin
  Almshouses [4] S11 . . 61 A2
Georgian Mews S60 . . . 57 A4
Gerald St S9 . . . . 43 B1
Gerard Ave S65 . . . . . . 24 A4
Gerard Cl [15] S8 . . . . . 74 A4
Gerard Rd S60 . . . . . . 33 B3
Gerard St S8 . . . . 74 A4
Gervase Ave S8 . . . . . . 96 C4
Gervase Dr S8 . . . . 96 C4
Gervase Pl S8 . . . . . . 96 C4
Gervase Rd S8 . . . . . . 96 C4
Gervase Wlk [2] S8 . . . . 96 C4
Gibbing Greaves Rd
  S65 . . . . 35 B2
Gibbons Dr S14 . . . . . . 86 C4
Gibbons Way S14 . . . . 86 C4
Gibbons Wlk S14 . . . . . 86 C4
Gibraltar Bldgs S3 . . . . . 106 A4
Gibraltar St S3 . . . . . . 106 A4
Gibson La S36 . . . . . . 3 B4
Gifford Rd S8 . . . . 62 B1
Gilbert Ct S2 . . . . 107 C2
Gilberthorpe Dr [2]
  S65 . . . . 34 A4
Gilberthorpe St S65 . . . 33 C4
Gilbert Row S2 . . . . . . 107 C3
Gilbert St S1 . . . . 106 B3
Gill Cl S6 . . . . 36 C1
Gill Croft [4] S6 . . . . . . 49 A4
Gilleyfield Ave S17 . . . . . 82 C1
Gill Mdws S6 . . . . 49 A4
Gillot Dell S66 . . . . . . 36 B1
Gillott La S66 . . . . 36 B1
Gillott Rd S6 . . . . 27 A2
Gilpin La S6 . . . . 51 C4
Gilpin St S6 . . . . 51 C4
Ginhouse La S61 . . . . . 20 C2
Gisborne Rd S11 . . . . . 72 A4
Glade Croft S12 . . . . . 75 C2
Glade Lea S12 . . . . 75 C2
Glade The S10 . . . . 60 C4
Gladstone Mews S10 . . . 59 C3
Gladstone Rd S10 . . . . 60 A3
Gladys Buxton Com Ed
  Ctr S18 . . . . 101 B4
Gladys St S65 . . . . . . 34 A4
Glasshouse St S60 . . . . 21 A1
GLEADLESS 75 C2
Gleadless Ave S12 . . . . 75 C2
Gleadless Bank S12 . . . . 75 B2
Gleadless Comm S12 . . . 75 C2
Gleadless Ct S2 . . . . . 74 A4
Gleadless Dr S12 . . . . . 75 B2
Gleadless Mount S12 . . . 75 C2
Gleadless Prim Sch
  S12 . . . . 76 A3
Gleadless Rd S12, S14,
  S2 . . . . 74 C3
Gleadless Rise
  [1] Sheffield, Gleadless
  Townend S12 . . . . . 75 C1
  Sheffield S12 . . . . . 75 B3
GLEADLESS
  TOWNEND 75 A1
GLEADLESS VALLEY . . . 75 A1
Gleadless View
  [2] Sheffield, Gleadless
  Townend S12 . . . . . 75 C1
  Sheffield S12 . . . . . 75 B3
Glebe Cres S13 . . . . . 23 B3
Glebelands Rd S36 . . . . 3 B2
Glebe Rd S10 . . . . 51 A1
Gledhill Cl S18 . . . . . . 100 C3
Glenalmond Rd S11 . . . 72 A4
Glencoe Dr S2 . . . . 107 C2
Glencoe Pl S2 . . . . . . 107 C2
Glencoe Rd S2 . . . . . . 107 C2
Glencroft [4] S11 . . . . . 60 B1
Glenholme Dr S13 . . . . 65 C1
Glenholme Pl S13 . . . . 64 A1
Glenholme Rd S13 . . . . . 64 A1
Glenholme Way S13 . . . 65 C1
Glenmore Croft S12 . . . 76 A4
Glenorchy Rd S7 . . . . . 72 C3
Glen Rd S7 . . . . 73 A4
Glen The S10 . . . . 60 C3
Glentilt Rd S7 . . . . 72 C3
Glen Vale S11 . . . . . . 99 C3
Glen View S11 . . . . 60 A2
Glen View Rd S11 . . . . 84 C2
Glenwood Cres S35 . . . . 7 C3

Glossop La S10 . . . . . . 105 B3
Glossop Rd S10 . . . . . . 105 B3
Glossop Row S35 . . . . . 13 B3
Gloucester Cres S10 . . . . 105 B2
Gloucester Rd S61 . . . . . 10 A1
Gloucester St S10 . . . . 105 B2
Glover Rd
  Sheffield, Highfield
  S8 . . . . 62 B1
  Sheffield, Totley Rise
  S17 . . . . 95 A3
Goathland Cl S13 . . . . . 67 B1
Goathland Dr S13 . . . . . 67 B1
Goathland Pl S13 . . . . . 67 B1
Goathland Rd S13 . . . . 67 B1
Goddard Ave S36 . . . . . 2 B4
Goddard Hall Rd S5 . . . . 42 A3
Godric Dr S60 . . . . . . 45 C3
Godric Gn S60 . . . . . . 45 C3
Godric Rd S5 . . . . 16 C1
Godstone Rd S60 . . . . . 33 B3
Goldcrest Wlk S61 . . . . . 9 B3
Golden Oak Dell S6 . . . . 38 A1
Goldsmith Dr S65 . . . . . 34 B4
Goldsmith Rd S65 . . . . 34 B4
Gomersal La S10 . . . . . 100 C3
Goodison Cres S6 . . . . 50 A4
Goodison Rise S6 . . . . . 50 A4
Goodwin Athletics Ctr
  (Univ of Sheffield) The
  S10 . . . . 104 A3
Goodwin Ave S62 . . . . . 12 A4
Goodwin Rd
  Rotherham S61 . . . . . 10 B2
  [7] Sheffield S8 . . . . . 73 C4
Goodwin Way S61 . . . . 10 B2
GOOLE GREEN 59 B1
Goore Ave S9 . . . . 64 C4
Goore Dr S9 . . . . 54 C1
Goore Rd S9 . . . . 64 C4
Goosebutt Ho S62 . . . . 12 A2
Goosebutt St S62 . . . . . 12 A2
Goosecroft Ave S65 . . . . 23 B4
Goose La S66 . . . . 36 C2
Gordon Ave S8 . . . . . . 85 B4
Gordon Rd [6] S11 . . . . 61 B2
Gordon Terr [5] S65 . . . 33 C4
Gordon Works S2 . . . . . 73 C4
Gorse Dr S21 . . . . 92 B1
Gorse La S10 . . . . 58 A1
Gorseland Ct S62 . . . . . 36 A2
Gorse The
  Rotherham,
  Herringthorpe S65 . . . 34 C3
  Rotherham, Wickersley
  S66 . . . . 36 B1
Gorsey Brigg S18 . . . . . 99 C3
Gorseybrigg Cty Jun Sch
  S18 . . . . 99 C3
Gorseybrigg Inf Sch
  S18 . . . . 99 C3
Gosber Rd S21 . . . . . . 103 B1
Gosber St S21 . . . . . . 103 A1
Gosforth Cl S18 . . . . . . 100 B3
Gosforth Cres S18 . . . . 100 B3
Gosforth Dr
  Dronfield, Dronfield
  Woodhouse S18 . . . . 99 C3
  Dronfield, Dronfield
  Woodhouse S18 . . . . 99 C3
  Dronfield, Gosforth Valley
  S18 . . . . 100 A3
Gosforth Gn S18 . . . . . 100 B3
Gosforth La S18 . . . . . 100 B3
GOSFORTH VALLEY . . . 100 A4
Gotham Rd S66 . . . . . . 46 A4
Gough Cl S65 . . . . 34 C2
Gower St S4 . . . . 53 A4
Grafton St S2 . . . . 107 C2
Grafton Way S65 . . . . . 21 B1
Graham Ave S60 . . . . . . 46 B1
Graham Ct S11 . . . . 60 A2
Graham Knoll S11 . . . . . 60 A2
Graham Rd S10 . . . . . . 60 A2
Graham Rise S11 . . . . . 60 A2
Grainger Cl S17 . . . . . . 59 C3
Grammar St S6 . . . . 40 B1
Granary The [1] S11 . . . 105 C1
Granby St S5 . . . . 42 B4
Grange Ave
  Aston S26 . . . . 69 A3
  Dronfield S18 . . . . . 100 A3

Grange Cliffe Cl S11 . . . 72 A2
Grange Cres S11 . . . . . 61 C2
Grange Crescent Rd
  S11 . . . . 61 C2
Grange Ct
  Rotherham S66 . . . . . 36 B2
  Sheffield S11 . . . . . 61 C2
Grange Dr S61 . . . . . . 19 A3
Grange Farm Cl S60 . . . 46 B1
Grange Farm Dr S26 . . . 81 A4
Grange La
  Brinsworth S60 . . . . 45 B4
  Rotherham S5, S61 . . . 17 C3
Grange Mill La S61 . . . . 30 A4
Grange Rd
  Rotherham S60 . . . . . 47 C4
  Sheffield, Beighton S20 79 C2
  Sheffield, Sharrow S11 . 61 C2
Grange The S11 . . . . . . 18 C4
Grange View Cres
  S61 . . . . 19 A2
Grange View Rd S61 . . . 19 A2
Granville Rd S2 . . . . . . 107 C2
Granville Sq S2 . . . . . . 107 B2
Granville St S2 . . . . . . 107 B2
Granville Terr [2] S65 . . . 33 C4
Grasby Ct S66 . . . . . . 25 A1
Grasmere Rd
  Dronfield S18 . . . . . 99 C3
  Sheffield S8 . . . . . . 73 A3
Grassdale View S12 . . . . 77 B1
Grassington Cl [2] S12 . . 78 A1
Grassington Dr S12 . . . . 78 A1
Grassington Way S35 . . . 7 A4
Grassmoor Cl S12 . . . . 75 B3
Grassthorpe Rd S12 . . . 76 A2
Grattan St S61 . . . . . . 31 B4
Graven Cl S35 . . . . . . 14 B2
Graves Art Gal [X] S1 . . . 107 B3
Graves Tennis & L Ctr
  S8 . . . . 85 C1
Graves Trust Homes
  Sheffield, Common Side
  S12 . . . . 75 C3
  Sheffield, Greenhill S8 . 85 A2
  Sheffield, Little Norton
  S8 . . . . 85 B2
  Sheffield S10 . . . . . 50 B1
Gray Ave S26 . . . . 69 B3
Gray Cl S65 . . . . 21 B2
Grayson Cl
  Rotherham S65 . . . . . 25 A2
  Stocksbridge S36 . . . 3 B2
Grayson Rd S61 . . . . . 10 B2
Gray St
  Sheffield, Mosborough
  S20 . . . . 90 A1
  Sheffield S3 . . . . . . 52 C4
Greasbro Rd S9 . . . . . 44 B4
GREASBROUGH 20 C4
Greasbrough Jun & Inf
  Sch S61 . . . . 10 C1
Greasbrough La S62 . . . 11 C3
Greasbrough Rd S62 . . . 11 C1
Greasbrough St S60 . . . 20 C1
Greaseborough Rd
  Rotherham, Northfield
  S60, S61 . . . . 21 A2
  [3] Rotherham S60 . . . 21 A1
Great Bank Rd S65 . . . . 34 C2
Great Croft S18 . . . . . . 99 C4
Great Eastern Way
  S62 . . . . 12 A1
Great Park Rd S61 . . . . 19 B2
Greaves Cl [7] S6 . . . . 49 A4
Greaves La
  Chapeltown S35 . . . . 5 B4
  Sheffield S6 . . . . . . 38 B1
Greaves Rd
  Rotherham S61 . . . . . 20 A1
  Sheffield S5 . . . . 16 A2
Greaves St S6 . . . . . . 40 B1
Greenacres S35 . . . . . 5 C2
Greenacres Cl S18 . . . . 101 B1
Green Bank Dr S66 . . . . 24 C2
Green Chase S21 . . . . . 102 C3
Greencroft
  Chapeltown S35 . . . . 5 B1

Greencroft continued
Rotherham S60. . . . . .33 C2
Greencroft Cl S60 . . . . . . .33 C1
Green Cross S18. . . . . . . .101 A4
Green Ct S66 . . . . .24 C1
Greendale Ct S18. . . . . . .101 A4
Greendale Sh Ctr
S18. . . . . .101 A4
Green Farm Hamlet
S36 .2 A3
Greenfield S62 . . . . .12 A3
Greenfield Cl
Rotherham S65. . . . . .23 A2
Sheffield S8 . . . . .85 A1
Greenfield Ct S66. . . . . . .36 B4
Greenfield Dr S8 . . . . . . .85 A1
Greenfield Gdns S66. . . . .36 B4
Greenfield Rd
Rotherham S65. . . . . .23 A2
Sheffield S8 . . . . .85 A1
Greenfields S21 . . . . .102 C1
Green Finch Cl S60 . . . . . .46 B2
Greengate Cl S13 . . . . . . .78 C4
Greengate La
Chapeltown S35 . . . . .5 C1
Sheffield S13 . . . . .78 C4
Greengate Lane Prim
Sch S35 . . . . .5 C1
Greengate Rd S13 . . . . . . .78 C4
Greenhall Rd S21 . . . . . . .102 C1
Greenhead Gdns S35 . . . . .7 B3
Greenhead La S35 . . . . . . .7 B3
GREENHILL. 84 C1
Greenhill Ave S8 . . . . . . .85 A2
Greenhill Main Rd S8. . . .85 A1
Greenhill Parkway S8. . . .96 B4
Greenhill Prim Sch
S8. . . . . .84 C1
Greenhill Rd S8 . . . . .85 A4
Greenhow St S6 . . . . .51 A3
Green La
Aston S26 . . . . .70 B1
Catliffe S60. . . . . .45 C1
Dronfield S18 . . . . .101 A4
Rawmarsh S62. . . . . .12 B3
Rotherham, Broom S60 . . . .47 B4
Rotherham, Dropping Well
S61. . . . . .18 C1
Rotherham, Listerdale
S66 . . . . .36 A3
Sheffield S3 . . . . .106 A5
Sheffield, St Michael's Field
S35. . . . . .16 C2
Stocksbridge S36 . . . . .2 A4
GREENLAND. 43 C1
Greenland Cl S9 . . . . .55 A3
Greenland Ct S9 . . . . .55 A4
Greenland Dr S9 . . . . .55 A4
Greenland Rd S9 . . . . .55 A4
Greenlands Jun & Inf
Schs S9. . . . . .55 A3
Greenland View S9 . . . . . .55 A3
Greenland Way
Sheffield, Greenland
S9. . . . . .44 A1
Sheffield S9 . . . . .55 A4
Greenland Wlk S9 . . . . . . .54 C4
Green Lea S18. . . . . .99 B4
Green Oak Ave S17 . . . . . .94 C2
Green Oak Cres S17 . . . . . .94 C2
Green Oak Dr S17 . . . . . . .94 C2
Green Oak Gr S17 . . . . . . .94 C2
Green Oak Rd S17 . . . . . . .94 C2
Greenock St S6 . . . . .39 C2
Green Pastures S17. . . . . .82 C1
Greenside S61. . . . . .10 C1
Greenside Mews S12 . . . . .78 A1
Greens Rd S65 . . . . .34 B4
Green St
Rotherham S61. . . . . .10 C2
Stocksbridge S36 . . . . .3 C3
Green The
Rotherham, Broom
S60 . . . . .33 C1
Rotherham S66. . . . . .24 C1
Rotherham, Whiston
S60 . . . . .47 C2
Sheffield S17 . . . . .94 B2

Greenway The
Sheffield S8 . . . . .85 A2
Stocksbridge S36 . . . . .4 A2
Greenwood Ave S9 . . . . . .54 C1
Greenwood Cl S9 . . . . .54 C1
Greenwood Cres
Rotherham S66. . . . . .36 C3
Sheffield S9 . . . . .54 B1
Greenwood Dr S9 . . . . . . .54 B1
Greenwood La S13 . . . . . . .67 B1
Greenwood Rd S9 . . . . . . .64 C4
Greenwood Way S9 . . . . . .54 B1
Greeton Dr S35 . . . . .13 C2
Gregg House Cres S5 . . . . .29 A4
Gregg House Rd S5 . . . . . .29 A3
Gregory Cl S8 . . . . .74 A4
Gregory Rd S8. . . . . .73 C4
Grenfolds Rd S35 . . . . . . .15 A2
Grenobank Rd S35. . . . . . .15 A2
Greno Cres S35 . . . . .15 A2
Greno Gate S35. . . . . .14 C3
Greno Ho S35 . . . . .14 C3
Grenomoor Cl S35. . . . . . .14 C3
GRENOSIDE 15 A2
Grenoside Com Prim Sch
S35. . . . . .14 C3
Greno View Rd S35 . . . . . . .5 C1
Greno Wood Ct S35. . . . . .14 C3
Gresham Ave S60. . . . . . . .46 B2
Gresham Rd S6 . . . . .51 A4
Gresley Rd S8 . . . . .96 C3
Gresley Wlk S8 . . . . .96 C3
Greyfriars S11. . . . . .60 B1
Greystock St S4 . . . . .53 C4
GREYSTONES. 60 B1
Greystones Ave S11. . . . . .60 C2
Greystones Cl S11 . . . . . . .60 B1
GREYSTONES CLIFFE 60 A1
Greystones Cres S11. . . . . .60 B1
Greystones Ct S11. . . . . . .60 B1
Greystones Dr S11. . . . . . .60 B1
Greystones Grange 1
S11. . . . . .60 B1
Greystones Grange Cres
2 S11 . . . . .60 B1
Greystones Grange Rd
S11. . . . . .60 B1
Greystones Hall Rd
S11. . . . . .60 B1
Greystones Prim Sch
S11. . . . . .60 C1
Greystones Rd
Rotherham S60. . . . . .48 B3
Sheffield S11 . . . . .60 B1
Greystones Rise 3
S11. . . . . .60 B1
Griffiths Cl S62 . . . . .12 A2
Griffiths Rd S35 . . . . .6 C1
GRIMESTHORPE 42 C3
Grimesthorpe Rd
Sheffield S4 . . . . .53 A4
Sheffield, Wood Hill S4. . . .42 B2
Grimesthorpe Rd S
S4. . . . . .53 A4
Grimsell Cl S6. . . . . .15 A1
Grimsell Cres S6 . . . . .15 A1
Grimsell Dr S6 . . . . .15 A1
Grimsell Wlk S6. . . . . .27 A4
Grinders Hill S2 . . . . .107 B2
Grindlow Cl S14 . . . . .74 B4
Grindlow Dr S14. . . . . .74 B4
Grisedale Wlk S18. . . . . . .100 A3
Grizedale Ave S20 . . . . . . .91 B4
Grizedale Cl 4 S20. . . . . .91 B4
Grosvenor Rd S65 . . . . . . .21 C2
Grosvenor Sq 7 S2. . . . . .62 A2
Grouse Croft S6 . . . . .51 B4
Grouse St S6 . . . . .40 A1
Grove Ave
Sheffield, Hillfoot
S17. . . . . .94 B3
Sheffield S6 . . . . .39 B4
Grove House Ct S17 . . . . . .94 C3
Grove Rd
Rotherham S60. . . . . .33 A3
Sheffield, Millhouses
S7. . . . . .72 B1
Sheffield, Totley Brook
S17. . . . . .95 A3
Stocksbridge S36 . . . . .4 B2
Grove Sq S6 . . . . .40 C1

Grove The
Rawmarsh S62. . . . . .12 B3
Rotherham, East Dene
S65. . . . . .22 B1
Rotherham, Wickersley
S66 . . . . .36 B2
Sheffield, Hillfoot S17 . . . .94 B3
Sheffield S6 . . . . .38 C2
Guernsey Rd S2 . . . . .62 B1
Guest Pl S60 . . . . .33 C2
Guest Rd
Rotherham S60. . . . . .33 C2
Sheffield S11 . . . . .61 A2
Guildford Ave S2 . . . . .63 B2
Guildford Rise S2 . . . . . . .63 C2
Guildford View S2 . . . . . . .63 C1
Guild Rd S65 . . . . .34 B4
GUILTHWAITE 47 C1
Guilthwaite Cres S60 . . . .47 B3
Gullingwood Dr S65 . . . . .24 A4
Gun La S3. . . . . .106 B4

H

Habershon Dr S35 . . . . .7 A4
Habershon Rd S61. . . . . . . .10 A1
Hackenforth Hall S12 . . . .78 A1
HACKENTHORPE 78 A2
Hackness La S60 . . . . .45 C3
Hackthorn Rd S8 . . . . .73 B1
Haddon Cl S18 . . . . .101 A4
Haddon St S3 . . . . .52 A4
Haddon Way S26 . . . . .70 A1
Haden St S6. . . . . .40 A2
Hadfield St S6. . . . . .51 A3
Hadleigh Cl S62 . . . . .12 A2
Hadrian Rd S60. . . . . .46 A4
Hafferty Cl S5 . . . . .29 B3
Haggard Rd S6 . . . . .40 B2
Hagg Hill
Sheffield, Birley Carr
S6. . . . . .26 B3
Sheffield S10 . . . . .50 A2
Hagg La S10. . . . . .49 C1
Haggonstones Dr S35. . . . .13 B2
Haggstones Rd S35. . . . . . .13 B2
Hague La S35 . . . . .5 A1
Hague Row S2 . . . . .107 C3
Haigh Memorial Homes
S8. . . . . .85 B1
Haigh Moor Cl 2 S13. . . .66 A3
Haigh Moor Rd S13. . . . . . .64 A2
Haigh Moor Way S26 . . . . .68 B1
Haigh Moor Wlk S13. . . . . .64 A2
Hail Mary Dr S13 . . . . .67 B2
Hail Mary Hill Wood
Nature Reserve ★
S60 . . . . .68 A4
Halcyon Cl S12 . . . . .77 B1
Haldane Rd S65 . . . . .22 A2
Hale St S8. . . . . .73 B4
Halesworth Rd S13 . . . . . . .66 A4
Half Acre La S18. . . . . . . .101 C2
HALFWAY. 91 A1
Halfway Ctr S20 . . . . .90 C1
Halfway Dr S20. . . . . .90 C1
Halfway Gdns S20 . . . . . . .90 C1
Halfway Inf Sch S20 . . . . . .91 A1
Halfway Jun Sch S20 . . . . .103 B4
Halifax Rd S6. . . . . .27 A3
Hallam Chase
Sheffield, Hallam Head
S10. . . . . .59 B4
Sheffield S10 . . . . .60 C3
Hallam Cl S26 . . . . .69 A3
Hallam Ct
Dronfield S18 . . . . .100 C2
Sheffield S10 . . . . .105 A1
Hallam FM Arena S9 . . . . . .43 C1
Hallamgate Rd S10 . . . . . .50 C1
Hallam Grange Cl S10 . . . .59 A2
Hallam Grange Cres
S10. . . . . .59 A3
Hallam Grange Croft
S10. . . . . .59 A3
Hallam Grange Rd
S10. . . . . .59 A3
Hallam Grange Rise
S10. . . . . .59 A3
HALLAM HEAD. 59 A4
Hallam La S1. . . . . .107 A2
Hallam Pl S62. . . . . .12 B3

Hallam Prim Sch S10 . . . . .59 A3
Hallam Rd S60 . . . . .47 B3
Hallam Rock S5 . . . . .41 C3
Hallamshire Cl S10 . . . . . .58 C2
Hallamshire Ct S11 . . . . . .61 C3
Hallamshire Dr S10. . . . . . .59 A2
Hallamshire Rd S10. . . . . . .58 C2
Hallam Way S10 . . . . .16 B2
Hallcar St S4 . . . . .53 A3
Hall Cl S18 . . . . .99 B4
Hall Close Ave S60 . . . . . .48 A3
Hall Cres S60 . . . . .47 C4
Hall Croft S66 . . . . .36 C2
Hall Farm Cl S26. . . . . . . .69 B4
Hallgate Rd S10 . . . . .50 B1
Hall Gr S60 . . . . .33 B3
Halliwell Cl S5 . . . . .27 A1
Halliwell Cres S5 . . . . . . .27 B1
Hall Meadow Croft
S20. . . . . .103 C3
Hall Meadow Dr S20. . . . .103 C3
Hall Meadow Gr S20. . . . .103 C3
HALLOWES 101 B2
Hallowes Ct S18 . . . . . . .101 A3
Hallowes Dr S18 . . . . . . .101 A2
Hallowes La
Dronfield S18 . . . . .101 A2
Dronfield S18 . . . . .101 A3
Hallowes Rise S18 . . . . . .101 B2
HALLOWMOOR 39 B3
Hallowmoor Rd S6 . . . . . . .39 B2
Hall Park Head S6 . . . . . . .49 C3
Hall Park Hill S6. . . . . . . .49 C3
Hall Park Mount S6. . . . . . .49 C3
Hall Rd
Aston S26 . . . . .69 B3
Rawmarsh S62. . . . . .12 C4
Rotherham S60. . . . . .33 B3
Sheffield, Handsworth
S13. . . . . .66 A4
Sheffield S9 . . . . .55 C1
Halls Ct S8 . . . . .73 B1
Hallside Ct S20 . . . . .103 A4
Hall St S60 . . . . .32 C4
Hall View S35. . . . . .7 B4
Hallwood Rd S35 . . . . .6 A3
Hallyburton Cl S2 . . . . . . .74 B4
Hallyburton Dr S2 . . . . . . .74 B4
Hallyburton Rd S2. . . . . . .74 B4
Halsall Ave S9. . . . . .55 A1
Halsall Dr S9 . . . . .55 A1
Halsall Rd S9 . . . . .55 A1
Halsbury Rd S65. . . . . .22 A2
Halton Ct S12 . . . . .78 B1
Hamer Wlk S65. . . . . .22 C1
Hamilton Rd S5 . . . . .42 B4
Hammerton Cl S6 . . . . .40 A1
Hammerton Rd S6 . . . . . . .40 A1
Hammond St S3 . . . . .104 B4
Hampton Rd S5 . . . . .42 A3
Hamstead Gn S61 . . . . .19 B3
Hanbury Cl S18. . . . . .100 B3
Handley St S3 . . . . .52 C3
Hands Rd S10 . . . . .51 A2
HANDSWORTH 65 C4
Handsworth Ave S9. . . . . . .55 B1
Handsworth Cres S9. . . . . .55 B1
Handsworth Grange Cl
S13. . . . . .66 B3
Handsworth Grange Cres
S13. . . . . .66 C3
Handsworth Grange Dr
S13. . . . . .66 C3
Handsworth Grange Rd
S13. . . . . .66 B3
Handsworth Grange Sch
S13. . . . . .66 C2
Handsworth Grange Way
S13. . . . . .66 C3
HANDSWORTH HILL 55 B2
Handsworth Rd S13,
S9. . . . . .66 A4
HANGING WATER 60 A2
Hangingwater Cl S10 . . . . .60 A2
Hangingwater Cotts
S11. . . . . .60 A1
Hangingwater Rd S11. . . . .60 A1
Hanley Cl S12 . . . . .78 A1
Hanmoor Rd S6 . . . . .49 A4
Hannah Rd S13. . . . . .67 B1
Hanover Ct S3 . . . . .105 B2
Hanover Sq S3 . . . . .105 C2

Hanover St S3 . . . . .105 C2
Hanover Way S3 . . . . . . .105 C2
Hanson Rd S6 . . . . .38 B2
Hanwell Cl S35 . . . . .16 B2
Harbord Rd S8 . . . . .84 C4
Harborough Ave S2 . . . . . .64 B3
Harborough Cl S2 . . . . . . .64 B4
Harborough Dr S2 . . . . . . .64 B4
Harborough Rd S2. . . . . . .64 B4
Harborough Rise S2. . . . . .64 B4
Harborough Way S2 . . . . . .64 B3
Harbury St S13 . . . . .67 C2
Harcourt Cres S10 . . . . . .104 A3
Harcourt Rd S10. . . . . . . .104 A4
Harcourt Rise S35 . . . . .7 C2
Harcourt Terr 3 S65. . . . .33 C4
Hardcastle Dr S13 . . . . . . .66 B1
Hardcastle Gdns S13 . . . . .66 B1
Hardcastle Rd S13. . . . . . .66 B1
Hardie Pl S62. . . . . .12 A4
Hardie St S21 . . . . .103 A1
Harding St S9 . . . . .54 C4
Hardwick Cl
Aston S26. . . . . .70 A1
Dronfield S18 . . . . .101 B4
Hardwick Cres S11 . . . . . . .61 A2
Hardwick Rd S65 . . . . .21 B2
Hardwick St S65. . . . . .61 A2
Hardy Pl S6 . . . . .51 B3
Hardy St S60 . . . . .20 C1
Harefield Rd 5 S11. . . . . .61 B2
Harehills Rd S60 . . . . .33 B3
Harewood Gr S66. . . . . . . .37 A4
Harewood Way S11 . . . . . . .83 B4
Hargrave Pl S65 . . . . .23 C4
Harland Rd S11. . . . . .61 C3
Harlech Cl S35 . . . . .7 A4
Harlech Fold S10 . . . . .58 A3
Harlech Gn S10. . . . . .58 A3
Harlech Gr S10 . . . . .58 A3
Harlech Mead S10. . . . . . . .58 A3
Harleston St S4 . . . . .53 B4
Harley Rd S11 . . . . .60 B1
Harmer La S1 . . . . .107 B3
Harmony Way S60 . . . . . . .57 A4
Harney Cl S9 . . . . .55 B1
Harold Croft S61 . . . . .11 A2
Harold St S6 . . . . .51 B4
Harrington Rd 10 S2. . . . . .62 B1
Harrison La S10 . . . . .58 B1
Harrison Rd S6 . . . . .39 C1
Harrison St S61 . . . . .32 A4
Harris Rd S6 . . . . .39 C4
Harrogate Rd S26 . . . . . . .80 B4
Harrowden Ct S9 . . . . .44 C4
Harrowden Rd S9 . . . . .44 C4
Harrow St S11 . . . . .105 C1
Harry Firth Cl 7 S9. . . . . .54 B3
Hartford Cl S8. . . . . .73 C1
Hartford Rd S8 . . . . .73 C1
Harthill Rd S13 . . . . .64 C1
Hartington Ave S7. . . . . . .72 B1
Hartington Cl S61 . . . . . . .32 A4
Hartington Ct S18 . . . . . .101 A4
Hartington Rd
Dronfield S18 . . . . .101 A4
Rotherham S65. . . . . .32 A4
Sheffield S7 . . . . .72 B1
Hartland Ave S20 . . . . .91 B4
Hartland Ct 6 S20. . . . . . .91 B4
Hartland Dr S20 . . . . .91 B4
Hartley Brook Ave S5 . . . . .28 C4
Hartley Brook Prim Sch
S5. . . . . .28 C4
Hartley Brook Rd S5 . . . . . .28 C4
Hartley La S61. . . . . .20 C1
Hartley St S2 . . . . .62 B1
Hartopp Ave S2. . . . . .74 B4
Hartopp Cl S2 . . . . .74 B4
Hartopp Dr S2. . . . . .74 C4
Hartopp Rd S2 . . . . .74 C4
Harts Head S1. . . . . .106 B4
Hartshead Sq S1 . . . . . . .106 B4
Harvest La S3 . . . . .52 B3
Harvest Rd S66 . . . . .36 B3
Harvey Clough Mews
S8. . . . . .74 A1
Harvey Clough Rd S8 . . . . .74 A1
Harvey Rd S35. . . . . .73 B1
Harvey St S36 . . . . .3 C3
Harwell Rd S2 . . . . .64 A3
Harwich Rd S2 . . . . .64 A3

Harwood Cl S2 . . . . 62 B2
Harwood Dr S20 . . . . 90 B3
Harwood Gdns S20 . . . . . . 90 C3
Harwood St 2 S2 . . . . 62 B2
Haslam Cres S8 . . . . 96 C4
Haslehurst Rd S2 . . . . 63 C4
Hassop Cl S18 . . . . 101 B4
Hastilar Cl S2 . . . . 64 C2
Hastilar Rd S2 . . . . 64 C2
Hastilar Rd S S13 . . . . 65 A1
Hastings Mount S7 . . . . . . 72 B2
Hastings Rd S7 . . . . 72 B2
Hatfield House Croft
S5 . . . . 29 A3
Hatfield House Ct S5 . . . . 29 A3
Hatfield House La S5 . . . . 29 A3
Hatfield Prim Sch S5 . . . . 29 A3
Hatherley Rd
Rotherham S65 . . . . 21 B2
Sheffield S9 . . . . 44 C4
Hatton Cl S18 . . . . 99 C2
Hatton Rd S6 . . . . 40 B1
Haugh La S11 . . . . 71 B3
Haughton Rd S8 . . . . 85 A4
Havelock St S10 . . . . 105 B2
Havercroft Rd
Rotherham S60 . . . . 34 C1
Sheffield S8 . . . . 73 A1
Havercroft Terr S21 . . . . . . 91 C1
Hawke St S9 . . . . 43 B2
Hawkins Ave S35 . . . . 6 C3
Hawkshead Ave S18 . . . . 100 A3
Hawkshead Rd S4 . . . . 43 A3
Hawksley Ave S6 . . . . 40 A2
Hawksley Mews S6 . . . . . . 40 A2
Hawksley Rd S6 . . . . 40 A2
Hawksley Rise S35 . . . . 13 B2
Hawksway S21 . . . . 102 B1
Hawksworth Cl S65 . . . . . . 22 C1
Hawksworth Rd
Rotherham S65 . . . . 23 A2
Sheffield S6 . . . . 51 B4
Hawley St
Rawmarsh S62 . . . . 12 A3
Sheffield S1 . . . . 106 A4
Haworth Bank S60 . . . . 47 A3
Haworth Cres S60 . . . . 47 A3
Hawthorn Ave S20 . . . . 90 B3
Hawthorn Ct S65 . . . . 22 B1
Hawthorne Ave
Dronfield S18 . . . . 97 B1
Rawmarsh S62 . . . . 12 B3
Stocksbridge S36 . . . . 2 B4
Hawthorne Cl S21 . . . . 92 B1
Hawthorne Pl S26 . . . . 69 C1
Hawthorne St S6 . . . . 50 C4
Hawthornes The S20 . . . . . 79 B2
Hawthorn Rd
Chapeltown S35 . . . . 5 C1
Sheffield S6 . . . . 39 C2
Hawthorn Terr 2 S10 . . . . 51 A1
Haxby Cl S13 . . . . 77 A4
Haxby Pl S13 . . . . 77 A4
Haxby St S13 . . . . 77 A4
Haybrook Ct S17 . . . . 94 C3
Haydon Gr S66 . . . . 36 B4
Hayes Ct S20 . . . . 103 B4
Hayes Dr S20 . . . . 103 B4
Hayfield Cl S18 . . . . 99 C3
Hayfield Cres S12 . . . . 76 C1
Hayfield Dr S12 . . . . 76 C1
Hayfield Pl S12 . . . . 76 C1
Hayfield View S21 . . . . . . 102 C1
Hayfield Wlk S61 . . . . 19 B3
Hayland St S9 . . . . 43 C4
Haymarket S1 . . . . 106 B4
Haywood Ave S36 . . . . 3 C3
Haywood Cl S65 . . . . 22 C1
Haywood La
Stocksbridge, Knoll Top
S36 . . . . 3 C3
Stocksbridge, Wood Royd
S36 . . . . 4 A3
Hazel Ave S21 . . . . 92 A1
Hazelbadge Cres S12 . . . . 77 A1
Hazel Cl S18 . . . . 101 A2
Hazel Ct
Dronfield S18 . . . . 101 A2
Rotherham S65 . . . . 25 B2
Hazel Gr
Chapeltown S35 . . . . 7 B2
Rotherham S66 . . . . 36 C3
Hazelshaw Gdns S35 . . . . . . 5 B1
Hazelwood Cl 5 S18 . . . . 99 B3
Hazlebarrow Cl S8 . . . . . . 98 A4
Hazlebarrow Cres S8 . . . . 86 A1
Hazlebarrow Ct S8 . . . . . . 85 C1
Hazlebarrow Dr S8 . . . . . . 85 C1
Hazlebarrow Gr S8 . . . . . . 86 A1
Hazlebarrow Rd S8 . . . . . . 85 C1
Hazlehurst Cl S65 . . . . 23 A3
Hazlehurst La S8 . . . . 87 A2
Headford Gdns S3 . . . . . . 105 C2
Headford Gr S3 . . . . 105 C2
Headford Mews S3 . . . . . 105 C2
Headford St S3 . . . . 105 C2
Headland Dr S10 . . . . 50 B1
Headland Rd S10 . . . . 50 B1
Heath Ave S21 . . . . 92 B1
Heathcote St 2 S4 . . . . . . 42 B3
Heather Cl S60 . . . . 33 B2
Heather Ct S66 . . . . 37 A2
Heather Lea Ave S17 . . . . . 82 A1
Heather Lea Pl S17 . . . . . . 82 A1
Heather Rd S5 . . . . 29 B1
Heathfield Cl
Dronfield S18 . . . . 100 B2
2 Dronfield S18 . . . . 100 B3
Heathfield Rd S12 . . . . 76 C2
Heath Rd
Sheffield S6 . . . . 27 A2
Stocksbridge S36 . . . . 3 C2
Heaton Cl S18 . . . . 99 C3
Heatons Bank S62 . . . . 12 B4
Heavygate Ave S10 . . . . . . 50 C4
Heavygate Rd S10 . . . . 51 A3
HEELEY 74 A4
Heeley Arches S2 . . . . 62 B1
Heeley Bank Rd S2 . . . . . . 62 C1
Heeley City Farm ★
S2 . . . . 62 C1
Heeley Gn S2 . . . . 74 A4
Heeley Ret Pk S8 . . . . 73 B3
Heighton View S26 . . . . 69 B3
Hellaby View S65 . . . . 25 A1
Helliwell Ct S36 . . . . 4 A1
Helliwell La S36 . . . . 4 A2
Helmsley Ave S20 . . . . 90 C1
Helmsley Cl S26 . . . . 80 B4
Helmton Dr S8 . . . . 85 B4
Helmton Rd S8 . . . . 85 A4
Helston Rise S7 . . . . 72 B2
Hemmingway Cl S60 . . . . . . 57 C1
Hemper Gr S8 . . . . 84 B1
Hemper La S8 . . . . 84 B1
HEMSWORTH 74 C1
Hemsworth Rd S8, S14 . . . 86 A4
Hendon St S13 . . . . 66 A3
Henley Ave S8 . . . . 86 A2
Henley Grove Rd S61 . . . . 20 B1
Henley Rise S61 . . . . 20 B1
Henley Way S61 . . . . 20 A1
Henry Ct
Rawmarsh S62 . . . . 12 A1
4 Rotherham S60 . . . . 21 A1
Henry Fanshawe Sch
S18 . . . . 101 A4
Henry St
Chapeltown S35 . . . . 5 A1
Eckington S21 . . . . 103 A1
Rotherham S65 . . . . 21 B1
Sheffield S3 . . . . 104 C5
Henson St S9 . . . . 54 C4
Heppenstall La S9 . . . . 54 A4
Hepworth Dr S26 . . . . 69 B1
Herbert Rd S7 . . . . 73 A4
Herbert St S61 . . . . 19 B1
HERDINGS 75 B1
Herdings Ct S12 . . . . 75 C1
Herdings Rd S12 . . . . 75 C1
Herdings View S12 . . . . 75 C1
Hereford St S1 . . . . 107 A1
Hereward Rd S5 . . . . 28 C2
Hereward's Rd S14 . . . . . . 86 B3
Hermitage St S2 . . . . 105 C1
Heron Hill S26 . . . . 81 A4
Heron Mount S2 . . . . 63 C4
Herries Ave S5 . . . . 28 A1
Herries Dr S5 . . . . 41 C4
Herries Pl S5 . . . . 41 B4
Herries Rd S5, S6 . . . . 40 B4
Herries Rd S S6 . . . . 40 B4
HERRINGTHORPE 34 A3
Herringthorpe Ave
S65 . . . . 34 B2
Herringthorpe Cl S65 . . . . 34 B3
Herringthorpe Gr S65 . . . . 34 C2
Herringthorpe Jun & Inf
Schs S65 . . . . 34 B2
Herringthorpe La S65 . . . . 34 C3
Herringthorpe Valley Rd
S60, S65 . . . . 34 C4
Herschell Rd S7 . . . . 62 A1
Hesley Bar S61 . . . . 8 C2
Hesley Gr S35 . . . . 8 A2
Hesley Grange S61 . . . . . . 18 C4
Hesley La S61 . . . . 8 C2
Hesley Mews S61 . . . . 18 C4
Hesley Rd S5 . . . . 17 A1
Hesley Terr S5 . . . . 17 B1
Heslow Gr S61 . . . . 8 C3
Hessey St S13 . . . . 77 B4
Hessle Rd S6 . . . . 39 C4
Hibberd Pl S6 . . . . 39 B2
Hibberd Rd S6 . . . . 39 C2
Hickmott Rd S11 . . . . 61 B2
Hicks St S3 . . . . 52 B4
Hides St S9 . . . . 43 C2
Highcliffe Ct S11 . . . . 60 B1
Highcliffe Dr
Oughtibridge S35 . . . . 13 B2
Sheffield S11 . . . . 60 A1
Highcliffe Pl S11 . . . . 71 B4
Highcliffe Rd S11 . . . . 71 B4
Highcroft 5 S11 . . . . 60 B1
High Ct S1 . . . . 106 B3
HIGHFIELD 62 B2
Highfield La S13, S60 . . . . 57 A1
Highfield Pl S2 . . . . 62 B2
Highfield Rd S61 . . . . 11 A1
Highfield Rise S6 . . . . 49 A4
Highfields Cres S18 . . . . . 100 C2
High Field Spring S60 . . . 56 B2
Highfields Rd S18 . . . . . . 100 C2
Highfield View S60 . . . . 57 A4
Highgate S9 . . . . 44 C4
Highgate Dr S18 . . . . 101 B1
Highgate La S18 . . . . 101 B1
High Greave S5 . . . . 28 C4
High Greave Ave S5 . . . . . . 16 C1
High Greave Ct S5 . . . . 28 C4
High Greave Jun & Inf
Schs S65 . . . . 22 C2
High Greave Pl S65 . . . . . . 22 C1
High Greave Rd S65 . . . . . 22 C2
HIGH GREEN 5 B1
High Green Prim Sch
S35 . . . . 5 B2
High Hazel Cres S60 . . . . . 57 A4
High Hazel Ct S60 . . . . 57 C2
High Hazel Rd S60 . . . . 57 C2
High Hazels Cl S9 . . . . 55 B2
High Hazels Mead S9 . . . . 55 B2
High House Terr S6 . . . . . . 40 B1
High La
Eckington S12 . . . . 88 C3
Sheffield S12 . . . . 89 A2
Highlow View S60 . . . . 46 A3
High Matlock Ave S6 . . . . 49 B4
High Matlock Rd S6 . . . . . 49 B4
Highnam Crescent Rd
S10 . . . . 51 A1
High Pavement Row 4
S2 . . . . 106 C4
High St
Aston S26 . . . . 69 A1
Dronfield S18 . . . . 100 C3
Eckington S21 . . . . 103 A1
Killamarsh S21 . . . . 92 B2
Rawmarsh S62 . . . . 12 A3
Rotherham, Kimberworth
S61 . . . . 19 B1
Rotherham S60 . . . . 33 A4
Rotherham, Whiston
S60 . . . . 47 C3
Sheffield, Beighton S20 . . . . 79 C2
Sheffield, Dore S17 . . . . 82 B1
Sheffield, Ecclesfield
S35 . . . . 16 B2
Sheffield, Mosborough
S20 . . . . 90 B1
Sheffield S3 . . . . 106 B3
High Storrs Cl S11 . . . . 71 C4
High Storrs Cres S11 . . . . 60 B1
High Storrs Dr S11 . . . . 60 B1
High Storrs Rd S11 . . . . . . 71 B4
High Storrs Rise S11 . . . . . 60 B1
High Storrs Sch S11 . . . . . 71 B4
High Street La S2 . . . . 106 C3
High Street Mews S20 . . . 90 A1
Highton St S6 . . . . 51 A4
High Trees
Rotherham S60 . . . . 34 B1
Sheffield S17 . . . . 82 B1
High View S5 . . . . 41 B2
HIGH WINCOBANK 29 B2
Highwood Pl S21 . . . . 102 C1
High Wray S11 . . . . 72 A2
High Wray Cl S11 . . . . 72 A2
Hilary Way S26 . . . . 69 B1
Hill Cl
Rotherham S65 . . . . 35 B2
Sheffield S6 . . . . 49 A4
Hillcote Cl S10 . . . . 59 B3
Hillcote Dr S10 . . . . 59 B3
Hillcote Mews S10 . . . . 59 B3
Hillcote Rise S10 . . . . 59 B3
Hillcrest Dr S35 . . . . 13 A2
Hillcrest Rd S36 . . . . 4 B2
Hill Crest Rd
Chapeltown S35 . . . . 7 A3
Rotherham S65 . . . . 22 B1
Hillcrest Rise S36 . . . . 4 B2
Hillcrest Way S66 . . . . 24 B2
HILLFOOT
Dronfield 94 B3
Sheffield 40 C1
Hillfoot Ct S17 . . . . 94 B2
Hillfoot Rd
Sheffield, Hillfoot
S17 . . . . 94 B3
Sheffield S3 . . . . 51 C4
HILLSBOROUGH 40 A3
Hillsborough Barracks
Bsns & Sh Ctr S6 . . . . . . 40 B2
Hillsborough Ctr Sh Arc
S6 . . . . 40 A2
Hillsborough Football
Ground S6 . . . . 40 A4
Hillsborough Pl S6 . . . . . . 40 A2
Hillsborough Prim Sch
S6 . . . . 40 A4
Hillsborough Rd S6 . . . . . . 40 A2
Hillside S20 . . . . 90 A1
Hill Side
Rotherham S60 . . . . 48 A3
Rotherham, Thorpe Hesley
S61 . . . . 9 A2
Hillside Ave
Dronfield S18 . . . . 100 C2
2 Dronfield S18 . . . . 100 C3
Sheffield S5 . . . . 28 B4
Hillside Ct S61 . . . . 21 A3
Hillside The S4 . . . . 43 B4
Hills Rd S36 . . . . 3 C3
Hill St S2 . . . . 62 B3
HILL TOP
100 C1
Oughtibridge 71 A3
Rotherham 30 C3
Hill Top Cl
Brinsworth S60 . . . . 45 C3
Rotherham S61 . . . . 31 A4
Hill Top Cres S20 . . . . 90 B4
Hilltop Gn S5 . . . . 27 C1
Hill Top La
Rotherham, Flanderwell
S65, S66 . . . . 36 A4
Rotherham, Richmond Park
S61 . . . . 31 A4
Sheffield S35 . . . . 14 B2
Hilltop Rd S18 . . . . 101 A1
Hill Top Rd S35 . . . . 15 A2
Hill Top Rise S35 . . . . 15 A2
Hilltop Way S18 . . . . 100 C1
Hill Turrets Cl S11 . . . . 71 B2
Hill View E S61 . . . . 19 A2
Hill View Rd S61 . . . . 19 A2
Hilton Dr S35 . . . . 16 B2
Hinde House 3-16 Sch
S5 . . . . 29 C2
Hinde House Cres S4 . . . . 42 C4
Hinde House Croft S4 . . . . 42 C4
Hinde House La S4 . . . . . . 42 C4
Hinde St S4 . . . . 42 C3
Hindewood Cl S4 . . . . 42 C4
Hind Rd S60 . . . . 48 A4
Hirst Common La S6 . . . . . 26 B4
Hirst Dr S65 . . . . 23 A1
Hobart St S11 . . . . 62 A2
Hobson Ave S6 . . . . 40 C1
Hobson Pl S6 . . . . 40 C1
Hodder Ct S35 . . . . 7 A4
Hodgson St S3 . . . . 105 C2
Hogarth Rise S18 . . . . 100 B2
Holbein Cl S18 . . . . 100 B2
Holberry Cl S10 . . . . 105 B2
Holberry Gdns S10 . . . . . 105 B2
Holbourne Gr S35 . . . . 5 B2
HOLBROOK 91 B2
Holbrook Ave S20 . . . . 91 B2
Holbrook Dr S13 . . . . 76 A4
Holbrook Gn S20 . . . . 91 B2
Holbrook Rd S13 . . . . 64 C1
Holbrook Rise S20 . . . . 91 B3
Holburn Ave S18 . . . . 100 C4
Holderness Dr S26 . . . . . . 69 B2
Holdings Rd S2 . . . . 63 B3
Hole House La S36 . . . . 3 A3
Holgate Ave S5 . . . . 27 C4
Holgate Cl S5 . . . . 27 C4
Holgate Cres S5 . . . . 28 A4
Holgate Dr S5 . . . . 28 A4
Holgate Meadows Com
Specl Sch S5 . . . . 28 B3
Holgate Rd S5 . . . . 28 A4
Holkham Rise S11 . . . . 83 A4
Holland Pl 8 S2 . . . . 62 B2
Holland Rd
Chapeltown S35 . . . . 5 B1
Sheffield S2 . . . . 62 B2
Holland St S1 . . . . 104 C3
Hollies Cl S18 . . . . 101 B2
HOLLIN BUSK 3 B1
Hollin Busk La S36 . . . . 3 B1
Hollin Busk Rd S36 . . . . 3 B2
Hollindale Dr S12 . . . . 76 B3
Holling Croft S36 . . . . 4 A3
Holling Hill La S66 . . . . 35 C2
Holling's La S65 . . . . 24 C2
Hollingswood Way
S66 . . . . 24 C1
Hollin Moor La S66 . . . . . . 36 A2
Hollin Rd S35 . . . . 13 A2
Hollins Cl S6 . . . . 50 A3
Hollins Ct S6 . . . . 50 A4
Hollins Dr S6 . . . . 50 B3
HOLLINS END 76 B3
Hollinsend Ave S12 . . . . . . 76 B3
Hollinsend Pl S12 . . . . 76 B3
Hollinsend Rd S12 . . . . 76 A3
Hollins La S6 . . . . 50 B4
Hollins Spring Ave
S18 . . . . 100 C2
Hollins Spring Rd
S18 . . . . 100 C2
Hollis Croft
Sheffield, Coisley Hill
S13 . . . . 77 C4
Sheffield, Netherthorpe
S1 . . . . 104 C4
Hollis Hospl S11 . . . . 82 C4
Hollowgate S60 . . . . 33 B3
Hollow Gate
Chapeltown S35 . . . . 6 B3
2 Rotherham S60 . . . . 47 C3
Hollow La
Sheffield, Mosborough
S20 . . . . 103 A4
Sheffield S20 . . . . 103 B4
Hollybank S12 . . . . 76 A4
Hollybank Ave S12 . . . . 76 B4
Hollybank Cl S12 . . . . 76 C4
Hollybank Cres S12 . . . . . . 76 B4
Hollybank Dr S12 . . . . 76 C4
Hollybank Rd S12 . . . . 76 B4
Hollybank Way S12 . . . . . . 76 C4
Hollybush St S62 . . . . 12 A1
Holly Cl
Chapeltown S35 . . . . 7 A2
Killamarsh S21 . . . . 92 A1
Holly Cres S66 . . . . 36 C4
Holly Gdns S12 . . . . 76 B4
Holly Gr S12 . . . . 76 B4
Holly House La S35 . . . . . . 14 B2
Holly La 2 S1 . . . . 106 A3

Holly Mount S66 . . . . 36 C2
Holly's House Rd S65 . . . . 25 C3
Holly St S1 . . . . 106 A3
Holly Terr S26 . . . . 69 A2
Hollythorpe Cres S8 . . . . . 73 C2
Hollythorpe Rd S8 . . . . 74 A2
Hollythorpe Rise S8 . . . . . 74 A2
Hollywell Hts S4, S9 . . . . . 43 B4
Holm Cl S18 . . . . 99 C4
Holme Cl S6 . . . . 40 A2
Holme Ct S60 . . . . 46 C4
Holme La S35 . . . . 15 A1
Holme Oak Way S6 . . . . . . 39 B2
HOLMES 32 A3
Holmes Cres S60 . . . . 57 C2
HOLMESDALE 101 B4
Holmesdale Cl S18 . . . . . . 98 A1
Holmesdale Inf Sch
  S18 . . . . 101 B4
Holmesdale Rd S18 . . . . . . 98 A1
Holmesfield S60 . . . . 32 A4
Holmesfield Rd
  Dronfield S18 . . . . 99 A3
  Oughtibridge S35 . . . . . . 13 B3
Holmes La S61 . . . . 32 B4
Holmes Rd S66 . . . . 37 C2
Holm Flatt St S62 . . . . 11 C1
Holmhirst Cl S8 . . . . 84 C4
Holmhirst Dr S8 . . . . 73 A1
Holmhirst Rd S8 . . . . 85 A4
Holmhirst Way S8 . . . . 73 A1
Holmley Bank S18 . . . . 97 B1
HOLMLEY COMMON . . . 97 B1
Holmley La S18 . . . . 97 B1
Holmshaw Dr S13 . . . . 65 C2
Holmshaw Gr S13 . . . . 65 C2
Holt House Gr S7 . . . . 72 C2
Holt House Ho S7 . . . . 72 C2
Holtwood Rd S4 . . . . 41 C1
Holy Gn S1 . . . . 107 A2
Holyoake Ave S13 . . . . 65 C2
Holyrood Ave S13 . . . . 58 A3
Holyrood Rise S66 . . . . 37 A4
Holyrood View S10 . . . . . . 58 A3
Holywell Pl **7** S65 . . . . . . 21 B1
Holywell Rd S4, S9 . . . . . . 43 B4
Homestead Cl S5 . . . . 29 A3
Homestead Dr S60 . . . . . . 45 C3
Homestead Rd S5 . . . . 29 A3
Honeysuckle Rd S5 . . . . . . 29 C1
Hoober Ave S11 . . . . 71 C3
Hoober Rd S11 . . . . 71 C3
Hoole La S10 . . . . 61 A4
Hoole Rd S10 . . . . 51 A1
Hoole St S6 . . . . 51 B4
Hooton La S65 . . . . 24 C5
Hopedale Rd S12 . . . . 76 C2
Hopefield Ave S12 . . . . 76 C2
Hope Rd S13 . . . . 13 C2
Hope St
  Rotherham S60 . . . . 20 C1
  Stocksbridge S36 . . . . 3 B3
Hope Street Extension
  S60 . . . . 20 C1
Horace St S60 . . . . 33 B3
Horbury La S35 . . . . 6 C2
Hornbeam Cl S35 . . . . 7 A2
Hornbeam Rd S66 . . . . 36 B4
Hornby Ct S11 . . . . 60 B1
Horndean Rd S5 . . . . 42 B3
Horner Cl S36 . . . . 3 A4
HORNER HOUSE 2 C4
Horner Rd **1** S7 . . . . 62 B1
Horninglow Cl S5 . . . . 28 C1
Horninglow Mount S5 . . . . 28 C1
Horninglow Rd S5 . . . . 29 A1
Horsewood Rd S13 . . . . . . 67 B2
Horton Cl S20 . . . . 90 C1
Horton Dr S20 . . . . 90 C1
Hounsfield Cres S65 . . . . . 23 A1
Hounsfield La S10 . . . . . . 105 B3
Hounsfield Rd
  Rotherham S65 . . . . 23 A1
  Sheffield S3 . . . . 105 B3
Housley La S35 . . . . 7 A3
Housley Pk S35 . . . . 7 B4
Houstead Rd S9 . . . . 55 B1
Hoveringham Ct S26 . . . . . 80 B4
HOWARD HILL 51 A3

Howard La S2 . . . . 107 B2
Howard Rd
  Rotherham S66 . . . . 37 B4
  Sheffield S6 . . . . 104 A5
Howard Sq S1 . . . . 107 B3
Howard St
  Rotherham S65 . . . . 33 B4
  Sheffield S1 . . . . 107 B2
Howarth Dr S60 . . . . 46 B1
Howarth Rd S60 . . . . 46 B1
Howbrook Cl S35 . . . . 5 A2
Howden Rd S9 . . . . 43 B1
Howlett Cl S60 . . . . 48 B3
Howlett Dr S60 . . . . 46 A1
Howson Cl S65 . . . . 25 B2
Howson Rd S36 . . . . 3 C3
Hoyland Rd S3 . . . . 40 C1
Hoyle St S3 . . . . 104 C5
Hucklow Dr S5 . . . . 29 A1
Hucklow Prim Sch S5 . . . . 42 A4
Hucklow Rd S5 . . . . 29 A1
Hudson Rd
  Rotherham S61 . . . . 19 B4
  Sheffield S13 . . . . 67 C2
Humphrey Rd S8 . . . . 84 C2
Hungerhill Cl S61 . . . . 19 A2
Hunger Hill La S60 . . . . . . 48 A3
Hungerhill Rd S61 . . . . 19 A3
Hunger Hill Rd S60 . . . . . . 48 A3
Hunsdon Rd S21 . . . . 102 C1
Hunshelf La S35 . . . . 16 B4
Hunshelf Pk S36 . . . . 3 B4
Hunshelf Rd
  Chapeltown S35 . . . . 7 B3
  Stocksbridge, Wood
    Willows S36 . . . . 3 B4
Hunsley St S4 . . . . 42 C2
Hunstone Ave S8 . . . . 85 B1
Hunter Cl S11 . . . . 60 C1
Hunter Hill Rd S11 . . . . . . 61 A2
Hunter House Rd S11 . . . . 61 A2
Hunter Rd S6 . . . . 39 C2
Hunter's Bar **3** S11 . . . . 61 A2
Hunter's Bar Jun & Inf
  Schs S11 . . . . 61 A2
Hunters Gdns S6 . . . . 38 B3
Hunter's La S13 . . . . 76 B4
Huntingdon Cres S11 . . . . 61 C2
Huntingtower Rd S11 . . . . 60 C1
Huntley Gr S11 . . . . 71 B4
Huntley Rd S11 . . . . 71 C4
Huntsman Rd S9 . . . . 55 B2
Huntsmans Gdns S9 . . . . . 44 A1
Hurl Dr S12 . . . . 75 B3
HURL FIELD 75 A3
Hurlfield Ct S12 . . . . 75 C4
Hurlfield Dr
  Rotherham S65 . . . . 25 A1
  Sheffield S12 . . . . 75 B4
Hurlfield Rd S12 . . . . 75 B3
Hurlingham Cl S11 . . . . . . 72 B3
Hursley Cl **4** S20 . . . . . . 91 B3
Hursley Dr S20 . . . . 91 B3
Hurst Gn S35 . . . . 5 B1
Hutchinson Ct S60 . . . . . . 33 B3
Hutchinson La S7 . . . . 72 C1
Hutchinson Rd
  Rawmarsh S62 . . . . 12 B4
  Sheffield S7 . . . . 72 C1
Hutcliffe Dr S8 . . . . 84 B4
Hutcliffe Wood Rd S8 . . . . 84 B4
Hutton Croft S12 . . . . 78 A1
Hutton Rd S61 . . . . 10 A1
Hyacinth Cl S5 . . . . 29 C1
Hyacinth Rd S5 . . . . 29 C1
Hyde Park Terr S2 . . . . . . 106 C3
Hyde Park Wlk S2 . . . . . . 106 C3

I

Ibbotson Rd S6 . . . . 51 A4
Ice Sheffield S9 . . . . 43 B1
ICKLES 32 B2
Ickles Way S60 . . . . 32 B1
Icknield Way S60 . . . . 46 A2
Ida's Rd S21 . . . . 103 A2
Idsworth Rd S5 . . . . 42 B4
Ilkley Cres S26 . . . . 80 B4
Ilkley Rd S5 . . . . 29 A2
Imperial Bldgs S60 . . . . . . 33 A4
Imperial Ho **2** S1 . . . . . 107 A2
Industry Rd S9 . . . . 55 A3

Industry St S6 . . . . 51 A4
Infield La S9 . . . . 55 B2
Infirmary Rd
  Rawmarsh S62 . . . . 12 B1
  Sheffield S6 . . . . 51 C3
Ingelow Ave S5 . . . . 28 B3
Ingfield Ave S9 . . . . 44 C4
Ingleborough Croft
  S35 . . . . 7 A4
Ingleby Cl S18 . . . . 99 B3
Inglewood Ave S20 . . . . . . 91 B3
Inglewood Ct **5** S20 . . . . 91 B3
Inglewood Dell **6**
  S20 . . . . 91 B3
Ingram Cl S2 . . . . 63 B4
Ingram Rd S2 . . . . 63 B4
Ingshead Ave S62 . . . . 12 B3
Inkersall Dr S20 . . . . 90 C2
INTAKE 76 A3
Intake Prim Sch S12 . . . . . 76 B4
Ironside Cl S14 . . . . 74 C1
Ironside Pl S14 . . . . 75 A1
Ironside Rd S14 . . . . 75 A1
Ironside Wlk S14 . . . . 86 B4
Irving St S9 . . . . 55 A2
Island Cl S65 . . . . 34 C1
Islay St S10 . . . . 50 C1
Ivan Brook Cl **4** S18 . . . . 99 B3
Ivanhoe Mews S26 . . . . . . 69 A2
Ivanhoe Rd S6 . . . . 50 B4
Ivy Cotts S11 . . . . 59 C1
Ivy Ct S8 . . . . 86 A4
Ivy Dr S10 . . . . 104 A4
Ivy Farm Croft S65 . . . . . . 23 A3
Ivy Gr S10 . . . . 104 A4
Ivy Hall Rd S5 . . . . 17 B1
Ivy La S20 . . . . 79 C2
Ivy Park Cl S10 . . . . 59 C4
Ivy Park Rd S10 . . . . 59 C3
Ivy Side Cl S21 . . . . 92 B2
Ivy Side Gdns S21 . . . . . . 92 B2

J

Jacobs Cl S5 . . . . 29 B2
Jacobs Dr S5 . . . . 29 C2
Jamaica St S4 . . . . 42 A1
James Andrew Cl S8 . . . . . 85 A1
James Andrew Cres
  S8 . . . . 84 C1
James Andrew Croft
  S8 . . . . 85 A1
James St
  Rotherham S60 . . . . 20 C1
  Sheffield S9 . . . . 55 B3
James Walton Ct S20 . . . . 91 A1
James Walton Dr S20 . . . . 91 A1
James Walton Pl S20 . . . . 91 A1
James Walton View
  S20 . . . . 91 A1
Janson St S9 . . . . 43 B2
Jardine Cl S9 . . . . 30 B2
Jardine St S9 . . . . 30 B2
Jarrow Rd S11 . . . . 61 B2
Jasmine Ave S20 . . . . 79 B1
Jaunty Ave S12 . . . . 76 B2
Jaunty Cl S12 . . . . 76 A1
Jaunty Cres S12 . . . . 76 B2
Jaunty Dr S12 . . . . 76 A1
Jaunty La S12 . . . . 76 A2
Jaunty Mount S12 . . . . 76 B1
Jaunty Pl S12 . . . . 76 A1
Jaunty Rd S12 . . . . 76 B1
Jaunty View S12 . . . . 76 B1
Jaunty Way S12 . . . . 76 A2
Jay La S26 . . . . 81 A4
Jedburgh Dr S9 . . . . 30 A2
Jedburgh St S9 . . . . 30 B2
Jeffcock Pl S35 . . . . 5 C1
Jeffcock Rd
  Chapeltown S35 . . . . 5 C1
  Sheffield S9 . . . . 55 A2
Jeffery Cres S36 . . . . 3 C2
Jeffery St **6** S2 . . . . 74 A4
Jenkin Ave S9 . . . . 43 B4
Jenkin Cl S9 . . . . 30 A1
Jenkin Dr S9 . . . . 43 B4
Jenkin Rd S5, S9 . . . . 30 A1
Jenkin Wood Cl S9 . . . . . . 24 C1
Jennings Cl S65 . . . . 21 B2
Jepson Rd S5 . . . . 29 C2
Jericho St S3 . . . . 104 C4

Jermyn Ave S12 . . . . 77 B2
Jermyn Cl S12 . . . . 77 B1
Jermyn Cres S12 . . . . 77 B2
Jermyn Dr S12 . . . . 77 B1
Jermyn Way S12 . . . . 77 B1
Jersey Rd S2 . . . . 62 B1
Jessamine Rd S5 . . . . 29 B2
Jessell St S9 . . . . 54 A3
Jessop St S1 . . . . 107 A2
Jewitt Rd S61 . . . . 19 B4
Jew La S1 . . . . 107 B3
Jockell Dr S62 . . . . 12 A3
John Calvert Rd S13 . . . . . 78 C4
John Eaton's
  Almshouses S8 . . . . 85 C4
John Hibbard Ave
  S13 . . . . 67 C1
John Hibbard Cl S13 . . . . . 67 C1
John Hibbard Cres
  S13 . . . . 67 C1
John Hibbard Rise
  S13 . . . . 67 C1
Johnson Ct S65 . . . . 33 C3
Johnson La
  Sheffield, Ecclesfield
    S35 . . . . 16 B3
  Sheffield S3 . . . . 106 B5
Johnson St
  Sheffield S3 . . . . 106 B5
  Stocksbridge S36 . . . . 3 C3
John St
  Eckington S21 . . . . 103 A1
  Rotherham S60 . . . . 32 C4
  Sheffield S2 . . . . 62 B3
John Trickett Ho S35 . . . . . 7 A3
John Ward St S13 . . . . 67 B1
John West St S36 . . . . 3 A2
Joiner St S3 . . . . 106 B4
JORDAN 31 C3
Jordan Cres S61 . . . . 31 B3
JORDANTHORPE 85 C1
  Jordanthorpe Ctr S8 . . . . 97 C4
Jordanthorpe Gn S8 . . . . . 98 A4
Jordanthorpe Parkway
  S8 . . . . 98 A4
Jordanthorpe View
  S8 . . . . 86 A1
Josephine Rd S61 . . . . 32 A4
Joseph Rd S61 . . . . 51 A3
Joseph St
  Eckington S21 . . . . 103 A1
  Rotherham S60 . . . . 20 C1
Joshua Rd S7 . . . . 73 A4
Josselin Ct S35 . . . . 7 A3
Jowitt Rd S11 . . . . 72 B4
Jubb Cl S65 . . . . 35 A2
Jubilee Cotts S60 . . . . 45 C3
Jubilee Cres S21 . . . . 92 C3
Jubilee Rd S9 . . . . 55 A4
Jubilee St S60 . . . . 33 A2
Judith Rd S26 . . . . 80 C4
Julian Rd S9 . . . . 30 B1
Julian Way S9 . . . . 30 B1
Jumble La S35 . . . . 17 B4
Junction Rd
  Sheffield S11 . . . . 61 A2
  Sheffield, Woodhouse
    S13 . . . . 67 C1
June Rd S13 . . . . 67 B1
Juniper Rise S21 . . . . 92 A1

K

Kashmir Gdns S9 . . . . 54 C3
Kaye Pl S10 . . . . 104 A4
Kearsley Rd S2 . . . . 62 B2
Keats Rd S6 . . . . 27 A4
Keepers Cl S5 . . . . 29 A2
Keeton's Hill **1** S2 . . . . . 62 A2
Keir Pl S62 . . . . 12 C4
Kelford St S61 . . . . 31 C4
Kelgate S20 . . . . 103 A4
Kelham Island S3 . . . . . . 106 A5
Kelham Island Ind Mus *
  S3 . . . . 106 A5
Kelvin Bdgs **3** S6 . . . . . 51 C4
Kelvin Ct S41 . . . . 18 C4
Kemp Cl S21 . . . . 92 A2
Kenbourne Gr S7 . . . . 61 C1
Kenbourne Rd S7 . . . . 61 C1
Kendal Dr S18 . . . . 100 A3
Kendal Rd S6 . . . . 39 C2

Kenilworth Ct S11 . . . . 71 B2
Kenilworth Rd S11 . . . . . . 61 A2
Kennedy Ct S10 . . . . 50 C1
Kennedy Rd S8 . . . . 84 C4
Kenneth St S65 . . . . 21 B1
Kenninghall Cl S2 . . . . 63 B1
Kenninghall Dr S2 . . . . 63 B1
Kenninghall Rd S2 . . . . . . 63 B1
Kensington Chase
  S10 . . . . 58 A2
Kensington Cl S10 . . . . 58 A2
Kensington Ct S10 . . . . 58 A2
Kensington Pk S10 . . . . . . 58 A2
Kent Grange **12** S8 . . . . . 74 A4
Kent House Cl S12 . . . . . . 88 C2
Kentmere Cl S18 . . . . 100 A3
Kent Rd
  Rotherham S61 . . . . 19 B3
  Sheffield S8 . . . . 74 A4
Kenwell Dr S17 . . . . 95 C3
Kenwood Ave S7 . . . . 61 C2
Kenwood Bank S7 . . . . 61 C2
Kenwood Chase **12**
  S7 . . . . 62 A2
Kenwood Cres S11 . . . . . . 61 B1
Kenwood Park Rd S7 . . . . 61 C1
Kenwood Rd S7 . . . . 61 C1
Kenwood Rise S66 . . . . . . 36 C4
Kenworthy Rd S36 . . . . 3 A2
Kenyon Alley **2** S3 . . . . 104 C4
Kenyon St S3 . . . . 104 C4
Keppel Dr S61 . . . . 18 B4
Keppel Hts S61 . . . . 18 B4
Keppel Pl S5 . . . . 29 B4
Keppel Rd
  Rotherham S61 . . . . 18 B4
  Sheffield S5 . . . . 17 C1
Keppel View Rd S61 . . . . . 19 A2
Kersal Lawns S10 . . . . 60 C4
Kerwin Cl S17 . . . . 82 A2
Kerwin Dr S17 . . . . 82 A2
Kerwin Rd S17 . . . . 82 A2
Kestrel Ave S61 . . . . 9 B3
Kestrel Cl S21 . . . . 91 C1
Kestrel Dr S21 . . . . 102 B1
Kestrel Gn S2 . . . . 63 C4
Kestrel Rise S26 . . . . 68 B1
Keswick Cl S6 . . . . 38 C2
Keswick Cres S60 . . . . 45 C2
Keswick Pl S18 . . . . 99 C3
Kettlebridge Rd S9 . . . . . . 54 B2
Ketton Ave S8 . . . . 74 A1
Kew Cres S12 . . . . 77 C4
Keyworth Pl S13 . . . . 77 C4
Keyworth Rd S6 . . . . 40 A3
Khartoum Rd S11 . . . . 61 B3
Kilburn Rd S18 . . . . 99 B3
Kildale Gdns S20 . . . . 90 B1
Kildonan Gr S12 . . . . 76 B1
KILLAMARSH 92 C2
  Killamarsh Inf Sch
    S21 . . . . 92 C3
  Killamarsh Jun Sch
    S21 . . . . 92 C3
Killamarsh La S21, S26 . . 93 C2
Kilner Way S6 . . . . 27 A1
Kiln Hill S18 . . . . 98 A1
Kiln Rd S61 . . . . 19 C2
Kiln St S8 . . . . 62 A1
Kilton Hill S3 . . . . 52 C4
Kilton Pl S3 . . . . 52 C4
Kilvington Ave S13 . . . . . . 64 C1
Kilvington Cres S13 . . . . . 64 C1
Kilvington Rd S13 . . . . 64 C1
Kimberley St S9 . . . . 54 A4
KIMBERWORTH 31 B4
  Kimberworth Com Prim
    Sch S61 . . . . 19 C1
  **KIMBERWORTH
    PARK** 10 A2
  Kimberworth Park Rd
    S61 . . . . 19 B4
Kimberworth Rd S61 . . . . . 32 A4
Kinder Gdns S5 . . . . 28 B3
King Ecgbert Rd S17 . . . . 94 C3
King Ecgbert Sch S17 . . . . 94 B4
King Edward VII Sch
  Sheffield S10 . . . . 105 A2
  Sheffield, Tapton Hill
    S10 . . . . 60 B4
Kingfield Rd S11 . . . . 61 B1
Kingfisher Gr S26 . . . . 68 B1

Kingfisher Rise S61 . . . . 9 B4
King James Apartments
 S6 . . . . 51 B4
King James St S6 . . . . 51 B4
Kings Coppice S17 . . . . . . 94 B4
Kings Ct S10 . . . . 60 B4
Kingscroft Cl S17 . . . . 82 C2
Kings Cl S10 . . . . 60 B4
Kingsley Park Ave S7 . . . 72 A2
Kingsley Park Gr S11 . . . 72 A2
Kings Mews S12 . . . . 103 B1
King St
 Aston S26 . . . . 69 A2
 Chapeltown S35 . . . . 7 B4
 Sheffield S3 . . . . 106 B4
Kingston St S4 . . . . 42 B1
Kings Way S60 . . . . 47 B4
Kingswood Ave S20 . . . . . 89 B4
Kingswood Cl ⑥ S20 . . . 89 B4
Kingswood Croft ⑨
 S20 . . . . 89 B4
Kingswood Gr ⑩ S20 . . . 89 B4
Kinharvie Rd S5 . . . . 27 C1
Kinnaird Ave S5 . . . . 28 C3
Kinnaird Pl S5 . . . . 28 C3
Kinnaird Rd S5 . . . . 28 C3
Kinsey Hts S35 . . . . 5 B1
Kinsey Rd S35 . . . . 5 A1
Kipling Cl S18 . . . . 101 B2
Kipling Rd S6 . . . . 40 A2
Kirby Cl S9 . . . . 55 A2
Kirby Dr S12 . . . . 75 C2
Kirby Rd S12 . . . . 75 C2
Kirby View S12 . . . . 75 C2
Kirby Way S12 . . . . 75 C1
Kirkcroft Ave
 Killamarsh S21 . . . . 92 B3
 Rotherham S61 . . . . 9 B3
Kirkcroft Cl S61 . . . . 9 A3
Kirkcroft Dr S21 . . . . 92 B2
Kirkcroft La S21 . . . . 92 B2
Kirkdale Cres S13 . . . . . . 66 C3
Kirkdale Dr S13 . . . . 66 C3
Kirkhill Sch S2 . . . . 63 A2
Kirklands Dr S62 . . . . 11 C4
Kirk St S4 . . . . 53 A4
Kirkstall Cl S60 . . . . 45 B3
Kirkstall Rd S11 . . . . 61 A2
Kirkstead Abbey Mews
 S61 . . . . 9 B1
Kirkstead Gdns S13 . . . . . 67 C1
Kirkstead Rd S61 . . . . 30 A4
Kirkstone Rd S6 . . . . 40 A1
Kirton Rd S4 . . . . 42 A2
Knab Cl S7 . . . . 72 B3
Knab Croft S7 . . . . 72 B3
Knab Rd S7 . . . . 72 B3
Knab Rise S7 . . . . 72 B3
Knapton Ave S62 . . . . 11 C4
Knaresboro Rd S7 . . . . . . 72 B1
Knaresborough Cl
 S26 . . . . 69 A1
Knoll Cl S18 . . . . 3 B3
Knoll The S18 . . . . 98 B1
KNOLL TOP 3 C3
Knowle Cl S6 . . . . 49 A4
Knowle Croft S11 . . . . . . 71 C3
Knowle Ct S11 . . . . 72 A3
Knowle Gn S17 . . . . 82 A1
Knowle La S11 . . . . 71 B3
Knowle Rd S5 . . . . 28 B4
Knowles Ave S36 . . . . 3 C2
KNOWLE TOP 49 A4
Knowle Top S20 . . . . 90 C1
Knutton Cres S5 . . . . 15 B1
Knutton Rd S5 . . . . 27 C4
Knutton Rise S5 . . . . 15 B1
Kyle Cl S5 . . . . 27 C2
Kyle Cres S5 . . . . 27 C2
Kynance Cres S60 . . . . . . 46 A1

Laburnum Ave S66 . . . . . 36 B4
Laburnum Cl S35 . . . . 7 B2
Laburnum Gr
 Killamarsh S21 . . . . 92 A1
 Stocksbridge S36 . . . . 3 A2
Laceby Cl S66 . . . . 25 A1
Ladies Spring Ct S17 . . . 83 B1
Ladies Spring Dr S17 . . . 83 B1
Ladies Spring Gr S17 . . . 83 B1

Ladybank Rd S20 . . . . . 103 A4
Lady Bank View S21 . . . . 103 A2
Ladybower Ct ⑦ S17 . . . 95 B3
Lady Ida's Dr
 Eckington S21 . . . . 102 C2
 Sheffield S21 . . . . 102 C3
Lady Oak Rd S65 . . . . 22 C2
Lady's Bridge S3 . . . . . . 106 B4
Ladysmith Ave S7 . . . . . . 72 C4
Laird Ave S6 . . . . 39 B3
Laird Dr S6 . . . . 39 B3
Laird Rd S6 . . . . 39 B3
Lakeside Cl S6 . . . . 24 C2
Lambcroft La S13 . . . . . . 78 B4
Lambcroft View S13 . . . . 78 B4
Lamb Dr S5 . . . . 27 A1
Lambert St S3 . . . . 106 A4
Lamb Hill Cl S13 . . . . 65 B1
Lamb Rd S5 . . . . 27 A1
Lancaster Rd S36 . . . . 3 A3
Lancaster St S3 . . . . 52 A3
Lancing Rd
 Sheffield, Highfield
 S2 . . . . 62 B2
 Sheffield S2 . . . . 62 C3
Landseer Cl
 ④ Dronfield S18 . . . . 100 A3
 Sheffield S14 . . . . 86 B4
Landseer Ct S66 . . . . 36 B4
Landseer Dr S14 . . . . 86 C4
Landseer Pl S14 . . . . 86 C4
Landseer Wlk S14 . . . . . . 86 C4
LANE END 7 B4
Lane End S35 . . . . 7 B4
Lane End Rd S60 . . . . 34 A1
Lane End View S60 . . . . . 34 A1
Lane Head Cl S62 . . . . . . 12 B4
Lane Head Rd S17 . . . . . . 94 A2
Lanes The S65 . . . . 22 B1
Langdale Dr S18 . . . . 98 A1
Langdale Rd S8 . . . . 73 A3
Langdon Rd S61 . . . . 19 B2
Langdon St S11 . . . . 62 A2
Langdon Wlk S61 . . . . . . 19 B2
Langley Cl S5 . . . . 23 A1
Langsett Ave S6 . . . . 26 A1
Langsett Cl S6 . . . . 40 B1
Langsett Cres S6 . . . . . . 40 B1
Langsett Gr S6 . . . . 51 B4
Langsett Rd S6 . . . . 40 B1
Langsett Rd N
 Oughtibridge S35 . . . . . 13 B4
 Wharncliffe Side S35 . . . 13 B4
Langsett Rd S S35 . . . . . 13 C2
Langsett Rise S6 . . . . 40 B1
Langsett Wlk S6 . . . . 40 B1
Lansbury Ave S35 . . . . 7 A3
Lansbury Ct S21 . . . . 103 A3
Lansdowne Rd ⑥ S11 . . 62 A3
Lapwater Rd S61 . . . . 10 A3
Lapwater Wlk S61 . . . . . . 10 A3
Lapwing Vale S61 . . . . 9 B4
Larch Ave
 Killamarsh S21 . . . . 92 A1
 Rotherham S66 . . . . 36 C3
Larch Gr
 Aston S26 . . . . 70 A2
 Chapeltown S35 . . . . 7 B2
Larch Hill S9 . . . . 55 C1
Larch Mews S65 . . . . 22 B2
Lark Ave S60 . . . . 46 B2
Larkhill Cl S62 . . . . 12 B1
Lark St S6 . . . . 50 C4
Latham Sq S11 . . . . 71 A3
Lathe Rd S60 . . . . 35 A1
Lathkill Cl S13 . . . . 65 A1
Lathkill Rd S13 . . . . 65 A1
Lauder St S4 . . . . 42 C4
Laudsdale Cl S65 . . . . . . 23 A2
Laudsdale Rd S65 . . . . . . 23 A2
Laughton Rd S9 . . . . 43 C4
Launce Rd S5 . . . . 27 C2
Laurel Ave S66 . . . . 37 A3
Laurel Ct S10 . . . . 60 C3
Laurel Dr S21 . . . . 92 A1
Laurel Ho S10 . . . . 60 A2
Laverack St S13 . . . . 66 A3
Laverdene Ave S17 . . . . . 95 B2
Laverdene Cl S17 . . . . . . 94 C2
Laverdene Dr S17 . . . . . . 95 A2
Laverdene Rd S17 . . . . . . 94 C2
Laverdene Way S17 . . . . 95 A2

Laverock Way S5 . . . . 29 A3
Lavinia Rd S35 . . . . 15 B2
Lawns The S11 . . . . 72 A4
Lawn The S18 . . . . 101 A4
Lawrence Cl S6 . . . . 36 B3
Lawrence St S9 . . . . 54 A4
Lawson Rd S10 . . . . 61 A4
Lawton La S60 . . . . 33 C1
Laxey Rd S6 . . . . 49 C3
Laycock Ave S26 . . . . 69 C1
Leabrook Rd S18 . . . . 99 B3
Leadbeater Dr S12 . . . . . 75 C3
Leadbeater Rd S12 . . . . . 75 C2
Leader Ct S6 . . . . 39 C3
Leader Rd S6 . . . . 39 C3
Leadmill Point S1 . . . . . 107 B2
Leadmill Rd
 Sheffield, Highfield
 S2 . . . . 107 B1
 Sheffield S1, S2 . . . . . . 107 B2
Leadmill St S1 . . . . 107 B2
Leake Rd S6 . . . . 40 A4
Leamington St S10 . . . . . 51 A2
Lea Rd S18 . . . . 100 C3
Lease Gate Rd S60 . . . . . 47 C4
Lea The S20 . . . . 90 B4
Leaton Cl S6 . . . . 38 B3
Leavy Greave ④ S10 . . 105 B3
Leavygreave Rd S3 . . . . 104 B3
Leawood Pl S6 . . . . 49 B4
Ledsham Rd S60 . . . . 34 A2
Ledstone Rd S8 . . . . 73 A2
Lee Ave S36 . . . . 3 C3
Leebrook Ave S20 . . . . . . 89 C3
Leebrook Ct S20 . . . . 89 C3
Leebrook Dr S20 . . . . 89 C3
Leebrook Rd S20 . . . . 89 C3
Lee Croft S1 . . . . 106 A4
Leedham Cl S5 . . . . 29 C2
Leedham Rd
 Rotherham S65 . . . . 35 A2
 Sheffield S5 . . . . 29 C2
Leeds Rd S9 . . . . 54 B4
Lee House La S36 . . . . 2 C2
Lee Rd S6 . . . . 38 B3
Lees Hall Ave S8 . . . . 74 A3
Lees Hall Pl S8 . . . . 74 A3
Lees Hall Rd S8 . . . . 74 A2
Lees House Ct S8 . . . . . . 73 C2
Lees Nook S8 . . . . 73 C2
Legh Dr S26 . . . . 69 C1
Leicester Way S9 . . . . . . 43 B1
Leighton Dr S14 . . . . 75 B1
Leighton Pl S14 . . . . 75 B1
Leighton Rd S14 . . . . 75 A2
Leighton View S14 . . . . . 75 A3
Lemont Rd S17 . . . . 94 C2
Lengdale Ct S62 . . . . 12 A3
Lennox Rd S6 . . . . 39 C3
Lenthall Inf Sch S18 . . . . 97 C1
Lenton St S2 . . . . 107 B1
Leonard Cl S2 . . . . 64 B1
Leopold St S1 . . . . 106 A3
Leppings La S6 . . . . 40 A4
Lescar La S11 . . . . 61 A2
Leslie Rd S6 . . . . 39 C3
Letard Dr S60 . . . . 46 A3
Letsby Ave S9 . . . . 55 C4
Leverton Dr S11 . . . . 62 A3
Leverton Gdns S11 . . . . . 62 A3
Leverton Way S65 . . . . . . 23 B3
Leveson St S4 . . . . 53 B3
Lewis Rd S13 . . . . 65 A1
Leybourne Rd S61 . . . . . . 19 B3
Leyburn Dr S26 . . . . 69 A2
Leyburn Gr S35 . . . . 7 B4
Leyburn Rd S8 . . . . 73 B4
Leyfield Rd S17 . . . . 82 B1
Liberty Cl S6 . . . . 49 C3
Liberty Dr S6 . . . . 49 C3
Liberty Hill S6 . . . . 49 C3
Liberty La S6 . . . . 49 C3
Liberty Pl S6 . . . . 49 C3
Liberty Rd S6 . . . . 49 C3
Library Cl S61 . . . . 10 B1
Lichfield Way S60 . . . . . . 46 B2
Lichford Rd S2 . . . . 74 B4
Lidget Cl S26 . . . . 80 A4
Lidget La S65 . . . . 25 B1
Lifestyle Ho ④ S10 . . . . 61 A4
Lifford St S9 . . . . 31 B1
LIGHTWOOD 87 A2

Lightwood House Hospl
 S8 . . . . 86 C3
Lightwood La S8 . . . . 87 A3
Lilac Ave S36 . . . . 3 A2
Lilac Farm Cl S66 . . . . . . 36 B2
Lilac Gr S66 . . . . 36 C3
Lilac Rd
 Sheffield, Beighton
 S20 . . . . 79 B1
 Sheffield, High Wincobank
 S5 . . . . 29 B1
Lilian St S60 . . . . 33 B3
Lilian St S60 . . . . 33 B3
Limb La S17 . . . . 82 B3
Limbrick Cl S6 . . . . 40 A1
Limbrick Rd S6 . . . . 40 A1
Lime Cl S65 . . . . 25 A4
Lime Gr
 Chapeltown S35 . . . . 7 B2
 Stocksbridge S36 . . . . 3 A2
Limegrove S60 . . . . 34 C2
Lime St
 Sheffield, Beighton
 S20 . . . . 79 B2
 Sheffield S6 . . . . 51 C4
Limes The S66 . . . . 34 A2
Limestone Cottage La
 S6 . . . . 26 B2
Lime Tree Ave S21 . . . . . 92 A1
Lime Tree Cres S62 . . . . 12 C4
Limpsfield Jun Sch
 S9 . . . . 43 B4
Limpsfield Rd S9 . . . . 43 B4
Linaker Rd S8 . . . . 50 C3
Linburn Rd S8 . . . . 85 A4
Lincoln St
 Rotherham S60 . . . . 21 A2
 Sheffield S9 . . . . 43 C4
Lincroft Dr S62 . . . . 12 B1
Linden Ave
 Dronfield S18 . . . . 97 C1
 Rotherham S66 . . . . 36 C4
 Sheffield S8 . . . . 84 C4
Linden Cres S36 . . . . 3 A3
Linden Ct
 Sheffield, Ecclesfield
 S35 . . . . 16 B3
 Sheffield, Meadow Head
 S8 . . . . 84 C4
Linden Rd S35 . . . . 16 B3
Lindholme Gdns S20 . . . . 90 A4
Lindisfarne Rd S18 . . . . 101 A2
Lindley Rd S5 . . . . 42 B4
Lindley St S65 . . . . 21 B2
Lindsay Ave S28 . . . . 28 B3
Lindsay Cl S5 . . . . 28 B3
Lindsay Cres S5 . . . . 28 B3
Lindsay Dr S5 . . . . 28 B3
Lindsay Pl S25 . . . . 69 B1
Lindsay Rd S5 . . . . 28 B3
Lindum Dr S66 . . . . 36 C2
Lindum Terr ① S65 . . . . 33 B4
Lingfield Cl S66 . . . . 37 B2
Lingfoot Ave S8 . . . . 97 C4
Lingfoot Cl S8 . . . . 97 C4
Lingfoot Cres S8 . . . . . . 98 A4
Lingfoot Dr S8 . . . . 98 A4
Lingfoot Pl S8 . . . . 97 C4
Lingfoot Wlk S8 . . . . 98 A4
Lings La S66 . . . . 36 C2
Lings The S66 . . . . 37 B2
Link Rd S65 . . . . 24 A4
Link Row ① S2 . . . . . . 106 C4
Links Rd S18 . . . . 101 A2
Linkswood Rd S65 . . . . . . 23 A3
Linley La S12, S13 . . . . . . 77 A3
Linnet Mount S61 . . . . 9 A3
Linscott Rd S8 . . . . 84 C4
Lipp Ave S21 . . . . 92 A3
Lisle Rd S60 . . . . 34 A2
Lismore Rd S8 . . . . 74 A3
Lister Ave S12 . . . . 76 A1
Lister Cl S12 . . . . 76 A1
Lister Cres S12 . . . . 76 A1
Lister La S13 . . . . 104 C5
Lister Pl S12 . . . . 76 A1
Lister Rd S6 . . . . 40 A1
Lister St S65 . . . . 33 C4

Lister Way S12 . . . . 76 A1
Little Attercliffe Rd S9 . . 54 C3
Little Common La
 Rotherham, Kimberworth
 S61 . . . . 19 A1
 Rotherham, Whiston
 S60 . . . . 48 C3
 Sheffield S11 . . . . 71 B1
Littledale Rd S9 . . . . 65 A4
Little La
 Sheffield, Grimesthorpe
 S4 . . . . 43 A3
 Sheffield, Woodthorpe
 Estate S12 . . . . 76 A4
 Wentworth S61 . . . . 8 C4
Little London Pl S8 . . . . . 73 B4
Little London Rd S8 . . . . 73 B3
Little Matlock Gdns
 S6 . . . . 49 B4
Little Matlock Way S6 . . 49 B4
Littlemoor S21 . . . . 103 B2
Littlemoor Bsns Ctr
 S21 . . . . 103 B2
LITTLE NORTON 85 B2
Little Norton Ave S8 . . . . 85 B2
Little Norton Dr S8 . . . . . 85 B2
Little Norton La S8 . . . . . 85 B2
Little Norton Way S8 . . . 85 B1
LITTLE SHEFFIELD 62 A3
Little Wood Dr S12 . . . . . 75 C1
Little Wood Rd S12 . . . . . 75 C1
Liverpool St S9 . . . . 43 B1
Livingstone Rd S35 . . . . . 6 C3
Livingston Rd S9 . . . . . . 53 C4
Lloyd St
 Rawmarsh S62 . . . . 12 A1
 Sheffield S4 . . . . 42 C3
Loakfield Dr S5 . . . . 15 C1
Lock House Rd S9 . . . . . . 44 A3
Lock La S9 . . . . 31 B1
Lock St S6 . . . . 51 C4
Lockton Cl S35 . . . . 5 A2
Lockwood Cl S65 . . . . 22 C1
Lockwood Rd S65 . . . . . . 22 C1
Lodge La
 Aston S26 . . . . 69 B1
 Rotherham S61 . . . . 9 A1
 Sheffield S10, S6 . . . . . . 58 B4
Lodge Moor Rd S10 . . . . 58 A2
Lodge The S11 . . . . 71 C3
Lodge Way S60 . . . . 46 A3
Logan Rd S9 . . . . 55 B2
Loicher La S35 . . . . 17 A3
Lomas Cl S6 . . . . 38 A1
Lomas Lea S6 . . . . 49 A4
London Rd S2 . . . . 62 A2
London Rd S S2 . . . . 62 B1
London Way S61 . . . . 8 C2
Longacre Cl S20 . . . . 91 B3
Longacre Rd S18 . . . . . . 100 C1
Long Acre View S20 . . . . 91 B2
Longacre Way S20 . . . . . 91 C3
Longcroft Ave S18 . . . . . 99 B4
Longcroft Cl S18 . . . . . . 99 B4
Longcroft Cres S18 . . . . . 99 B4
Longcroft Rd S18 . . . . . . 99 B4
Longfellow Dr S65 . . . . . 34 B3
Longfield Dr S65 . . . . 25 A2
Longfield Rd S10 . . . . 50 C3
Longford Cl S17 . . . . 95 B3
Longford Cres S17 . . . . . 95 B3
Longford Dr S17 . . . . 95 A2
Longford Rd S17 . . . . 95 B2
Longford Spinney S17 . . 95 A2
Long Henry Row S2 . . . 107 C3
Long La
 Killamarsh S21 . . . . 93 A3
 Oughtibridge S35 . . . . . 13 A3
 Rotherham S60 . . . . 47 B1
 Sheffield, Loxley S6,
 S35 . . . . 38 B4
 Sheffield S10 . . . . 50 A4
 Stocksbridge S36 . . . . . . 2 A2
Longley Ave W S5 . . . . . . 41 A4
Longley Cl S5 . . . . 41 C4
Longley Cres S5 . . . . 28 B1
Longley Dr S5 . . . . 41 A4
LONGLEY ESTATE 28 B1
Longley Farm View
 S5 . . . . 41 C4

Longley Hall Gr S5 . . . . 42 A4
Longley Hall Rd S5 . . . . 42 A4
Longley Hall Rise S5 . . . . . . 28 B1
Longley Hall Way S5 . . . . . . 42 A4
Longley La S5 . . . . 28 B1
Longley Park Sixth Form
 Coll S5 . . . . 28 C1
Longley Prim Sch S5 . . . . 41 B4
Longstone Cres S12 . . . . . . 76 C2
Longwood Cl S66 . . . . 24 B2
Lonsdale Rd S6 . . . . 40 A1
Loosemore Dr S12 . . . . 75 B3
Lopham Cl S4 . . . . 53 B4
Lopham St S3 . . . . 52 C3
Lord St S65 . . . . 22 A1
Lorne Cl S18 . . . . 99 C4
Louden Cl S61 . . . . 18 B4
Louden Rd S61 . . . . 18 B4
Lound Inf Sch S35 . . . . 7 A4
Lound Jun Sch S35 . . . . 7 B4
Lound Rd S9 . . . . 55 B1
Lound Side S35 . . . . 7 B3
Louth Rd S11 . . . . 60 C2
Lovell Rd S4 . . . . 53 B3
Love St S3 . . . . 106 A4
Lovetot Ave S26 . . . . 69 B2
Lovetot Rd
 Rotherham S61 . . . . 19 B4
 Sheffield S9 . . . . 53 C3
Lowburn Rd S13 . . . . 65 A1
LOWEDGES 97 B4
Low Edges S8 . . . . 97 B4
Lowedges Cres S8 . . . . 97 A4
Lowedges Dr S8 . . . . 97 A4
Lowedges Pl S8 . . . . 97 B4
Lowedges Prim Sch
 S8 . . . . 96 C4
Lowedges Rd S8 . . . . 96 C4
LOWER BRADWAY 96 A4
LOWER CRABTREE 42 A2
Lower Meadow Prim Sch
 S8 . . . . 97 B3
LOWER WALKLEY 40 A1
LOWFIELD 62 C2
Lowfield Ave
 Eckington S12 . . . . 88 C2
 Rotherham S61 . . . . 11 A1
Lowfield Com Prim Sch
 S2 . . . . 62 B1
Lowfield Ct 4 S2 . . . . 62 B1
Lowgreave S65 . . . . 22 C2
Lowhouse Rd S5 . . . . 17 B1
Low La S61 . . . . 20 A2
Low Matlock La S6 . . . . . . 38 C2
Low Rd
 Oughtibridge S35 . . . . 13 B3
 Sheffield S6 . . . . 50 B4
Low Riddings S66 . . . . 36 C4
Lowry Dr S18 . . . . 100 B3
Lowther Rd S6 . . . . 40 B3
LOW WINCOBANK 30 A2
LOXLEY 38 B3
Loxley Ct
 Rotherham S60 . . . . 47 A4
 Sheffield, Loxley S6 . . . . . 39 A3
 Sheffield S6 . . . . 40 A1
Loxley New Rd S6 . . . . 39 C1
Loxley Pk S6 . . . . 39 B1
Loxley Prim Sch S6 . . . . . . 38 C3
Loxley Rd S6 . . . . 38 C2
Loxley View Rd S10 . . . . . . 50 C3
Loy Cl S61 . . . . 10 B1
Lucas St S4 . . . . 42 A1
Lucknow Ct S7 . . . . 73 A4
Ludlam Ho S2 . . . . 75 A4
Luke La S6 . . . . 39 A3
Lumley St
 Sheffield S4, S9 . . . . 53 B2
 Sheffield S9 . . . . 54 A2
Lump La S35 . . . . 14 C3
Luna Croft S12 . . . . 87 A4
Lund Rd S35 . . . . 13 B1
Lundwood Cl S20 . . . . 90 A4
Lundwood Dr S20 . . . . 90 A4
Lundwood Gr S20 . . . . 90 A4
Lundy Rd S18 . . . . 101 A2
Lupton Cres S8 . . . . 97 A4
Lupton Dr S8 . . . . 97 A4
Lupton Rd S8 . . . . 97 A4

Lupton Wlk S8 . . . . 97 B4
Luterel Dr S26 . . . . 69 B2
Lyceum Theatre ★
 S1 . . . . 107 B3
LYDGATE 50 B1
Lydgate Ct S10 . . . . 50 C1
Lydgate Hall Cres S10 . . . 50 B1
Lydgate Inf Sch S10 . . . . . 50 B1
Lydgate La S10 . . . . 60 B4
Lydgate La S10 . . . . 50 C1
Lyme St S60 . . . . 32 C4
Lyminster Rd S6 . . . . 27 A2
Lyminton La S60 . . . . 57 C2
Lymister Ave S60 . . . . 47 A3
Lyncroft Cl S60 . . . . 46 B2
Lyndhurst Cl S11 . . . . 72 B4
Lyndhurst Rd S11 . . . . 72 C4
Lynmouth Rd S7 . . . . 73 A3
Lynn Pl S9 . . . . 43 C2
Lynton Ave S60 . . . . 34 B1
Lynton Rd 9 S11 . . . . 61 B2
Lynwood Cl 1 S18 . . . . 99 C3
Lyons Rd S4 . . . . 42 A1
Lyons St S4 . . . . 42 B1
Lytton Ave S5 . . . . 27 B3
Lytton Cres S5 . . . . 27 B3
Lytton Ct S5 . . . . 27 C3
Lytton Dr S5 . . . . 27 C3
Lytton Rd S5 . . . . 27 B3

M

Mabel St S60 . . . . 33 C3
Machin La S36 . . . . 2 A4
Machins Ct S18 . . . . 100 C4
Machon Bank S7 . . . . 73 A4
Machon Bank Rd S7 . . . . . . 73 A4
McIntyre Rd S36 . . . . 3 A3
Mackenzie Cres
 Chapeltown S35 . . . . 6 C2
 Sheffield S10 . . . . 105 B2
Mackenzie St S11 . . . . 61 C2
Madehurst Gdns S2 . . . . . . 62 C1
Madehurst Rd S2 . . . . 62 C1
Madehurst Rise S2 . . . . . . 62 C1
Madehurst View S2 . . . . . . 62 C1
Mafeking Pl S35 . . . . 7 B4
Magna Cl S66 . . . . 36 B4
Magna Cres S66 . . . . 36 A4
Magna La S65 . . . . 23 B3
Magna Science
 Adventure Pk ★ S60 . . . 31 C2
Magnolia Ct S10 . . . . 59 C2
Magpie Gr S2 . . . . 63 C4
Mahon Ave S62 . . . . 12 A4
Maidstone Rd S6 . . . . 27 A2
Main Ave S17 . . . . 94 C2
Main Rd
 Dronfield S18 . . . . 99 A3
 Eckington, Ridgeway
  S12 . . . . 88 C2
 Sheffield, Darnall S9 . . . . 55 A2
 Sheffield, Handsworth Hill
  S9 . . . . 55 B2
Main St
 Aston, Aughton S26 . . . . . 69 A4
 Aston, Swallownest
  S26 . . . . 69 A1
 Catliffe S60 . . . . 57 B4
 Ravenfield S65 . . . . 25 A4
 Rawmarsh S62 . . . . 12 B4
 Rotherham, Bramley
  S66 . . . . 37 A3
 Rotherham, Greasbrough
  S61 . . . . 11 A1
 Rotherham S60 . . . . 33 A4
 Sheffield, Grenoside
  S35 . . . . 14 C2
 Sheffield, Hackenthorpe
  S12 . . . . 78 A1
 Sheffield S35 . . . . 14 C3
Mair Ct S60 . . . . 47 B3
Malham Gdns S20 . . . . 90 B1
Malham Gr S20 . . . . 90 C1
Malham Pl S35 . . . . 7 A4
MALINBRIDGE 39 B1
Malin Bridge Prim Sch
 S6 . . . . 39 C2
Malinda St S3 . . . . 104 C5
Malinder Cl S21 . . . . 92 B2
Malin Rd
 Rotherham S65 . . . . 23 A2

Malin Rd continued
 Sheffield S6 . . . . 39 B1
Mallard Cl S61 . . . . 9 B3
Mallard Dr S21 . . . . 91 C1
Mallory Ave S62 . . . . 11 C4
Mallory Rd S65 . . . . 22 C2
Maltby St S9 . . . . 43 B1
Maltings The
 Rotherham S60 . . . . 33 A3
 4 Sheffield S11 . . . . 105 C1
Maltkiln St S60 . . . . 33 A3
Malton Dr S26 . . . . 69 C1
Malton St S4 . . . . 42 A1
Maltravers Cl S2 . . . . 63 C4
Maltravers Cres S2 . . . . . . 53 C1
Maltravers Pl S2 . . . . 53 C1
Maltravers Rd S2 . . . . 53 C1
Maltravers Terr S2 . . . . 63 C4
Maltravers Way S2 . . . . 53 C1
Malvern Dr S66 . . . . 24 B1
Malvern Rd S9 . . . . 54 C3
Malvern Way S66 . . . . 24 B1
Manchester Rd
 Sheffield S10, S6 . . . . 49 B1
 Stocksbridge S36 . . . . 3 B3
Mandeville St S9 . . . . 55 A3
Mangham Rd S61, S62 . . . 21 B4
Mangham Way S61 . . . . . . 21 A3
Manners St S3 . . . . 52 A4
Manor App S61 . . . . 19 C1
Manor Bglws S18 . . . . 100 B3
Manor Cres
 Brinsworth S60 . . . . 45 C2
 Dronfield S18 . . . . 100 B3
Manor Ct S65 . . . . 23 A2
Manor Dev Ctr S9 . . . . 64 C3
Manor Dr S60 . . . . 48 A3
MANOR ESTATE 64 C2
Manor Farm Cl S26 . . . . . . 69 B4
Manor Farm Ct
 Killamarsh S21 . . . . 92 B1
 4 Sheffield S20 . . . . 79 C1
Manor Farm Mews 2
 S20 . . . . 79 C1
Manor Fields S61 . . . . 19 B2
Manor Ho S6 . . . . 49 A4
Manor House Rd S61 . . . . 19 B2
Manor La S2 . . . . 64 A4
Manor Laith Rd S2 . . . . 64 A4
Manor Lodge Com Prim
 Sch S2 . . . . 63 C3
Manor Oaks Cl S2 . . . . 53 C1
Manor Oaks Ct S2 . . . . 53 B1
Manor Oaks Dr S2 . . . . 53 B1
Manor Oaks Gdns S2 . . . . 53 B1
Manor Oaks Pl S2 . . . . 63 C4
Manor Oaks Rd S2 . . . . 53 B1
MANOR PARK 64 A4
Manor Park Ave S2 . . . . . . 64 A3
Manor Park Cl S2 . . . . 64 A3
Manor Park Cres S2 . . . . . 64 A3
Manor Park Ct S2 . . . . 64 A4
Manor Park Ctr S2 . . . . 64 A4
Manor Park Dr S2 . . . . 64 A4
Manor Park Pl S2 . . . . 64 A4
Manor Park Rd S2 . . . . 64 A4
Manor Park Rise S2 . . . . . . 64 A4
Manor Park Way S2 . . . . . . 64 A3
Manor Pl S62 . . . . 12 B3
Manor Rd
 Brinsworth S60 . . . . 45 C2
 Killamarsh S21 . . . . 92 C1
Manor View S60 . . . . 90 C1
Manor Way S2 . . . . 54 A1
Mansel Ave S5 . . . . 27 B4
Mansel Cres S5 . . . . 27 A4
Mansel Ct S5 . . . . 27 B4
Mansel Prim Sch S5 . . . . . 15 B1
Mansel Rd S5 . . . . 27 A4
Mansfield Rd
 Aston S26 . . . . 81 B1
 Killamarsh S21 . . . . 93 A2
 Rotherham S60 . . . . 33 B4
 Sheffield S12 . . . . 76 A4
 Wales S26 . . . . 81 B1
Mansfield View S12 . . . . . . 76 A4
Manton St S2 . . . . 107 B1
Manvers Cl S26 . . . . 69 B1
Manvers Rd
 Aston S26 . . . . 69 A1
 Sheffield, Beighton S20 . . 79 B2

Manvers Rd continued
 Sheffield S6 . . . . 40 A1
Maplebeck Dr S9 . . . . 45 A4
Maplebeck Rd S9 . . . . 45 A4
Maple Croft Cres S9 . . . . . 30 A1
Maple Croft Rd S9 . . . . 29 C1
Maple Ct S62 . . . . 12 B3
Maple Dr
 Killamarsh S21 . . . . 92 A1
 Rotherham S66 . . . . 36 B4
Maple Gr
 Aston S26 . . . . 70 A2
 Sheffield S9 . . . . 55 C1
 Stocksbridge S36 . . . . 3 A2
Maple Pl S35 . . . . 7 B2
Maplewood Ave S66 . . . . . 24 B2
Mapperley Rd S18 . . . . 99 B3
Mappin Ct 8 S11 . . . . 105 C3
Mappin's Rd S60 . . . . 57 B3
Mappin St S1 . . . . 104 C3
Mapplebeck Rd S35 . . . . . . 5 C1
Marcham Dr S20 . . . . 79 C2
March Flatts Rd S65 . . . . . 24 A4
March St S9 . . . . 43 C1
Marchwood Ave S6 . . . . . . 49 C4
Marchwood Dr S6 . . . . 38 C1
Marchwood Rd S6 . . . . 38 C1
Marcliff Cl S66 . . . . 35 C2
Marcliff Cres S66 . . . . 35 C2
Marcliff La S66 . . . . 35 C2
Marden Rd S7 . . . . 73 A4
Margaret Cl S26 . . . . 80 C4
Margaret St S1 . . . . 107 A1
Margate Dr S4 . . . . 42 B2
Margate St S4 . . . . 42 C2
Margetson Cres S5 . . . . . . 27 C4
Margetson Dr S5 . . . . 27 C4
Margetson Rd S5 . . . . 27 C4
Marigold Cl S5 . . . . 29 B1
Marion Rd S6 . . . . 39 C4
Markbrook Dr S35 . . . . 5 A2
Market Pl
 Chapeltown S35 . . . . 7 C3
 Rotherham S60 . . . . 33 A4
 Sheffield S1 . . . . 106 B4
Market Sq
 9 Rotherham S65 . . . . . . 21 B1
 Sheffield S13 . . . . 78 B4
Market St
 Chapeltown S35 . . . . 7 C3
 Eckington S21 . . . . 103 B1
 Rotherham S60 . . . . 33 A4
 Sheffield S13 . . . . 78 B4
Markfield Dr S66 . . . . 36 B3
Mark Gr S66 . . . . 36 B3
Markham Terr S8 . . . . 73 B4
Marlborough Rd S10 . . . . 104 A3
Marlborough Rise
 S26 . . . . 81 A4
Marlcliffe Com Prim Sch
 S6 . . . . 39 C4
Marlcliffe Rd S6 . . . . 39 C4
Marlfield Croft S35 . . . . . . 16 B2
Marlow Cl S66 . . . . 37 A2
Marlowe Dr S65 . . . . 34 B3
Marlowe Rd S65 . . . . 34 B3
Marmion Rd S11 . . . . 60 C2
Marples Cl 7 S8 . . . . 62 A1
Marples Dr 8 S8 . . . . 62 A1
Marrick Ct S35 . . . . 7 A3
Marrion Rd S62 . . . . 12 B4
Marriott La S7 . . . . 72 C1
Marriott Rd S7 . . . . 72 C1
Marrison Dr S21 . . . . 90 A2
Marr Terr S10 . . . . 60 A3
Marsden La S3 . . . . 104 C4
Marsden Rd S36 . . . . 3 B3
Marshall Cl S62 . . . . 12 A2
Marshall Rd S8 . . . . 85 A4
Marsh Ave S18 . . . . 97 C1
Marsh Cl S20 . . . . 102 C3
Marsh House Rd S11 . . . . . 71 C3
Marsh La S10 . . . . 50 B1
Marsh St
 Rotherham S60 . . . . 33 B3
 Stocksbridge S36 . . . . 3 C3
Marsh Wlk S2 . . . . 53 B2
Marston Cl S18 . . . . 99 C2
Marstone Cres S17 . . . . . . 95 A3
Marston Rd S10 . . . . 50 C2
Martin S6 . . . . 104 B5
Martin Cl S26 . . . . 69 A4

Martin Cres S5 . . . . 28 B4
Martin Ct S21 . . . . 102 C1
Martin Rise
 Eckington S21 . . . . 102 C1
 Rotherham S61 . . . . 9 B4
Martin St S6 . . . . 104 B5
Maryfield S7 . . . . 73 A4
Maryhill Cl S60 . . . . 57 D2
Mary St
 Eckington S21 . . . . 103 A1
 5 Rotherham S60 . . . . . . 20 C1
 Sheffield S1 . . . . 107 A1
Marys Wlk S2 . . . . 53 B2
Mary Tozer Ho S10 . . . . . . 50 C1
MASBROUGH 32 B4
Masbrough St S60 . . . . 32 C4
Masefield Rd S13 . . . . 76 B4
Mason Ave S26 . . . . 69 B3
Mason Cres S13 . . . . 76 C4
Mason Dr S26 . . . . 69 B3
Mason Gr S13 . . . . 65 B1
Mason Lathe Rd S5 . . . . . . 29 B4
Massey Rd S13 . . . . 78 C3
Masters Cres S5 . . . . 28 B3
Masters Rd S5 . . . . 28 B3
Mather Ave S9 . . . . 54 C1
Mather Cres S9 . . . . 54 C1
Mather Ct S9 . . . . 54 C1
Mather Dr S9 . . . . 54 C1
Mather Rd S9 . . . . 54 C1
Mather Wlk S9 . . . . 54 C1
Matilda La S1 . . . . 107 B2
Matilda St S1 . . . . 107 A2
Matilda Way S1 . . . . 107 A2
Matlock Rd S6 . . . . 51 A3
Matthews Dr S66 . . . . 36 B1
Matthews Fold S8 . . . . 86 A3
Matthews La S8 . . . . 86 A3
Matthew St S3 . . . . 104 C5
Maugerhay S8 . . . . 86 A3
Mauncer Cres S13 . . . . 66 C1
Mauncer Dr S13 . . . . 66 C1
Mauncer La S13 . . . . 78 A4
Maun Way S5 . . . . 28 C1
Maurice St S62 . . . . 12 A1
Mawfa Ave S14 . . . . 86 B4
Mawfa Cres S14 . . . . 86 B4
Mawfa Dr S14 . . . . 86 B4
Mawfa Rd S14 . . . . 86 B4
Mawfa Wlk S14 . . . . 86 B4
Maxey Pl S8 . . . . 73 C4
Maxfield Ave S10 . . . . 51 A1
Maxwell St S4 . . . . 53 A4
Maxwell Way S4 . . . . 53 A4
Maycock Ave S61 . . . . 19 A4
Mayfield Ct S10 . . . . 59 A2
Mayfield Hts S10 . . . . 59 B3
Mayflower Ct S12 . . . . 76 A4
Maynard Rd S60 . . . . 48 A4
May Rd S6 . . . . 39 C2
May Tree Cl S20 . . . . 90 C3
May Tree Croft 8
 S20 . . . . 90 C3
May Tree La S20 . . . . 90 C3
Meadow Bank Ave S7 . . . . 61 B1
Meadowbank Cl S61 . . . . . 32 A4
Meadow Bank Rd
 Rotherham S61 . . . . 31 B3
 Sheffield S11 . . . . 61 B1
Meadowbrook Ind Est
 S20 . . . . 91 B2
Meadow Cl
 Dronfield S18 . . . . 98 A2
 Rotherham S65 . . . . 23 B3
Meadowcourt S9 . . . . 43 C4
Meadow Cres S20 . . . . 89 C3
Meadowcroft Cl S60 . . . . . 47 C2
Meadowcroft Gdns
 S20 . . . . 90 C2
Meadowcroft Glade
 S20 . . . . 90 C2
Meadowcroft Rise 2
 S20 . . . . 90 C2
Meadow Dr S35 . . . . 6 C3
Meadow Gate Ave
 S20 . . . . 91 C4
Meadow Gate Cl S20 . . . . 91 C4
Meadow Gate La S20 . . . . 91 C4
Meadowgate Pk S21 . . . . . 92 B2
Meadow Gr S17 . . . . 94 C2
Meadow Grove Rd
 S17 . . . . 94 B3

MEADOWHALL 30 C1
Meadowhall Ctr S9. . . . . . 44 A4
Meadowhall Dr S9. . . . . . 43 C4
Meadowhall
(Interchange) Sta
S9 . . . . 30 C1
Meadowhall Jun Sch
S61. . . . . 31 B4
Meadowhall Rd
Rotherham S61. . . . . 31 A3
Sheffield S9 . . . . 43 C4
Meadowhall Ret Pk
S9 . . . . 44 A2
Meadowhall Riverside
Ind Est S9. . . . . 30 B1
Meadowhall Way S9 . . . . 44 A4
Meadowhead S8 . . . . 85 A2
MEADOW HEAD 84 C3
Meadow Head Ave S8. . . 85 A2
Meadow Head Cl S8 . . . . 84 C1
Meadow Head Dr S8. . . . 85 A2
Meadowhead Sch S8. . . . 85 B1
Meadow House Dr
S10. . . . . 59 B3
Meadow St
Rotherham S61. . . . . 32 A4
Sheffield S3 . . . . 104 C4
Meadows The S21 . . . . . . 92 B2
Meadow Terr 5 S11 . . . . 61 A2
Meadow View Dr S65 . . . 25 B2
Meadow View Rd S8 . . . . 85 A2
Meads The S8 . . . . 85 C2
Meadway Dr S17 . . . . 82 B1
Meadway The S17 . . . . . . 82 B1
Medhomes S65. . . . . 21 C1
Medlock Cl S13. . . . . 66 B3
Medlock Cres S13. . . . . . 66 B4
Medlock Croft S13. . . . . . 66 B4
Medlock Dr S13. . . . . 66 B3
Medlock Rd S13. . . . . 66 B3
Medlock Way S13. . . . . . 66 B4
MEERSBROOK 74 A3
Meersbrook Ave S8. . . . . 73 B3
MEERSBROOK BANK. . . 73 C3
Meersbrook Bank Prim
Sch S8. . . . . 73 B3
Meersbrook Park Rd
S8 . . . . 73 C3
Meersbrook Rd S8. . . . . . 74 A3
Meersbrook Works
S2 . . . . 73 C4
Meersdale S2 . . . . 74 A4
Meetinghouse Croft
S13 . . . . 78 B4
Meetinghouse La
Sheffield S1. . . . . 106 B4
Sheffield, Woodhouse
S13 . . . . 78 A4
Mekyll Cl S66. . . . . 36 B4
Melbeck Ct S35. . . . . 6 C3
Melbourne Ave
Aston S26. . . . . 69 C2
Dronfield S18 . . . . 99 A3
Sheffield S10 . . . . 61 A4
Melbourne Rd S36. . . . . . . 2 C3
Melbourn Rd S10. . . . . . . 51 A2
Melciss Rd S66. . . . . 36 A2
Melfort Glen S10 . . . . 49 C1
Mellington Cl S8 . . . . 86 A4
Mellor Lea Farm Chase
S35 . . . . 16 B4
Mellor Lea Farm Cl
S35 . . . . 16 B4
Mellor Lea Farm Dr
S35 . . . . 16 B4
Mellor Lea Farm Garth
S35 . . . . 16 B4
Melrose Cotts S60. . . . . . 48 A3
Melrose Gr S60. . . . . 47 B4
Melrose Rd S3 . . . . 41 C1
Melton Ct S26. . . . . 70 B1
Melton Gr S20. . . . . 89 B4
Melville Dr S2. . . . . 64 B2
Mendip Rise S60 . . . . 46 B1
Merbeck Dr S5 . . . . 5 C3
Merbeck Gr S5 . . . . 5 C2
Merchants Cres S3 . . . . 106 B4
Mercia Dr S17. . . . . 94 C4
Meredith Rd S6 . . . . 39 C2
Merlin Way
Rotherham S61. . . . . 9 B4
Sheffield S5 . . . . 28 C1

Merton La S9. . . . . 30 B2
Merton Rd S9 . . . . 30 B2
Merton Rise S9. . . . . 30 B2
Metcalfe Ave S21 . . . . . . 92 A2
Methley Cl S12 . . . . 75 B4
Mews The S10 . . . . 60 A3
Meynell Com Prim Sch
S5. . . . . 27 B2
Meynell Cres S5 . . . . 27 A2
Meynell Rd S5. . . . . 27 A2
Meynell Way S21 . . . . . . 92 A2
MICKLEY 95 C1
Mickley La S17, S18 . . . . 95 A2
Middle Ave S62. . . . . 12 A4
Middlecliff Cl S20 . . . . . . 90 C3
Middlecliff Ct 2 S20 . . . . 90 C3
Middlecliff Rise 1
S20 . . . . 90 C3
Middle Dr S60. . . . . 47 A3
Middlefield Cl S17. . . . . . 82 A1
Middlefield Croft S17. . . . 82 A1
Middlefield Rd S60 . . . . . 47 C4
Middlefields Dr S60 . . . . 48 A3
Middle Hay Cl S14 . . . . . 75 A2
Middle Hay Pl S14 . . . . . 75 A2
Middle Hay Rise S14. . . . 75 A2
Middle Hay View S14. . . . 75 A2
Middle La
Rotherham S65. . . . . 34 A4
Sheffield, Grenoside
S35. . . . . 14 B3
Sheffield S6 . . . . 50 B4
Middle La S65 . . . . 34 A3
Middle Ox Cl S20 . . . . . 103 C4
Middle Ox Gdns S20 . . . 103 C4
Middle Pl S65 . . . . 22 B1
Middleton La S35. . . . . . 15 A2
Middleton Rd S65 . . . . . . 33 C4
Middlewood Chase
S6. . . . . 26 A1
Middlewood Dr
Rotherham S61. . . . . 18 C4
Sheffield S6 . . . . 26 A1
Middlewood Dr E S6. . . . 26 A1
Middlewood Rd S6 . . . . . 26 B1
Midfield Rd S10 . . . . 50 C2
Midhill Rd S2. . . . . 62 C1
Midhurst Rd S6. . . . . 26 B3
Midland Ct S60. . . . . 32 B4
Midland Rd S61 . . . . 23 C4
Midland St
Rotherham S62. . . . . 21 C4
Sheffield S1 . . . . 107 A1
Midland Sta S1. . . . . . . 107 B2
Midvale Ave S6. . . . . 51 C4
Midvale Cl S4 . . . . 51 C3
Milburn Cl S20 . . . . 91 B3
Milburn Gr S20. . . . . 91 B3
Milden Rd S6. . . . . 39 B4
Mile Oak Rd S60. . . . . . . 34 A1
Miles Cl S5 . . . . 41 B3
Miles Rd
Chapeltown S35 . . . . 5 C1
Sheffield S5 . . . . 41 B3
Milford St S9 . . . . 43 C2
Milgrove Cres S35 . . . . . . 5 B2
Millais Rise S66 . . . . 24 B1
Millbank Cl S5 . . . . 6 B4
Mill Cl S60 . . . . 32 C2
Mill Ct S35 . . . . 16 B3
Milldale Rd S17 . . . . 95 A3
Milldyke Cl S5. . . . . 48 B3
Miller Croft S13 . . . . 77 C4
Miller Dale Dr S60. . . . . . 46 B1
Miller Rd 6 S8 . . . . 62 A1
Miller St S13 . . . . 4 B3
Mill Hill S60. . . . . 48 A3
Millhouse Ct S65 . . . . . . 22 C3
MILLHOUSES 72 B1
Millhouses Ct S11. . . . . . 72 A2
Millhouses Glen S11. . . . 72 A2
Millhouses La S7, S11 . . 72 A2
Mill La
Dronfield S18 . . . . 101 A3
Sheffield S17 . . . . 95 A3
Stocksbridge S36 . . . . 4 B3
Treeton S60 . . . . 57 B2
Mill Meadow Cl S20 . . . . 91 C3
Mill Meadow Gdns
S20 . . . . 91 C3
Millmoor La S60. . . . . . . 32 B4

Millmoor (Rotherham
Utd FC) S60. . . . . 32 B4
Millmount Rd S7 . . . . 73 B3
Mill Rd
Eckington S21. . . . . 103 B2
Sheffield S35 . . . . 16 B3
Treeton S60 . . . . 57 B2
Mill Road Cl S35 . . . . 16 B3
Millsands S3 . . . . 106 A4
Mill St
Rotherham, Greasbrough
S61 . . . . 10 C2
Rotherham S60. . . . . 33 A3
Millstone Cl 1 S18 . . . . . 99 C4
Millstone Dr S26 . . . . 69 B1
Millthorpe Rd S5 . . . . 29 A2
Mill Wood View S6. . . . . 38 A1
Milner Cl S66. . . . . 37 B4
Milnrow Cres S5. . . . . . . 27 C4
Milnrow Dr S5. . . . . 27 C4
Milnrow Rd S5. . . . . 27 C4
Milnrow View S5. . . . . . . 27 C4
Milton Cl S61. . . . . 10 C2
Milton La S1 . . . . 105 C2
Milton Rd
Chapeltown S35 . . . . 6 B3
Rotherham S65. . . . . 21 C2
Sheffield S7 . . . . 62 A1
Milton St
Rotherham S60. . . . . 21 A2
Sheffield S1, S3 . . . . . . 105 C2
Minden Cl S66. . . . . 36 B2
Minna Rd S3 . . . . 41 C1
Minster Cl S35. . . . . 16 C2
Minster Rd S35. . . . . 16 B2
Minto Rd S6. . . . . 39 C2
Mitchell Rd S8 . . . . 85 A4
Mitchell St S3 . . . . 104 B4
Moat Cl S66. . . . . 24 C1
Moffatt Rd S2 . . . . 62 C1
Molineaux Cl S5. . . . . . . 29 A3
Molineaux Rd S5. . . . . . . 29 A3
Molloy Pl 12 S8. . . . . 73 C4
Molloy St 18 S8. . . . . 73 C4
Mona Ave S10 . . . . 51 A2
Mona Rd S10. . . . . 51 A2
Monckton Rd S5. . . . . . . 29 C1
Moncrieffe Rd S7. . . . . . . 73 A4
Monks Cl S66. . . . . 18 C4
Monmouth St S3 . . . . . . 105 B2
Montague St S11. . . . . . . 61 C3
Monteney Cres S5 . . . . . . 16 A2
Monteney Gdns S5 . . . . . 16 A1
Monteney Prim Sch
S5 . . . . 16 A1
Monteney Rd S5. . . . . . . 16 A2
Montfort Dr S7. . . . . 72 C1
Montgomery Ave S7. . . . 61 C1
Montgomery Ct S11. . . . . 71 C3
Montgomery Dr S7 . . . . . 61 C1
Montgomery Rd S7. . . . . 61 C1
Montgomery Terrace Rd
S6. . . . . 104 C5
Montrose Ct S11. . . . . . . 71 B2
Montrose Pl S18. . . . . . . 99 C4
Montrose Rd S7 . . . . 72 B3
Moonpenny Way
S18. . . . . 100 C3
Moonshine La S5. . . . . . . 27 C1
Moonshine Way S5 . . . . . 41 A4
Moorbank Cl S10. . . . . . . 59 B4
Moorbank Dr S10 . . . . . . 49 C1
Moorbank Rd S10 . . . . . . 49 B1
Moor Cres S20. . . . . 90 A1
Moorcroft Ave S10. . . . . . 58 C1
Moorcroft Cl S10 . . . . . . 58 C1
Moorcroft Dr S10. . . . . . . 58 C1
Moorcroft Rd S10. . . . . . . 58 C1
Moor End Rd S10. . . . . . . 51 A2
Moore St S3. . . . . 105 C1
Moor Farm Ave S20. . . . . 89 C2
Moor Farm Garth S20. . . 90 A2
Moor Farm Rise S20 . . . . 89 C2
Moorfield Ave S65. . . . . . 25 A1
Moorfield Cl S65. . . . . . . 25 A1
Moorfield Gr S65 . . . . 25 A1
Moorfields S3 . . . . 106 A4
Moorfields Flats S3. . . . 106 A4
Moorgate Ave
Rotherham S60. . . . . 33 B2
Sheffield S60 . . . . 104 A4

Moorgate Bsns Ctr
S60 . . . . 33 A3
Moorgate Chase S60. . . . 33 B3
Moorgate Cres S18 . . . . 101 A2
Moorgate Gr S60 . . . . . . 33 C2
Moorgate La S60 . . . . 33 B2
Moorgate Rd S60 . . . . . . 33 B2
Moorgate St S60. . . . . . . 33 A4
Moor Head S1 . . . . 107 A2
MOORHOLE 89 B3
Moorhouse Cl S60 . . . . . 48 B3
Moorhouse La S60. . . . . . 48 B3
Moor La N S65. . . . . 25 A3
Moorland Dr S36 . . . . 2 C3
Moorland Pl S6. . . . . 49 A4
Moorlands S66 . . . . 35 C2
Moorlands Cres S60 . . . . 48 B3
Moorland View
Aston S26. . . . . 69 C1
Sheffield S12 . . . . 87 B4
Moor La S65 . . . . 25 A1
Moor Oaks Rd S10 . . . . . 51 A1
Moor Rd S65 . . . . 34 B4
Moorside S10 . . . . 58 B2
Moorside Cl S20. . . . . . . 90 A2
Moorsyde Ave S10. . . . . . 50 C3
Moorsyde Cres S10 . . . . 50 C2
Moor The S1. . . . . 107 A2
Moorthorpe Dell S20. . . . 89 C3
Moorthorpe Gdns 2
S20 . . . . 89 B4
Moorthorpe Gn S20. . . . . 89 A4
Moorthorpe Rise S20 . . . 89 C3
Moorthorpe View S20. . . 89 C3
Moorthorpe Way
Sheffield, Birley S20. . . . 89 B4
Sheffield S20 . . . . 90 A4
Moor Valley S20 . . . . 89 B3
Moor Valley Cl S20. . . . . 89 B3
Moorview S61 . . . . 31 A4
Moorview Ct
Rotherham S61. . . . . 31 A4
2 Sheffield S17. . . . . 95 C3
Moor View Dr S8 . . . . 84 C4
Moor View Rd S8. . . . . . . 84 C4
Moor View Terr S11. . . . . 71 A3
Moorwinstow Croft
S17 . . . . 82 C1
Moorwoods Ave S35. . . . . 7 B3
Moorwoods La S35 . . . . . 7 B3
Moray Pl S18. . . . . 99 C4
Mordaunt Rd S2 . . . . 75 B4
Morgan Ave S5. . . . . 27 B1
Morgan Cl S5 . . . . 27 C1
Morgan Rd S5. . . . . 41 A4
Morland Cl S14. . . . . 75 B1
Morland Dr S14 . . . . 75 B1
Morland Pl S14 . . . . 75 B1
Morland Rd S14 . . . . 75 B1
Morley Cl S18 . . . . 99 B3
Morley Rd S61. . . . . 19 B3
Morley St
Rawmarsh S62. . . . . 12 A2
Sheffield S3 . . . . 40 A1
Morpeth Gdns S3. . . . . . 104 C4
Morpeth St
Rotherham S65. . . . . 33 B4
Sheffield S3 . . . . 104 C4
Morrall Rd S5. . . . . 16 A1
Mortain Rd S60. . . . . 47 A4
Morthen Rd S66. . . . . 36 C1
Mortimer St S1 . . . . 107 B2
Mortlake Rd S5 . . . . 42 B4
MORTOMLEY 5 C1
Mortomley Cl S35. . . . . . . 5 C1
Mortomley Hall Gdns
S35 . . . . 5 C2
Mortomley La S35 . . . . . . 5 C1
Morton Gdns S20. . . . . . 103 C4
Morton Mount S20 . . . . . 91 A1
Morton Pl S35. . . . . 14 C2
MOSBOROUGH 90 B1
Mosborough Hall Dr
S20 . . . . 103 A4
Mosborough Hall Farm
S20 . . . . 103 A4
Mosborough Moor
S20 . . . . 90 A1
Mosborough Prim Sch
Sheffield S20 . . . . 90 A1
Sheffield S20 . . . . 90 B1
Mosborough Rd S13 . . . . 64 C1

Moscrop Cl S13 . . . . 67 A1
Mossbrook Ct S21 . . . . . 103 B2
Mossbrook Sch S8 . . . . . 86 A2
Moss Cl S66 . . . . 36 B2
Mossdale Ave S20 . . . . . 90 B1
Moss Dr S21. . . . . 90 B1
Moss Gr S12. . . . . 78 C1
Moss Rise Pl S21 . . . . . 102 C1
Moss View S20 . . . . 102 C4
Moss Way S20 . . . . 90 A1
Motehall Dr S2 . . . . 64 B3
Motehall Pl S2 . . . . 64 C3
Motehall Rd S2. . . . . 64 C3
Motehall Way S2 . . . . . . 64 B3
Motehall Wlk 2 S2. . . . . 64 C3
Motte The S61 . . . . 19 C2
Mountbatten Dr S35. . . . . 6 B3
Mountenoy Rd S60 . . . . . 33 B3
Mountford Croft S17. . . . 94 C3
Mount Pleasant S35 . . . . . 7 B4
Mount Pleasant Cl S35 . . 7 B4
Mount Pleasant Rd
Rotherham S61. . . . . 20 B1
Sheffield S11 . . . . 62 A2
Mount Rd
Chapeltown S35 . . . . 6 C3
Sheffield S3 . . . . 41 A1
Mount St
Rotherham S61. . . . . 20 B1
Sheffield S11 . . . . 62 A3
Mount The S66 . . . . 24 B1
Mount View Ave S8 . . . . 73 C1
Mount View Gdns S8 . . . 73 C1
Mount View Lodge 2
S8. . . . . 73 C1
Mount View Rd S8 . . . . . 74 A1
Mousehole Cl S65 . . . . . . 23 B3
Mousehole La S65 . . . . . 23 B3
Mowbray Gdns S65 . . . . 22 C2
Mowbray Pl S65 . . . . 22 C2
Mowbray St
Rotherham S65. . . . . 22 C2
Sheffield S3 . . . . 52 B3
Mowson Cres S35 . . . . . 13 B1
Mowson Dr S35 . . . . 13 B1
Mowson Hollow S35 . . . . 13 C1
Mowson La S35 . . . . 13 C1
Moxon Cl S36 . . . . 4 A2
Mucky La S36 . . . . 2 B1
Mulberry Cl S62 . . . . 12 B1
Mulberry St S1. . . . . 106 B3
Mulehouse Rd S10. . . . . 50 C2
Mundella Pl S8 . . . . 73 C1
Mundella Prim Sch
S8 . . . . 73 C1
Munro Cl S21. . . . . 92 B2
Munro Ct S11. . . . . 72 A3
Munsbrough La S61 . . . . 20 B4
Munsbrough Rise S61 . . 10 C1
Munsdale S61 . . . . 10 C1
Murdock Rd S5 . . . . 27 C2
Murrayfield Dr 6
S20 . . . . 103 B4
Murray Rd
Killamarsh S21 . . . . 92 C3
Rawmarsh S62. . . . . 12 B4
Sheffield S11 . . . . 60 C1
Musard Way S21. . . . . . . 92 A2
Musgrave Cres S5 . . . . . 41 B3
Musgrave Dr S5 . . . . 41 B3
Musgrave Pl S5. . . . . 41 B3
Musgrave Rd S5. . . . . . . 41 A3
Musgrave Way S5. . . . . . 24 A4
Mushroom La S3,
S10. . . . . 104 A4
Muskoka Ave S11. . . . . . 71 A3
Muskoka Dr S11. . . . . . . 71 A3
Myers Ave S35. . . . . 13 B4
Myers Grove La S6. . . . . 38 C1
Myers Grove Sch S6. . . . 39 A1
Mylnhurst RC Prep Sch
S11. . . . . 72 A2
Mylnhurst Rd S11. . . . . . 72 A3
Mylor Rd S11. . . . . 71 C4
Myrtle Cres S66 . . . . 36 C3
Myrtle Rd S2 . . . . 62 C1
Myrtle Springs S12 . . . . 75 B3
Myrtle Springs Dr S12 . . 75 B3

Myrtle Springs Sch
S2 . . . . .75 B4
Myton Rd S9 . . . . .54 B2

N

Nabeel Ct S60 . . . . .33 B3
Nairn Dr S18 . . . . .99 C3
Nairn St S10 . . . . .50 C1
Nanny Hill S36 . . . . 3 B3
Napier St S11 . . . . .62 A3
Nascot Cl S66 . . . . .37 C1
Nascot Gdns S26 . . . . .69 A4
Naseby St S9 . . . . .43 B4
Nathan Ct S20 . . . . .91 A3
Nathan Dr S20 . . . . .91 A4
Nathan Gr S20 . . . . .90 C4
Navan Rd S2 . . . . .64 B1
Naylor Gr S35 . . . . .13 A2
Naylor Rd S18 . . . . .13 A3
Naylor St S62 . . . . .12 A1
Nearcroft Rd S61 . . . . .19 C2
Needham Way S7 . . . . .72 B3
NEEPSEND 52 A4
Neepsend La S3 . . . . .52 A4
Neill Rd S11 . . . . .61 A2
Nelson Cl S60 . . . . .46 B2
Nelson Mandela Wlk **3**
S2 . . . . .64 C3
Nelson Pl S35 . . . . 6 B3
Nelson Rd S6 . . . . .50 A4
Nelson St S65 . . . . .21 B1
Nesfield Way S5 . . . . .29 A2
Nether Ave
Killamarsh S21 . . . . .92 A2
Sheffield S35 . . . . .15 A3
Netherby Manor S17 . . . . . .83 B1
Nether Cres S15 . . . . .15 A3
Netherdene Rd S18 . . . . . . .100 C3
NETHER EDGE 73 A4
Nether Edge Hospl
S11 .72 B4
Nether Edge Rd S7 . . . . .73 A4
Netherfield Cl S36 . . . . .43 B1
Netherfield La S62 . . . . .12 A2
Netherfield Rd S10 . . . . .50 C2
Netherfields Cres
S18 . . . . .100 C2
NETHERGATE 49 A3
Nethergate S6 . . . . .49 A3
NETHER GREEN
Killamarsh 92 B3
Sheffield 59 C2
Nethergreen Ave S21 . . . . . .92 B3
Nethergreen Ct S21 . . . . . .92 B3
Nethergreen Gdns
S21 .92 B3
Nether Green Inf Sch
S10 .59 B2
Nether Green Jun Sch
S10 .59 C2
Nethergreen Rd S11 . . . . . . .60 A2
NETHER HAUGH 11 A4
Nether La S35 . . . . 7 C1
Nether Ley Ave S35 . . . . 7 B3
Nether Ley Croft S35 . . . . . . 7 B3
Nether Ley Ct S35 . . . . 7 B3
Nether Ley Gdns S35 . . . . . . 7 B3
Nethermoor Ave S21 . . . . . .92 B3
Nethermoor Cl S21 . . . . .92 B3
Nethermoor Dr S21 . . . . .92 B3
Nethermoor La S21 . . . . .92 B3
Nether Oak Cl S20 . . . . .91 C4
Nether Oak Dr S20 . . . . .91 C4
Nether Oak View S20 . . . . . .91 C4
Nether Rd S35 . . . . .16 B3
Nether Shire La S5 . . . . .29 A4
NETHERTHORPE
Aston 70 B1
Sheffield 104 C4
Netherthorpe Cl S21 . . . . . .92 A3
Netherthorpe La S21 . . . . . .92 A3
Netherthorpe Pl S3 . . . . . .104 C4
Netherthorpe Prim Sch
S3 .104 C4
Netherthorpe Rd S3 . . . . . .104 C4
Netherthorpe St S3 . . . . . .104 C4

Netherthorpe Wlk
S3 .104 C4
Nether Wheel Row
S13 .77 B3
Nettleham Rd S8 . . . . .73 B1
Neville Cl S3 . . . . .52 C3
Neville Dr S3 . . . . .52 C4
Neville Rd S61 . . . . .10 A1
Neville St S60 . . . . .21 A1
Newark **8** S20 . . . . .90 C2
Newark St S9 . . . . .43 B1
Newbiggin Cl S62 . . . . .11 C2
Newbiggin Dr S62 . . . . .11 C2
Newbould Cres S20 . . . . .79 C1
Newbould La S10 . . . . .105 A2
New Brinsworth Rd
S60 .57 B4
Newburn Dr S9 . . . . .44 C4
Newbury Rd S10 . . . . .50 C2
Newcastle St S1 . . . . .104 C3
Newcroft Cl S20 . . . . .80 A1
New Cross Dr S13 . . . . .77 C4
New Cross Way S13 . . . . .77 C4
New Cross Wlk S13 . . . . .66 B1
New Droppingwell Rd
S61 .30 B4
Newent La S10 . . . . .50 C2
Newfield Cres S17 . . . . .82 A1
Newfield Croft S17 . . . . .82 A2
Newfield Ct S10 . . . . .50 C2
Newfield Farm Cl S14 . . . . . .75 A3
NEWFIELD GREEN 74 C3
Newfield Green Rd S2 . . . . . .74 C4
Newfield La S17 . . . . .82 A1
Newfield Pl S17 . . . . .82 A1
Newfield Sch S8 . . . . .74 B1
Newgate St S35 . . . . 5 C1
New Hall Cres S36 . . . . 2 B4
New Hall La S36 . . . . 2 A3
Newhall Rd S9 . . . . .43 A1
New Haven Gdns S17 . . . . . .94 C2
Newington Dr S26 . . . . .69 C1
Newington Rd S11 . . . . .61 A2
Newlands Ave S12 . . . . .75 C4
Newlands Dr S12 . . . . .75 C4
Newlands Gr S12 . . . . .76 A4
Newlands Rd S12 . . . . .75 C4
Newlyn Pl S8 . . . . .73 C1
Newlyn Rd S8 . . . . .73 B1
Newman Cl S9 . . . . .30 B2
Newman Ct
Rotherham S60 . . . . .47 B4
Sheffield S9 . . . . .30 B2
Newman Dr S9 . . . . .30 A2
Newman Rd
Rotherham S60 . . . . .47 C4
Sheffield S9 . . . . .30 A2
Newman Sch S60 . . . . .47 B3
Newmarch St S9 . . . . .31 B1
New Rd
Sheffield, Hill Top
S61 .30 B3
Stocksbridge S36 . . . . 3 C3
New School Cl S20 . . . . .90 A1
New School Ct S20 . . . . .90 A1
New School Rd S20 . . . . .90 A1
Newsham Rd S8 . . . . .73 B2
New St
Catliffe S60 . . . . .57 B4
Chapeltown S35 . . . . 5 B2
Rawmarsh S62 . . . . .12 A3
Rotherham, Greasbrough
S61 .10 C2
Rotherham, Thorpe Hesley
S61 . . . . 9 A2
Sheffield, Holbrook S20 . . . . .91 B2
Sheffield S1 . . . . .106 A4
Stocksbridge S36 . . . . 4 A3
Newstead Ave
Oughtibridge S35 . . . . .13 B4
Sheffield S12 . . . . .77 A1
Newstead Cl
Dronfield S18 . . . . .99 B3
Sheffield S12 . . . . .77 A1
Newstead Dr S12 . . . . .88 C4
Newstead Gr S12 . . . . .77 A1
Newstead Pl S12 . . . . .88 C4
Newstead Rd S12 . . . . .77 B1
Newstead Rise S12 . . . . .89 A4
Newstead Way S12 . . . . .88 C4
New Street Bus Link
S20 .91 B2

New Street La S2 . . . . .106 C4
Newton Ave S36 . . . . 2 B4
Newton Croft S13 . . . . .78 A4
Newton Dr S65 . . . . .34 A4
Newton La
Sheffield S1 . . . . .107 A2
Stocksbridge S36 . . . . 2 B4
Newton Pl S61 . . . . 9 A1
Newton Rd S35 . . . . 5 C1
Newton St S65 . . . . .34 A4
NEW TOTLEY 94 C2
Newwen Ho S65 . . . . .21 C1
New Wortley Rd S60,
S61 .20 B1
NEW YORK 32 C3
Niagara Rd S6 . . . . .26 C1
Nicholson St **9** S8 . . . . .74 A4
Nicholson Pl **7** S8 . . . . .74 A4
Nicholson Rd S8 . . . . .73 C4
Nichols Rd S6 . . . . .50 B3
Nickerwood Dr S26 . . . . .80 C4
Nickleby Ct S60 . . . . .56 C4
Nidderdale Pl S66 . . . . .36 C4
Nidderdale Rd S61 . . . . .10 A3
Nidd Rd S9 . . . . .54 B3
Nidd Rd E S9 . . . . .54 C3
Nightingale Cl S60 . . . . .33 B3
Nightingale Croft S61 . . . . . . 9 B4
Nightingale Ct S60 . . . . .33 B3
Nightingale Rd S35 . . . . .15 A2
Nile St S10 . . . . .61 A4
Nodder Rd S13 . . . . .65 A1
Noehill Pl S2 . . . . .64 C3
Noehill Rd S2 . . . . .64 C3
Nook End S6 . . . . .49 B4
Nook La S6 . . . . .49 A4
Nook Lane Jun Sch
S6 . . . . .49 A4
Nook The S10 . . . . .104 A4
Norborough Rd S9 . . . . .31 B1
Norbrook Way S60 . . . . .48 B3
Norburn Dr S21 . . . . .92 B2
Norbury Cl S18 . . . . .99 C3
Norfolk Com Prim Sch
Sheffield S2 . . . . .63 B2
Sheffield S2 . . . . .63 C1
Norfolk Ct **8** S65 . . . . .21 B1
Norfolk Hill S35 . . . . .14 C3
Norfolk Hill Croft S35 . . . . . .14 C3
Norfolk La S1 . . . . .107 A3
Norfolk Park Ave S2 . . . . . . .63 B2
Norfolk Park Dr S2 . . . . .63 B2
Norfolk Park Rd S2 . . . . . . .107 C1
Norfolk Park Sch S2 . . . . . . .63 A3
Norfolk Park Students
Residence S2 . . . . .63 B3
Norfolk Rd S2 . . . . .107 C2
Norfolk Row S1 . . . . .106 A3
Norfolk St
Rotherham S65 . . . . .21 B1
Sheffield S1 . . . . .106 B3
Norfolk Way S60 . . . . .47 B4
Norgreave Way S20 . . . . .90 C1
Normancroft Cres S2 . . . . . . .65 A3
Normancroft Ct S2 . . . . .64 C3
Normancroft Dr S2 . . . . .64 C3
Normancroft Way S2 . . . . . . .65 A3
NORMANDALE 38 C2
Normandale Ave S6 . . . . .38 C1
Normandale Rd **2** S6 . . . . . .40 B1
Norman St S9 . . . . .43 B1
Normanton Gdns S4 . . . . . . .42 A1
Normanton Gr S13 . . . . .77 B4
Normanton Hill S13 . . . . .76 C4
NORMANTON
SPRING 77 B4
Normanton Spring Ct
S13 .77 B4
Normanton Spring Rd
S13 .77 B3
Normanville Ave S60 . . . . . . .45 C3
Norrel's Croft S60 . . . . .33 C2
Norrels Dr S60 . . . . .33 C2
Norris Rd S6 . . . . .39 C2
Norroy St S4 . . . . .53 B4
Norstead Cres S60 . . . . .37 B3
North Church St S1 . . . . . . .106 A4
Northcote Ave S2 . . . . .74 A4
Northcote Ho S8 . . . . .73 B1
Northcote Rd S2 . . . . .74 A4
North Cres
Killamarsh S21 . . . . .92 C4

North Cres continued
Rotherham S65 . . . . .22 A1
North Dr S60 . . . . .21 A2
Northern Ave S2 . . . . .63 C1
Northern Comm S18 . . . . . . .99 A4
Northern General Hospl
S5 . . . . .42 A4
North Farm Ct S26 . . . . .70 A1
NORTHFIELD 21 A2
Northfield Ave S10 . . . . .50 C3
Northfield Cl S10 . . . . .51 A3
Northfield Ct
Rotherham S66 . . . . .36 B2
Sheffield S10 . . . . .50 C3
Northfield Jun Sch
S18 .98 A1
Northfield La S66 . . . . .36 B3
Northfield Rd
Rotherham S60 . . . . .21 A2
Sheffield S10 . . . . .50 C3
Northgate Ho S21 . . . . .103 A1
North Hill Rd S5 . . . . .27 C2
Northlands Rd S5 . . . . .27 C2
North Pitt St S61 . . . . .31 C4
North Pl S65 . . . . .22 A1
North Quadrant S5 . . . . .29 A2
North Rd S65 . . . . .22 B2
Northside S3 . . . . .28 C3
North St S60 . . . . .20 C1
Northumberland Rd
S10 .104 A3
Northwood S35 . . . . .26 A2
Northwood Dr S6 . . . . .26 A2
Northwood Pl S6 . . . . .26 A1
NORTON 85 C2
Norton Ave S14 . . . . .86 C4
Norton Church Glebe
S6 . . . . .86 A3
Norton Church Rd S8 . . . . . . .85 C3
Norton Free CE Prim Sch
S8 . . . . .86 A3
Norton Green Cl S8 . . . . .86 A3
Norton Hall S8 . . . . .85 C3
Norton Hall Ct S8 . . . . .85 C3
Norton Hammer La **1**
S8 . . . . .73 A2
Norton La S8 . . . . .86 A3
Norton Lawns S8 . . . . .86 A3
NORTON LEES 73 C2
Norton Lees Cl S8 . . . . .73 C1
Norton Lees Cres S8 . . . . . . .73 C1
Norton Lees Glade S8 . . . . . .73 C2
Norton Lees La S8 . . . . .73 C2
Norton Lees Rd S8 . . . . .73 C2
Norton Lees Sq S8 . . . . .73 C1
Norton Mews S8 . . . . .86 A3
Norton Park Ave S8 . . . . .85 C2
Norton Park Cres S8 . . . . . . .85 B2
Norton Park Dr S8 . . . . .85 B2
Norton Park Rd S8 . . . . .85 C2
Norton Park View S8 . . . . . . .85 C2
NORTON
WOODSEATS 85 B4
Norwich Row S11 . . . . .107 C3
NORWOOD 93 A4
Norwood Ave S5 . . . . .41 C4
Norwood Cl S5 . . . . .41 C3
Norwood Cres S21 . . . . .93 A3
Norwood Dr S5 . . . . .41 C3
Norwood Grange Dr
S5 . . . . .41 C4
Norwood Ind Est S21 . . . . . . .92 C4
Norwood Pl S21 . . . . .93 A3
Norwood Rd S5 . . . . .41 C3
Norwood St S65 . . . . .23 A3
Notre Dame High RC
High Sch S10 . . . . .60 B3
Nottingham Cliff S13 . . . . . . .52 C4
Nottingham St
Rotherham S65 . . . . .21 B1
Sheffield S3 . . . . .52 C4
Nowill Ct **2** S8 . . . . .73 C4
Nowill Pl **3** S8 . . . . .73 C4
Nunnery Cres S60 . . . . .57 A4
Nunnery Dr S2 . . . . .54 A1
Nunnery Terr S2 . . . . .54 A1
Nursery Dr
Catliffe S60 . . . . .57 A4
Sheffield S35 . . . . .16 B2
Nursery Gr S35 . . . . .16 B2
Nursery La S3 . . . . .106 B5
Nursery Rd S26 . . . . .69 A2

Nursery St S3 . . . . .106 B5
Nuttall Pl S2 . . . . .53 B1
Nutwood Trad Est S6 . . . . . .26 B3

O

Oak Apple Wlk S6 . . . . .38 A1
Oakbank Ct S17 . . . . .94 C3
Oakbrook Ct S11 . . . . .60 A2
Oakbrook Rd S11 . . . . .60 A2
Oakbrook Wlk **3** S65 . . . . . .22 B2
Oakburn Ct S10 . . . . .105 A1
Oak Cl
Killamarsh S21 . . . . .92 A1
Rotherham S66 . . . . .36 B4
Oakdale Ct S7 . . . . .72 C4
Oakdale Pl S61 . . . . .31 C4
Oakdale Rd
Rotherham S66 . . . . .31 C4
Sheffield S7 . . . . .72 C4
Oakdell S18 . . . . .98 B1
Oaken Wood Cl S61 . . . . 9 B3
Oaken Wood Rd S61 . . . . 9 A3
Oakes Gn S9 . . . . .54 A4
Oakes Park Sch S8 . . . . .86 A4
Oakes Park View S14 . . . . . .86 B3
Oakes St S9 . . . . .30 B2
Oakes The S8 . . . . .86 B3
Oakfern Gr S35 . . . . 5 B2
Oak Grove Gn S17 . . . . .94 C2
Oakham Dr S3 . . . . .52 A4
Oakhill Rd
Dronfield S18 . . . . .98 A1
Sheffield S7 . . . . .72 C4
Oakholme Mews S10 . . . . . . .61 A3
Oakholme Rd S10 . . . . .61 A3
Oakland Ct S6 . . . . .39 C2
Oakland Rd S6 . . . . .39 C2
Oaklands S66 . . . . .36 C1
Oak Lea S61 . . . . .10 C1
Oakley St S13 . . . . .65 C4
Oak Lodge Rd S35 . . . . 5 A1
Oak Mdws S65 . . . . .22 B2
Oak Pk S10 . . . . .60 C4
Oak Rd
Sheffield, Beighton
S20 .79 B2
Sheffield, Gleadless
Townend S12 . . . . .87 B4
Oaks Ave S36 . . . . 2 C3
Oaks Fold S5 . . . . .29 B4
Oaks Fold Ave S5 . . . . .29 B3
Oaks Fold Rd S5 . . . . .29 B4
Oaks La
Rotherham S61 . . . . .19 C3
Sheffield S5 . . . . .29 B3
Oak St
Sheffield, Heeley S8 . . . . .62 B1
Sheffield S20 . . . . .90 A2
Oaks The **2** S10 . . . . .60 C4
Oak Terr S26 . . . . .68 C2
Oak Tree Cl S66 . . . . .36 C3
Oakwood Ave S5 . . . . .15 C1
Oakwood Cres S35 . . . . .13 B1
Oakwood Dr S60 . . . . .34 A2
Oakwood Flats S5 . . . . .41 C3
Oakwood Gr S60 . . . . .34 A1
Oakwood Hall Dr S60 . . . . . .47 A4
Oakwood Rd E S60 . . . . .34 A1
Oakwood Rd W S60 . . . . .33 C1
Oakwood Tech Coll
S60 .33 C3
Oakworth Cl **1** S20 . . . . . .103 A3
Oakworth Dr S20 . . . . .103 A4
Oakworth Gr S20 . . . . .103 A4
Oakworth View S20 . . . . . . .103 A4
Oates Ave S62 . . . . .12 B3
Oates Cl S61 . . . . .20 A1
Oates St S61 . . . . .20 A1
Oats Orch S20 . . . . .103 A4
Oborne Cl S65 . . . . .25 B2
Occupation La
Sheffield, Birley S12 . . . . .77 B3
Sheffield, Loxley S6 . . . . .38 B3
Occupation Rd S62 . . . . .11 C2
Ochre Dike Cl S20 . . . . .90 C4
Ochre Dike La S20 . . . . .90 B4
Ochre Dike Wlk S61 . . . . . . .10 B2
Octagon Ctr ★ S10 . . . . . .105 B3
Octavia Cl S60 . . . . .46 A4
Odom Ct S2 . . . . .74 A4
Oil Mill Fold S60 . . . . .33 A4

Oldale Cl S13 . . . . 78 B3
Oldale Ct S13 . . . . 78 B4
Oldale Gr S13 . . . . 78 B4
Old Clifton La S65 . . . . . . 33 C3
Old Cottage Cl S13 . . . . . 67 B1
Oldfield Ave S6 . . . . 49 B4
Oldfield Cl S6 . . . . 49 B4
Oldfield Gr S6 . . . . 49 B4
Oldfield Rd
  Rotherham S65 . . . . 23 A1
  Sheffield S6 . . . . 49 B3
Oldfield Terr S6 . . . . 49 B3
Old Forge Bsns Pk 5
  S2 . . . . 62 B1
Old Fulwood Rd S10 . . . . 59 B1
Old Garden Dr S65 . . . . . 22 A1
Oldgate La S65 . . . . 23 B4
Old Hall Cl S66 . . . . 37 A3
Old Hall Dr S66 . . . . 37 A3
Old Hall Farm S61 . . . . . . 19 B1
Old Hall Mews S66 . . . . . 37 A3
Old Hall Rd S9 . . . . 43 B1
Oldhay Cl S17 . . . . 94 B4
Old Hay Gdns S17 . . . . . . 94 A4
Old Hay La S17 . . . . 94 A4
Old La S20 . . . . 91 B1
Old Park Ave S8 . . . . 84 B1
Old Park Rd S8 . . . . 84 B1
Old Retford Ct S13 . . . . . 67 A3
Old Retford Rd S13 . . . . . 67 A2
Old School Cl S61 . . . . . . 11 A2
Old School Dr S5 . . . . 28 B3
Old School La S60 . . . . . . 57 B4
Old Sheffield Rd S60 . . . . 33 A3
Old St S2 . . . . 106 C4
Old Station Dr S7 . . . . . . 72 C1
Oldwell Cl S17 . . . . 94 B2
Old Wheel S6 . . . . 38 A1
Old Wortley Rd S61 . . . . . 19 B2
Olive Cl S26 . . . . 69 B1
Olive Cres S12 . . . . 87 B4
Olive Grove Rd S2 . . . . . . 62 C2
Olive Rd
  Sheffield S20 . . . . 90 B1
  Stocksbridge S36 . . . . . . 3 A3
Oliver Rd S7 . . . . 72 B2
Olivers Dr S9 . . . . 55 B2
Olivers Mount S9 . . . . . . 55 C2
Olivers Way S6 . . . . 56 C4
Olive Terr S6 . . . . 38 B1
Olivet Rd S8 . . . . 73 B1
Onchan Rd S6 . . . . 49 C3
Onslow Rd S11 . . . . 60 C1
Orange St S1 . . . . 104 C3
Orchard Cl
  Catliffe S60 . . . . 57 B4
  Sheffield S5 . . . . 16 B1
Orchard Cres S5 . . . . 16 B1
Orchard Flatts Cres
  S61 . . . . 20 A4
Orchard La
  Sheffield, Beighton
  S20 . . . . 91 A4
  Sheffield S1 . . . . 106 A3
Orchard Lea Dr S26 . . . . . 69 B1
Orchard Pl
  Killamarsh S21 . . . . 92 B2
  Rotherham S60 . . . . 32 C4
Orchard Rd S6 . . . . 51 A4
Orchard Sq
  Dronfield S18 . . . . 99 C4
  Sheffield S1 . . . . 106 A3
Orchard St
  Oughtibridge S35 . . . . . . 13 B3
  Sheffield S1 . . . . 106 A3
  Stocksbridge S36 . . . . . . 4 B2
Orchard Way S60 . . . . . . 46 A1
Orchard Wells S66 . . . . . 36 C2
Ordnance Terr S61 . . . . . 31 C4
ORGREAVE 66 C4
Orgreave Cl S13 . . . . 67 A3
Orgreave Cres S13 . . . . . 67 A3
Orgreave Dr S13 . . . . 67 A3
Orgreave La S13 . . . . 66 C4
Orgreave Pl S13 . . . . 66 C3
Orgreave Rd
  Catliffe S60 . . . . 57 A3
  Orgreave S13 . . . . 66 C3
Orgreave Rise S13 . . . . . 67 B2
Oriel Mount S10 . . . . 59 A1
Oriel Rd S10 . . . . 59 B1
Ormesby Cl S18 . . . . 99 B3

Ormesby Way S66 . . . . . . 37 B2
Ormes Mdw S20 . . . . 90 A4
Ormond Cl S8 . . . . 97 C4
Ormond Dr S8 . . . . 97 C4
Ormond Rd S8 . . . . 85 C1
Ormond Way S8 . . . . 85 C1
Orpen Dr S14 . . . . 86 C4
Orpen Ho S8 . . . . 86 B4
Orpen Way S14 . . . . 86 C4
Orphanage Rd S3 . . . . . . 41 C2
Osberton Pl S11 . . . . 61 B2
Osberton St S62 . . . . 12 C4
Osberton Way S65 . . . . . 22 C3
Osbert Rd S60 . . . . 47 C4
Osborne Ave S26 . . . . . . 69 C2
Osborne Cl S11 . . . . 61 A1
Osborne Ct S11 . . . . 61 A1
Osborne Mews S11 . . . . . 61 B1
Osborne Rd S11 . . . . 61 B1
Osgathorpe Cres S4 . . . . 42 A2
Osgathorpe Dr S4 . . . . . . 42 B2
Osgathorpe Rd S4 . . . . . . 42 A2
Osmaston Rd S8 . . . . 85 A4
Osmund Ct S21 . . . . 102 C1
Osmund Rd S21 . . . . 102 C1
Osprey Gdns S2 . . . . 63 C4
Osprey Rd S2 . . . . 81 A4
Oswestry Rd S5 . . . . 28 C2
Otley Wlk S6 . . . . 51 B4
Otter St S9 . . . . 54 A4
OUGHTIBRIDGE 13 C3
Oughtibridge La S35. . . . . 14 A1
Oughtibridge Prim Sch
  S35 . . . . 13 B3
Oughton Way S4 . . . . 42 B1
Oulton Ave S66 . . . . 37 B4
Ouseburn Croft S9 . . . . . 54 B3
Ouseburn Rd S9 . . . . 54 B2
Ouseburn St S9 . . . . 54 B3
Ouse Rd S9 . . . . 54 B3
Outram Rd S2 . . . . 63 C4
Oval Rd S65 . . . . 22 B1
Oval The S5 . . . . 29 A1
Overcroft Rise S17 . . . . . 94 B2
Overdale Gdns S17 . . . . . 94 B4
Overdale Rise S17 . . . . . . 94 A4
Overend Cl S14 . . . . 74 C2
Overend Dr S14 . . . . 74 C2
Overend Rd S14 . . . . 74 C2
Overend Way S14 . . . . . . 74 C2
Oversley St S31 . . . . 31 B1
Overton Rd S6 . . . . 39 C4
Owen Cl
  Rotherham S65 . . . . 21 B2
  Sheffield S6 . . . . 27 A4
Owen Pl S6 . . . . 27 A4
Owen Wlk S6 . . . . 15 A1
Owler Brook Inf Sch
  S4 . . . . 42 C3
Owler La S4 . . . . 42 B3
OWLERTON 40 B4
Owlerton Gn S6 . . . . 40 B2
Owlerton Stadium S7. . . . 40 B4
Owlings Pl S6 . . . . 39 B2
Owlings Rd S6 . . . . 39 B3
OWLTHORPE 89 C4
Owlthorpe Ave S20 . . . . . 89 C2
Owlthorpe Cl S20 . . . . . . 89 C2
Owlthorpe Dr S20 . . . . . . 89 C2
Owlthorpe Gr S20 . . . . . . 89 C2
Owlthorpe Greenway
  Sheffield S20 . . . . 90 C3
  Sheffield, Waterthorpe
  S20 . . . . 90 C3
Owlthorpe La S20 . . . . . . 89 C2
Owlthorpe Rise S20. . . . . 89 C2
Ox Close Ave
  Rotherham S61 . . . . 10 A1
  Sheffield S17 . . . . 95 B3
Oxclose Dr 2 S18 . . . . . . 99 B3
Oxclose La S18 . . . . 99 B3
Oxclose Park Gdns
  S20 . . . . 103 C4
Oxclose Park Rd S20. . . . 103 C4
Oxclose Park Rd N
  S20 . . . . 91 A1
Oxclose Park View
  S20 . . . . 103 C4
Oxford S6 . . . . 104 B4
Oxford Cl S11 . . . . 11 A1
Oxford St
  Rotherham S65 . . . . 22 A1

Oxford St continued
  Sheffield, Port Mahon
  S6 . . . . 104 B4
Oxley Cl S36 . . . . 2 C3
Oxley Ct S60 . . . . 33 C2
Oxley Gr S60 . . . . 33 C2
Oxspring Bank S5 . . . . . . 40 B4
Oxted Rd S9 . . . . 43 B4

P

Paces High Green Sch
  S35 . . . . 5 C2
Pack Horse La S35 . . . . . . 5 C2
Packmans Cl S35 . . . . . . 14 C3
Packmans Way S35 . . . . . 14 C3
Paddock Cres S2 . . . . . . 75 A3
Paddock Dr S66 . . . . 24 C1
Paddocks The
  Aston S26 . . . . 69 C1
  Rotherham S66 . . . . 25 B2
  Rotherham, Thrybergh
  S65 . . . . 24 A4
Paddock The S61 . . . . 9 C2
Paddock Way S18 . . . . . . 97 C1
Padley Way S5 . . . . 29 A2
Padley Wlk S5 . . . . 29 A2
Page Hall Rd S4 . . . . 42 B3
Pagenall Dr S26 . . . . 69 B2
Paget St S9 . . . . 43 A1
Palgrave Cres S5 . . . . . . 27 B2
Palgrave Rd S5 . . . . 27 B2
Palmer Cres 3 S18. . . . . 101 A3
Palmer Rd S9 . . . . 55 A4
Palmer St S9 . . . . 54 A3
Palmerston Rd S10 . . . . . 105 A3
Palm Hollow Cl S66 . . . . . 35 C2
Palm La S6 . . . . 51 A4
Palm St S6 . . . . 51 A4
Paper Mill Rd S5 . . . . 17 B1
Paradise La S1 . . . . 106 A4
Paradise Sq S1 . . . . 106 A4
Paradise St S1 . . . . 106 A4
Park Ave
  Chapeltown S35 . . . . 7 B2
  Dronfield S18 . . . . 101 A4
  Rotherham S60 . . . . 48 A4
  Sheffield S10 . . . . 60 C2
  Treeton S60 . . . . 57 D2
Park Cl S65 . . . . 23 C4
Park Cres
  Sheffield, Broomfield
  S10 . . . . 105 A2
  Sheffield, Ecclesfield
  S35 . . . . 16 B2
Park Ct S35 . . . . 14 C2
Park Dale S62 . . . . 12 A3
Park Dr
  Aston S26 . . . . 68 C1
  Stocksbridge S36 . . . . . . 3 A3
Park Drive Way S36 . . . . . 3 A4
Parkers La S17 . . . . 82 B2
Parker's La S11 . . . . 51 A1
Parker's Rd S10 . . . . 51 A1
Park Farm S18 . . . . 99 B4
Parkfield Ct S62 . . . . 12 A1
Parkfield Pl S2 . . . . 62 B2
Parkfield Rd S66 . . . . 33 C4
PARKGATE 21 C4
Parkgate Ct S18 . . . . . . 101 B4
Parkgate Cl S20 . . . . 89 B2
Parkgate Croft S20 . . . . . 89 B2
Parkgate Ct S62 . . . . 21 B4
Parkgate Dr S20 . . . . 89 B3
Park Gr
  Rotherham S66 . . . . 37 A3
  Stocksbridge S36 . . . . . . 3 A4
Park Grange Croft S2 . . . . 63 A2
Park Grange Ct S2 . . . . . 63 A2
Park Grange Dr S2 . . . . . 63 A2
Park Grange Mount
  S2 . . . . 63 B1
Park Grange Rd S2 . . . . . 63 B1
Park Grange Rise S2 . . . . 63 B2
Park Grange View S2 . . . . 63 B2
PARKHEAD 71 B1
PARK HEAD 49 C3
Parkhead Cres S11 . . . . . 71 B2
Parkhead Ct S11 . . . . 71 B2
Parkhead Rd S11 . . . . . . 71 B1
PARK HILL 107 C3

Park Hill
  Aston S26 . . . . 68 C1
  Eckington S21 . . . . 103 B1
Park Hill Gdns S26 . . . . . 68 C1
Park House La S9 . . . . . . 45 A2
Park La
  Rotherham S65 . . . . 23 C4
  Sheffield, Broomfield
  S10 . . . . 105 A2
  Stocksbridge S36 . . . . . . 4 A4
Parklands Ct S9 . . . . 44 A1
Parklands View S26 . . . . 81 A3
Park Mount S65 . . . . 33 B4
Park Nook S65 . . . . 23 B4
Park Pl S65 . . . . 22 B1
Park Rd
  Rotherham S65 . . . . 22 B1
  Sheffield S6 . . . . 50 A4
PARK SIDE 49 B3
Parkside La S6 . . . . 49 B3
Parkside Rd S6 . . . . 49 A4
Parkside Sh Ctr S21 . . . . 92 B3
Parkson Rd S60 . . . . 47 C4
Park Spring Dr S2 . . . . . . 63 A2
Park Spring Pl S2 . . . . . . 63 A2
Park Spring Way S2 . . . . . 63 A2
Park Sq S2 . . . . 106 C4
Park St
  Aston S26 . . . . 69 A1
  Rawmarsh S62 . . . . 12 A4
  Rotherham S61 . . . . 20 B1
  Parkstone Delph S12 . . . 87 B4
Park Terr
  Chapeltown S35 . . . . 7 C2
  Rotherham S65 . . . . 23 B4
Park Vale Dr S65 . . . . 23 C4
Park View
  Rotherham, Greasbrough
  S61 . . . . 10 C1
  Rotherham, Thorpe Hesley
  S61 . . . . 8 C2
Park View Ave S20 . . . . . 90 C1
Park View Ct S8 . . . . 85 B4
Parkview Lodge S6 . . . . . 39 C3
Park View Rd
  Chapeltown S35 . . . . 7 B2
  Rotherham S61 . . . . 30 C4
  Sheffield S6 . . . . 40 A3
Parkway Ave S9 . . . . 54 A2
Parkway Cl S9 . . . . 54 A2
Parkway Dr S9 . . . . 54 C1
Park Wlk S2 . . . . 63 A3
Parkwood High Sch S5,
  S6 . . . . 40 C4
Parkwood Ind Est S3 . . . . 52 A4
Parkwood Rd S3 . . . . 40 C3
Parkwood Rd N S5 . . . . . 41 A4
PARKWOOD
  SPRINGS 41 A1
Parliament St S11 . . . . . . 61 C3
Parsley Hay Cl S13 . . . . . 66 A3
Parsley Hay Dr S13 . . . . . 66 A3
Parsley Hay Gdns S13 . . . 66 A3
Parsley Hay Rd S13 . . . . . 66 A3
Parsonage Cl S20 . . . . . 103 A4
Parsonage Cres S6 . . . . . 51 A4
Parsonage Ct S6 . . . . . . 51 A4
Parsonage St S6 . . . . 51 A4
PARSON CROSS 27 C3
Parson Cross CE Prim
  Sch S6 . . . . 27 A2
Parson Cross Rd S6 . . . . 27 A2
Partridge Cl S21 . . . . . . 102 B1
Partridge Pl S26 . . . . 81 A4
Partridge View S2 . . . . . 63 C4
Passhouses Rd S4 . . . . . 41 C2
Pasture Gr S21 . . . . 102 C1
Paternoster Row S1 . . . . 107 B2
Paterson Cl S36 . . . . 2 C4
Paterson Cl S36 . . . . 2 C4
Paterson Ct S36 . . . . 2 C4
Paterson Gdns S36 . . . . . 2 C4
Patmore Rd S5 . . . . 29 A2
Patterdale Cl 2 S18 . . . . 100 A3
Pavement The S2 . . . . . 106 C3
Pavilion La S60 . . . . 45 C4
Pavilion Way S5 . . . . 29 A2
Paxton Ct S14 . . . . 75 B2
Paxton La S10 . . . . 105 A4
Payler Cl S2 . . . . 64 B2

Peacock Cl
  Killamarsh S21 . . . . 92 B2
  Rotherham S61 . . . . 9 A4
Peacock Trad Est S6 . . . . 40 B2
Peak Cl S66 . . . . 24 B1
Peakdale Cres S12 . . . . . 77 A3
Peaks Mount S20 . . . . . . 79 A1
Peak Sq S20 . . . . 90 C4
Peakstone Mews S62 . . . 12 A3
Pearce Rd S5 . . . . 55 A1
Pearce Wlk S9 . . . . 55 A2
Pearl St S11 . . . . 61 C2
Pea Royd La S36 . . . . 3 B4
Pearson Bldg (Sheffield
  Hallam Univ) S10. . . . . 105 A1
Pearson Pl S8 . . . . 73 B2
Pearson's Cl S65 . . . . . . 34 C2
Pearson St S36 . . . . 3 A4
Pear St S11 . . . . 61 C3
Pear Tree Ave S66 . . . . . 37 A3
Pear Tree Cl
  Brinsworth S60 . . . . 46 B2
  Killamarsh S21 . . . . 92 A1
Pear Tree Rd S5 . . . . 29 A4
Peashill St S62 . . . . 12 A3
Peatfield Rd S21 . . . . 93 A3
Peckham Rd S5 . . . . 7 A4
Pedley Ave 4 S20 . . . . . . 90 C2
Pedley Cl 5 S20 . . . . 90 C2
Pedley Dr S20 . . . . 90 C2
Pedley Gr 6 S20 . . . . 90 C3
Peel Gdns S18 . . . . 100 B3
Peel St S10 . . . . 61 A4
Peel Terr S10 . . . . 105 B3
Pembrey Cl S20 . . . . 91 B4
Pembroke Cres S35. . . . . 6 C4
Pembroke Rd
  Dronfield S18 . . . . 100 C2
  4 Dronfield S18 . . . . . . 100 C2
Pembroke St
  Rotherham S61 . . . . 31 C4
  Sheffield S11 . . . . 61 C3
Pendeen Rd S11 . . . . 60 A2
Pendle Croft S20 . . . . . . 91 C3
Penistone Rd
  Chapeltown S35 . . . . 6 B2
  Sheffield S3 , S6 . . . . . . 40 C1
Penistone Rd N S6 . . . . . 40 A4
Penley St S11 . . . . 62 B2
Pennine Ctr The S1 . . . . 106 A4
Pennine View S36 . . . . . . 3 A1
Pen Nook Cl S36 . . . . 4 A1
Pen Nook Ct S36 . . . . 4 A1
Pen Nook Dr S36 . . . . 4 A1
Pen Nook Gdns S36 . . . . . 4 A1
Penns Rd S2 . . . . 74 B4
Penny Engine La S21 . . . 103 B2
Penny La S11 . . . . 94 A3
Penrhyn Rd S11 . . . . 61 A1
Penrith Cl S5 . . . . 40 C4
Penrith Cres S5 . . . . 40 C4
Penrith Rd S5 . . . . 40 C4
Penrose Pl S13 . . . . 77 C4
Penthorpe Cl S12 . . . . . . 76 A4
Pentland Gdns S20 . . . . . 90 B4
Pentland Rd S18 . . . . 99 C3
Penton St S1 . . . . 106 A4
Penwood Wlk S66 . . . . . . 24 B2
Penyghent Cl S35 . . . . . . 7 A4
Pepper Cl S61 . . . . 19 A4
Percy St
  Rotherham S65 . . . . 33 B4
  Sheffield S3 . . . . 52 A3
Perigree Rd S8 . . . . 73 A1
Periwood Ave S8 . . . . . . 73 A1
Periwood Cl S8 . . . . 73 A1
Periwood Dr S8 . . . . 73 A1
Periwood Gr S8 . . . . 73 A1
Periwood La S8 . . . . 73 A1
Perkyn Rd S5 . . . . 17 A1
Perkyn Terr S5 . . . . 17 A1
Peterborough Cl S10 . . . . 58 B2
Peterborough Dr S10 . . . . 58 B3
Peterborough Rd S10 . . . . 58 B3
Peter St S61 . . . . 19 B1
Petre Dr S4 . . . . 42 C2
Petre St S4 . . . . 42 B2
Petworth Dr S11 . . . . 83 A4

Peveril Rd
Eckington S21 ... 103 B1
Sheffield S11 ... 60 C1
Pexton Rd S4 ... 42 A2
PHILADELPHIA ... 52 A4
Philadelphia Dr 6 S6 ... 51 C3
Philadelphia Gdns S6 ... 51 C3
Philadelphia Gr 5 S6 ... 51 C3
Phillimore Com Prim Sch S9 ... 54 C4
Phillimore Rd S9 ... 54 C4
Phillips Rd S6 ... 38 B3
Phoenix Ct
Eckington S12 ... 88 C3
1 Sheffield S1 ... 107 A3
Phoenix Gr S60 ... 45 C3
Phoenix Rd
Eckington S12 ... 88 C3
Rotherham S9 ... 31 B2
Pickard Cres S13 ... 65 B2
Pickard Dr S13 ... 65 B2
Pickering Cres S26 ... 69 A1
Pickering Rd S3 ... 41 A1
Pickering St S9 ... 43 C2
Pickmere Rd S10 ... 50 C2
Pickwick Dr S60 ... 56 C4
Piece End S35 ... 5 B2
Piece End Cl S35 ... 5 B2
Pieces N The S60 ... 47 C2
Pieces S The S60 ... 47 C2
Pighills La S18 ... 97 C2
Pike Rd S60 ... 46 A3
Pilgrim St S3 ... 41 C1
Pinchfield Ct S66 ... 36 B1
Pinchfield Holt S66 ... 36 B1
Pinchfield La S66 ... 36 B1
Pinchwell View S66 ... 36 B1
Pine Cl
Killamarsh S21 ... 92 A1
Rotherham S66 ... 36 C4
Pine Croft S35 ... 7 B2
Pinecroft Way S35 ... 7 B2
Pines The
Rotherham S66 ... 36 C1
Sheffield S10 ... 58 B2
Pinewood Cl S65 ... 23 A3
Pinfold La
Rotherham S60 ... 33 B3
Sheffield S3 ... 41 C1
Pinfold St
Eckington S21 ... 103 A1
Sheffield S1 ... 106 A3
Pingle Ave S7 ... 72 B1
Pingle La S65 ... 24 C4
Pingle Rd
Killamarsh S21 ... 92 C3
Sheffield S7 ... 72 B1
Pingles Cres S65 ... 23 C4
Pinner Rd S11 ... 61 A2
Pinsent 4 S3 ... 106 B5
Pinstone Chambers 5 S1 ... 107 A3
Pinstone St S1 ... 107 A3
Piper Cl S5 ... 28 A1
Piper Cres S5 ... 28 A1
Piper Ct S5 ... 28 A1
Piper La S26 ... 70 A2
Piper Rd S5 ... 41 C4
Pipworth Gr S2 ... 65 A3
Pipworth Jun & Inf Schs S2 ... 64 C3
Pipworth La S21 ... 103 C2
Pipworth Rd S2 ... 64 C3
Pisgah House Rd S10 ... 51 A1
PISMIRE HILL ... 29 A2
Pitchford La S10 ... 59 B3
Pit La
Rotherham S61 ... 9 A1
Sheffield S12 ... 75 C4
Treeton S60 ... 57 D2
PITSMOOR ... 42 A1
Pitsmoor Rd
Sheffield S3 ... 41 C2
Sheffield, Woodside S3 ... 52 B4
Pitt Cl S1 ... 105 C3
Pitt La S1 ... 104 C3
Pitt St
Rotherham S61 ... 31 C4
Sheffield S1 ... 105 C3
Plane Dr S66 ... 36 C2
Plank Gate S35 ... 13 C4
Plantation Rd 8 S8 ... 73 C4
Plantin Rise S20 ... 90 C1
Plantin The S20 ... 90 C1
Platts Dr S20 ... 79 C2
Platts La S35 ... 13 C4
Platt St S3 ... 52 B4
Pleasant Cl S12 ... 76 A4
Pleasant Rd S12 ... 76 A4
Plover Croft S61 ... 9 B4
Plover Ct S2 ... 63 C4
Plowmans Way S61 ... 10 A3
Plowright Cl S14 ... 74 C3
Plowright Dr S14 ... 74 C3
Plowright Mount S14 ... 74 C3
Plowright Way S14 ... 74 C3
PLUMBLEY ... 102 A4
Plumbley Hall Mews S20 ... 102 C4
Plumbley Hall Rd S20 ... 102 C4
Plumbley La S20 ... 102 B4
Plumb Leys S60 ... 57 C2
Plum La S3 ... 106 A4
Plumper's Rd S9 ... 44 B4
Plum St S3 ... 106 A4
Plymouth Rd S7 ... 73 A3
Polka Ct S3 ... 52 B4
Pollard Ave S5 ... 27 B1
Pollard Cres S5 ... 27 B1
Pollard Rd S5 ... 27 B1
Pollard St S61 ... 31 B4
Pomona St S11 ... 61 C3
Pond Cl S6 ... 49 B4
Pond Hill S1 ... 106 B3
Pond Rd S6 ... 49 B4
Ponds Forge International Sports Ctr S1 ... 106 B3
Pond St S1 ... 107 B3
Poole Pl S9 ... 55 A2
Poole Rd S9 ... 55 A2
Pool Sq S1 ... 107 A3
Poplar Ave
Rotherham S65 ... 23 B4
Sheffield S20 ... 79 B3
Stocksbridge S36 ... 3 A2
Poplar Cl
Dronfield S18 ... 101 B1
Killamarsh S21 ... 92 A1
Oughtibridge S35 ... 13 A3
Poplar Dr S60 ... 45 C2
Poplar Glade S66 ... 36 B2
Poplar Gr S65 ... 25 B2
Poplar Rd S35 ... 13 A3
Poplar Way S60 ... 56 C3
Popple St S4 ... 42 B3
Porter Brook View S11 ... 61 B2
Porter Croft CE Prim Sch S11 ... 61 C3
Porter Terr 6 S11 ... 61 A2
Portland Ave S26 ... 69 C1
Portland Bdgs 7 S6 ... 51 C3
Portland Bsns Pk S13 ... 65 C4
Portland Ct S6 ... 51 C4
Portland La S1 ... 105 C3
Portland Rd S20 ... 79 C1
Portland St 2 S6 ... 51 C3
PORT MAHON ... 104 B5
Portobello S1 ... 104 C3
Portobello La 2 S1 ... 104 C3
Portobello St S1 ... 104 C3
Portsea Rd S6 ... 39 C2
POT HOUSE ... 3 A2
Pot House La S36 ... 3 A3
Potter Hill S61 ... 11 A1
Potter Hill La S35 ... 5 A1
Potters Gate S35 ... 5 A1
Pottery Cl S62 ... 12 A3
Pottery La S62 ... 12 C3
Pottery Row S61 ... 32 A4
Poucher St S61 ... 31 A4
Powell Dr S21 ... 92 A2
Powell St S3 ... 104 B4
Powley Rd S6 ... 27 A3
Poynton Wood Cres S17 ... 95 B4
Poynton Wood Glade S17 ... 95 B4
Prescott Rd S6 ... 39 B4
President Way S4 ... 53 B4
Preston St S8 ... 62 B1
Prestwich St S9 ... 30 B2
Prestwood Gdns S35 ... 6 C3
Priestley St S2 ... 62 C3
Primrose Ave
Brinsworth S60 ... 46 B1
Sheffield S5 ... 29 B2
Primrose Cl S21 ... 92 C3
Primrose Cres S20 ... 79 B1
Primrose Dr S35 ... 16 B2
Primrose Hill
Rotherham S60 ... 21 A2
Sheffield S6 ... 51 B4
Primrose La S21 ... 92 C3
Prince Edward Prim Sch S12 ... 64 B1
Prince Of Wales Rd S2, S9 ... 65 A4
Princess Ct S2 ... 64 C2
Princess Dr S36 ... 3 B2
Princess Rd S18 ... 101 A4
Princess St S4 ... 53 B4
Princes St S60 ... 32 B4
Pringle Rd S60 ... 45 C2
Priory Ave S7 ... 62 A2
Priory Cl S35 ... 16 A3
Priory Pl S7 ... 62 A2
Priory Rd
Sheffield, Ecclesfield S35 ... 16 A3
Sheffield, Sharrow Head S7 ... 62 A2
Priory Terr 10 S7 ... 62 A2
Priory Way S26 ... 69 C1
Pritchard Cl S12 ... 78 A1
Proctor Pl S6 ... 40 A2
Progress Dr S66 ... 37 A3
Prominence Way S66 ... 24 B1
Prospect Cl S66 ... 37 A2
Prospect Ct 1 S17 ... 95 C3
Prospect Dr S17 ... 95 A3
Prospect Pl S17 ... 95 B3
Prospect Rd
Dronfield S18 ... 98 A1
Sheffield, Bradway Bank S17 ... 95 B3
Sheffield, Lowfield S2 ... 62 B1
Providence Rd S6 ... 50 C4
Providence St
Rotherham, Greasbrough S61 ... 11 A1
Rotherham, New York S60 ... 32 C4
Provincial Park S35 ... 16 C4
Psalter Croft S11 ... 60 C1
Psalter Ct S11 ... 61 A1
Psalter La S11 ... 61 A1
Psalters La
Rotherham, Holmes S61 ... 32 A4
Rotherham, Kimberworth S61 ... 31 C4
Purbeck Ct S20 ... 90 B4
Purbeck Gr S20 ... 90 B4
Purbeck Rd S20 ... 90 B4
Purslove Cl S66 ... 37 B2
Pye Bank CE Prim Sch S3 ... 52 C4
Pye Bank Cl S3 ... 52 B4
Pye Bank Dr S3 ... 52 B4
Pye Bank Rd S3 ... 52 B4

Q

Quadrant The S17 ... 94 C3
Quail Rise S2 ... 63 C4
Quarry Cl S60 ... 45 B2
Quarry Field La S66 ... 36 B1
Quarry Fields S66 ... 36 B1
Quarry Head Lodge S11 ... 61 A1
Quarry Hill
Rotherham S60 ... 33 A4
Sheffield S20 ... 89 B2
Quarry La
Rotherham S61 ... 20 C2
Sheffield S11 ... 72 B4
Quarry Rd
Killamarsh S21 ... 92 A3
Sheffield, Handsworth S13 ... 55 C1
Quarry Rd *continued*
Sheffield, Totley Brook S17 ... 94 C3
Quarry St S62 ... 12 A4
Quarry Vale Gr S12 ... 76 B2
Quarry Vale Rd S12 ... 76 B2
Queen Anne Ct S14 ... 75 A1
Queen Elizabeth Ct S14 ... 75 A1
Queen Mary Cl S2 ... 64 B1
Queen Mary Cres S2 ... 64 B2
Queen Mary Ct S2 ... 64 B2
Queen Mary Mews S2 ... 64 B1
Queen Mary Rd S2 ... 64 C2
Queensgate S35 ... 15 A2
Queens Gdns S2 ... 63 A2
Queens Mews S2 ... 63 A2
Queens Rd
Aston S26 ... 69 A1
Sheffield, Lowfield S2 ... 62 C2
Sheffield S2 ... 107 B1
Queen's Rd S20 ... 79 B2
Queens Ret Pk S2 ... 62 C2
Queen's Row S3 ... 104 C4
Queens Stables S2 ... 63 A2
Queen St
Chapeltown S35 ... 7 B3
Eckington S21 ... 103 B1
Rotherham S65 ... 22 A1
Sheffield, Mosborough S20 ... 90 A1
Sheffield S1 ... 106 A4
Queens View S2 ... 63 A2
Queensway S60 ... 47 A4
Queenswood Cl S6 ... 26 A1
Queen Victoria Rd S17 ... 95 A3
Quintec Ct S61 ... 21 B3
Quoit Gn S18 ... 101 A3
QUOIT GREEN ... 101 A3

R

Raby St S9 ... 31 B1
Racker Way S6 ... 39 C1
Radbourne Comm 4 S18 ... 99 C3
Radford Cl S65 ... 25 B2
Radford St S3 ... 104 C4
Radley Ave S66 ... 36 B3
Radnor Cl S20 ... 91 B4
Raeburn Cl S14 ... 86 C4
Raeburn Pl S14 ... 75 A1
Raeburn Rd S14 ... 75 A1
Raeburn Way S14 ... 86 C4
Rail Mill Way S62 ... 21 C4
Railway Ave S60 ... 57 A3
Railway Cotts S60 ... 57 A4
Railway Terr S60 ... 32 C4
Rainbow Ave S12 ... 78 B2
Rainbow Cl S12 ... 78 B2
Rainbow Cres S12 ... 78 B2
Rainbow Dr S12 ... 78 B2
Rainbow Forge Prim Sch S12 ... 78 B1
Rainbow Gr S12 ... 78 B2
Rainbow Pl S12 ... 78 B2
Rainbow Rd S12 ... 78 B2
Rainbow Way S12 ... 78 B2
Rainbow Wlk 2 S12 ... 78 A2
Raisen Hall Pl S5 ... 41 B4
Raisen Hall Rd S5 ... 28 A1
Raleigh Dr S35 ... 6 B3
Raleigh Rd S2 ... 74 A4
Ralph Ellis Dr S36 ... 3 A2
Ralston Croft S20 ... 103 B4
Ralston Ct S20 ... 103 A4
Ralston Gr S20 ... 103 A4
Ralston Pl S20 ... 103 A4
Rampton Rd 1 S7 ... 62 A1
Ramsden Rd S60 ... 33 B3
Ramsey Rd S10 ... 51 A2
Ranby Rd S11 ... 60 C1
Randall Pl 4 S2 ... 62 A2
Randall St S2 ... 62 B3
Ranelagh Dr S11 ... 72 A3
Ranfield Ct S65 ... 25 B2
Rangeley Rd S6 ... 50 B3
RANMOOR ... 60 A3
Ranmoor Chase S10 ... 60 C3
Ranmoor Cliffe Rd S10 ... 60 A3
Ranmoor Cres S10 ... 60 A3
Ranmoor Ct S10 ... 60 B2
Ranmoor Grange S10 ... 60 A3
Ranmoor House (Sheffield Univ) S10 ... 60 B4
Ranmoor Park Rd S10 ... 60 A3
Ranmoor Rd S10 ... 60 A3
Ranmoor Rise S10 ... 60 A3
Ranskill Ct S9 ... 44 A1
Ranulf Ct S7 ... 72 B1
Ranworth Rd S66 ... 37 B3
Raseby Ave S20 ... 90 C4
Raseby Cl S20 ... 90 C4
Raseby Pl S20 ... 90 C4
Ratcliffe Rd 7 S11 ... 61 B2
Ravencar Rd S21 ... 102 B1
Ravencarr Pl S2 ... 64 B3
Ravencarr Rd S2 ... 64 B3
Raven Dr S61 ... 9 B4
Ravenfield Cl S20 ... 89 B4
Ravenfield Prim Sch S65 ... 25 A3
Raven Rd S7 ... 72 C4
Ravenscroft Ave S13 ... 65 C2
Ravenscroft Cl S13 ... 65 C2
Ravenscroft Cres S13 ... 65 C2
Ravenscroft Ct S13 ... 65 C2
Ravenscroft Dr S13 ... 65 C1
Ravenscroft Oval S13 ... 65 C2
Ravenscroft Pl S13 ... 65 C2
Ravenscroft Rd S13 ... 65 C1
Ravenscroft Way S13 ... 65 C2
Ravensdale Rd S18 ... 99 C3
Ravenswood Dr S66 ... 24 B2
Ravine The S5 ... 17 B1
Rawlins Ct S18 ... 98 A2
RAWMARSH ... 11 C3
Rawmarsh Ashwood Jun & Inf Sch S62 ... 12 A1
Rawmarsh Com Sch S62 ... 11 C4
Rawmarsh Hill S62 ... 12 A2
Rawmarsh Ho S62 ... 12 A2
Rawmarsh Rd S60 ... 21 A2
Rawmarsh Ryecroft Inf Sch S62 ... 12 B4
Rawmarsh St Mary's CE Prim Sch S62 ... 12 A3
Rawmarsh Sh Ctr S62 ... 12 A3
Rawson Rd S65 ... 21 B1
Rawsons Almshouses S6 ... 39 B4
Rawsons Bank S35 ... 16 B2
Rawson Spring Rd S6 ... 40 B4
Rawson Spring Way S6 ... 40 B4
Rawson St S6 ... 40 C1
Raybould Rd S61 ... 10 A1
Raynald Rd S2 ... 64 B3
Reaper Cres S35 ... 6 C4
Reasby Ave S65 ... 25 A2
Rectory Cl
Eckington S21 ... 103 B2
Stocksbridge S36 ... 3 B3
Rectory Gdns S21 ... 92 B2
Rectory Rd S21 ... 92 B1
Rectory St S62 ... 12 A2
Redbrook Croft 6 S20 ... 77 C1
Redbrook Gr 5 S20 ... 77 C1
Redcar Rd S10 ... 51 A1
Redfern Ave S20 ... 90 B3
Redfern Ct S20 ... 90 B3
Redfern Dr S20 ... 90 B3
Redfern Gr S20 ... 90 B3
Red Fern Gr S36 ... 3 A2
Redgrave 5 S3 ... 106 B5
Redgrave Pl S66 ... 36 B4
Red Hill S1 ... 104 C3
Red La S10 ... 61 A3
Redland La S7 ... 72 C1
Redmires Rd S10 ... 58 C3
Redmires Way S10 ... 58 A3
Red Oak La S6 ... 38 A1
Redrock Rd S60 ... 47 B4
Redscope Cres S61 ... 19 A3
Redscope Prim Sch S61 ... 19 B3
Redscope Rd S61 ... 19 A3
Redthorn Rd S13 ... 64 A2
Redwood Ave S21 ... 92 A1
Redwood Glen S35 ... 7 A2

Reedham Dr S66 . . . . 37 B3
Regent Cl S6 . . . . 40 A2
Regent St
 Rotherham S61. . . . . 31 C4
 Sheffield S1 . . . . 105 C3
Regents Way S26 . . . . 69 C1
Regent Terr S3 . . . . 105 C3
Reignhead Prim Sch
 S20 . . . . 79 C1
Rembrandt Dr S18. . . . . . 100 A3
Remington Ave S5. . . . . . . 15 C1
Remington Dr S5. . . . . 15 C1
Remington Rd S5. . . . . 15 C1
Remount Rd S61 . . . . 19 A4
Remount Way S61 . . . . 19 A4
Renathorpe Rd S5. . . . . . . 29 A4
Rencliffe Ave S60. . . . . . . 33 C1
Reneville Cl S60 . . . . 33 B2
Reneville Cres S5. . . . . . . 16 A2
Reneville Ct S5. . . . . 16 A2
Reneville Dr S5. . . . . 16 A2
Reneville Rd S60 . . . . 33 B2
Reney Ave S8. . . . . 96 B4
Reney Cres S8. . . . . 96 B4
Reney Dr S8. . . . . 96 B4
Reney Rd S8 . . . . 84 C1
Reney Wlk S8 . . . . 96 B4
Renishaw Ave S60 . . . . . . 47 C4
Renshaw Cl S35 . . . . 5 A2
Renshaw Rd S11. . . . . 71 C4
Renway Rd S60. . . . . 34 A1
Repton Pl S18 . . . . 99 B3
Reresby Cres S60. . . . . . . 48 A4
Reresby Dr S60 . . . . 48 A4
Reresby Rd
 Rotherham, Thrybergh
 S65. . . . . 24 A4
 Rotherham, Whiston
 S60. . . . . 48 A4
Reservoir Rd S10 . . . . 51 A1
Retail Shop WA Ctr &
 Trad Est S60. . . . . 21 C3
Retford Rd
 Aston S13. . . . . 67 C2
 Orgreave S13. . . . . 66 C3
 Sheffield, Woodhouse Mill
 S13. . . . . 67 C2
Revell Cl S60 . . . . 23 A1
Revill La S13 . . . . 78 B4
Rex Ave S7. . . . . 72 B2
Reynard La S2. . . . . 49 A3
Reynolds Cl
 Dronfield S18. . . . . 100 A2
 Rotherham S66. . . . . 36 B4
Rhodes Ave S61 . . . . 19 B4
Rhodes Dr S60 . . . . 48 A4
Rhodes St S35 . . . . 107 C3
Rianstorth S35 . . . . 17 B4
Ribble Croft S35. . . . . 7 B4
Ribblesdale Dr S12 . . . . . . 89 A3
Ribble Way S5. . . . . 28 C1
Riber Cl S6. . . . . 49 B4
Ribston Ct S9 . . . . 54 C2
Ribston Mews S9 . . . . 54 C2
Ribston Pl S9 . . . . 54 C2
Ribston Rd S9 . . . . 54 C2
Ribston Wlk S9 . . . . 54 C2
Richard Rd S60. . . . . 33 B3
Richards Ct 2 S2. . . . . . . 74 A4
Richards Rd S2 . . . . 74 A4
Richards Way S62 . . . . . . 12 B4
RICHMOND. 65 C1
Richmond Ave S13. . . . . . 64 A2
Richmond Ct S13. . . . . . . 65 B1
Richmond Farm Mews
 S13. . . . . 65 B1
Richmond Dr S13 . . . . 65 C2
Richmond Hall Ave
 S13. . . . . 65 B2
Richmond Hall Cres
 S13. . . . . 65 B1
Richmond Hall Dr S13 . . . 65 B2
Richmond Hall Rd
 S13. . . . . 65 B2
Richmond Hall Way
 S13. . . . . 65 B1
Richmond Hill Ho S13 . . . 65 B1
Richmond Hill Rd S13 . . . 65 B1
RICHMOND PARK. 31 A4
Richmond Park Ave
 Rotherham S61. . . . . 31 A4
 Sheffield S13 . . . . 65 C4

Richmond Park Cl
 S13. . . . . 65 C3
Richmond Park Cres
 S13. . . . . 65 C4
Richmond Park Croft
 S13. . . . . 65 C4
Richmond Park Dr
 S13. . . . . 65 C3
Richmond Park Gr
 S13. . . . . 65 C3
Richmond Park Rd
 S13. . . . . 65 C3
Richmond Park Rise
 S9 . . . . 65 B4
Richmond Park View
 S13. . . . . 65 C3
Richmond Park Way
 S13. . . . . 65 C3
Richmond Pl S13 . . . . 65 B1
Richmond Rd
 Rotherham S61. . . . . 31 B4
 Sheffield S13. . . . . 65 B1
Richmond St S13 . . . . 52 C4
Richworth Rd S13 . . . . . . 64 A2
Rickard Cl S26 . . . . 69 B3
Ridal Ave S36. . . . . 2 C4
Ridal Cl S36 . . . . 2 C4
Ridal Croft S36 . . . . 2 C4
Riddings Cl S2 . . . . 64 B1
Rider Rd S6 . . . . 40 A2
Ridge Ct
 Rotherham S65. . . . . 21 B1
 Sheffield S10. . . . . 59 A4
Ridgehill Ave S12. . . . . . . 76 A3
Ridgehill Gr S12. . . . . 76 A3
Ridge Rd S65 . . . . 21 C1
Ridge The S10 . . . . 59 A3
Ridge View Cl S9 . . . . 30 A1
Ridge View Dr S9 . . . . 30 A1
RIDGEWAY. 88 C2
Ridgeway
 Dronfield S18. . . . . 98 B1
 Rotherham S65. . . . . 23 A1
Ridgeway Cl S65. . . . . 23 A1
Ridgeway Craft Ctr ★
 S12. . . . . 88 C2
Ridgeway Cres S12. . . . . . 75 C4
Ridgeway Dr S12. . . . . . . 75 C4
RIDGEWAY MOOR. 88 C1
Ridgeway Prim Sch
 S12. . . . . 88 C2
Ridgeway Rd
 Brinsworth S60 . . . . 46 A2
 Sheffield S12 . . . . 75 C3
Riding Cl S66. . . . . 36 A3
Rig Cl S61 . . . . 10 A1
Rimmington Ho S36 . . . . . 4 B2
Ringstead Ave S10. . . . . . 49 C1
Ringstead Cres S10. . . . . 50 A1
Ringwood Cres S20. . . . . 91 B4
Ringwood Dr S20. . . . . . . 91 B4
Ringwood Gr S20. . . . . . . 91 B4
Ringwood Rd 3 S20. . . . . 91 B4
Ripley St S6 . . . . 40 A1
Ripon St S9 . . . . 54 A3
Rippon Cres S6. . . . . 39 C2
Rippon Dr S6. . . . . 39 C2
Rippon Rd S6 . . . . 39 C2
Rising St S3 . . . . 52 C4
Rivelin Bank S6 . . . . 39 C1
Rivelin Glen Cotts S6 . . . 49 C2
Rivelin Park Cres S6. . . . . 50 B4
Rivelin Park Dr S6. . . . . . . 50 B4
Rivelin Park Rd S6. . . . . . 50 B4
Rivelin Prim Sch S6 . . . . 40 A1
Rivelin Rd S6. . . . . 50 B4
Rivelin St S6 . . . . 50 C4
Rivelin Terr S6 . . . . 50 B4
Rivelin Valley Rd S6. . . . . 49 A2
River Bank S35 . . . . 13 C3
River Ct S17 . . . . 83 B1
Riverdale Ave S10 . . . . . . 60 B2
Riverdale Dr S10 . . . . 60 B3
Riverdale Rd S10 . . . . 60 B3
River Rivelin Trail ★
 S6 . . . . 49 B2
Riverside S6 . . . . 39 B1
Riverside Cl S6. . . . . 39 A2
Riverside Ct S9 . . . . 43 A1
Riverside Mews 3 S6 . . . 40 A2
Riverside Pk S2 . . . . 107 B1

Riverside Studios
 S18. . . . . 101 A2
Riverside Way S60 . . . . . . 32 C3
River Terr S6 . . . . 40 A2
River View Rd S35 . . . . . . 13 C3
Roach Rd S11 . . . . 61 A1
Robert Rd S8. . . . . 85 B1
Roberts Gr S26 . . . . 69 C1
Robertshaw 1 S13 . . . . 104 B3
Robertshaw Cres S36. . . . 3 C3
Robertson Dr S6 . . . . 50 B4
Robertson Rd S6 . . . . 50 C4
Robert St S60 . . . . 32 B4
Robey St S4 . . . . 42 C3
Robinets Rd S61. . . . . 10 B1
Robin Hood Chase S6. . . . 38 A1
Robin Hood Rd S9 . . . . . . 30 A2
Robin La S20 . . . . 79 B2
Robin Pl S26 . . . . 81 A4
Robins Ct S26 . . . . 69 C1
Robinson Ct S11. . . . . 19 C1
Robinson Rd S2 . . . . 107 C2
Robinson St S60. . . . . 33 A2
Robinson Way S21. . . . . . 92 A2
Roche 3 S20. . . . . 90 C2
Rocher Ave S35 . . . . 15 B1
Rocher Cl S35. . . . . 15 B1
Rocher Gr S35. . . . . 15 B1
Rochester Cl S10 . . . . 58 B3
Rochester Rd S10. . . . . . . 58 B3
Rochester Rd S10 . . . . . . 58 B3
Rockcliffe Rd S62 . . . . . . 12 A3
Rockingham 11 S20 . . . . . 90 C2
Rockingham Cl
 3 Dronfield S18 . . . . . . 99 B3
 Sheffield S1 . . . . 107 A2
Rockingham Gate 1
 S1. . . . . 107 A2
Rockingham Ho S62 . . . . . 12 B4
Rockingham Jun & Inf
 Sch S61. . . . . 10 A3
Rockingham La S1 . . . . . 107 A3
Rockingham Rd S62 . . . . . 12 B4
Rockingham St S11. . . . . 104 C3
Rockingham Way
 Rotherham S61. . . . . 10 A3
 Sheffield S1 . . . . 107 A2
Rockland Villas S65 . . . . . 23 B4
Rockley Rd S6 . . . . 39 C4
Rock Mount S10 . . . . 60 A3
Rock Mount Rd S9. . . . . . 30 B2
Rock Pl S36 . . . . 3 C3
Rock St S3 . . . . 52 C4
Rockwood Cl S35. . . . . 6 C3
Rodger Rd S13 . . . . 78 C4
Rodger St S60. . . . . 20 C1
Rodman Dr S13. . . . . 67 B2
Rodman St S13 . . . . 67 C2
Rod Moor Rd S17, S18. . . 95 C2
Rodney Hill S6 . . . . 38 C3
Rodwell Cl S60 . . . . 57 C2
Roebuck Rd S6 . . . . 104 A4
Roehampton Rise S60 . . . 45 B3
Roe La S3 . . . . 41 C2
Roewood Ct S3. . . . . 41 C2
Rojean Rd S35. . . . . 15 A2
Rokeby Dr S5. . . . . 28 B4
Rokeby Rd S5 . . . . 28 A4
ROLLESTONE. 74 C3
Rolleston Rd S5 . . . . 29 A2
Rollin Dr S6 . . . . 39 C3
Roman Cres
 Brinsworth S60 . . . . 46 A4
 Rawmarsh S62. . . . . 11 C4
Roman Ct S61 . . . . 31 B4
Romandale Gdns S2 . . . . 63 A3
Roman Ridge Rd S9 . . . . . 30 B1
Romney Cl S66 . . . . 36 B4
Romney Dr S18. . . . . 100 A3
Romney Gdns S2 . . . . . . 74 A4
Romsdal Rd S10. . . . . 51 A2
Ronald Rd S9. . . . . 55 A2
Ronksley Cres S5 . . . . . . 29 A4
Ronksley Rd S5. . . . . 29 A4
Rookery Bank S6 . . . . 4 B2
Rookery Chase S36 . . . . . 4 B2
Rookery Cl S36 . . . . 4 B2
Rookery Dell S36 . . . . 4 B2
Rookery Rise S36 . . . . 4 B1
Rookery The S36 . . . . 4 B2
Rookery Vale S36 . . . . 4 B2
Rosamond Ave S17 . . . . . 95 B4

Rosamond Cl S17. . . . . . . 95 B4
Rosamond Ct S17. . . . . . . 95 B3
Rosamond Dr S17 . . . . . . 95 B4
Rosamond Glade S17 . . . 95 B4
Rosamond Pl S17. . . . . . . 95 B4
Rosa Rd S10. . . . . 51 A2
Roscoe Bank S6 . . . . 49 C3
Roscoe Ct S6. . . . . 50 A4
Roscoe Dr S6 . . . . 50 A3
Roscoe Mount S6 . . . . . . 50 A3
Roscoe Rd S3 . . . . 104 C5
Roscoe View S6. . . . . 50 A3
Rose Ave S20. . . . . 79 B1
Rosebery St S61 . . . . 32 A4
Rose Cl S60 . . . . 46 B1
Rose Cres S62 . . . . 12 C4
Rose Ct S66 . . . . 36 A2
Rosedale Ave S62. . . . . . . 12 A4
Rosedale Cl S26 . . . . 69 C2
Rosedale Gdns S11 . . . . . 61 B2
Rosedale Rd
 Aston S26. . . . . 69 C2
 Sheffield S11 . . . . 61 B2
Rosedale Way S66 . . . . . . 36 C4
Rose Dr S66. . . . . 36 C3
Rose Garth Ave S26. . . . . 69 C2
Rose Hill S20. . . . . 89 C2
Rose Hill Ave S20 . . . . . . 89 C2
Rose Hill Cl S20 . . . . 89 C2
Rose Hill Dr S20 . . . . 89 C2
Rosehill Rd S62 . . . . 12 A4
Rose Hill Mews S20. . . . . 89 C2
Rosehill Rd S62 . . . . 12 A4
Rose Hill View S20 . . . . . . 89 C2
Roselle St S6 . . . . 40 A2
Rosemary Ct
 1 Sheffield, Norton
 Woodseats S8 . . . . . . 73 C1
 Sheffield S8 . . . . 51 A3
Rosemary Rd
 Rotherham S66. . . . . 36 A3
 Sheffield S20 . . . . 79 B2
Rose Way S21 . . . . 92 B1
Rosewell Ct S65. . . . . 22 B2
Roslin Rd S10 . . . . 51 A1
Rosser Ave S12. . . . . 87 A4
Rossetti Mount S66 . . . . . 36 B4
Rossington Rd S11. . . . . . 61 A2
Rossiter Rd S61 . . . . 11 A2
Rosslyn Ave S26 . . . . 69 C2
Ross St S9 . . . . 55 B2
Roston Cl 3 S18 . . . . 99 C3
Rothay Cl
 Dronfield S18. . . . . 100 A2
 Dronfield S18. . . . . 100 A3
Rothay Rd S4. . . . . 43 A3
Rothbury Cl S20. . . . . 91 B4
Rothbury Ct 5 S20. . . . . . 91 B4
Rothbury Way S60. . . . . . 46 A3
Rother Cres S60. . . . . 57 C2
ROTHERHAM 33 C4
Rotherham Central Sta
 S60. . . . . 33 A4
Rotherham Cl S21 . . . . . . 93 A4
Rotherham Coll of Arts &
 Tech S65. . . . . 21 B1
Rotherham District
 General Hospl S60 . . . . 47 A4
Rotherham Rd
 Aston S26. . . . . 69 A1
 Catliffe S60. . . . . 57 B4
 Eckington S20, S21. . . . 103 C4
 Killamarsh S21. . . . . 93 A4
 Orgreave S13. . . . . 66 C3
 Rotherham S62. . . . . 21 B4
 Sheffield, Beighton S20 . . 79 C3
 Sheffield S20, S21. . . . . 103 C4
Rotherham Rd N S20 . . . . 91 A2
Rotherham St S9 . . . . 43 B1
Rotherhill Cl S65. . . . . 22 A1
Rother Rd S60. . . . . 33 A1
Rotherside Rd S21. . . . . . 103 C2
Rotherstoke Cl S60. . . . . . 33 B2
Rother Terr S60. . . . . 33 A1
Rothervale Cl S20 . . . . . . 79 C2
Rother Valley Way
 S20 . . . . 91 C2
Rother View Cl S65 . . . . . . 68 B1
Rother View Gdns S26 . . . 68 B1
Rother View Rd S60 . . . . . 33 A2
Rotherway S60 . . . . 46 C2
Rotherwood S13 . . . . 67 B2

Ree–Ryd 127

Rotherwood Rd S21 . . . . . 92 C3
Rough La S35 . . . . 14 B3
Roughwood Gn S61. . . . . . 10 B1
Roughwood Prim Sch
 S61. . . . . 19 B4
Roughwood Rd S61. . . . . . 19 B4
Roughwood Way S61 . . . . 19 B4
Roundel St S9. . . . . 54 A3
Roundwood Gr S62 . . . . . . 12 C3
Rowan Cl S35 . . . . 7 B2
Rowan Dr S66. . . . . 36 A3
Rowan Sch The S17 . . . . . 94 C4
Rowan Tree Cl S21 . . . . . . 92 A1
Rowan Tree Dell S17 . . . . 94 C1
Rowan Tree Rd S21 . . . . . 92 A1
Rowdale Cres S12 . . . . . . 76 C3
Rowel La S6. . . . . 38 A2
Rowland Rd 8 S2 . . . . 62 B2
Rowland St S3 . . . . 52 B3
Rowley Way S66 . . . . 24 B2
Rowsley St S2 . . . . 62 C3
Roxton Ave 2 S8 . . . . 85 A2
Roxton Rd S8. . . . . 84 C3
Royale Cl S21 . . . . 103 B1
Royal Exchange S3 . . . . . 106 B4
Royal Hallamshire Hospl
 S10 . . . . 105 A2
Royal Victoria Bldgs
 S3 . . . . 106 B4
ROYD 4 A1
Roydfield Cl S20. . . . . 90 B4
Roydfield Dr S20 . . . . 90 B4
Roydfield Gr S20 . . . . 90 B4
Royd Inf Sch S36 . . . . 4 A2
Royd La S36 . . . . 3 C1
Royds Ave S60. . . . . 48 A4
Royds Close Cres S65 . . . 23 B4
Royds La S4 . . . . 53 C4
Royd The S36. . . . . 3 C1
Royston Ave S20. . . . . . . 89 B4
Royston Cl 5 S20 . . . . 89 B4
Royston Croft 11 S20 . . . . 89 B4
Royston Gr 4 S20 . . . . . . 89 B4
Rubens Cl S18. . . . . 100 B3
Rubens Row 2 S2. . . . . . 106 C4
Ruby Ho S8 . . . . 74 A3
Rudston Prep Sch
 S60 . . . . 33 C3
Rudyard Ct 4 S6. . . . . . . 40 A2
Rudyard Rd S6 . . . . 40 A2
Rufford Ct S20. . . . . 91 B4
Rufford Rise S20 . . . . 91 B4
Rugby St S3 . . . . 52 B4
Rundle Dr S7. . . . . 61 C1
Rundle Rd
 Sheffield S7. . . . . 61 C1
 Stocksbridge S36 . . . . . . 3 A3
Rupert Rd S7. . . . . 73 A4
Rural La S6 . . . . 39 A4
Rushby St S4 . . . . 42 B3
Rushdale Ave S8 . . . . 74 A3
Rushdale Mount 4
 S8. . . . . 73 C3
Rushdale Rd S8 . . . . 74 A3
Rushdale Terr 3 S8 . . . . . 73 C3
Rushleigh Ct S17 . . . . 82 B1
Rushley Ave S17. . . . . . . 82 B2
Rushley Cl S17 . . . . 82 B2
Rushley Dr S17 . . . . 82 B1
Rushley Rd S17 . . . . 82 B1
Ruskin Ho S6. . . . . 50 C4
Ruskin Sq S8 . . . . 73 C4
Russell Cl S26 . . . . 68 C1
Russell Ct S11. . . . . 83 B4
Russell St
 Rotherham S65. . . . . 21 B2
 Sheffield S3 . . . . 106 A5
Rustlings Cl S11 . . . . 60 A2
Rustlings Rd S11 . . . . 60 C2
Ruthin St S4. . . . . 42 C2
Ruth Sq S10 . . . . 105 B2
Rutland Ct S10 . . . . 105 A2
Rutland Pk S10. . . . . 61 A4
Rutland Rd S3 . . . . 52 B4
Rutland Way S3 . . . . 52 A3
Ryan Dr S13 . . . . 67 C1
Ryan Pl S62 . . . . 12 A2
Rydal Cl S18. . . . . 99 C3
Rydalhurst Ave S6 . . . . . . 39 B4

Rydal Rd S8 . . . . .73 A3
Rye Bank S60. . . . . .48 B3
RYECROFT 12 B4
Ryecroft Glen Rd S17 . . .83 B2
Ryecroft View S17 . . . . . .82 B2
Ryefield Gdns S11 . . . . . .71 C3
Ryegate Cres S10 . . . . . . .50 C1
Ryegate Rd S10 . . . . .50 C1
Ryeview Gdns S61 . . . . . .20 B4
Ryhill Dr S20 . . . . .89 B4
Ryle Rd S7 . . . . .61 C1
Rylstone Ct S12 . . . . .89 C4
Rylstone Gr S12 . . . . .89 C4

S

Sackerville Terr S21. . . . . .91 C1
Sackville Rd S10. . . . . . . .50 C2
Sacred Heart RC Prim
  Sch S6. . . . . .40 A1
Saddler Ave S20 . . . . .90 B3
Saddler Cl S20 . . . . .90 B3
Saddler Gn S20. . . . . .90 B3
Saddler Gr S20 . . . . .90 B3
St Aidan's Ave S2. . . . . . .63 B2
St Aidan's Dr S2. . . . . . . .63 C2
St Aidan's Pl S2 . . . . .63 C2
St Aidan's Rd S2. . . . . . . .63 C2
St Aidan's Way S2 . . . . . .63 C2
St Albans CE Prim Sch
  S66. . . . . .36 B2
St Albans Cl S10 . . . . .59 A3
St Albans Ct S66. . . . . . . .36 B2
St Albans Dr S10 . . . . . . .58 C3
St Albans Rd S10 . . . . . . .59 A3
St Alban's Way S66. . . . . .36 B2
St Andrew Rd S36 . . . . . . .4 A2
St Andrews Cl S66 . . . . . .24 C1
St Andrew's Cl S11 . . . . . .61 B1
St Andrew's Prim Sch
  S18 . . . . .99 C3
St Andrew's Rd S11. . . . . .61 B1
St Andrews Wlk S60 . . . . .45 B3
ST ANN'S 21 A2
St Ann's Jun & Inf Sch
  S65. . . . . .21 C1
St Ann's RC Prim Sch
  S36 . . . . .3 A2
St Ann's Rd
  Rotherham S61. . . . . . . .21 B1
  Stocksbridge S36. . . . . . .3 C3
St Anthony Rd S10. . . . . . .50 B2
St Barnabas Ho [12] S2. . . .62 B2
St Barnabas La [4] S2. . . . .62 B2
St Barnabas Rd [5] S2. . . . .62 B2
St Bede's RC Prim Sch
  S61 . . . . .19 B2
St Bede's Rd S60 . . . . .32 C4
St Benedicts Ct S2. . . . . . .63 B2
St Bernard's RC High Sch
  S65 . . . . .34 C3
St Catherine's RC Prim
  Sch S4. . . . . .41 C2
St Charles St S9 . . . . .53 C4
St Clements Ct S13 . . . . . .78 A4
St David Rd S36 . . . . .4 A2
St Davids Dr S60. . . . . . . .45 B3
St Elizabeth Cl S2 . . . . . . .62 C2
St Francis Cl
  Rotherham S66. . . . . . . .24 C1
  Sheffield S10 . . . . .59 C4
St George Rd S36. . . . . .4 A2
St George's Church
  S1. . . . . .104 C3
St George's Cl S3. . . . . . . .104 B3
St George's Ct S1. . . . . . . .104 C3
St George's Dr S60 . . . . . .45 B2
St George's Terr S1 . . . . . .104 C3
St Gerard's RC Prim Sch
  S65 . . . . .23 B4
St Giles CE Prim Sch
  S21 . . . . .92 A2
St Giles Sq S35 . . . . .7 A3
St Helen Rd S36 . . . . .4 A1
St Helens Cl S60. . . . . . . .57 D1
St Hilda Cl S36 . . . . .4 A1
St James' Row [3] S1. . . . .106 A3
St James' St S1. . . . . .106 A3
St James Wlk S13 . . . . . . .67 B2

St Joan Ave S36 . . . . .4 A1
St John Fisher RC Prim
  Sch S2. . . . . .77 C1
St Johns Ave S66 . . . . . . .36 C4
St John's Ave S60 . . . . . . .20 B1
St John's Cl S65 . . . . .22 A2
St Johns Ct S60 . . . . .32 B4
St John's Ct S66 . . . . .36 C4
St John's Gn S61 . . . . .19 B3
St John's Rd
  Rotherham S65. . . . . . . .22 A2
  Sheffield S2 . . . . .53 B2
  Stocksbridge S36. . . . . . .4 B2
St Joseph's RC Prim Sch
  Rawmarsh S62. . . . . . . .12 B3
  Sheffield S13 . . . . .66 A3
St Joseph's Rd S13 . . . . . .66 A3
St Lawrence Ave S65 . . . .24 A4
St Lawrence Rd S9 . . . . . .44 C4
St Leonards Ave S65 . . . . .28 B1
St Leonards Cl S35 . . . . . .28 B1
St Leonard's La S65 . . . . . .21 C1
St Leonard's Pl S65. . . . . .21 C1
St Leonard's Rd S65 . . . . .21 C1
St Luke's Hospice S11 . . . .71 B1
St Margaret Ave S36 . . . . . .4 A2
St Margaret's Rd S35 . . . .16 B1
St Maries RC Prim Sch
  S10 . . . . .60 B3
St Mark Rd S36. . . . . .4 A2
St Mark's Cres S10 . . . . . .105 A2
St Martin Cl S36 . . . . .4 A2
St Mary Cres S36 . . . . .4 B1
St Mary's CE Prim Sch
  S6. . . . . .51 B4
St Mary's Cl S35 . . . . .16 A3
St Mary's Dr S60. . . . . . . .57 A4
St Mary's Gate S2, S3 . . . .105 C1
St Mary's La S35. . . . . . . .16 A3
St Mary's RC Prim Sch
  S65 . . . . .34 C4
St Mary's RC Prim Sch
  High Green S35 . . . . .5 C2
St Mary's Rd
  Rawmarsh S62. . . . . . . .12 B3
  Sheffield S2, S9 . . . . . . .107 B1
St Mary's Sq S2 . . . . .105 C1
St Mary's View S10 . . . . . .10 C1
St Matthias Rd S36 . . . . . . .4 A2
St Michael's Cl S35 . . . . . .16 B2
St Michael's Cres S35. . . . .16 B1
ST MICHAEL'S FIELD 16 C2
St Michael's Rd S35 . . . . . .16 B1
St Nicolas Rd S62. . . . . . . .12 B4
St Nicolas Wlk S62 . . . . . .12 C4
St Patrick Rd S36. . . . . .4 A2
St Patrick's RC Prim Sch
  S5 . . . . .28 C2
St Paul Cl S36 . . . . .4 A2
St Paul's Par S1 . . . . .107 A3
St Peter Ave S36. . . . . .4 B2
St Peter's Cl
  Brinsworth S60 . . . . .45 B2
  Sheffield S10 . . . . .106 A4
St Philip's La S3. . . . . .104 C5
St Philip's Rd S3. . . . . .104 B4
St Quentin Cl S17. . . . . . . .95 C3
St Quentin Dr S17 . . . . . . .95 C3
St Quentin Mount S17 . . . .95 C3
St Quentin Rise S17. . . . . .95 C3
St Quentin View S17 . . . . .95 C3
St Ronan's Rd S7 . . . . .62 A1
St Stephen's Dr S26 . . . . . .69 B2
St Stephens Rd S3. . . . . . .104 B4
St Stephen's Rd S65 . . . . .21 B1
St Stephen's Wlk S3. . . . . .104 B4
St Theresa's RC Prim Sch
  S2 . . . . .64 C1
St Thomas More RC Prim
  Sch S35. . . . . .15 B1
St Thomas of Canterbury
  RC Prim Sch S8 . . . . . . .85 A2
St Thomas Rd S10 . . . . . . .50 C1
St Thomas St S1 . . . . .104 C3
St Veronica Rd S36. . . . . . .4 B1
St Wandrilles Cl S35 . . . . .16 B3
St Wilfrid's RC Prim Sch
  S7 . . . . .72 B2
St Wilfrid's Rd [11] S2. . . . .62 B2
Sale Hill S10 . . . . .60 C4
Salisbury Ave S18 . . . . . . .100 C1

Salisbury Rd
  Dronfield S18 . . . . .101 A2
  Sheffield S10 . . . . .50 C2
Salmon St [5] S11. . . . . . . .62 A2
Salt Box Gr S35. . . . . .14 C1
Salt Box La S35 . . . . .15 A1
Samson St S2 . . . . .107 C2
Samuel Cl S2. . . . . .63 B1
Samuel Dr S2 . . . . .63 B1
Samuel Pl S2 . . . . .63 B1
Samuel Rd S2 . . . . .63 B2
Sandal Ct S61 . . . . .20 B1
Sandbeck Pl S11 . . . . .61 B2
Sandbed Rd S3. . . . . .40 C1
Sandbergh Rd S61. . . . . . .19 B4
Sandby Croft S14. . . . . . . .86 C4
Sandby Ct S14. . . . . .86 C4
Sandby Dr S14 . . . . .86 C4
Sandeby Dr S65 . . . . .25 A1
Sanderson St S9 . . . . .43 A1
Sandford Grove Rd
  S7 . . . . .73 A4
Sandhurst Pl S10 . . . . .51 A2
Sandiron Ho S7 . . . . .83 C3
Sandon View S10 . . . . . . .105 B2
Sandpiper Rd S61 . . . . .9 A4
Sandringham Ave S60 . . . .47 C3
Sandringham Pl
  Rotherham S65. . . . . . . .25 A2
  Sheffield S10 . . . . .58 A3
Sandringham Rd S9 . . . . . .30 A2
Sands Cl S14 . . . . .75 A2
Sandstone Ave S9 . . . . . . .43 A4
Sandstone Cl S9. . . . . .30 A1
Sandstone Dr S9 . . . . .43 A4
Sandstone Rd S9 . . . . .30 A1
Sandy Acres Cl S20 . . . . . .91 A3
Sandy Acres Dr S20 . . . . . .91 A3
SANDYGATE 59 C4
Sandygate Cl S10. . . . . . . .59 B4
Sandygate Gr S10 . . . . . . .59 B4
Sandygate Grange Dr
  S10 . . . . .59 C4
Sandygate Park Cres
  S10 . . . . .59 B4
Sandygate Park Rd
  S10 . . . . .59 B4
Sandygate Pk S10 . . . . . . .59 B4
Sandygate Rd S10 . . . . . . .59 C4
Sandy La S66. . . . . .37 C1
Sarah St S61 . . . . .32 B4
Sark Rd S2 . . . . .62 B1
Saunders Pl S2. . . . . .53 C1
Saunders Rd S2 . . . . .53 C1
Savage La S17. . . . . .82 B1
Savile St S4 . . . . .53 B4
Savile St E S4 . . . . .106 C5
Saville Rd S60 . . . . .47 C3
Saville St S65 . . . . .22 C3
Sawdon Rd S11 . . . . .61 C3
Saxonlea Ave S2 . . . . .65 A3
Saxonlea Cres S2 . . . . . . .65 A3
Saxonlea Ct S2. . . . . .65 A3
Saxonlea Dr [4] S2 . . . . . . .64 C3
Saxon Rd
  Rotherham S61. . . . . . . .31 A4
  Sheffield S2 . . . . .73 C4
Saxton Dr S60 . . . . .47 A3
Scammadine Cl S60 . . . . . .46 B2
Scampton Lodge S5 . . . . . .41 C4
Scarborough Rd
  Rotherham S66. . . . . . . .36 B3
  Sheffield S9 . . . . .55 A3
Scarlett Oak Mdw [5]
  S6. . . . . .49 A4
Scarsdale Cl S18 . . . . .101 A2
Scarsdale Cross [1]
  S18 . . . . .101 A3
Scarsdale Rd
  [2] Dronfield S18 . . . . . . .101 A3
  Sheffield S8 . . . . .73 B1
Schofield Rd S36 . . . . .3 C2
Sch of Nursing &
  Midwifery S3. . . . . .104 B4
SCHOLES 9 C2
Scholes Field Cl S61 . . . . . .18 C4
Scholes La S61 . . . . .9 C2
Scholes Rise S35 . . . . .16 B2
Scholes View S35 . . . . . . .16 B3
Scholey Rd S66. . . . . .36 B3
Scholey St S3 . . . . .106 B5
School Ave S20. . . . . .91 A1

School Cl S20 . . . . .91 A1
School Gr S20. . . . . .69 C1
School Green La S10. . . . . .58 C1
School Hill S60. . . . . .47 C3
School Ho S35. . . . . .13 A3
School La
  Dronfield S18 . . . . .100 C3
  Rawmarsh S62. . . . . . . .12 B1
  Sheffield, Greenhill S8 . . .85 A1
  Sheffield, Grenoside
    S35. . . . . .14 C3
  Sheffield, Park Hill S2 . . .107 C3
  Sheffield S8 . . . . .86 A3
  Sheffield, Stannington
    S6. . . . . .49 A3
School Lane Cl S8 . . . . . . .86 A3
School Rd
  Chapeltown S35 . . . . .7 A4
  Sheffield S10 . . . . .51 A2
  Sheffield, Sothall S20. . . .80 A1
School St
  Aston S26. . . . . .69 A1
  Eckington S21. . . . . .103 A1
  Rotherham S65. . . . . . . .23 B4
  Sheffield S20 . . . . .90 B1
Scotland St S3 . . . . .106 A4
Scott Rd S4 . . . . .42 A2
Scott St S4 . . . . .42 C2
Scott Way S35. . . . . .7 A2
Scowerdons Cl S12 . . . . . .77 B3
Scowerdons Dr S12. . . . . .77 B3
Scraith Wood Dr S5 . . . . . .40 C4
Scrooby Dr S61. . . . . .11 A1
Scrooby La S62. . . . . .11 B1
Scrooby Pl S61 . . . . .11 A1
Scrooby St S61 . . . . .11 A1
Sea Breeze Terr S13 . . . . . .65 B2
Seabrook Rd S2 . . . . .63 B4
Seagrave Ave S12 . . . . . . .76 A2
Seagrave Cres S12 . . . . . . .76 A2
Seagrave Dr S12. . . . . .76 A2
Seagrave Rd S12. . . . . .76 A2
Searby Rd S66. . . . . .25 A1
Seaton Cl S2 . . . . .64 A4
Seaton Cres S2 . . . . .64 A4
Seaton Pl S2 . . . . .64 A4
Seaton Way S2 . . . . .64 A4
Sebastian View S60 . . . . . .46 A4
Sedan St S4 . . . . .42 A1
Sedge Cl S66 . . . . .37 B2
Sedgley Rd S6. . . . . .40 B2
Sefton Ct S10 . . . . .59 B1
Sefton Rd S10. . . . . .59 C1
Selborne Rd S10. . . . . .50 B1
Selborne St S65 . . . . .21 B2
Selby Cl S26. . . . . .69 A1
Selby Rd S4 . . . . .42 B3
Selig Par S12. . . . . .88 A4
Sellars Rd S61. . . . . .19 B3
Sellars Row S35 . . . . .5 C2
Sellers St S8 . . . . .62 A1
Selly Oak Gr S8. . . . . .98 A4
Selly Oak Rd S8. . . . . .98 A4
Selwood S65 . . . . .21 C1
Selwyn St S65. . . . . .21 B2
Senior Rd S9 . . . . .55 A2
Seniors Pl S35. . . . . .7 A4
Serpentine Wlk S8 . . . . . . .85 C2
Sevenairs Fold S20 . . . . . .79 A1
Sevenairs Rd S20. . . . . . . .79 A1
Sevenairs View S20 . . . . . .79 A1
Sevenfields Ct S6. . . . . . . .39 B3
Sevenfields La S6 . . . . .39 B3
Severn Cl S10 . . . . .105 A3
Severn Rd S10. . . . . .105 A3
Severndale Dr S13. . . . . . .66 B1
Severndale Gdns S13 . . . . .66 B1
Severndale Pl S13 . . . . . . .66 B1
Severndale Wlk S13 . . . . . .77 C4
Sewell Rd S20 . . . . .103 C4
Sexton Dr S66 . . . . .37 A2
Seymore Rd S26. . . . . .81 A4
Shafton Rd S60 . . . . .47 C4
Shaftsbury Sq S65 . . . . . . .21 B1
Shakespeare Cres
  S18 . . . . .101 B1
Shakespeare Rd S65 . . . . .21 C2
Shaldon Gr S26. . . . . .69 B1
Shalesmoor S3 . . . . .104 C5
Sharpe Ave S8. . . . . .84 C2
Sharrard Cl S12 . . . . .76 A3
Sharrard Dr S12 . . . . .76 A3

Sharrard Gr S12 . . . . .76 A4
Sharrard Rd S12. . . . . .76 A3
SHARROW. 61 C1
Sharrow Inf Sch S7. . . . . . .62 A2
Sharrow Jun Sch S7. . . . . .62 A2
Sharrow La S11 . . . . .62 A2
Sharrow Rd S11. . . . . .62 A2
Sharrow St S11. . . . . .62 A2
Sharrow Vale Rd S11. . . . . .61 B2
Sharrow View S7 . . . . .61 C2
Shaw Rd S65 . . . . .22 A2
Shawsfield Rd S60. . . . . . .33 C1
Shaw St S18. . . . . .98 A2
SHAY HOUSE 3 A2
Shay House La S36 . . . . . . .3 A2
Shay Rd S36. . . . . .3 B3
Sheaf Bank S2 . . . . .62 B1
Sheaf Bank Bsns Pk
  S2 . . . . .62 B1
Sheaf Gardens Terr
  S2 . . . . .107 A3
Sheaf Gdns S2 . . . . .107 B1
Sheaf Sq S1 . . . . .107 B2
Sheaf St S1 . . . . .107 B3
Sheards Cl S18 . . . . .100 B3
Sheards Dr S18. . . . . .100 A3
Sheards Way S18. . . . . . . .100 B3
Shearman Ave S61. . . . . . .19 B4
Shearwood Rd S10 . . . . . .105 B3
Sheepcote Hill S21. . . . . . .92 B2
Sheepcote Rd S21 . . . . . . .92 A2
Sheep Cote Rd S60 . . . . . .35 B1
SHEFFIELD 53 B1
Sheffield Airport Bsns Pk
  S9, S60 . . . . .55 C3
Sheffield Cath [*] S1 . . . . .106 A4
Sheffield Childrens
  Hospl S10. . . . . .105 A3
Sheffield City Airport
  S60 . . . . .56 B4
Sheffield Coll
  (Bannerdale Ctr) The
  S7 . . . . .72 C2
Sheffield Coll Loxley Ctr
  The S6. . . . . .39 A1
Sheffield Coll (Norton
  Coll) The S8. . . . . .85 C1
Sheffield Coll Peaks Ctr
  S20 . . . . .78 C1
Sheffield Coll The
  (Castle Ctr N) S2. . . . . .107 C2
Sheffield Coll The
  (Castle Ctr S) S2. . . . . .107 C1
Sheffield Coll The
  (Frecheville Ctr)
  S12 . . . . .76 B2
Sheffield Fire & Police
  Mus [*] S1. . . . . .106 A4
Sheffield Hallam Univ
  Sheffield, Little Sheffield
  S11 . . . . .62 A3
  Sheffield S1 . . . . .107 B3
Sheffield Hallam Univ
  (Psalter Lane Campus)
  S11 . . . . .61 B1
Sheffield High Sch
  S10 . . . . .61 A4
Sheffield La S60 . . . . .57 A3
SHEFFIELD LANE
  TOP 28 C3
SHEFFIELD PARK 63 C2
Sheffield Parkway
  Catliffe S60. . . . . .56 C4
  Sheffield S9 . . . . .65 B4
Sheffield Rd
  Aston S13. . . . . .68 B2
  Dronfield S18 . . . . .97 A1
  Eckington S20, S21. . . . .103 B3
  Killamarsh S21. . . . . . . .92 B3
  Rotherham S60. . . . . . . .32 B2
  Sheffield, Coisley Hill
    S13 . . . . .78 A4
  Sheffield, Hackenthorpe S12,
    S20. . . . . .77 C1
  Sheffield, Meadowhall
    S9 . . . . .44 A3
  Sheffield S20, S21. . . . . .103 B3
  Sheffield, Templeborough
    S9, S60 . . . . .43 C3
Sheffield Science Park
  S2 . . . . .107 B2
Sheffield Ski Village [*]
  S3 . . . . .41 A1

Sheffield Sta S1	107 B2
heldon La 8 S6	49 A4
heldon Rd	
Sheffield S7	73 A4
Stocksbridge S36	3 B3
heldon Row S3	106 B4
heldon St S2	62 B3
heldrake Cl S61	9 A3
helley Dr	
Dronfield S18	101 B1
Rotherham S65	34 B4
helley Rd S65	34 C4
henstone Dr S65	34 B2
henstone Rd	
Rotherham S65	34 B2
Sheffield S6	40 A4
hepcote La S9	44 A2
hepcote Way S9	44 B1
hepherd Dr S35	6 C4
hepherd St S3	104 C4
hepley Croft S35	6 C4
hepperson Rd S6	39 C3
herbourne Ave S66	37 B1
herburn Gate S35	7 A4
herde Rd S6	51 C3
herdn Dr S65	34 C4
heringham Cl S35	5 B1
heringham Gdns S35	5 B1
herwood Chase S17	94 C3
herwood Cres S60	33 B4
herwood Glen S7	83 C3
herwood Pl 2 S18	99 C3
herwood Rd	
Dronfield S18	99 C3
Killamarsh S21	92 C3
hetland Rd S18	101 A2
hip Hill S60	33 A4
hipman Ct S20	90 B1
hipton St S6	104 B5
hirebrook Ct S2	73 C4
hirebrook Rd S8	73 C4
HIRECLIFFE	41 B3
hirecliffe Cl S3	41 C1
hirecliffe Jun Sch	
S	40 C4
hirecliffe La S3	41 B1
hirecliffe Rd S3	41 B3
HIREGREEN	29 A4
hiregreen La S5	29 C2
hiregreen Terr S5	29 A2
hirehall Cres S5	29 B4
hirehall Rd S5	17 A1
hireoaks Rd S18	101 B4
hirland Ct S9	54 C3
hirland La S9	54 B3
hirland Mews 4 S9	54 B3
hirland Pl S9	54 C3
hirle Hill Hospl & Sch	
S	61 B1
hirley Rd S3	41 C1
hooter's Grove Prim	
ch S6	50 A4
hore Ct S10	60 C4
horeham Ave S60	47 B3
horeham Dr S60	47 A3
horeham Rd S60	47 A3
horeham St S1	107 B2
hore La S10	60 B4
horland Dr S60	57 D2
hortbrook Bank 10	
20	90 C2
hortbrook Cl S20	91 A2
hortbrook Com Prim	
ch S20	90 C2
hortbrook Croft 6	
20	91 A2
hortbrook Dr S20	90 C2
hortbrook Rd S20	90 C2
hortbrook Way 13	
20	90 C2
hortbrook Wlk 12	
20	90 C2
hortridge St S9	54 A4
hrewsbury Hospl	
lmshouses S2	107 C2
hrewsbury Rd S2	107 B2
hrewsbury Terr	
Sheffield S61	31 C3
heffield S17	94 B2
hrogswood Rd S60	35 A1
hubert Cl S13	66 C2
ude Hill S1	106 B3

Sibbering Row S36	4 B2
Sicey Ave S5	29 A3
Sicey La S5	29 A4
Siddall St S1	104 C3
Sidney St S1	107 A2
Sidons Cl S61	19 B4
Siemens Cl S9	44 C4
Silkstone Cl S12	77 A2
Silkstone Cres S12	77 A2
Silkstone Dr S12	76 C2
Silkstone Pl S12	77 A2
Silkstone Rd S12	77 A2
Silver Birch Ave S10	59 A1
Silverdale Cl S11	71 C2
Silverdale Cres S11	71 C3
Silverdale Croft S11	71 C2
Silverdale Ct 1 S11	72 A2
Silverdale Gdns 2	
S11	72 A2
Silverdale Glade 3	
S11	72 A2
Silverdale Rd S11	71 C2
Silverdale Sch S11	71 A2
Silver Hill Rd S11	72 A3
Silver Mill Rd S2	62 B2
Silvermoor Dr S65	25 A2
Silver St	
Rotherham S65	23 B4
Sheffield S1	106 A4
Silver Street Head	
S1	106 A4
Silverwood Cl S66	24 B1
Silverwood Wlk S66	36 B4
Simcrest Ave S21	92 B1
Simmonite Rd S61	10 A1
Simon Ct S11	60 A2
Sims St S1	106 A4
Singleton Cres S6	40 A1
Singleton Gr S6	40 A1
Singleton Rd S6	40 A1
Sir Frederick Mappin	
Blgd (Univ of	
Sheffield) S1	104 C3
Sir Harold Jackson Prim	
Sch S17	95 C3
Sitwell 14 S20	90 C2
Sitwell Ave S36	2 C3
Sitwell Dr S60	34 A1
Sitwell Gr S60	47 B4
Sitwell Jun & Inf Schs	
S60	34 B1
Sitwell La S66	36 B3
Sitwell Park Rd S60	35 A1
Sitwell Pl 15 S7	62 A2
Sitwell Rd S7	62 A2
Sitwell St S21	102 C1
Sitwell Terr S66	36 B3
Sitwell View S60	48 B3
Skelton Cl S13	78 B3
Skelton Dr S13	78 B4
Skelton Gr S13	78 A4
Skelton La	
Sheffield, Beighton	
S20	79 B1
Sheffield, Coisley Hill	
S13	78 A4
Skelton Rise S8	73 C3
Skelton Rise S13	13 B2
Skelton Way S13	78 A4
Skelton Wlk S13	78 B4
Skelwith Cl 2 S4	43 A3
Skelwith Dr S4	43 A3
Skelwith Rd S4	43 A3
Skew Hill La S35	14 B1
Skinnerthorpe Rd S4	42 B3
Skipton Rd	
Aston S26	69 A4
Sheffield S4	42 A2
Skye Edge Ave S2	63 C4
Skye Edge Rd S2	63 B4
Slacks La S66	37 A1
Slaidburn Ave S35	7 A4
Slate St S2	62 C2
Slayleigh Ave S10	59 B2
Slayleigh Delph S10	59 A2
Slayleigh Dr S10	59 B2
Slayleigh La S10	59 B2
Sleaford St S9	54 A4
Sledgate Dr S66	35 C1
Sledgate La S66	36 A2
Slinn St S10	51 A3

Slitting Mill La S9	54 A4
Sloade La S12	88 B1
Smallage La S13	68 A3
Smalldale Rd S12	76 C2
Smeaton Cl S65	25 B2
Smeaton St 11 S61	19 B1
Smelter Wood Ave	
S13	65 C1
Smelter Wood Cl S13	65 C1
Smelter Wood Cres	
S13	64 A1
Smelter Wood Ct S13	65 C1
Smelter Wood Dr S13	65 C1
Smelter Wood La S13	65 C1
Smelter Wood Pl S13	64 A1
Smelter Wood Rd S13	65 C1
Smelter Wood Rise	
S13	64 A1
Smelter Wood Way	
S13	65 C1
Smithey Cl S35	6 B4
Smithfield	
Sheffield, Netherthorpe	
S3	106 A4
15 Sheffield S1	105 C3
Smithfield Rd S12	75 C1
Smith Rd S36	3 A3
Smith St S35	7 B3
Smithy Carr Ave S35	7 A3
Smithy Carr Cl S35	7 A3
Smithy Cl S61	10 A1
Smithy Croft S18	99 C4
SMITHY MOOR	2 B4
Smithy Moor Ave S36	2 B4
Smithy Moor La S36	2 A5
Smithy Wood Cres	
Sheffield S8	73 A2
Sheffield S8	73 B2
Smithy Wood Rd	
Chapeltown S61	8 B2
Sheffield S8	73 B2
Snail Hill S60	33 A4
Snaithing La S10	59 C3
Snaithing Park Cl S10	59 C3
Snaithing Park Rd	
S10	59 C3
SNAPE HILL	100 C4
Snape Hill S18	100 C4
Snape Hill Cl S18	97 B1
Snape Hill Cres S18	97 B1
Snape Hill Dr S18	97 C1
Snape Hill La S18	100 C4
Snelston Cl S18	99 C3
Snig Hill S3	106 B4
Snowdon Way S60	46 B1
Snow La S3	106 A4
Soaper La S18	100 C4
Soap House La S13	79 B4
Solly St S1	104 C4
Solway Rise S18	99 C4
Somercotes Rd S12	76 C3
Somerset Rd S12	52 C4
Somerset St S3	52 C4
Somerville Terr S6	51 C4
Sopewell Rd S61	31 A4
Sorby Rd S26	68 C1
Sorby St S4	53 A3
Sorby Way S66	36 B1
Sorrel Rd S60	46 C2
Sorrelsykes Cl S60	47 C2
SOTHALL	91 C3
Sothall Cl S20	79 B1
Sothall Ct S20	79 B1
Sothall Gn S20	79 B1
Sothall Green Farm	
S20	79 B1
Sothall Mews S20	79 B1
Sough Hall Ave S61	9 A3
Sough Hall Cl S61	9 A3
Sough Hall Cres S61	9 A3
Sough Hall Rd S61	9 A2
Southall St 10 S8	73 C4
Southbourne Ct S17	94 B4
Southbourne Mews	
S10	61 A3
Southbourne Rd S10	61 A3
Southcote S18	99 C3
South Cres	
Killamarsh S21	92 C3
Rotherham S65	22 C1
Southcroft Gdns 1	
S7	73 B4

Southcroft Wlk 2 S7	73 B4
South Ct S17	82 C1
Southend Pl S2	63 C4
Southend Rd S2	63 C4
Southey Ave S5	28 A1
Southey Cl S5	27 C1
Southey Cres S5	28 A1
Southey Dr S5	28 A1
SOUTHEY GREEN	27 B1
Southey Green Cl S5	27 C1
Southey Green Com Prim	
Sch S5	27 C1
Southey Green Rd S5	27 B1
Southey Hall Dr S5	28 A1
Southey Hall Rd S5	28 A2
Southey Hill S5	27 C2
Southey Pl S5	27 C1
Southey Rise S5	27 C1
Southfield Dr S18	101 B2
Southfield Mount	
S18	101 B2
Southgate S21	103 B1
Southgate Ct S21	103 B1
Southgrove Rd S10	105 A1
South La S11	107 A1
Southlands Way S26	69 C1
South Par S3	106 A5
South Rd	
Chapeltown S35	5 B1
Rotherham S61	19 B1
Sheffield S6	51 A4
Southsea Rd S13	77 C4
South St	
Rawmarsh S62	12 B4
Rotherham, Greasbrough	
S61	11 A1
Rotherham, Kimberworth	
S61	31 B4
Sheffield S20	103 A4
South Street Pk S2	107 C3
South Vale Dr S65	23 C4
South View	
Aston S26	69 B1
Sheffield S20	91 B1
South View Cl S6	38 C3
South View Cres S7	62 A1
South View Rd S7	62 A2
South View Rise S6	38 C3
South View Terr S60	57 A3
Southwell Gdns S26	68 B1
Southwell Rd	
Rawmarsh S62	12 C4
6 Sheffield S4	43 A3
South West Ctr The 3	
S8	73 A2
Southwood S6	26 A1
Southwood Ave S18	101 A1
Southwood Gr S6	26 A1
South Yorkshire Fresh	
Produce & Flower Ctr	
S9	54 C2
Spa Brook Cl S12	77 B2
Spa Brook Dr S12	77 B3
Spa La S13	78 B4
Spa Lane Croft S13	78 B4
Spalton Rd S62	12 A2
Spa View Ave S12	77 B1
Spa View Dr S12	77 B1
Spa View Pl S12	77 B1
Spa View Rd S12	77 B1
Spa View Terr S12	77 B1
Spa View Way S12	77 B1
Speeton Rd S6	40 A1
Spencer Ct S60	48 B3
Spencer Dr S65	25 A1
Spencer Gn S60	48 B3
Spencer Rd S2	62 B1
Spenser Rd S65	34 B3
SPINK HALL	3 A2
Spink Hall Cl S36	3 B2
Spink Hall La S36	3 A2
Spinkhill Ave S13	65 A2
Spinkhill Dr S13	65 B2
Spinkhill Rd S13	65 B2
Spinney Cl S60	34 B1
Spinneyfield S60	47 B4
Spitalfields S3	106 B5
Spital Hill S4	53 A3
Spital La S3	53 A3
Spital St S3	52 C3
Spofforth Rd S9	54 B3
Spooner Dr S21	92 A2

Spooner Rd S10	61 A4
Spoon Glade 2 S6	49 A4
Spoonhill Rd S6	50 A4
Spoon Mews S6	49 A4
Spoon Oak Lea 3 S6	49 A4
Spoon Way S6	49 A4
Spotswood Cl S14	75 A2
Spotswood Dr S14	75 A3
Spotswood Mount	
S14	75 A2
Spotswood Pl S14	74 C2
Spotswood Rd S14	74 C3
Spout Copse S6	49 A4
Spout La S6	38 A1
Spout Spinney S6	49 A4
Spring Cl S60	48 A3
Spring Close Dell S14	75 B2
Spring Close Mount	
S14	75 B2
Spring Close View	
S14	75 B2
Spring Croft S61	10 A1
Springfield Ave S7	72 B2
Springfield Cl	
Eckington S21	102 C1
Rotherham S61	21 A3
Sheffield S7	72 B2
Springfield Dr S65	24 A4
Springfield Glen S7	72 A2
Springfield Prim Sch	
S3	105 A2
Springfield Rd	
Rotherham S66	36 A2
Sheffield S7	72 B2
Springfield Way S35	6 B3
Spring Hill S10	51 A2
Spring Hill Rd S10	51 A2
Spring House Rd S10	51 A2
Spring La S2	63 C2
Spring St	
Rotherham S65	21 B1
Sheffield S3	106 A4
Springvale Rd S10	51 A2
Springvale Wlk S10	104 B5
Spring View Rd S10	51 A2
Spring Water Ave S12	77 C1
Spring Water Cl 3	
S12	77 C1
Spring Water Dr 1	
S12	77 C1
Springwater Ho S12	78 A1
Springwell Ave S20	79 A2
Springwell Cres S20	79 A2
Springwell Dr S20	79 A2
Springwell Gr S20	79 A2
Spring Wlk S25	81 C3
Springwood Ave S26	69 A3
Springwood Ct S26	69 B3
Springwood La S35	6 B4
Springwood Rd S8	73 C4
Spruce Ave S66	36 C3
Spruce Rise S21	92 A1
Spurley Hey Gr S36	3 B2
Spurr St S2	62 C2
Square E The S66	24 C1
Square W The S66	24 B1
Squirrel Croft S61	10 A4
Stacye Ave S13	78 C4
Stacye Rise S13	78 C3
Stadium Ct S62	21 B4
Stadium Way	
Rotherham S60	21 C3
Sheffield S9	54 A3
Stafford Cl S18	99 B4
Stafford Cres S60	47 A3
Stafford Dr S60	47 A3
Stafford La S2	63 B4
Stafford Mews S2	63 B4
Stafford Rd S2	63 B4
Stafford St S2	107 C2
Stafford Way S35	7 A3
Stag Cl S60	34 C1
Stag Cres S60	34 C1
Stag La S60	34 B1
Stag Willow Cl S60	34 B1
Staindrop View S35	7 B4
Stainmore Ave S20	91 B4
Stainton Rd S11	60 C2
Stair Rd S4	42 A2

Stalker Lees Rd S11 . . . . . **61** B2
Stamford Rd S66 . . . . **24** B2
Stamford St S9 . . . . **43** A1
Stanage Rise S12 . . . . **77** A3
Standish Ave S5 . . . . **41** B2
Standish Bank S5 . . . . **41** B2
Standish Cl S5 . . . . **41** B3
Standish Dr S5 . . . . **41** B3
Standish Gdns S5 . . . . **41** B2
Standish Rd S5 . . . . **41** B3
Standish Way S5 . . . . **41** B2
Standon Cres S9 . . . . **30** A3
Standon Dr S9 . . . . **30** A3
Standon Rd S9 . . . . **30** A3
Staneford Ct S20 . . . . **90** B3
Stanford Rd S18 . . . . **99** B3
Stanhope Rd S12 . . . . **76** B3
Staniforth Ave S21 . . . . . **102** B1
Staniforth Rd S9 . . . . **54** C3
Staniforth Wks S12 . . . . **78** A1
Stanley Gr S26 . . . . **70** A2
Stanley La S3 . . . . **106** B5
Stanley Rd
　Chapeltown S35 . . . . **6** C4
　Sheffield S8 . . . . **74** A3
　Stocksbridge S36 . . . . **3** B3
Stanley St
　Killamarsh S21 . . . . **92** B3
　Rotherham S60 . . . . **33** A4
　Sheffield S3 . . . . **106** B5
STANNINGTON **49** A3
Stannington Glen S6 . . . . **49** C4
Stannington Inf Sch
　S6 . . . . **49** A4
Stannington Rd S6 . . . . . . **49** B4
Stannington Rise S6 . . . . . **39** B1
Stannington View Rd
　S10 . . . . **50** C2
Stanton Cres S12 . . . . **76** C2
Stanwell Ave S9 . . . . **30** A2
Stanwell Cl S9 . . . . **30** A2
Stanwell St S9 . . . . **30** A2
Stanwell Wlk S9 . . . . **30** A2
Stanwood Ave S6 . . . . **50** A4
Stanwood Cres S6 . . . . **50** B4
Stanwood Dr S6 . . . . **50** A4
Stanwood Mews S6 . . . . . . **50** A4
Stanwood Rd S6 . . . . **50** A4
Staple Gn S65 . . . . **24** A4
Starling Mead S2 . . . . **63** C4
Starnhill Cl S35 . . . . **16** C3
Station La
　Oughtibridge S35 . . . . **13** B3
　Sheffield S9 . . . . **43** B4
Station Rd
　Catliffe S60 . . . . **57** A4
　Chapeltown S35 . . . . **7** C4
　Rotherham S60 . . . . **32** C4
　Sheffield, Darnall S9 . . . . . **55** A2
　Sheffield, Ecclesfield
　　S35 . . . . **16** C3
　Sheffield S20 . . . . **90** C1
　Sheffield, Woodhouse
　　S13 . . . . **67** B1
　Stocksbridge S36 . . . . **4** C3
　Treeton S60 . . . . **57** C2
Station Works S35 . . . . **16** C3
Staton Ave S20 . . . . **79** C2
Statutes The S60 . . . . **33** A4
Staveley Rd S8 . . . . **62** B1
Steade Rd S7 . . . . **62** A1
Stead Mews S21 . . . . **103** A1
Stead St S21 . . . . **103** A1
STEEL BANK **50** C2
Steel Bank Villas S6 . . . . . **104** A4
Steel Hill S6, S35 . . . . **14** C1
Steelhouse La S3 . . . . **106** A4
Steel Rd S11 . . . . **61** A2
Steel St S61 . . . . **32** A3
Stemp St S11 . . . . **62** A2
Stenton Rd S8 . . . . **85** A1
Stephen Dr
　Sheffield, Grenoside
　　S35 . . . . **14** B2
　Sheffield S10 . . . . **50** A1
STEPHEN HILL **50** A1
Stephen Hill S10 . . . . **50** A1
Stephen Hill Rd S10 . . . . . . **50** B1
Stephen La S35 . . . . **14** B2

Stepney St S2 . . . . **106** C4
Stepping La S35 . . . . **14** B3
Sterndale Rd S7 . . . . **72** B1
Steven Cl S35 . . . . **7** A2
Steven Cres S35 . . . . **7** A3
Steven Pl S35 . . . . **7** A3
Steven Pl S35 . . . . **7** A2
Stevenson Dr S65 . . . . **34** B3
Stevenson Rd S9 . . . . **53** C4
Stevenson Way S9 . . . . **54** A4
Steventon Rd S65 . . . . **24** A4
Stewart Rd S11 . . . . **61** B2
Stewarts Rd S62 . . . . **12** C4
Stirling Way S2 . . . . **64** B2
Stock Rd S2 . . . . **63** C3
STOCKSBRIDGE **3** B4
Stocksbridge High Sch
　S36 . . . . **3** A3
Stocksbridge Inf Sch
　S36 . . . . **3** A3
Stocksbridge Jun Sch
　S36 . . . . **3** A2
Stocks Green Ct S17 . . . . . **94** B2
Stocks Green Dr S17 . . . . . **94** B2
Stocks Hill S35 . . . . **16** A3
Stock's La S62 . . . . **12** A3
Stockton Cl S3 . . . . **52** C3
Stoke St S9 . . . . **53** C3
Stoneacre Ave S12 . . . . **78** A1
Stoneacre Cl **5** S12 . . . . . **78** A1
Stoneacre Dr S12 . . . . **89** C4
Stoneacre Rise S12 . . . . . . **78** A1
Stone Bank Ct S18 . . . . . **101** A3
Stone Cl
　Dronfield S18 . . . . **98** A1
　Rotherham S65 . . . . **25** A1
Stonecliffe Dr S36 . . . . **3** A1
Stonecliffe Pl S2 . . . . **64** B3
Stonecliffe Rd S2 . . . . **64** B3
Stonecliffe Wlk **1** S2 . . . **64** C3
Stone Cres S66 . . . . **36** B3
Stonecroft Rd S17 . . . . **95** A3
Stonedale Cl S20 . . . . **90** B1
Stone Delf S10 . . . . **59** B3
Stonegravels Croft **7**
　S20 . . . . **103** B4
Stonegravels Way
　S20 . . . . **103** C4
Stone Hill Dr S26 . . . . **69** B1
Stone La S13 . . . . **78** A3
Stoneley Cl S12 . . . . **87** C3
Stoneley Cres S12 . . . . **87** C3
Stoneley Dell S12 . . . . **87** C3
Stoneley Dr S12 . . . . **87** C3
Stonelow Cres S18 . . . . . **101** B4
Stonelow Gn S18 . . . . **101** A4
Stonelow Jun Sch
　S18 . . . . **101** B4
Stonelow Rd S18 . . . . **101** B4
Stonely Brook S65 . . . . **37** A4
Stone Moor Rd S36 . . . . **3** A1
Stone Rd S18 . . . . **98** A1
Stonerow Way S60 . . . . **21** C3
Stones Inge S35 . . . . **5** B1
Stone St S20 . . . . **90** B1
Stonewood Ct S10 . . . . **59** B4
Stonewood Gr S10 . . . . **59** B4
Stoney Gate S35 . . . . **5** B2
Stony Wlk **2** S6 . . . . **51** A4
Stowe Ave S7 . . . . **72** B2
Stradbroke Ave S13 . . . . . . **65** B1
Stradbroke Cl S13 . . . . **65** C1
Stradbroke Cres S13 . . . . . **65** C1
Stradbroke Dr S13 . . . . **65** C1
Stradbroke Pl S13 . . . . **65** C1
Stradbroke Prim Sch
　S13 . . . . **65** B1

Stradbroke Rd S13 . . . . **77** A4
Stradbroke Way S13 . . . . . **65** C1
Stradbroke Wlk S13 . . . . . **65** B1
Strafford Pl S61 . . . . **8** C3
Strafford Rd S61 . . . . **19** B4
Strafford Rd S10 . . . . **59** B3
Stratford Way S66 . . . . **37** B2
Strathtay Rd S11 . . . . **60** C1
Strawberry Ave S5 . . . . **28** B4
Straw La S6 . . . . **51** C3
Streetfield Cres S20 . . . . . **103** A4
Streetfields S20 . . . . **103** B4
Strelley Ave S8 . . . . **84** C3
Strelley Rd S8 . . . . **84** C3
Stretton Rd S11 . . . . **61** A1
Stringers Croft S60 . . . . **48** B3
Struan Rd S7 . . . . **72** C3
Strutt Rd S3 . . . . **41** B1
Stuart Gr S35 . . . . **7** C2
Stuart Rd S35 . . . . **7** C2
STUBBIN **3** C2
Stubbing House La S6,
　S35 . . . . **14** B1
Stubbin La S5 . . . . **29** A2
Stubbs Cres S61 . . . . **10** A1
Stubbs Wlk S61 . . . . **10** A1
Stubley Cl S18 . . . . **100** A4
Stubley Croft S18 . . . . **99** C4
Stubley Dr S18 . . . . **100** A4
Stubley Hollow S18 . . . . . . **97** A1
Stubley La S18 . . . . **99** C4
Stubley Pl S18 . . . . **100** A4
Stubley Rise S6 . . . . **39** A2
Studfield Cres S6 . . . . **39** A2
Studfield Dr S6 . . . . **39** A3
Studfield Gr S6 . . . . **39** A2
STUDFIELD HILL **39** A2
Studfield Hill S6 . . . . **39** A2
Studfield Rd S6 . . . . **39** A3
Studfield Rise S6 . . . . **39** A2
Studio Theatre ★ S1 . . . . **106** B3
Studley Cl S8 . . . . **55** A2
Studmoor Rd S61 . . . . **19** A4
Studmoor Wlk S61 . . . . **19** A4
STUMPERLOWE **59** B2
Stumperlowe Ave S10 . . . . **59** C2
Stumperlowe Cl S10 . . . . . **59** C2
Stumperlowe Crescent
　Rd S10 . . . . **59** C2
Stumperlowe Croft
　S10 . . . . **59** B2
Stumperlowe Hall Chase
　S10 . . . . **59** B3
Stumperlowe Hall Rd
　S10 . . . . **59** B2
Stumperlowe La S10 . . . . . **59** B2
Stumperlowe Mansions
　S10 . . . . **59** B2
Stumperlowe Park Rd
　S10 . . . . **59** C2
Stumperlowe View
　S10 . . . . **59** B3
Stupton Rd S9 . . . . **43** B4
Sturge Croft **3** S2 . . . . . . **74** A4
Sturton Cres S13 . . . . **88** C4
Sturton Rd S4 . . . . **42** A2
Sudbury Dr S26 . . . . **69** C1
Sudbury St S3 . . . . **104** C5
Suffolk Rd S2 . . . . **107** B2
SUMMERFIELD **61** A4
Summerfield S65 . . . . **33** B4
Summerfield Rd S18 . . . . . . **97** C1
Summerfield St S11 . . . . . . **61** B3
Summer La S17 . . . . **94** B2
Summer St S35 . . . . **104** B4
Summerwood La S18 . . . . . **97** A1
Summerwood Pl S18 . . . . **100** B4
Sumner Rd S65 . . . . **21** C2
Sunderland St S11 . . . . **61** C3
Sundew Croft S5 . . . . **5** B2
Sundew Gdns S35 . . . . **5** B2
Sundown Pl S13 . . . . **64** A2
Sundown Rd S13 . . . . **64** A2
Sunlea Flats S65 . . . . **21** C1
Sunningdale Mount
　S11 . . . . **72** B3
Sunny Bank
　Chapeltown S35 . . . . **5** B1
　Sheffield S10 . . . . **105** B1
Sunnybank Cres S60 . . . . . **46** A3
SUNNYSIDE **24** B1
Sunnyvale Ave S17 . . . . **94** B2
Sunnyvale Rd S17 . . . . **94** B2

Surbiton St S9 . . . . **43** C2
Surrey La S1 . . . . **107** B2
Surrey Pl S1 . . . . **107** B3
Surrey St S1 . . . . **107** A3
Sussex Rd
　Chapeltown S35 . . . . **7** B3
　Sheffield S4 . . . . **106** C5
Sussex St S4 . . . . **106** C4
Suthard Cross Rd S10 . . . . **50** C2
Sutherland Rd S4 . . . . **53** A4
Sutherland St S4 . . . . **53** B3
Sutton St S3 . . . . **104** B3
Swale Dr S35 . . . . **6** C3
Swaledale Rd S7 . . . . **72** C3
Swale Gdns S9 . . . . **55** A2
Swale Rd S61 . . . . **10** B1
Swallow Cres S62 . . . . **12** C3
Swallow La S26 . . . . **81** A4
SWALLOWNEST **69** A1
Swallownest Prim Sch
　S26 . . . . **69** A1
Swallow Wood Cl S60 . . . . **57** C2
Swallow Wood Ct S13 . . . . **77** C4
Swallow Wood Rd
　S26 . . . . **68** C1
Swamp Wlk S6 . . . . **40** B1
Swanbourne Pl S5 . . . . **28** C2
Swanbourne Rd S5 . . . . **28** C3
Swan Rd S26 . . . . **81** A4
Swan St S60 . . . . **33** A3
Swarcliffe Rd S9 . . . . **54** B3
Sweeny Ho S36 . . . . **2** C3
Swift Rd S60 . . . . **34** A1
Swift Rd S35 . . . . **15** A2
Swift Rise S61 . . . . **9** B4
Swift Way S2 . . . . **63** C2
Swinburne Pl S65 . . . . **34** B3
Swinton St S3 . . . . **106** A5
Sycamore Ave
　Dronfield S18 . . . . **97** B1
　Rotherham S66 . . . . **36** C3
Sycamore Ct
　Oughtibridge S35 . . . . **13** B3
　Sheffield S11 . . . . **61** A1
Sycamore Ctr S65 . . . . **22** B3
Sycamore Dr S21 . . . . **92** A1
Sycamore Farm Cl
　S66 . . . . **36** B1
Sycamore House Rd
　S5 . . . . **29** C4
Sycamore Rd
　Rotherham S65 . . . . **22** B3
　Sheffield S5 . . . . **16** B2
　Stocksbridge S36 . . . . **2** C2
Sycamore St
　Sheffield, Beighton
　　S20 . . . . **79** B2
　Sheffield S20 . . . . **90** A2
Sycamores The S13 . . . . . . **76** B4
Sydney Rd S6 . . . . **104** A4
Sylvester Gdns S1 . . . . **107** A2
Sylvester St S1 . . . . **107** A2
Sylvia Cl S13 . . . . **67** B1
Symons Cres S5 . . . . **27** C2

T

Tadcaster Cres S8 . . . . **73** B2
Tadcaster Rd S8 . . . . **73** B2
Tadcaster Way **1** S8 . . . . . **73** B2
Talbot Cres S2 . . . . **107** C2
Talbot Gdns S2 . . . . **107** C2
Talbot Pl S2 . . . . **107** C3
Talbot Rd S2 . . . . **107** C3
Talbot Sch S8 . . . . **86** A4
Talbot St S2 . . . . **107** C2
Talmont Rd S11 . . . . **72** A4
Tanfield Rd S6 . . . . **40** B3
Tanfield Way S66 . . . . **36** B2
Tannery Cl S13 . . . . **78** A4
Tannery St S13 . . . . **78** A4
Tansley Dr S9 . . . . **30** B2
Tansley St S9 . . . . **30** B2
Taplin Rd S6 . . . . **39** C2
Tapton Bank S10 . . . . **60** B4
Tapton Crescent Rd
　S10 . . . . **60** C4
Tapton Ct **1** S10 . . . . **60** C4
TAPTON HILL **60** C4
Tapton Hill Rd S10 . . . . **60** B4

Tapton House Rd S10 . . . . **60** C
Tapton Mews S10 . . . . **50** C
Tapton Mount Cl S10 . . . . **60** C
Tapton Park Gdns S10 . . . **60** B
Tapton Park Rd S10 . . . . . . **60** B
Tapton Sch S10 . . . . **60** B
Tapton (Univ of
　Sheffield) S10 . . . . **51** A
Taptonville Cres S10 . . . . . **61** A
Taptonville Rd S10 . . . . **61** A
Tapton Wlk S10 . . . . **60** C
Tasker Rd S10 . . . . **50** C
Taunton Ave S9 . . . . **30** B
Taunton Gr S9 . . . . **30** B
Taverner Cl S35 . . . . **5** F
Taverner Croft S35 . . . . **5** C
Taverner Way S35 . . . . **5** C
Tavistock Rd S7 . . . . **62** A
Tay Cl S13 . . . . **99** C
Taylors Cl S62 . . . . **21** B
Taylors Ct S62 . . . . **21** C
Taylors La S62 . . . . **21** C
Tay St S6 . . . . **104** A
Teesdale Rd
　Rotherham S61 . . . . **10** A
　Sheffield S12 . . . . **89** A
TEMPLEBOROUGH . . . . . . **31** C
Templeborough Ent Pk
　S60 . . . . **32** C
Temple Cres S66 . . . . **37** A
Temple Rd S9 . . . . **31** C
Ten Acre Rd S61 . . . . **19** C
Tennyson Rd
　Rotherham S65 . . . . **34** B
　Sheffield S6 . . . . **51** B
Tenterden Rd S5 . . . . **29** C
Tenter St
　Rotherham S60 . . . . **20** C
　Sheffield S1 . . . . **106** A
Terminus Rd S7 . . . . **72** B
Terrace Rd S62 . . . . **12** A
Terrey Rd S17 . . . . **94** C
Terry St S9 . . . . **43** C
Tetney Rd S10 . . . . **60** A
Teynham Dr S5 . . . . **41** A
Teynham Rd S5 . . . . **40** C
Thames St S60 . . . . **20** C
Thatch Pl S61 . . . . **10** B
THE CROSS . . . . **16** C
THE WHEEL . . . . **15** C
Thirlmere Dr S18 . . . . **100** C
Thirlmere Rd S8 . . . . **73** A
Thirlwell Rd S8 . . . . **73** C
Thomas Rotherham Coll
　S60 . . . . **33** B
Thomas St S1 . . . . **105** C
Thompson Gdns S35 . . . . . . **5** A
Thompson Hill S35 . . . . **5** A
Thompson Rd S11 . . . . **61** B
Thoresby Cl S26 . . . . **70** A
Thoresby Rd S6 . . . . **40** A
Thornborough Cl S2 . . . . . **63** A
Thornborough Pl S2 . . . . . . **63** A
Thornborough Rd S2 . . . . . **63** A
Thornbridge Ave S12 . . . . . **76** C
Thornbridge Cl S12 . . . . . . **76** C
Thornbridge Cres S12 . . . . **77** A
Thornbridge Dr S12 . . . . . . **76** C
Thornbridge Gr S12 . . . . . . **76** C
Thornbridge La S12 . . . . . . **77** A
Thornbridge Pl S12 . . . . . . **76** C
Thornbridge Rd S12 . . . . . . **76** C
Thornbridge Rise S12 . . . . **77** A
Thornbridge Way S12 . . . . **77** A
Thornbrook Cl S35 . . . . **7** C
Thornbrook Gdns S35 . . . . . **7** C
Thornbrook Mews S35 . . . . **7** C
Thornbury Hospl S10 . . . . . **60** B
Thorncliffe Cl S26 . . . . **80** A
Thorndale Rise S60 . . . . . . **46** B
Thorne Rd S7 . . . . **73** A
THORN HILL . . . . **20** C
Thornhill Ave S60 . . . . **46** A
Thornhill Edge **1** S60 . . . **20** C
Thornhill Prim Sch
　S61 . . . . **20** B
Thornsett Ct S7 . . . . **61** C
Thornsett Gdns S17 . . . . . . **83** A
Thornsett Rd S7 . . . . **61** C
Thornton Pl **1** S18 . . . . . . **99** B
Thornton St S61 . . . . **31** B
Thornton Terr S61 . . . . **31** B

horntree Cl S61 . . . . 9 A2
horntree Rd S61. . . . . 9 A1
hornwell La S61. . . . . 9 A1
horpe Ct S2 . . . . 62 B2
horpe Ave S18 . . . . 98 A2
THORPE COMMON. 8 C1
horpe Dr S20. . . . . 90 C3
horpefield Cl S61. . . . . 9 A3
horpefield Dr S61 . . . . 9 A3
horpe Gn S20 . . . . 90 B3
THORPE HESLEY 8 C1
horpe Hesley Inf Sch
S61 . . . . 8 C2
horpe Hesley Jun Sch
S61 . . . . 8 C2
horpe House Ave S8. . 74 A2
horpe House Rd S8. . . 74 A2
horpe House Rise
S8 . . . . 74 A2
horpe St S61. . . . . 9 A3
hreshfield Way 3
S12 . . . . 78 A1
hrush Ave S60. . . . . 46 B2
hrush St S6 . . . . 50 C4
hrrybergh Prim Sch
S65 . . . . 23 B4
hundercliffe Rd S61 . . 30 B4
hurstan Ave S8. . . . . . . 84 C2
ber View S60 . . . . 46 A4
deswell Rd S5 . . . . 28 C1
dewell St S5 . . . . 28 C1
lford Rd S13. . . . . 78 B4
llotson Cl 1 S8. . . . . . 73 C4
llotson Rise S8 . . . . . . 73 C4
inker La S10, S6. . . . . . . 50 C3
inker Rd S62 . . . . 12 C4
INSLEY 44 B4
Sheffield, Greenland
S9 . . . . 55 A4
Sheffield, Tinsley S9. . . . 44 B3
nsley Inf Sch S9 . . . . . . 44 C4
nsley Jun Sch S9 . . . . . . 44 C4
nsley Park Rd S9 . . . . . 43 C1
nsley Park Rd S9 . . . . . . 44 C4
pton St S9. . . . . 43 B4
the Barn Ave S13 . . . . . 67 A1
the Barn Cl S13. . . . . . . 67 A1
the Barn La S13. . . . . . . 67 A1
the Barn Way S13. . . . . 66 C1
tterton Cl S9 . . . . 54 B4
tterton St S9 . . . . 54 B4
ackwith Rd S9. . . . . 54 C3
dwick Rd S8 . . . . 73 A1
fts La S6 . . . . 49 A2
ftwood Ave S10 . . . . . . 50 B2
ftwood Rd S10 . . . . 50 C2
ll Bar Ave S12 . . . . 75 A3
ll Bar Cl S12 . . . . 75 A3
ll Bar Dr S12 . . . . 75 B3
ll Bar Rd
otherham S65. . . . . 35 B2
heffield S12 . . . . 75 A3
ll Cl S3 . . . . 41 C1
ll House Mead S20 . . . 90 A1
oker Rd S60. . . . . 33 B3
p Field La S65. . . . . 23 A2
ppham Dr S8 . . . . 97 A4
ppham Rd S8 . . . . 97 A4
ppham Way S8 . . . . 97 A4
p Rd S35. . . . . 13 B1
p Side S15 . . . . 14 B2
p Terr 1 S10 . . . . 51 A1
rbay Rd S4. . . . . 42 B1
rksey Rd S5. . . . . 29 A2
rksey Rd W S5 . . . . 29 A2
rry Ct S3 . . . . 78 B4
r Way S60 . . . . 46 B2
rwood Dr S8 . . . . 84 C1
TLEY 94 C2
tley All Saints CE Prim
ch S17. . . . . 94 B2
TLEY BROOK 94 C3
tley Brook Cl S17. . . . . . 94 B3
tley Brook Croft
S17 . . . . 94 B3
tley Brook Glen
S17 . . . . 94 B3
tley Brook Gr S17 . . . . . 94 B3
tley Brook Rd S17 . . . . . 94 C3
tley Brook Way S17. . . . 94 B3

Totley Grange Cl S17 . . . 94 B2
Totley Grange Dr S17. . . 94 B2
Totley Grange Rd S17. . . 94 B2
Totley Hall Croft S17. . . . 94 B1
Totley Hall Dr S17 . . . . . . 94 B1
Totley Hall La S17. . . . . . 94 B2
Totley Hall Mead S17 . . . 94 B1
Totley La S17. . . . . 95 B3
Totley Prim Sch S17. . . . . 94 B1
TOTLEY RISE 95 A3
Tower Cl S2 . . . . 63 A2
Tower Dr S2. . . . . 63 A2
Tower Ho S2 . . . . 63 A2
TOWN END
Sheffield. 49 C3
Stocksbridge 4 B2
Townend Ave S35 . . . . . . 23 B3
Townend Cl S60 . . . . 57 C2
Townend La S36. . . . . 4 A1
Town End Rd S35 . . . . . . 16 A2
Townend St S10 . . . . 51 A2
Town Fields Ave S35. . . . 16 C2
Towngate Gr S35 . . . . . . 13 B1
Towngate Rd S35 . . . . . . 13 B1
TOWNHEAD 82 A1
Townhead Rd S17 . . . . . . 82 A1
Townhead St S1 . . . . 106 A3
Town St
Rotherham S60. . . . . 33 A2
Sheffield S9 . . . . 44 B4
Toyne St S10 . . . . 50 C2
Traditional Heritage
Mus ★ S11. . . . . 61 A1
Trafalgar Rd S6. . . . . 26 C2
Trafalgar St S1 . . . . 105 C2
Trap La S11 . . . . 71 A4
Traso Bsns Pk S18. . . . . 101 C3
Travey Rd S2 . . . . 64 B1
Travis Pl S10 . . . . 105 B2
Treefield Cl S61 . . . . 10 B1
Tree Root Wlk S10 . . . . . 105 A3
TREETON. 57 D2
Treeton CE Prim Sch
S60 . . . . 57 D1
Treeton Ent Ctr S60 . . . . 57 C1
Treeton La
Aston S26. . . . . 69 A4
Catliffe S60. . . . . 57 B3
Treeton Wood Nature
Reserve ★ S26 . . . . 68 B4
Treetown Cres S60. . . . . 57 C3
Treherne Rd S60. . . . . . . 33 C3
Trent Gr S18. . . . . 97 C1
Trentham Cl S60. . . . . . . 46 B2
Trenton Cl S13 . . . . 78 C4
Trenton Rise S13 . . . . . . 78 C4
Trent St S9 . . . . 44 C4
Treswell Cres S6. . . . . . . 40 A2
Trickett Rd
Chapeltown S35 . . . . 5 A2
Sheffield S6 . . . . 40 A1
Trinity Croft CE Jun & Inf
Sch S65 . . . . 23 A2
Trinity St S3 . . . . 106 A4
Trippet Ct S10 . . . . 60 B2
Trippet La S1 . . . . 107 A3
Tristford Cl S60. . . . . 57 B4
Trough Dr S65. . . . . 24 A4
Troutbeck Rd S7. . . . . . . 73 A2
Truman Gr S26 . . . . 4 B3
Truswell Ave S10 . . . . . . 50 C2
Truswell Rd S10 . . . . 50 B1
Tudor Sq S1. . . . . 107 B3
Tuffolds Cl S2 . . . . 64 B1
Tulip Tree Ct S20. . . . . . . 79 C3
Tullibardine Rd S11. . . . . 72 A4
Tummon Rd S2. . . . . 63 C4
Tummon St S61 . . . . 32 B4
Tunwell Ave S5. . . . . 16 B1
Tunwell Dr S5 . . . . 16 B1
Tunwell Greave S5 . . . . . 16 B1
Turie Ave S5. . . . . 28 A4
Turie Cres S5. . . . . 28 A4
Turner Bsns Pk S13. . . . . 65 C3
Turner Cl
Dronfield S18. . . . . 100 B3
Rawmarsh S62. . . . . 12 B2
Turner La S60 . . . . 47 C2
Turners La S10 . . . . 61 A4
Turner St S2 . . . . 107 B2
Turnpike Croft S35 . . . . . 14 C3

Turnshaw Ave S26 . . . . . 69 A3
Turnshaw Rd S26 . . . . . . 69 C4
Twelve O'Clock Ct S4 . . . 53 B3
Twentylands The S60 . . . 57 C1
Twentieth Ct S17. . . . . . . 83 B1
Twentieth Dr S17. . . . . . . 95 C4
Twentieth La S17. . . . . . . 95 C4
Twentieth Rd S17 . . . . . . 95 C3
Twentieth Rise S17. . . . . 95 C4
Twentieth View S17. . . . . 95 C4
Twickenham Cl 11
S20. . . . . 103 B4
Twickenham Cres
S20. . . . . 103 C4
Twickenham Ct 8
S20. . . . . 103 B4
Twickenham Glade 10
S20. . . . . 103 B4
Twickenham Glen
S20. . . . . 103 C3
Twickenham Gr 9
S20. . . . . 103 B4
Twitchill Dr S13 . . . . 77 C4
Tyas Rd S5 . . . . 16 B1
Tye Rd S20 . . . . 79 C1
Tyler St S9 . . . . 30 B1
Tyler Way S9 . . . . 30 B1
Tylney Rd S2 . . . . 63 B4
Tynker Ave S20 . . . . 79 C1
Tyzack Rd S8 . . . . 84 C4

U

Ulley Cres S13. . . . . 64 C1
Ulley La S26. . . . . 69 C2
Ulley Rd S13. . . . . 64 C1
Ulley View S26. . . . . 69 B4
Ullswater Ave S20 . . . . . 103 B4
Ullswater Cl
Dronfield S18. . . . . 100 A4
Sheffield S20 . . . . 103 B4
Ullswater Dr S18 . . . . . . 100 A4
Ullswater Pk S18 . . . . . . 100 A4
Ullswater Pl S18. . . . . . . 100 A4
Ulverston Rd S8 . . . . 73 A2
Undercliffe Rd S6 . . . . . . 50 A4
Underhill La S6. . . . . 26 B3
Underwood Rd S8 . . . . . . 73 B2
Union Dr S11. . . . . 72 C4
Union La S1 . . . . 107 A2
Union Rd S11. . . . . 72 C4
Union St
Rotherham S65. . . . . 32 B4
Sheffield S1 . . . . 107 A2
Unity Pl S60 . . . . 33 A4
Universe Works S1 . . . . . 107 A1
Univ of Sheffield
S10. . . . . 104 B3
Unsliven Rd S36 . . . . 2 B5
Unstone Dronfield By-
Pass S18 . . . . 97 A1
Unstone Hill S18. . . . . . . 101 C1
Unstone St S1. . . . . 62 B3
Uplands Way S62. . . . . . 11 C4
Upper Albert Rd S8. . . . . 74 A3
Upper Allen St S3 . . . . . 104 C4
UPPER BRADWAY. 95 C2
Upper Castle Folds
S3. . . . . 107 B4
Upper Clara St S61 . . . . . 31 C4
UPPER CRABTREE 41 C3
UPPER GATE. 49 A4
Upper Gate Rd S6 . . . . . . 49 A4
Upper Hanover St
S3. . . . . 105 B3
Upper Ley Ct S35 . . . . . . 7 B3
Upper Ley Dell S35. . . . . 7 B3
Upper Millgate S60 . . . . . 33 A4
Upper Rye Cl S60 . . . . . . 48 B3
Upper School La
8 Dronfield S18 . . . . 100 C3
Dronfield S18. . . . . 101 A2
UPPERTHORPE 92 B1
Upperthorpe S6 . . . . 104 A5
Upperthorpe Glen
S6. . . . . 104 A5
Upperthorpe Rd S6. . . . . 104 B5
Upperthorpe Villas
S21. . . . . 92 B1
Upper Valley Rd S8 . . . . . 74 A3
UPPER WHISTON 48 B1
Upper Whiston La S60 . . . 48 B1

Upper Wortley Rd S61 . . . 18 B4
Upwell Hill S4 . . . . 42 C3
Upwell La S4 . . . . 42 C3
Upwell St S4 . . . . 43 A3
Upwood Rd S6 . . . . 39 C3
Utah Terr S12. . . . . 78 B1
Uttley Cl S9 . . . . 54 C4
Uttley Croft S9 . . . . 54 C4
Uttley Dr S9 . . . . 54 C4

V

Vainor Rd S6 . . . . 39 B4
Vale Ave S65 . . . . 23 C4
Vale Cl S18 . . . . 101 A3
Vale Cres S5 . . . . 23 C4
Vale Ct S5 . . . . 23 C4
Vale Gr S6. . . . . 38 C2
Valentine Cl S5 . . . . 28 C3
Valentine Cres S5 . . . . . . 28 C3
Valentine Rd S5 . . . . 28 C3
Vale Rd
Rotherham S65. . . . . 24 A4
Sheffield S3 . . . . 41 A1
Valetta Ho S62 . . . . 12 A2
Valley Dr S21. . . . . 92 B3
Valley Park Com Sch
S14. . . . . 87 A4
Valley Rd
Chapeltown S35 . . . . 6 C1
Killamarsh S21. . . . . 92 B3
Sheffield, Hackenthorpe
S12. . . . . 78 B1
Sheffield, Heeley S8. . . . . 73 C4
Valley Works
Sheffield, Greenland
S9 . . . . 44 A1
Sheffield S5 . . . . 17 C2
Varley Gdns S66 . . . . 36 B4
Vaughton Hill S36 . . . . . . 4 B3
Vauxhall Cl S9 . . . . 30 B2
Vauxhall Rd S9 . . . . 30 B2
Ventnor Ct 13 S7 . . . . . . 62 A2
Ventnor Pl S7 . . . . 62 A2
Venus Ct S60 . . . . 46 A4
Verdant Way S5 . . . . 29 A3
Verdon St S3 . . . . 52 C3
Verelst Ave S26 . . . . 69 B2
Vere Rd S6 . . . . 40 A4
Vernon Delph S10 . . . . . . 50 A1
Vernon Dr S7 . . . . 7 B3
Vernon Rd
Rotherham S60. . . . . 34 B1
Sheffield S17 . . . . 95 A4
Vernon Terr S10 . . . . 60 B4
Vesey St S62 . . . . 12 A2
Vicarage Cl
Rotherham S65. . . . . 23 A2
Sheffield S35. . . . . 14 C2
Vicarage Cres S35 . . . . . 14 C2
Vicarage Ct S60 . . . . 46 B1
Vicarage La
Rotherham S60. . . . . 33 A4
Sheffield S17 . . . . 82 B1
Vicarage Rd
Sheffield, Grenoside
S35. . . . . 14 C2
Sheffield S9 . . . . 54 A4
Vicar Ct S13. . . . . 78 A4
Vicar La
Sheffield, Coisley Hill
S13. . . . . 66 C1
Sheffield S1 . . . . 106 A3
Vickers Dr S5. . . . . 29 A1
Vickers Rd
Chapeltown S35 . . . . 5 B1
Sheffield S5 . . . . 42 B4
Victoria Ave S65 . . . . 33 C4
Victoria Cl S36 . . . . 3 A3
Victoria Ct S11 . . . . 72 C4
Victoria Ho 13 S3. . . . . . 105 C3
Victoria Rd
Rawmarsh S62. . . . . 12 B2
Sheffield, Beighton S20 . . . 79 B2
Sheffield, Broomhill
S10. . . . . 105 B1
Stocksbridge S36. . . . . 3 B3
Victoria St
Catliffe S60. . . . . 57 B4
Dronfield S18. . . . . 100 B4
Rotherham S60. . . . . 32 B4
Sheffield S3 . . . . 105 C3

Victoria St continued
Stocksbridge S36. . . . . 3 B3
Victoria Station Rd
S4. . . . . 106 C4
Victoria Villas S6 . . . . . . 104 B5
Victor Rd S17. . . . . 83 A1
Victor St 3 S6 . . . . 40 B1
Viewlands Cl S66 . . . . . . 37 B2
View Rd
Rotherham S65. . . . . 22 A2
Sheffield S2 . . . . 62 B1
Vikinglea Cl S2. . . . . 64 C2
Vikinglea Dr S2. . . . . 64 C2
Vikinglea Glade S2 . . . . . 64 C3
Vikinglea Rd S2. . . . . 64 C3
Villiers Cl S2 . . . . 75 A4
Villiers Dr S2 . . . . 75 A4
Vincent Rd
Rotherham S65. . . . . 25 A1
Sheffield S7 . . . . 62 A2
Vine Cl S60. . . . . 32 C4
Viola Bank S36 . . . . 3 A3
Violet Ave S20 . . . . 79 B1
Violet Bank Rd S7 . . . . . . 73 A4
Vista S60. . . . . 33 B3
Vivian Rd S5 . . . . 42 B4
Vulcan Ho 2 S65 . . . . . . 22 A1
Vulcan Rd S9. . . . . 44 B4

W

Wadbrough Rd S11 . . . . . 61 B3
Waddington Way S65 . . . 22 A4
Wade Cl S60. . . . . 33 C2
Wade Mdw S6 . . . . 39 B3
Wade St S4. . . . . 42 C3
WADSLEY 39 A4
WADSLEY BRIDGE 26 C1
Wadsley La S6. . . . . 39 C4
Wadsley Park Cres S6 . . 39 B3
Wadsworth Ave S12 . . . . 76 C3
Wadsworth Cl S12 . . . . . 76 C3
Wadsworth Dr S12. . . . . . 76 C3
Wadsworth Rd
Rotherham S66. . . . . 37 A2
Sheffield S12 . . . . 76 B3
Wadworth Rise S65 . . . . 23 B3
Wagon Rd S61. . . . . 20 B4
Waingate S3 . . . . 106 B4
Wainwright Ave S65 . . . . 65 B2
Wainwright Cres S13 . . . 65 B2
Wainwright Rd S61 . . . . . 10 A1
Wake Rd S7 . . . . 61 C1
Walden Rd S2 . . . . 62 C1
Walders Ave S6. . . . . 39 B4
WALES COMMON 81 A1
Wales Pl S6 . . . . 51 B4
WALESWOOD. 80 C1
Waleswood Rd S20,
S26. . . . . 80 B2
Waleswood View S26 . . . 80 C4
Waleswood Villas S26 . . . 81 B1
Waleswood Way S26. . . . 81 B1
Walford Rd S21. . . . . 92 A2
Walker Cl S35 . . . . 14 C2
Walker La S65 . . . . 21 B1
Walker Rd S61. . . . . 10 A1
Walkers La S21 . . . . 92 B2
Walker St
Rawmarsh S62. . . . . 12 C4
Sheffield S3 . . . . 106 B5
Walker View S62. . . . . . . 12 C4
WALKLEY 51 B4
WALKLEY BANK 50 C4
Walkley Bank Cl S6 . . . . 40 C1
Walkley Bank Rd S6 . . . . 39 C1
Walkley Crescent Rd
S6. . . . . 50 C4
Walkley La S6 . . . . 40 A1
Walkley Prim Sch S6 . . . 51 B4
Walkley Rd S6. . . . . 51 A4
Walkley St S6 . . . . 51 B3
Walkley Terr S6 . . . . 50 B4
Wallace Rd S3. . . . . 41 A1
Waller Rd S6 . . . . 50 B3
Walling Rd S9. . . . . 43 C4
Walling Rd S9 . . . . 43 C4
Walnut Dr S21. . . . . 92 A1
Walnut Pl S35 . . . . 7 A2

Walpole Gr S26. . . . . 69 B3
Walsham Gr S35. . . . . 13 A1
Walshaw Rd S35. . . . . 13 B1
Walter St
Rotherham S60. . . . . 20 C1
Sheffield S6 . . . . 40 B1
Waltham Gdns **1** S20. . . 91 B4
Waltheof Rd S2. . . . . 64 B2
Waltheof Sch S2 . . . . 64 C4
Walton Cl
Chapeltown S35 . . . . 5 A2
Dronfield S18 . . . . 99 B4
Walton Ct S8 . . . . 84 C2
Walton Rd S11. . . . . 61 B3
Wannop St S62 . . . . 12 A1
Wansfell Rd S4 . . . . 43 A3
Warburton Cl S2. . . . . 63 A1
Warburton Gdns S2. . . . . . 63 A1
Warburton Rd S2 . . . . 63 A1
Warde-Aldam Cres
S66 . . . . 36 A3
Warden St S60 . . . . 33 A1
Wardlow Rd S12. . . . . 76 C3
Ward Pl **16** S7. . . . . 62 A2
Wardsend Rd S6. . . . . 40 B4
Wardsend Rd N S6. . . . . . . 26 C1
Ward St S3. . . . . 106 A5
Wards Yd S18. . . . . 100 C3
Wareham Ct S20. . . . . 91 B4
Warley Rd S2. . . . . 63 C3
Warminster Cl S8. . . . . 73 C2
Warminster Cres S8 . . . . . 74 A2
Warminster Dr S8 . . . . 74 A1
Warminster Gdns S8. . . . . 73 C1
Warminster Pl S8. . . . . 85 C4
Warminster Rd S8. . . . . . . 73 C1
Warner Rd S6 . . . . 39 C3
Warren Dr S61 . . . . 19 C2
Warreners Dr S65 . . . . 24 A4
Warren Hill S61 . . . . 19 C2
Warren House Cl S66 . . . . 37 A3
Warren Mount S61 . . . . . . 19 C2
Warren Rd S66 . . . . 36 B3
Warren Rise S18. . . . . 98 A1
Warren St
Sheffield S4 . . . . 53 B3
Sheffield S4 . . . . 53 C3
Warrington Rd S10 . . . . . 104 A4
Warris Cl S61. . . . . 19 B3
Warris Pl S2. . . . . 53 B1
Warwick St S60. . . . . 33 B3
Warwick St
Rotherham S60. . . . . 33 B3
Sheffield S10 . . . . 51 A2
Warwick Terr S10 . . . . 51 A2
Wasdale Ave **5** S20. . . 103 B4
Wasdale Cl S20. . . . . 103 B4
Washfield Cres S60 . . . . . . 57 C2
Washfield La S60 . . . . 57 C2
Washford Rd S9 . . . . 53 C3
Washington Rd
Sheffield, Ecclesfield
  S35 . . . . 16 B3
Sheffield, Sharrow Head
  S11. . . . . 62 A2
Watch St S13 . . . . 67 C2
Waterfield Mews **8**
S20. . . . . 90 C3
Waterford Rd S3. . . . . 40 C1
Waterhouse Cl S65 . . . . . . 23 B3
Water La
Rotherham S60. . . . . 33 A3
Sheffield S17 . . . . 83 A1
Waterloo Wlk S3 . . . . 52 A3
Watermead Inf Sch
S5 . . . . 41 A4
Waterside Ct S9 . . . . 43 B2
Waterside Dr S66. . . . . 24 C2
Waterside Gdns S35 . . . . . 13 B3
Water Slacks Cl S13 . . . . . 78 A4
Water Slacks Dr S13 . . . . . 78 A3
Water Slacks Rd S13. . . . . 78 A3
Water Slacks Way
S13. . . . . 78 A4
Water Slacks Wlk S13. . . . 78 A4
Watersmeet Rd S6. . . . . . . 39 C1
Water St
6 Rotherham S65. . . . . . . 21 A1
Sheffield S3 . . . . 106 A4

WATERTHORPE 90 C4
Waterthorpe Cl **4**
S20. . . . . 91 A2
Waterthorpe Cres S20 . . . 91 A2
Waterthorpe Gdns **3**
S20. . . . . 91 A2
Waterthorpe Glade **5**
S20. . . . . 91 A2
Waterthorpe Glen **2**
S20. . . . . 91 A2
Waterthorpe Greenway
S20. . . . . 78 C1
Waterthorpe Inf Sch
S20. . . . . 90 C3
Waterthorpe Rise **1**
S20. . . . . 91 A2
Watery St S3 . . . . 104 C5
Wath Rd S7 . . . . 73 A4
Watkinson Gdns S20. . . . . 91 A3
Watson Cl S61. . . . . 19 C2
Watson Glen S61 . . . . 18 C2
Watson Rd
Rotherham S61. . . . . 19 C2
Sheffield S10 . . . . 105 A2
Watsons Wlk S3 . . . . 106 B4
Watt La S10 . . . . 60 A4
Waverley Cotts S13 . . . . . . 56 A1
Waverley Rd S9 . . . . 55 A2
Waverley View S60. . . . . . . 57 C4
Waverley Works S4. . . . . . 53 B3
Wayford Ave S66 . . . . 37 B4
Wayland Rd S11 . . . . 61 B2
Weakland Cl S12 . . . . 77 B1
Weakland Cres S12 . . . . . . 77 B1
Weakland Dr S12 . . . . 77 B1
Weakland Way S12 . . . . . . 77 B1
Weavers Cl S35. . . . . 14 C3
Webb Ave S36 . . . . 4 A2
Webbs Ave S6 . . . . 49 C4
Webster Cl S61 . . . . 19 A2
Webster Cres S61. . . . . 19 A2
Webster St S9 . . . . 43 C3
Wedgewood Cl S62 . . . . . . 12 A3
Weedon St S9 . . . . 43 C3
Weetwood Dr S11 . . . . 72 A3
Weetwood Gdns S11. . . . . 71 C3
Weetwood Rd S60 . . . . 47 B4
Weigh La S2. . . . . 107 C3
Weir Head S9 . . . . 43 C3
Welbeck Cl S18. . . . . 99 B4
Welbeck Dr S26 . . . . 70 A1
Welbeck Mews S66 . . . . . . 36 B1
Welbeck Rd S6 . . . . 50 C4
Welbury Gdns S20 . . . . . 103 B4
Welby Pl S8 . . . . 73 B3
Welham Dr S60. . . . . 33 B2
Welland Cl S3 . . . . 52 A4
Wellbourne Cl S35. . . . . . . 8 A2
Wellcarr Rd S8 . . . . 85 B4
Wellcliffe Cl S66. . . . . 36 C4
Well Croft S35 . . . . 5 B1
Wellcroft Gdns S66 . . . . . . 37 B2
Well Ct S12. . . . . 78 A1
Well Dr S65 . . . . 24 A4
Wellesley Rd S10 . . . . 105 A3
Wellfield Cl
Eckington S12. . . . . 88 C3
Sheffield S6 . . . . 104 A5
Wellfield Lodge S61 . . . . . 19 B3
Wellfield Rd
Rotherham S61. . . . . 19 B3
Sheffield S6 . . . . 104 A5
Wellgate S60. . . . . 33 B4
Wellgate Mount S60 . . . . . 33 B4
Wellgate Terr **4** S60. . . . 33 C4
Well Green Rd S6. . . . . 49 A3
Wellhead Rd **4** S8. . . . . . 73 C4
Wellington Pl S9 . . . . 55 A2
Wellington Rd S6. . . . . 49 C4
Wellington St S1 . . . . 105 C2
Welling Way S61. . . . . 19 B1
Well La
Aston S26. . . . . 69 A4
Rotherham S60. . . . . 47 C3
Sheffield S35 . . . . 16 B2
Sheffield, Wadsley S6. . . . 39 A4
Treeton S60 . . . . 57 C3
Upper Whiston S60 . . . . . . 48 B1
Well Meadow Dr **1**
S3 . . . . 104 C4
Well Meadow St S3 . . . . . 104 C4
Well Rd S8 . . . . 73 C4

Well View Rd S61 . . . . 19 A2
Wellway The S66. . . . . 24 C1
Welney Pl S6 . . . . 26 C2
Welwyn Cl S12 . . . . 76 A2
Welwyn Pl S12 . . . . 76 A2
Welwyn Rd S12 . . . . 76 A2
Wenlock St S13. . . . . 66 A3
Wensley Cl S4 . . . . 42 C4
Wensley Croft S4 . . . . 42 C4
Wensley Ct
Rotherham S60. . . . . 47 A4
Sheffield S4 . . . . 42 C4
Wensleydale Dr S60 . . . . . 46 B1
Wensleydale Rd S61 . . . . . 10 A3
Wensley Gdns S4. . . . . 42 C4
Wensley Gn S4 . . . . 42 C4
Wensley St S4 . . . . 42 C4
Wentworth S6. . . . . 104 B5
Wentworth Ave
Aston S26. . . . . 70 A1
Sheffield S11 . . . . 83 B4
Wentworth Cl S61 . . . . 8 C3
Wentworth Ct S61. . . . . . . 10 C2
Wentworth Dr S62. . . . . . . 12 A2
Wentworth Pl S61 . . . . 18 C4
Wentworth Rd
Dronfield S18 . . . . 99 B3
Rotherham S61. . . . . 9 B3
Wesley Ave S26. . . . . 69 B2
Wesley Ct S61 . . . . 9 A3
Wesley La S10 . . . . 50 C1
Wesley Rd S35. . . . . 5 A1
Wessex Gdns S17 . . . . 94 B3
West Ave S62. . . . . 12 A4
Westbank Cl S18 . . . . 97 C2
Westbank St S18 . . . . 98 A2
West Bar S3. . . . . 106 A4
Westbar Gn S1 . . . . 106 A4
West Bawtry Rd S60 . . . . . 46 B3
Westbourne Rd S10. . . . . . 61 A4
Westbourne St S10 . . . . . . 61 A4
Westbrook Bank S11. . . . . 61 B2
Westbrook Cl S11. . . . . 61 C2
Westbrook Rd S35. . . . . . . 7 B3
Westbury Ave S35 . . . . 7 C2
Westbury St S9 . . . . 54 A3
Westby Cl S65 . . . . 55 B2
Westby Cres S60 . . . . 47 C3
Westby Wlk S66 . . . . 37 B3
West Cl S61 . . . . 19 B2
West Cres S36 . . . . 2 C3
Westcroft Cres S20 . . . . . . 90 C2
Westcroft Dr S20 . . . . 90 C1
Westcroft Gdns S20 . . . . . 90 C2
Westcroft Glen S20 . . . . . . 90 C1
Westcroft Gr S20 . . . . 90 C1
West Don St S6. . . . . 51 C4
Western Bank S10 . . . . . . 105 A3
Western Rd
Rotherham S65. . . . . 34 B4
Sheffield S10 . . . . 51 A2
Westerton Dr S66. . . . . 37 C2
West Farm La S65 . . . . 23 A2
WESTFIELD 91 A2
Westfield Ave
Aston S26. . . . . 69 A3
Sheffield S12 . . . . 78 B1
Westfield Craft Pk
S62 . . . . 11 C2
Westfield Cres S20 . . . . . . 90 A2
Westfield Ctr S20 . . . . 90 C2
Westfield Gr **4** S12. . . . . 78 A1
Westfield Northway
S20. . . . . 90 C2
Westfield Rd
Dronfield S18 . . . . 101 B2
Killamarsh S21. . . . . 92 A1
Rawmarsh S62. . . . . 11 C2
Rotherham S65. . . . . 37 A3
Westfield Sch S20 . . . . 90 B2
Westfield Southway
S20. . . . . 90 C2
Westfield Sta S20 . . . . 91 A2
Westfield Terr S1 . . . . 105 C3
Westgate S60 . . . . 33 A4
Westgate Mews S26 . . . . . 69 A3
West Hill S60 . . . . 30 C4
Westhill La S60 . . . . 33 C2
West Ho S8. . . . . 73 C2
West La S26. . . . . 68 C3
Westland Cl S20 . . . . 90 C3
Westland Gdns S20 . . . . . . 90 B3

Westland Gr **3** S20. . . . . 90 C2
Westland Rd **1** S20. . . . . 90 C2
Westminster Ave S10 . . . . 58 C3
Westminster Chambers
6 S3 . . . . 105 B3
Westminster Cl
Rotherham S66. . . . . 37 B2
Sheffield S10 . . . . 58 C3
Westminster Cres S10 . . . 58 C3
Westmoreland St **1**
S6 . . . . 51 C3
Westnall Ho S35 . . . . 13 B3
Westnall Rd S5 . . . . 17 A1
Westnall Terr S5 . . . . 17 A1
West One Aspect **1**
S3 . . . . 105 C2
West One Central **9**
S1. . . . . 105 C3
West One Cube **4**
S1. . . . . 105 C2
West One Peak **12**
S1. . . . . 105 C3
West One Plaza **10**
S1. . . . . 105 C3
West One Reflect **2**
S3 . . . . 105 C2
West One Space **3**
S1. . . . . 105 C3
West One Twr **11** S1. . . 105 C3
Weston Park Hospl
S10. . . . . 105 A3
Weston Park Mus★
S10. . . . . 104 A3
Weston St S3. . . . . 104 B4
Weston View **4** S10. . . . 51 A1
Westover Rd S10 . . . . 59 C4
West Park Dr S26. . . . . 68 C1
West Quadrant S5 . . . . 29 A1
West St
Dronfield S18 . . . . 100 B4
Sheffield, Beighton S20 . . . 79 C1
Sheffield S1 . . . . 104 C3
West Street La S1 . . . . . . 106 A3
Westthorpe Rd S21 . . . . . . 92 B1
West Vale Gr S65 . . . . 23 C4
West View Cl S17 . . . . 95 A4
West View La S17 . . . . 95 A4
West View Rd S61. . . . . 30 C4
Westways Middle Sch
S10. . . . . 51 A2
Westwell Pl S20 . . . . 103 A4
Westwick Cres S8 . . . . 84 B1
Westwick Gr S8 . . . . 84 C1
Westwick Rd S8 . . . . 84 C1
Westwood Ct S35. . . . . 5 B2
Westwood Ctry Pk★
S35 . . . . 5 A2
Westwood New Rd S35 . . . 5 A1
Westwood Rd
Chapeltown S35 . . . . 5 B1
Sheffield S11 . . . . 60 A2
Wetherby St S9. . . . . 55 A2
Wetherby Dr S26 . . . . 80 B4
Wharfedale Dr S35 . . . . . . 6 C3
Wharf Rd S9 . . . . 31 A1
Wharf St S2 . . . . 106 B4
Wharncliffe Ave S26 . . . . . 69 C2
Wharncliffe Ind Complex
S36 . . . . 4 C3
Wharncliffe Rd
Chapeltown S35 . . . . 5 B1
Sheffield S10 . . . . 105 B2
Wharncliffe St S65 . . . . . . 33 B4
Wharton Ave S26 . . . . 69 B3
Wheatacre Rd S36. . . . . . . 3 B3
Wheata Dr S5 . . . . 16 B1
Wheata Pl S5. . . . . 16 A1
Wheata Rd S5 . . . . 16 A1
Wheatcroft Rd S62 . . . . . . 12 C4
Wheatfield Cres S5 . . . . . . 29 A4
Wheathill St S60. . . . . 33 A3
Wheatley Gr S13. . . . . 65 C3
Wheatley Rd S61 . . . . 19 B3
Wheats La **1** S1. . . . . . . 106 A4
Wheeldon St S1 . . . . 104 C3
Wheel La
Oughtibridge S35 . . . . 13 A3
Sheffield S35 . . . . 15 A2
Wheel The S35 . . . . 15 C2
Wheldrake Rd S5. . . . . 42 B4
Whernside Ave S35 . . . . . . 7 A4

Whinacre Cl S8. . . . . 97 C
Whinacre Pl S8. . . . . 97 B
Whinacre Wlk S8 . . . . 97 B
Whinfell Ct S11. . . . . 82 C
Whinmoor Rd
Chapeltown S35 . . . . 5 A
Sheffield S5 . . . . 29 C
WHINNEY HILL . . . . 23 A
Whins The S61, S62. . . . . . 11 A
WHIRLOW . . . . 83 A
Whirlow Court Rd
S11. . . . . 83 A
Whirlowdale Cl S11. . . . . . 83 A
Whirlowdale Cres S7 . . . . 72 A
Whirlowdale Rd S7,
S11. . . . . 83 A
Whirlowdale Rise S11 . . . 83 A
Whirlow Farm Mews
S11. . . . . 83 A
Whirlow Gn S11. . . . . 82 C
Whirlow Gr S11 . . . . 83 A
Whirlow Grange Ave
S11. . . . . 82 C
Whirlow Grange Dr
S11. . . . . 82 C
Whirlow La S11. . . . . 71 B
Whirlow Mews S11 . . . . . . 71 B
Whirlow Park Rd S11 . . . . 83 A
WHISTON . . . . 48 A
Whiston Brook View
S60 . . . . 48 B
Whiston Gn S60 . . . . 47 C
Whiston Gr S60. . . . . 33 C
Whiston Grange S60 . . . . . 47 B
Whiston Grange Sch
S60 . . . . 47 C
Whiston Jun & Inf Sch
S60 . . . . 47 C
Whiston Vale S60 . . . . 47 C
Whiston Worry Goose
Jun & Inf Sch S60 . . . . . . 48 A
Whitby Rd S9. . . . . 55 A
White Croft S1 . . . . 106 A
Whitecroft Cres S60 . . . . . 46 A
Whitegate Wlk S61 . . . . . . 10 A
Whitehall Rd S61 . . . . 10 B
Whitehall Way S61 . . . . . . 10 B
White Hart Cnr S21 . . . . . 103 A
Whitehead Ave S36 . . . . . . 3 C
WHITE HILL . . . . 46 A
Whitehill Ave S60. . . . . 46 A
Whitehill Dr S60 . . . . 46 A
Whitehill La S60. . . . . 46 A
Whitehill Rd S60 . . . . 46 A
Whitehouse La S6. 51
Whitehouse Rd S6. 51
White La S12. . . . . 88 A
Whiteley La S10 59
Whiteley Wood Cl
S11. 60
Whiteleywood Ho S11 . . . 59
Whiteley Wood Rd
S11. . . . . 59 A
White's La S2 53
White Thorns Cl S8 . . . . . . 97 A
White Thorns Dr S8 . . . . . 97 A
White Thorns View
S8 . . . . 97 A
Whiteways Cl S4 42
Whiteways Dr S4 42
Whiteways Gr S4 42
Whiteways Jun Sch
S4 42
Whiteways Rd S4. 42
Whitfield Rd S10 105
Whitham Rd S10. 105
Whiting St **9** S8. 73
WHITLEY 15
Whitley Carr S35 15
Whitley Croft S35. 16
Whitley La S35 15
Whitley View S35 16
Whitley View Rd S61. 30
Whitwell Cres S36 3
Whitwell La S36 2
Whitwell St S9 55
Whitworth La S9 43
Whitworth Rd S10 60
Whybourne Gr S60 33
Whybourne Terr **5**
S60 33
Wicker S3. 106

Wicker La S3 ....106 B4
WICKERSLEY 36 C2
Wickersley Northfield
Prim Sch S66 ....36 B3
Wickersley Rd S60 .....34 C2
Wickersley Sch & Sports
Coll S66 ....36 C2
Wickfield Cl S12 ....77 B3
Wickfield Dr S12 ....77 B3
Wickfield Gr S12 ....77 A2
Wickfield Pl S12 ....77 B3
Wickfield Rd S12 ....77 B3
Widdop Cl S13 ....65 B2
Widdop Croft S13 ......65 B2
Wigfull Rd S11 ....61 A3
Wignall Ave S66 ....35 C2
Wilcox Cl S6 ....27 A3
Wilcox Gn S61 ....10 B2
Wilcox Rd S6 ....27 A3
Wilding Cl S61 ....19 B2
Wilding Way S61 ....19 B2
Wilfred Cl S9 ....54 B3
Wilfred Dr S9 ....54 B3
Wilfred St S60 ....33 A4
Wilfrid Rd S9 ....54 B3
Wilkinson La S10 ......105 B3
Wilkinson St 5 S10 ...105 B3
Willan Dr S60 ....57 A3
Willbury Dr S12 ....75 C4
Willey St S3 ....106 B4
William Cl S20 ....103 A4
William Cres S20 ....103 A4
William Levick Prim Sch
S18 ....99 B4
Williamson Rd S11 .....61 B1
William St
Eckington S21 ....103 A1
Rawmarsh S62 ....12 B2
Rotherham S60 ....33 B4
Sheffield S10 ....105 B2
Willingham Cl S20 ....91 B3
Willingham Gdns S20 ...91 B4
Willington Rd S5 ......28 C2
Willis Rd S6 ....39 C3
Willoughby St S4 ......42 C4
Willow Ave S60 ....12 B4
Willow Beck 4 S65 ...22 B2
Willow Cl
Brinsworth S60 ....46 B1
Rotherham S66 ....36 C4
Willow Cres S35 ....7 B2
Willow Ct
Rawmarsh S62 ....12 B4
Rotherham S66 ....36 B2
Willow Dr
Rotherham S66 ....36 C4
Sheffield S9 ....55 C1
Willow Garth S62 ......12 B4
Willowgarth Ave S60 ...46 A2
Willow Gr S26 ....70 A2
Willow Rd
Killamarsh S21 ....92 A1
Stocksbridge S36 ......3 A1
Willows The
Rotherham, Dropping
Well S61 ....19 A4
Rotherham S66 ....33 C3
Wilson Ave S62 ....11 C4
Wilson Carlile College of
Evangilism S3 ....105 C3
Wilson Dr S65 ....23 B3
Wilson Pl 6 S8 ....62 B1
Wilson Rd
Eckington S18 ....98 A2
Sheffield S61 ....61 A2
Stocksbridge S36 ......4 B2
Wilson St
Dronfield S18 ....101 A2

Wilson St continued
Sheffield S3 ....52 B4
Wilthorpe Gdns 7
S20 ....77 C1
Wilton Cl S62 ....12 A3
Wilton Ct S61 ....20 A1
Wilton Gdns 20 A1
Wilton La S61 ....32 A4
Wilton Pl S10 ....105 B2
Winchester Ave S10 ...58 C2
Winchester Cres S10 ..58 C2
Winchester Ct 4 S65 ..21 B1
Winchester Dr S10 ....58 C2
Winchester Rd S10 ....58 C2
Winchester Way S60 ...45 B3
WINCOBANK 30 B1
Wincobank Ave S5 .....29 C1
Wincobank Cl S5 ......29 C1
Wincobank Inf Sch S9 .30 A2
Wincobank La S4 ......43 A3
Wincobank Rd S5 .....29 C1
Winco Rd 8 S4 ....43 A3
Winco Wood La S5 ....29 C1
Windermere Ave
S18 ....100 A3
Windermere Rd 8 S8 ..73 A3
Windmill Ct S61 ......9 B1
Windmill Greenway
S20 ....103 B3
Windmill Hill La S35 ...7 A2
Windmill Hill Prim Sch
S35 ....7 A2
Windmill La S5 ....29 B1
Windsor Cl S66 ....37 A4
Windsor Ct S11 ....71 B2
Windsor Dr S18 ....99 B3
Windsor Rd
Rotherham S66 ....9 A2
Sheffield S8 ....73 B4
Windsor Rise S26 .....81 A4
Windsor St
Sheffield S4 ....53 B4
Sheffield S4 ....53 C3
Windy House La S2 ....64 B2
Windy Ridge S26 .....69 A3
Wingerworth Ave S8 ...84 B2
WINGFIELD 10 A3
Wingfield Cl
6 Dronfield S18 .....99 B3
Rotherham S66 ....10 B1
Wingfield Cres S12 ...76 B3
Wingfield Rd S61 .....10 A2
Wingfield Sch S61 ....20 A4
Winifred St S60 ......20 C1
Winkley Terr S5 ......29 B1
Winlea Ave S65 ......35 B2
Winn Cl S6 ....26 B1
Winn Dr S6 ....26 B1
Winn Gdns S6 ....26 B1
Winn Gr S6 ....26 B1
Winsford Rd S6 ......26 C3
Winster Rd S6 ....40 A3
Winston Ave S6 ......2 B4
Winter Hill La S61 ...19 B1
Winterhill Rd S61 ....19 B1
Winterhill Sch S61 ...19 B1
Winterton Gdns S12 ..78 B1
Wiseton Ct 1 S11 ....61 A2
Wiseton Rd 2 S11 ....61 A2
WISEWOOD 39 A2
Wisewood Ave S6 .....39 A2
Wisewood La S6 ......39 B2
Wisewood Pl S6 ......39 A2
Wisewood Prim Sch
S6 ....39 B3
Wisewood Rd S6 .....39 B2

Wisewood Sch & Com
Sports Coll S6 ....39 B3
Wishing Well Gn S26 ..68 C1
Withens Ave S6 ....39 C4
Witney St S8 ....62 B2
Woburn Pl S11 ....83 A4
Wolfe Dr S6 ....27 A3
Wolfe Rd S6 ....27 A3
Wolfson Flats S10 ....61 A3
Wollaton Ave S10 ....95 B3
Wollaton Dr S17 ......95 B3
Wollaton Rd S17 .....95 B3
Wolseley Rd 2 S8 ...62 B1
Wolverley Rd S13 .....77 C4
Woodall Rd
Killamarsh S21 ....93 A1
Rotherham S65 ....34 C2
Woodall Rd S S65 ....34 C2
Woodbank Cres S8 ...73 B3
Woodbank Ct S17 ....83 B1
Woodbine Rd S9 .....43 A1
Woodbourn Hill S9 ...54 A3
Woodbourn Rd S9 ....54 A2
Woodbury Dr S35 ....8 A2
Woodbury Rd S9 .....30 A3
Woodbury Rd S9 .....30 A3
Wood Cl
Chapeltown S35 ......8 A2
Rotherham S65 ....24 C2
Woodcock Cl S61 .....10 A2
Woodcock Pl S2 ......53 B1
Wood Croft S61 .....10 A1
Wood End S35 ....10 A4
Woodend Dr S6 ......39 B1
Woodend Dr S6 ......39 B1
Woodfarm Ave S6 ....50 A4
Woodfarm Cl S6 ......49 C4
Woodfarm Dr S6 .....49 C4
Woodfarm Pl S6 .....49 C4
Woodfield Rd S10 ....50 C3
Wood Fields S66 .....37 B2
Wood Fold S3 ....41 B1
Woodfoot Rd S60 .....47 A3
Woodgrove Rd
Rotherham S65 ....22 C1
Sheffield S9 ....30 B2
Woodhead Rd S2 .....62 B2
WOOD HILL 42 B2
Woodholm Pl S11 .....72 A3
Woodholm Rd S11 ....72 A3
WOODHOUSE 78 C4
Woodhouse Ave S20 ..79 B2
Woodhouse Cres S20 .79 B2
Woodhouse Ct S20 ...79 B2
Woodhouse Gdns S13 .78 B4
Woodhouse La S13 ...79 B3
WOODHOUSE MILL 67 B2
Woodhouse Rd S12 ...76 A4
Woodhouse Sta S13 ..67 B1
Woodhouse West Prim
Sch S13 ....77 C4
Wood La
Catliffe S60 ....45 B1
Rotherham, Canklow
S60 ....33 A1
Rotherham, Wickersley S66 36 C1
Sheffield S6 ....49 C4
Woodlaithes Rd S66 ..24 C1
Woodland Cl
Catliffe S60 ....57 A3
Rotherham S66 ....36 C1
Woodland Dr S12 .....87 C4
Woodland Pl S17 .....95 A3
Woodland Rd S8 .....74 A1
Woodlands S60 ....34 C1
Woodlands Ave S20 ..79 B3
Woodlands Cl S26 ...69 B3
Woodlands Farm S60 .57 C2

Woodlands The S10 ......60 B4
WOODLAND VIEW 50 B4
Woodland View
Sheffield, Abbeydale Park
S17 ....83 B1
Sheffield, Charnock Hill
S12 ....87 C4
Woodland View Rd S6 ..50 B4
Woodland Way S65 ...35 A2
Wood Lane Cl S6 ....49 C4
Wood Nook S35 ......14 C3
Woodpecker Cl S26 ...81 A4
Wood Rd
Rotherham S66 ....10 A1
Sheffield S6 ....39 C2
Woodrove Ave S13 ...64 C1
Woodrove Cl S13 ....64 C1
WOOD ROYD 4 A3
Wood Royd Rd S36 ...4 A2
WOOD SEATS 6 B1
Wood Seats S35 .....6 B1
Woodseats Cl S8 ....73 A2
Woodseats House Rd
S8 ....85 A4
Woodseats Prim Sch
S8 ....73 B1
Woodseats Rd S8 .....73 B2
WOODSIDE 52 B4
Woodside Ave S21 ....93 A3
Woodside Cl S66 ....36 C1
Woodside La
Sheffield, Grenoside
S35 ....14 C3
Sheffield S3 ....52 B4
Woodside Wlk S61 ...10 C1
Wood Spring Ct S4 ..42 C2
Wood St
Rotherham S65 ....23 B4
Sheffield S6 ....51 C4
Woodstock Rd
Sheffield, Normandale S6 .38 C2
Sheffield S7 ....73 A4
Wood Terr S60 ....33 A1
Woodthorpe Cres S13 .65 A2
WOODTHORPE
ESTATE 65 A1
Woodthorpe Prim Sch
S13 ....65 A1
Woodthorpe Rd S13 ..65 A1
Woodvale Flats S10 ..60 C3
Woodvale Rd S10 ....60 C3
Wood View Ho S21 ...102 C1
Wood View Pl S6 ....33 A1
Woodview Rd S6 .....40 A1
Woodview Terr S10 ..59 C2
Woodway The S66 ....24 B1
WOOD WILLOWS 3 C4
Woofindin Ave S11 ..59 C1
Woofindin Rd S10 ...59 B1
Wooldale Cl S20 .....89 B4
Wooldale Croft S20 ..89 B4
Wooldale Dr S20 ....89 B4
Wooldale Gdns S20 ..89 B4
Woollen La 8 S6 .....51 C3
Woolley Rd S36 ......2 C3
Woolley Wood Rd S5 .17 C1
Woolley Wood Sch S5 29 B4
Wootton Ct S65 .....23 B4
Worcester Cl S10 ....58 C3
Worcester Dr S10 ....58 C3
Worcester Rd S10 ...58 C3
Wordsworth Ave S5 ..27 B3
Wordsworth Cl S5 ...27 B4
Wordsworth Cres S5 .27 B2
Wordsworth Dr
Rotherham S65 ....34 A4
Sheffield S5 ....27 B2

Workhouse La S3 ......106 A4
Worksop Rd
Aston S26 ....69 C1
Sheffield S9 ....54 B4
Worral Ave S60 ....57 C2
WORRALL 13 B1
Worrall Dr S35 ....13 B1
Worry Goose La S60 ..48 B4
Worthing Rd S9 ......53 C3
Wortley Cl S35 ....5 B1
Wortley Dr S35 ....13 C3
Wortley Mews S61 .....8 C2
Wortley Rd
Chapeltown S35 ....5 B2
Rotherham S61 ....19 C2
Stocksbridge S36 .....4 C3
Wostenholm Rd S7 ....62 A2
Wragby Rd S11 ....60 B2
Wragg Rd S2 ....63 C3
Wreakes La S18 ......100 B4
Wren Bank S2 ....63 C4
Wren Park Cl S12 ....88 C2
Wright's Hill 2 S2 ...62 A2
Wroxham Cl S66 ......37 B3
Wroxham Dr S66 .....37 B3
Wroxham Way S66 ....37 B3
Wulfric Rd
Eckington S21 ....102 C1
Sheffield S2 ....64 B2
Wyatt Ave S11 ....72 B4
WYBOURN 53 C1
Wybourn Com Prim Sch
S2 ....53 C1
Wybourn House Rd
S2 ....53 C1
Wybourn Terr S2 .....53 C1
Wychwood Croft 8
S20 ....91 B4
Wychwood Glen 7
S20 ....91 B4
Wychwood Gr 6 S20 .91 B4
Wyedale Croft S20 ...79 B2
Wyndthorpe Ct S60 ..34 C2
Wynyard Rd S6 ......39 C3
Wyvern Gdns S17 .....94 C4

Yardley Sq S3 ....104 B4
Yarmouth St S9 ......43 C3
Yates Cl S66 ....36 A1
Yeomans Rd S6 ......51 C3
Yew Greave Cres S5 .15 C1
Yew La S5 ....15 C1
Yewlands Sch Tech Coll
S35 ....15 B1
Yews The S65 ....21 C1
Yew Tree Dr
Killamarsh S21 ....92 A1
Sheffield S9 ....45 A3
Yoredale Ave S35 ....7 A4
York Rd
Rotherham S65 ....21 B1
Sheffield S9 ....55 A3
Stocksbridge S36 .....3 A3
York Rise S26 ......69 A1
York St S1 ....106 A4
Youlgreave Dr S12 ...76 C3
Young St S3 ....105 C1

Zion La S9 ....54 A4
Zion Pl S9 ....54 A4

List of numbered locations

In some busy areas of the maps it is not always possible to show the name of every place.

Where not all names will fit, some smaller places are shown by a number. If you wish to find out the name associated with a number, use this listing.

The places in this list are also listed normally in the Index.

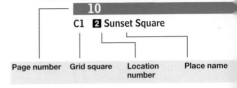

10

C1 **2** Sunset Square

Page number | Grid square | Location number | Place name

16
A2 1 Eva Ratcliffe Ho
4 Brailesford Ct

20
C1 1 Thornhill Edge
2 Chemist La
3 Garden La
4 Amen Cnr
5 Mary St

21
A1 1 Amen Cnr
2 George St
3 Greasebrough Rd
4 Henry Ct
5 Effingham Sq
6 Water St
7 College Wlk
B1 1 Archer Ho
2 Fletcher Ho
3 Arrowsmith Ho
4 Winchester Ct
5 Carlisle Pl
6 Spring Wlk
7 Holywell Pl
8 Norfolk Ct
9 Market Sq
10 Elliott Ct

22
A1 1 Bishopstoke Ct
2 Vulcan Ho
3 Eastleigh
B2 2 Eastwood View
3 Oakbrook Wlk
4 Willow Beck

33
B4 1 Lindum Terr
2 Catherine St
3 Beeversleigh
4 Wellgate Terr
5 Whybourne Terr
C4 1 Badsley Ct
2 Granville Terr
3 Harcourt Terr
4 Ellesmere Terr
5 Gordon Terr

34
A4 2 Gilberthorpe Dr
B3 1 Canterbury Cl
2 Browning Ct
3 Barrat Cnr

39
C2 1 Dykes Hall Gdns

40
A2 2 Cheadle St

3 Riverside Mews
4 Rudyard Ct
B1 1 Blackburne St
2 Normandale Rd
3 Victor St
4 Channing Gdns

42
B3 1 Bolsover Rd E
2 Heathcote St
3 Barretta St
4 Earl Marshal Cl
5 Earl Marshal Dr

43
A3 1 Farcroft Gr
2 Skelwith Cl
3 Brathay Cl
4 Brathay Rd
5 Birdwell Rd
6 Southwell Rd
8 Winco Rd
9 Carlisle Bsns Pk

47
C3 2 Hollow Gate

49
A4 1 Albanus Croft
2 Spoon Glade
3 Spoon Oak Lea
4 Gill Croft
5 Scarlett Oak Mdw
6 Durmast Gr
7 Greaves Ct
8 Sheldon La

50
C2 1 Flodden St
2 Bosworth St

51
A1 1 Top Terr
2 Hawthorn Terr
3 Bank Terr
4 Weston View
A4 1 Gresham Rd
2 Stony Wlk
3 Chapel Bank Apartments
C3 1 Westmoreland St
2 Portland St
3 Woollen La
4 Midvale Ct
5 Philadelphia Gr
6 Philadelphia Dr
7 Portland Bdgs
C4 1 Balaclava La
2 Cross Gilpin St
3 Kelvin Bdgs

54
B3 1 Fearnehough St
2 Chinley St
3 Garth Cl
4 Shirland Mews
5 Faranden Rd
6 Cattal St
7 Harry Firth Cl
B4 2 Beverley St
3 Bootle St
4 Chapel La

60
B1 1 Greystones Grange
2 Greystones Grange Cres
3 Greystones Rise
4 Glencroft
5 Highcroft
C4 1 Tapton Ct
2 Oaks The
3 Fairfield Hts

61
A2 1 Wiseton Ct
2 Wiseton Rd
3 Hunter's Bar
4 George Woodfin-din Almshouses
5 Meadow Terr
6 Porter Terr
7 Carmel Ct
A4 2 Beech Hill Rd
3 Ashgate La
4 Lifestyle Ho
B2 3 Harefield Rd
5 Dyson Pl
6 Gordon Rd
7 Ratcliffe Rd
8 Berresford Rd
9 Lynton Rd

62
A1 1 Rampton Rd
2 Farrar Rd
3 Ainsty Rd
5 Gamston Rd
6 Miller Rd
7 Marples Cl
8 Marples Dr
9 Dalton Ct
10 Frederick Rd
A2 1 Keeton's Hill
2 Wright's Hill
3 Bennett St
4 Randall St
5 Salmon St
6 Clarke Sq
7 Grosvenor Sq
10 Priory Terr
11 Smeaton St
12 Kenwood Chase
13 Ventnor Ct
14 Asher Rd

15 Sitwell Pl
16 Ward Pl
A3 2 Club Garden Wlk
6 Lansdowne Rd
7 Forge Student Village
B1 1 Horner Rd
2 Wolseley Rd
3 Alderney Rd
4 Lowfield Ct
5 Old Forge Bsns Pk
6 Wilson Pl
B2 2 Harwood St
3 Rowland Rd
4 St Barnabas La
5 St Barnabas Rd
6 Belgrave Sq
7 Crowther Pl
8 Holland Pl
9 Batt St
10 Harrington Rd
11 St Wilfrid's Rd
12 St Barnabas Ho

64
C3 1 Stonecliffe Wlk
2 Motehall Wlk
3 Nelson Mandela Wlk
4 Saxonlea Dr
5 Normancroft Ct

66
A3 1 Ashbourne Gr
2 Haigh Moor Cl

72
A2 1 Silverdale Ct
2 Silverdale Gdns
3 Silverdale Glade

73
1 Norton Hammer La
2 Acorn Bsns Pk
3 South West Ctr The
A3 1 Arnside Rd
2 Coniston Terr
3 Windermere Rd
4 Crummock Rd
B2 1 Tadcaster Way
2 Denton Rd
B4 1 Southcroft Gdns
2 Southcroft Wlk
3 Avenue Rd
4 Belper Rd
C1 1 Rosemary Ct
2 Mount View Lodge
3 Abbey View Hts
C3 1 Cross Park Rd
2 Brooklyn Pl

3 Rushdale Terr
4 Rushdale Mount
5 Brooklyn Rd
C4 1 Tillotson Cl
2 Nowill Ct
3 Nowill Pl
4 Wellhead Rd
7 Goodwin Rd
8 Plantation Rd
9 Whiting St
10 Southall St
11 Molloy St
12 Molloy Pl

74
A4 1 Bradwell St
2 Richards Ct
3 Sturge Croft
4 Denson Cl
5 Farish Pl
6 Jeffery St
7 Nicholson Pl
8 Carrfield Ct
9 Nicholson Ct
10 Gregory Ct
11 Carter Grange
12 Kent Grange
13 Cambridge St
14 Cambridge Lodge
15 Gerard Cl

75
C1 1 Gleadless Rise
2 Gleadless View
C2 3 Crispin Rd

77
C1 1 Spring Water Dr
3 Spring Water Cl
4 Fairmount Gdns
5 Redbrook Gr
6 Redbrook Croft
7 Wilthorpe Gdns

78
A1 1 Brookside Cl
2 Grassington Cl
3 Threshfield Way
4 Westfield Gr
5 Stoneacre Ct
6 Brookhouse Ct
A2 1 Birley Spa Wlk
2 Rainbow Wlk
3 Carter Lodge Wlk
4 Carr Forge Wlk

79
C1 1 Copper Beech Cl
2 Manor Farm Mews
3 Broomwood Cl
4 Manor Farm Ct

85

2 **2** Roxton Ave

89

1 Cranford Ct
2 Moorthorpe Gdns
3 Brampton Ct
4 Royston Gr
5 Royston Cl
6 Kingswood Cl
7 Deanhead Ct
8 Deanhead Dr
9 Kingswood Croft
10 Kingswood Gr
11 Royston Croft

90

1 Westland Rd
2 Meadowcroft Rise
3 Westland Gr
4 Pedley Ave
5 Birchwood Rise
6 Birchwood Gdns
7 Birchwood Cl
8 Newark
9 Roche
10 Shortbrook Bank
11 Rockingham
12 Shortbrook Wlk
13 Shortbrook Way
14 Sitwell
15 Garland Mount
16 Birchwood Way
3 **1** Middlecliff Rise
2 Middlecliff Ct
3 May Tree Croft
5 Pedley Cl
6 Pedley Gr

8 Waterfield Mews

91

A2 **1** Waterthorpe Rise
2 Waterthorpe Glen
3 Waterthorpe Gdns
4 Waterthorpe Cl
5 Waterthorpe Glade
6 Shortbrook Croft
7 Eastcroft Way
B3 **1** Collingbourne Dr
2 Bramshill Ct
3 Milburn Ct
4 Hursley Cl
5 Inglewood Ct
6 Inglewood Dell
B4 **1** Waltham Gdns
2 Charnwood Ct
3 Ringwood Rd
4 Grizedale Cl
5 Rothbury Ct
6 Hartland Ct
7 Wychwood Glen
8 Wychwood Croft
9 Wychwood Gr

95

B3 **3** Everard Glade
4 Ladybower Ct
5 Derwent Ct
C3 **1** Prospect Ct
2 Moorview Ct

96

C4 **1** Atlantic Cres
2 Gervase Wlk

99

B3 **1** Thornton Pl
2 Oxclose Dr
3 Rockingham Cl
4 Ivan Brook Cl
5 Hazelwood Cl
6 Wingfield Cl
C3 **1** Lynwood Cl
2 Sherwood Pl
3 Roston Cl
4 Radbourne Comm
C4 **1** Millstone Cl
2 Buckingham Cl

100

A3 **1** Castlerigg Way
2 Patterdale Cl
3 Constable Cl
4 Landseer Cl
B3 **2** Heathfield Cl
C3 **2** Hillside Ave
4 Pembroke Rd
5 Upper School La

101

A3 **1** Scarsdale Cross
2 Scarsdale Rd
3 Palmer Cres

103

B4 **1** Oakworth Cl
2 Borrowdale Cl
3 Borrowdale Ave
4 Ennerdale Ave
5 Wasdale Ave
6 Murrayfield Dr

7 Stonegravels Croft
8 Twickenham Ct
9 Twickenham Gr
10 Twickenham Glade
11 Twickenham Cl

104

B3 **1** Robertshaw
2 Cornhill
3 Adamfield
C3 **2** Portobello La
C4 **1** Well Meadow Dr
2 Kenyon Alley

105

B3 **4** Leavy Greave
5 Wilkinson St
6 Westminster Chambers
C1 **1** Granary The
2 Barley Ho
3 Draymans Ct
4 Maltings The
C2 **1** West One Aspect
2 West One Reflect
3 West One Space
4 West One Cube
C3 **3** Charlotte La
4 Devonshire La
5 Canning St
6 Mappin Ct
7 Cavendish Ho
8 West One City
9 West One Central
10 West One Plaza
11 West One Twr

12 West One Peak
13 Victoria Ho
14 Forum The
15 Smithfield

106

A3 **2** Holly La
3 St James' Row
A4 **1** Wheats La
2 Fig Tree La
B5 **4** Pinsent
5 Redgrave
6 Cracknell
7 Foster
C4 **1** Link Row
2 Rubens Row
3 Bernard Gdns
4 High Pavement Row

107

A2 **1** Rockingham Gate
2 Imperial Ho
3 Exchange Works
A3 **1** Phoenix Ct
4 Cambridge Ct
5 Pinstone Chambers

PHILIP'S MAPS
the Gold Standard for drivers

◆ **Philip's street atlases cover every county in England, Wales, Northern Ireland and much of Scotland**

◆ Every named street is shown, including alleys, lanes and walkways

◆ Thousands of additional features marked: stations, public buildings, car parks, places of interest

◆ Route-planning maps to get you close to your destination

◆ Postcodes on the maps and in the index

◆ Widely used by the emergency services, transport companies and local authorities

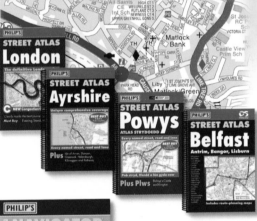

For national mapping, choose
Philip's Navigator Britain
the most detailed road atlas available of England, Wales and Scotland. Hailed by Auto Express as 'the ultimate road atlas', the atlas shows every road and lane in Britain.

'The ultimate in UK mapping'
The Sunday Times

Street atlases currently available

England	
Bedfordshire	East Sussex
Berkshire	West Sussex
Birmingham and West Midlands	Tyne and Wear
	Warwickshire
Bristol and Bath	Birmingham and West Midlands
Buckinghamshire	Wiltshire and Swindon
Cambridgeshire	Worcestershire
Cheshire	East Yorkshire Northern Lincolnshire
Cornwall	North Yorkshire
Cumbria	South Yorkshire
Derbyshire	West Yorkshire
Devon	
Dorset	**Wales**
County Durham and Teesside	Anglesey, Conwy and Gwynedd
Essex	Cardiff, Swansea and The Valleys
North Essex	Carmarthenshire, Pembrokeshire and Swansea
South Essex	
Gloucestershire	Ceredigion and South Gwynedd
Hampshire	
North Hampshire	Denbighshire, Flintshire, Wrexham
South Hampshire	
Herefordshire Monmouthshire	Herefordshire Monmouthshire
Hertfordshire	Powys
Isle of Wight	
Kent	**Scotland**
East Kent	Aberdeenshire
West Kent	Ayrshire
Lancashire	Dumfries and Galloway
Leicestershire and Rutland	Edinburgh and East Central Scotland
Lincolnshire	
London	Fife and Tayside
Greater Manchester	Glasgow and West Central Scotland
Merseyside	Inverness and Moray
Norfolk	Lanarkshire
Northamptonshire	Scottish Borders
Northumberland	
Nottinghamshire	**Northern Ireland**
Oxfordshire	County Antrim and County Londonderry
Shropshire	County Armagh and County Down
Somerset	
Staffordshire	Belfast
Suffolk	County Tyrone and County Fermanagh
Surrey	

How to order

Philip's maps and atlases are available from bookshops, motorway services and petrol stations. You can order direct from the publisher by phoning **0207 531 8473** or online at **www.philips-maps.co.uk**
For bulk orders only, e-mail philips@philips-maps.co.uk